Educational Policy in Australia and America: Comparative Perspectives

Education Policy Perspectives

General Editor: Professor Ivor Goodson, Faculty of Education, University of Western Ontario, London, Canada N6G 1G7

Education policy analysis has long been a neglected area in the United Kingdom and, to an extent, in the USA and Australia. The result has been a profound gap between the study of education and the formulation of education policy. For practitioners such a lack of analysis of the new policy initiatives has worrying implications particularly at such a time of policy flux and change. Education policy has, in recent years, been a matter for intense political debate — the political and public interest in the working of the system has come at the same time as the consensus on education policy has been broken by the advent of the 'New Right'. As never before the political parties and pressure groups differ in their articulated policies and prescriptions for the education sector. Critical thinking about these developments is clearly necessary.

All those working within the system also need information on policy making, policy implementation and effective day-to-day operation. Pressure on schools from government, education authorities and parents has generated an enormous need for knowledge amongst those on the receiving end of educational policies.

This series aims to fill the academic gap, to reflect the politicalization of education, and to provide the practitioners with the analysis for informed implementation of policies that they will need. It will offer studies in broad areas of policy studies. Beside the general section it will offer a particular focus in the following areas: School organization and improvement (David Reynolds, University College, Cardiff, UK); Critical social analysis (Professor Philip Wexler, University of Rochester, USA); Policy studies and evaluation (Professor Ernest House, University of Colorado-Boulder, USA); and Education and training (Dr Peter Cuttance, University of Edinburgh, UK).

Educational Policy in Australia and America
Comparative Perspectives

Edited by

William Lowe Boyd
Pennsylvania State University

and

Don Smart
Murdoch University

 The Falmer Press

(A member of the Taylor & Francis Group)
New York Philadelphia and London

UK	The Falmer Press, Falmer House, Barcombe, Lewes, East Sussex, BN8 5DL
USA	The Falmer Press, Taylor & Francis Inc., 242 Cherry Street, Philadelphia, PA 19106-1906

© Selection and editorial material copyright W. L. Boyd and D. Smart 1987

First published 1987

Library of Congress Cataloguing in Publication Data is available on request

ISBN 1-85000-198-7
ISBN 1-85000-199-5 (pbk.)

6 33 80883

Jacket design by Caroline Archer

Typeset in 10/12 Bembo by
Imago Publishing Ltd, Thame, Oxon

Printed in Great Britain by Taylor & Francis (Printers) Ltd, Basingstoke

Contents

Contents

Foreword

In large measure, this book is the product of the increasing international ferment in policy studies in education. More specifically, it is the product of the growing interest in 'bilateral trans-Pacific' comparative studies of education policy which has sprung up between colleagues in the United States and Australia in the past decade.

These developments, of course, parallel the growing US interest in things Australian, from movies to pop groups — an interest that is reflected at a more serious level by the growing number of Australian Studies Centers springing up in American universities and in such related phenomena as the establishment, in March 1986 at Columbia University in New York, of the American Association for Australian Literary Studies.

In recent years there has been a growing awareness among scholars and policy makers of the productive comparisons to be made between Australia and the United States in the sphere of educational policy issues and problems. Our purpose in producing this book has been to highlight *national*, *state*, and *local level* policy trends and problems in education that the two nations share by collecting together in one volume a set of papers by eminent scholars of educational policy, politics, and the law.

In one sense this volume's existence is directly attributable to the Fulbright Fellowships that provided each of the editors with his initial opportunity to visit the other's country (Smart to the US in 1979 and Boyd to Australia in 1984) and to discover the stimulation and policy salience of Australia-US comparative study at close hand. Following our personal contact in Australia during Boyd's visit in 1984, the opportunity came to jointly organize, in 1985 and again in 1986, a series of symposia on particular aspects of Australia-US educational policy. These symposia were held as part of the program of the annual meetings of the American Educational Research Association, in Chicago in 1985 and San Francisco in 1986.

The revised versions of the papers we commissioned for the symposia in San Francisco constitute the four sections of this book. The integration of the volume has been greatly enhanced by the thematic organization of the symposia and by the fact that each group of papers was discussed by a symposium critic. The commentary of the critics is included at the end of each section and provides valuable assistance in identifying and highlighting common issues and themes.

We clearly owe a debt of gratitude to all those who agreed to participate in these symposia and to the American Educational Research Association for providing us with the opportunity to include the symposia within its meeting program.

While we are expressing thanks, we wish also to pay tribute to the many scholars who have stimulated interest in this relatively new field and have given us encouragement in our endeavors. In this respect, the long-term contributions to the field of Grant Harman, Michael Kirst, and Fred Wirt deserve special mention. Americans also owe a vote of thanks to the numerous globetrotting educational leaders from 'down under', such as Bill Walker, Colin Moyle and Richard Bates, who have made extraordinary contributions in fostering travel and interchange between our two nations.

We also would be remiss not to mention the seminal influence of the US-Australia Education Policy Project (serviced from Stanford University, 1977–1983) on the growth of studies in this area. That project, jointly funded by the Ford Foundation and the Australian government, provided an initial stimulus for more research in this area and many of the contributors to this volume had an association with that project. A successor US-Australia Education Policy Project began in 1985–86 and is being jointly coordinated by the University of Wollongong, New South Wales, and Teachers College, Columbia University, New York. Its first major meeting was held in Washington, DC in May 1987. We wish this new project and its participants well in their endeavors.

William Boyd
Don Smart
June, 1987

A Pen Portrait of Australia

Janice Dudley

Australia occupies an area of 3 million square miles and is almost the same size as the USA (excluding Alaska and Hawaii). Of great geological age, it is the lowest and flattest of the continents and is also very dry. The centre and western half is either arid or semi-arid.

The Commonwealth of Australia is a federation of states — New South Wales, Victoria, Queensland, South Australia, Western Australia, Tasmania — together with territories which are administered by the Commonwealth — the most important of these are the Northern Territory and the Australian Capital Territory, where the nation's capital, Canberra, is located.

In spite of Australia's image as an outback nation, where laconic bushmen muster sheep and cattle, most of Australia's 16 million people live in large coastal cities — either the state capitals or major cities on the south and east coasts. It is a multicultural nation with over 20 per cent of its people having been born overseas — most of these were born in either the United Kingdom or Ireland, but a significant proportion of those arriving in recent decades are from Southern Europe and the Middle East. Indo-Chinese refugees constitute the greatest proportion of Australia's refugee intake during the 1980s. The indigenous peoples of Australia — Aborigines and Torres Strait Islanders — make up about 1 per cent of Australia's population. Like their American Indian counterparts they tend to live in rural or outback areas (especially in Queensland, New South Wales, Western Australia and the Northern Territory) rather than in major cities.

Political System

Australia has a Westminster style political system. The government is formed by the political party which achieves a majority in the directly elected lower house of the Parliament. The head of the government — the Prime Minister — is the leader of that party. Under the Australian constitution, which came into effect on 1 January 1901, the Parliament of the Commonwealth of

Australia consists of the Sovereign (the Queen of the United Kingdom), the Senate and the House of Representatives. The Sovereign is represented throughout the nation by the Governor-General, whilst in each state there is a State Governor. The Governor-General and state governors play an essentially symbolic and non-political role, although on several occasions, such as November 1975 when the Governor-General dismissed the Whitlam government (that is, withdrew the Labor Party's Leader, Gough Whitlam's commission to form a government), the latent political powers of the governors and Governor-General have been implemented.

In the Parliament's upper house, the Senate, twelve senators are elected from each state — each state constitutes an electorate. Members of the lower house, the House of Representatives, are directly elected and represent separate electorates. Voting is compulsory and preferential. Although preferences are significant only in marginal seats, preferential voting has enabled minority parties to exercise considerable influence over government policies by trading preferences for policy concessions.

The legislatures in most of the states are also bicameral. State upper houses are legislative councils whilst lower houses are either legislative assemblies or houses of assembly. Thus with seven parliamentary houses and over 800 politicians, Australia has the remarkable statistic of one politician per 20,000 people!

History

Australia was first settled by ancestors of today's Aborigines at least 40,000 years ago. Theirs was a nomadic hunter-gatherer society. European settlement began in 1788, when a convict penal settlement, which was to become the city of Sydney, was established on the east coast of Australia. Cook had claimed this region for the British crown in 1770 and named it New South Wales (NSW). A further convict colony was established at Hobart in Tasmania in 1803.

During the first half of the nineteenth century the agricultural productivity of the country became the source of considerable wealth and power for the squatters (pastoralists) who were to become Australia's elite. At the same time free settlers arrived to take up land whilst ex-convicts were able to take a place in the new society in ways which would have been impossible in Great Britain. Between 1824 and 1836, the colonies which were to become Queensland, Victoria, Western Australia (WA) and South Australia (SA) were established by free settlers. Self-government was granted to New South Wales in the 1820s.

The discovery of gold and the subsequent gold rushes of the 1850s and 1860s almost tripled the population and prepared the way for the rise of the new urban middle class in the latter half of the nineteenth century. 'Responsible government' had been granted to all the colonies (except WA) during the

1850s, and rail links between the colonies (with the exception of WA) were completed during the 1880s. As native born Australians began to outnumber immigrants, a new sense of nationalism began to emerge. During the 1890s political labour movements — an extension of the unionism which had developed during the 1880s, partly as a response to the introduction of Pacific Islanders as cheap labour for Queensland's sugar-cane fields — began to grow. The labour movement's aims were essentially reformist and the ideals of the early nineteenth century Utopian socialists were strong — the slogan 'equal opportunity for all' was used in Queensland as early as 1883. Thus, by the mid-1890s, although many in the six separate colonies were in favour of retaining their individual identities, the economic, nationalistic and political pressures for some form of national unity were strong.

A federal nation emerged from the constitutional conventions of the late 1890s with the most important powers, including taxation, being retained by the states. The Australian constitution was passed by the British Parliament in 1900 and the Commonwealth of Australia came into being on 1 January 1901. Australia's political parties were divided not only by philosophy but also by religion — the Labor party was dominantly Irish Catholic whilst the parties with either conservative and/or liberal outlook were dominated by pro-British protestants. A series of conservative or conservative/liberal Federal governments were followed in 1908 by a Labor government which enacted Australia's first social welfare legislation — invalid and old age pensions.

Between 1914 and 1918 Australia was involved in the First World War. The ALP (Australian Labor Party) was divided over military conscription and in 1916/17 the party split over the issue. Together with the rise of the Country Party over the period 1917 to 1920, this ensured a series of conservative/Country Party coalition governments during the 1920s. Thus, the pattern of Australian politics which continues today had been established — a coalition of interests between the conservative and business-oriented parties of both city and country opposed to the Labor Party which was concerned with social welfare, the interests of the 'working man', and the creation of state (Australian) owned enterprises which were free of overseas control.

Australian soldiers fought in Europe, Africa and the Pacific during World War II. Robert Gordon Menzies, the leader of the United Australia Party, the then conservative, free enterprise party, was Prime Minister between 1939 and 1941. When Labor came to power in 1941 John Curtin became Prime Minister. He died in office in 1945 and was succeeded by Benedict (Ben) Chifley, who was Prime Minister from 1945 to 1949. It was under Curtin's prime ministership that Australia's close relationship with the USA developed. Curtin turned to the US when he became aware of Great Britain's inability, or lack of commitment, to defend Australia from the Japanese.

Under Labor, in 1943, as a 'temporary war-time measure', the states ceded their personal taxation powers to the Commonwealth. However, the

Commonwealth did not relinquish this newly acquired source of power and influence at the end of the war. The financial arrangement whereby all income tax, company tax, etc is gathered by the Commonwealth and a proportion returned to the states under negotiated agreements permanently changed the balance of power between the federal and state governments and has been a strong centralizing influence in Australia's political life since World War II.

During the 1940s Labor either introduced or improved a whole range of social welfare measures such as child endowment, hospital benefits, invalid and old age pensions, maternity allowances, unemployment and sickness benefits and widow's pension. In 1946 a referendum to amend the constitution was passed. The new Section 51 (xxiiiA) empowered the Commonwealth to provide social welfare benefits to a wide range of groups — including students.

Menzies had founded the Liberal Party in 1944, and in 1949 the Liberals were elected to power and Menzies became Prime Minister — a post he was to occupy for seventeen years. Amid a McCarthyist style anti-Communist climate, Menzies attempted to ban the Communist Party of Australia in 1950. However, in 1951, the Communist Party Dissolution Act was declared unconstitutional and hence invalid by the High Court (c.f. US Supreme Court), and the subsequent referendum to change the Constitution was defeated. Evatt, the Labor leader, had campaigned strongly against the referendum and this added to the widening rift between the socialist left wing and the conservative, Catholic, anti-Communist right wing of the Labor Party. The split became a schism, and in 1957 the Catholic conservative wing of the party left the ALP to form the Democratic Labor Party (DLP). The DLP's preferences were directed to the Liberal Party and so, with the clergy from the pulpit urging good Catholics to vote DLP, the DLP's 10 per cent of the vote was a significant contributory factor in the Liberal/Country Party coalition retaining power until 1972.

Menzies retired in 1966 and the Liberal Party was then racked by a series of leadership upheavals. Gough Whitlam was elected to the leadership of the ALP in 1970 and presided over a series of major policy reforms aimed at the ALP achieving government rather than remaining on the high moral ground of principled opposition. Together with the demise of the DLP, these policies and the sense of the timeliness of a change in Australian political life, which was summed up in the Labor slogan 'It's Time!', resulted in the Labor Party being elected to government in 1972 — Australia's first Labor government for twenty-three years.

The new Labor government, with its agenda for social reform after years in the political wilderness, attempted to change Australian society almost overnight. Within days of being elected, the government had withdrawn Australian troops from Vietnam, had recognized the People's Republic of China and had established a Royal Commission into Aboriginal Land Rights. Major educational innovations of the 1972 to 1975 Whitlam government included the elimination of tertiary (university and college) tuition fees, complete Commonwealth funding of tertiary education (rather than shared funding with the states) and the establishment of an independent Federal Schools Commission to oversee the Labor Party's policy of extensive federal aid to schools on the basis of need.

Malcolm Fraser had been elected Leader of the Liberal Party in March 1975 and by October 1975, amid a sense of growing economic crisis — rapidly rising inflation and unemployment — the Liberal/Country Party controlled Senate refused to pass the Whitlam government's money supply bills (that is, it refused to release federal monies to the government). Thus the government was unable to pay its bills or its employees and was effectively unable to govern. The crisis continued for four weeks until, on 11 November 1975, the Governor-General dissolved both Houses of Parliament and installed Fraser as caretaker Prime Minister until elections in December. The Liberal/Country Party coalition was elected and thus Fraser, with his new federalism policies of greater power to the states and a reversal of the centralism of the Whitlam government, became Prime Minister.

In 1982, hampered by the lack of a majority in the Senate, Fraser requested the Governor-General to declare a double dissolution of Parliament and bring on an election. On the same day Bob Hawke was elected parliamentary leader of the ALP. Hawke's background was the union movement and he had both a national reputation for the resolution of difficult industrial disputes and an exceptional personal popularity.

The Hawke ALP government was elected in March 1983 under the banner of 'Bringing Australians Together'. This slogan reflected the divisions and polarizations within Australian society during the previous decade — or at least since 1975 — and the conciliatory consensus style of government which the Hawke government professed to espouse. Hawke, in particular, was very impressed by the Swedish model of government by consensus and was very concerned to distance both himself and his government from the perceived 'crash through or crash' style of the former Whitlam Government.

Hawke's government was re-elected in 1984. His personal popularity continues to be one of the government's major assets. However, the pragmatism and 'recession thinking' of senior ministers has caused many, both within and without the party, to consider that the government has been co-opted by monetarist economic policy. The traditional platforms of social reforms and social change appear to be under threat and rifts within the party are growing. It remains to be seen whether Hawke and the Labor Party can resist the party's seemingly irresistible 'death wish' to split over issues of principle, and achieve an historic third term of government in 1987.

Australian Education

As in the US, education is constitutionally a responsibility 'reserved' to the states. Nevertheless in both countries, the federal government has become heavily involved in education. Furthermore, in Australia, the High Court has ruled that federal aid to church schools is constitutionally valid. Within the Australian states, schooling in government schools is controlled by State Education Departments headed by a Director-General of Education and responsible to a government minister. Centralization is a feature of the administration of public education in all states of Australia — staffing, curriculum planning, buildings, resources are all the responsibility of 'The Department'. This has the goal of equality of opportunity for all children, be they urban or rural, but has tended to be expressed in a uniformity of practices throughout each state and indeed throughout the nation. The public schools are financed not as in the US through local taxes but through redistribution of federal income tax.

Approximately 25 per cent of Australian schools are non-government schools. Most of these are Catholic parochial schools which are centrally administered by a Catholic Education Commission in each state, whilst the remainder are independent schools which are autonomous institutions often under the auspices of the Protestant churches. The educational offerings in most of these schools are essentially similar. There is also a small number of schools offering an education alternative to the mainstream education offered by both the systemic schools (government and Catholic) and the independent schools. Approximately 75 per cent of Australian school students are enrolled at government (public) schools, 18 to 20 per cent are enrolled in Catholic schools and about 5 per cent are enrolled in independent schools. All private schools are financed through a mixture of fairly generous federal and state aid and parental/private contributions.

Children attend a primary (elementary) school for the first six to seven years of their education. High schools in both the government and non-government sector are comprehensive and coeducational, although there are still some few single sex independent schools.

Australia's nineteen universities and forty-five colleges of advanced education are autonomous institutions established under Acts of State Parliament and are the only institutions empowered to confer degrees. Thus there are, to date, no private universities or colleges in Australia.[1] However, although the establishment of universities and colleges is a state responsibility and they were traditionally state funded, tertiary education is almost completely funded by the Commonwealth. Under a series of trade-off agreements in 1974, the Commonwealth undertook total funding responsibilities for the tertiary sector in order to achieve its policy objective of free tertiary education. Thus, since 1975 there have been no tertiary tuition fees. However, in the 1986/87 budget the Hawke government introduced a $250 'administrative charge'. Some senior ministers in the Hawke Cabinet wish to reintroduce tertiary fees as a solution to the burgeoning cost of the tertiary sector, but others argue that the party should adhere to its fee-free platform. The issue of tertiary fees nicely illustrates the conflict in the party between pragmatism and principle.

Technical and Further Education (TAFE) colleges (somewhat akin to US community colleges), which are essentially vocationally oriented and also provide adult education both vocational and non-vocational, are funded mainly by the states (75 per cent state, 25 per cent Commonwealth).

Federal Education Commissions — the Schools Commission (SC) and the Commonwealth Tertiary Education Commission (CTEC) — formulate and administer federal education policy *within government financial guidelines.* CTEC is a particularly influential body because the Commonwealth holds the purse-strings. The Commonwealth Department of Education was established in 1966 and has major responsibility for student aid and international education.

Note

1 *Editors note:* Since this was written a private university, Bond University in Queensland, has been founded.

Introduction

1 Introduction and Overview: The Badger and the Bandicoot

William Lowe Boyd and Don Smart

In their admirable book, *Contemporary Issues in Educational Policy: Perspectives from Australia and USA* (1983) — undoubtedly the first of its kind comparing education policy in our two countries — Greg Hancock, Michael Kirst and David Grossman chose as the title for their introductory chapter, 'The kangaroo and the bald eagle'. In an endeavour not to claim too much for comparative study, and to avoid overinflating the expectations of readers of this second foray into US-Australia comparative education policy, we have chosen the more modest subtitle, 'The badger and the bandicoot'. In so doing we simply wish to remind policy-makers, policy-analysts and administrators that educational problems are complex and are heavily embedded in a cultural and structural context. For this reason we would caution against expectations of easy answers and instantly transferable solutions from 'down under' to 'up over' and vice versa.[1]

Having said that, however, in this time of major statewide reforms in both nations, we want to strongly argue that the benefits to policy-makers of comparative studies such as this are substantial and that they are primarily in the realm of broadened perspective, enhanced insight, reduced 'parochialism' and the promotion of innovative change.

Justification for the Book

It is just four years since Hancock, Kirst and Grossman's seminal edited volume on US-Australia education policy was published. Because our book is in many respects a companion and up-date volume to that earlier book, we do not intend to retraverse the familiar terrain which the editors covered in their detailed justification of comparative study and explication of comparative methodology.[2]

Suffice it to say here that it is human nature to compare and, for many scholars, the intellectual stimulation of comparison is justification enough. Nevertheless, in these utilitarian times when 'relevance' is commonly demanded of scholarly research, there are even better reasons for comparative studies of policy issues.

As Hancock *et al.* noted in justifying their study, comparison is fundamental to the search for general principles — principles which presumably we must seek if we are to improve education policy-making:

> ... in many areas of thought, comparison is the precondition of explicit understanding ... without attempts at rigorous comparison, there would be no taxonomy. Without taxonomy there would be no science. Without science there would be no disciplined general principles from which logic could tease reasonable inferences. Without reasonable inferences, creative thought of a rigorous nature would atrophy (Hancock *et al.*, 1983, p. 313).

In his commentary in this current volume (chapter 6), Frederick Wirt illustrates the vital role which comparative study of education policy plays in providing 'a check on parochialism in thinking about policy and theory'. Thus, policies which we might at first sight give credit to a national leader for 'choosing' may, on closer international comparison, prove to have been simply thrust on the leader by international forces over which he/she had little control.

In this way, Wirt sees an important role of comparative study to be that of enhancing awareness and reducing blind spots which were due to a previously more limited perspective. The essence of the argument for comparative study, though, is the simple fact that our two nations — while unquestionably significantly different — are alike in so many important respects that it is possible for analysts to conceive of each nation as an interesting 'policy laboratory' for the other.

For example, to cite some of the most obvious similarities: both are 'relatively young English-speaking pioneering countries settled primarily by European migrants'; both are of approximately similar total area; furthermore they 'both have democratic representative governments cast in the federal mould'; and they have 'mixed economies' and are 'affluent industrialized societies' (Porter, 1983, p. 49). As Tannock noted a decade ago, when we look specifically at education, the similarities between our countries are great:

> Both have highly developed education systems which extend from pre-school through higher education. In both countries, although public education constitutes the major sector, private initiatives remain important at all levels, and show signs of increasing support. The co-existence of public and private education, and the forms of support, controls, and interrelationship between the sectors remain important issues for public policy. Both countries also have constitutional provisions and legal and administrative traditions which often confusingly divide responsibility for education between state and

federal governments. Both face major and often conflicting educational goals such as equality of opportunity, minimum standards, choice and diversity, etc. Within the context of such aims, both countries must deal with the difficult realities of federal-state relations, large ethnic minorities (both indigenous and immigrant), sharply declined birth rates, high levels of youth unemployment, widespread disaffection about traditional and even current education values, and the fact that funds for education no longer take precedence over most other areas of public resource allocation (Grossman, 1983, p. 26, citing Tannock).

Enough has been said, then, to show that there are some striking similarities between our two nations and their education systems. There are, nevertheless, equally striking dissimilarities which we must bear in mind as we seek to compare. Porter (1983) has usefully contrasted the US and Australia on two continuums — those of homogeneity-heterogeneity and centralization-decentralization.

In almost every respect one can think of, the US is much more diverse and heterogeneous. Australia, by contrast, is much more geologically, geographically and demographically uniform — its people (until recently) very largely Anglo-Saxon in origin with more than three-quarters of them concentrated in the six major capital cities dotted around the coastline of the southern and eastern seaboard. Unlike the US, much of the vast hinterland is unoccupied desert. So far as schools are concerned, the state (or public) schools which educate roughly 75 per cent of all Australian children are remarkably homogeneous and uniform by American standards. This stems from the comparatively highly centralized administration of schools by large state education department bureaucracies located in the capital city of each state. These departments have traditionally controlled all resources, staffing and curriculum. Thus, in much the same way as the centralized French system, school programs, textbooks and syllabi within states until very recently have been remarkably homogeneous.

Despite the strong criticisms of such dull Australian uniformity and centralization leveled by the American educator, Freeman Butts (1955), thirty years ago, it is only comparatively recently, particularly since the advent of the Federal (Commonwealth) Schools Commission (1973), that the values of diversity and devolution of control have been strongly promoted and have led to some (so far mostly minor) changes in administration and practice. One of the sections (part 4) of this book is largely dedicated to exploring the current experiences in Victoria — the state which has gone furthest down this devolutionary track — as attempts are made to promote devolution of administration.

The past decade has produced an accelerating curve of interest and activity among scholars and policy-makers in the fruitful comparisons to be made between Australia and the US in the sphere of educational policy issues and problems. This should come as no surprise for it parallels the growth of interest in more general Australian and American studies in the learning centers of our respective countries. Nor should it be assumed that the recent quantum leap in American interest in Australia is confined simply to pop culture (to pop groups such as 'Men at Work' and to movie/TV stars such as Paul 'Crocodile Dundee' Hogan) or to sport (for example, Australian Rules Football and America's Cup Yachting). For the record shows a steady growth of serious academic interest in Australia too. Apart from the now well-established Australian Studies Center at Pennsylvania State University and the Endowed Chair of Australian History at Harvard, there have been recent Australian Studies developments at the Universities of Oregon, Texas at Austin, and Columbia in New York. Reference has already been made to the original US-Australian Education Policy Project (1977–83) housed at Stanford and its recently established successor Project which is being jointly coordinated from the University of Wollongong in New South Wales and Teachers College, Columbia University in New York.

Such developments augur well for the future of US-Australian collaborative study generally, and for comparative education policy specifically. It would reveal a lack of historical perspective, however were we to assume that substantial interchange between our relatively youthful countries was only of comparatively recent origin. It sometimes comes as a surprise to citizens of both countries to discover that there was a substantial interchange of people, possessions, and plants between the goldfields of California and Australia as long ago as the 1850s. It is not by accident that the coast of California is sprinkled with glorious eucalyptus trees of Australian origin!

But, returning to education, it is true that there have been growing links in education between our two countries throughout most of this century. Thus, it was Carnegie Foundation money that helped establish the Australian Council for Educational Research (ACER) in 1929. In the post-war years many of Australia's most eminent educators established a tradition of undertaking their doctoral studies in the US. Perhaps one of the most symbolic influences of all, however, was the six months visit of the American Professor, R. Freeman Butts, to ACER in 1955. At the end of his visit, Butts produced a report for ACER entitled *Assumptions Underlying Australian Education*. This remarkable document, which is still widely known and used in teacher education courses today, clearly established the great insights to be had from a comparative perspective. Coming as an outsider, Butts was able to identify with forceful clarity some of the most striking (even damning!) but hitherto unstated assumptions underlying much of Australia's education system and practice. Since that time, the flow of visiting educators in each direction has become a torrent — this edited set of papers being the product of but one set of conference interactions in San Francisco.

The Contents of the Book

This book is structured into four discrete parts, each of the first two ending with a discussion chapter which seeks to tie together the threads and draw out common themes. Parts 3 and 4 share a common discussion chapter.

Part 1 provides a national perspective and examines both Federal government policy in the US and Australia and the role of the courts in relation to education in both countries. Part 2 deals with the specific issue of recent policy concerning public and private schools in Australia. It seeks to explore the implications of Australian private school funding policies for the US and raises questions about the Australian approach and its long-term consequences for Australian society.

Part 3 examines the way in which teachers unions influence and in turn are influenced by education policy in each country. And, finally, in part 4 a diverse range of Australian issues, including the role of senior executive level administrators and the complex issues of state-wide administrative reform and coordination in the state of Victoria, are explored. Each of these issues has policy relevance for the US — indeed the Australian data on senior executives resonates with similar data collected by Wirt in the US.

We will now touch briefly on some relevant aspects of the substantive papers to whet the reader's appetite and to highlight some significant policy issues. In part 1, the chapters by Don Smart and by David Clark and Terry Astuto, both bring the reader quickly to grips with an understanding of the pendulum swing from left to right in educational values and policies that has occurred in recent years in both countries. As if by magic, the strong educational equity agendas of the Whitlam Labor and Carter Democratic administrations were rapidly swept aside and replaced by the conservative agendas of Fraser and Reagan. These latter agendas stressed a reduced federal role and reduced federal expenditure (New Federalism) and sought to replace equity with excellence and freedom of choice as the chief educational values. In seeking to explain these changes, the authors emphasize the effects of international recession and the emergence of the powerful 'neo-conservatism' or 'New Right' forces which have exercised such a strong influence over economic policy and ideology in recent years, not only in the US and Australia, but also in Thatcher's UK. Smart sought to test the prediction that, with the replacement of the conservative Fraser government by the Hawke socialist government in 1983, Australia would witness yet another pendulum swing back towards equity as the predominant value. He was forced to conclude, however, that national and international constraining factors — especially the state of the economy (Federal budgetary deficit) and the increasingly conservative outlook of the Australian electorate — had led (or forced) Hawke to adopt a range of unpredictably conservative policies more in keeping with his opposition, Fraser, than with the ideology and policies of his socialist predecessor, Gough Whitlam.

As noted earlier, in his summary of these two chapters Wirt seized on this discovery to emphasize one valuable lesson of this comparative study — that sometimes the policies which leaders adopt are not (as we normally expect) dictated by their ideology but rather by powerful external forces largely beyond their control.

In the other two complementary chapters in part 1, written by Betsy Levin and Ian Birch respectively, a stark contrast is revealed in the relationship between the American and Australian judicial systems and education. Born of the independence struggle, the constitution of the USA and its amendments have made provision for the maintenance of individual rights against the rights of the states, though not exclusively. By contrast, the Australian constitution virtually eschewed the notion of rights with the founding fathers (sic) voting against the inclusion of provisions for individual rights in the constitution.

It is not surprising, therefore, to find in Levin's chapter a considerable range of constitutional interests impacting on education, with the consequent reference to numerous cases decided in the courts. Nor is it unexpected to read of the paucity of case law impinging on education in Birch's chapter. In canvassing their separate jurisdictions both writers allude to the variety of government legislative influences on education at national, state and local level. They also note the inconclusive, if not unsatisfactory, aspects of some judicial decisions. Clearly these decisions bring to bear an important influence on education policy development in the USA and Australia.

Part 2 deals with complex policy issues concerning the highly sensitive issue of public and private schools, their funding and function, in our two countries. While only 10 per cent of US students attend private schools, a substantially greater 26 per cent of Australian students do so. This difference is largely attributable to the strong and enduring Roman Catholic school system in Australia, which dates back to the nineteenth century. Eighty per cent of all private school students in Australia attend Roman Catholic schools. Whereas the constitutional 'wall of separation' between church and state has been deemed by the Supreme Court to preclude public funding of private schools in the US, the Australian experience has been to the contrary. Despite a very similarly worded clause in the Australian Constitution (portions of which were modeled after the US Constitution), federal and state governments have been providing extensive aid to private schools since 1963 and the High Court (equivalent to the US Supreme Court) has ruled such aid to be constitutional.

In chapter 7, Smart examines the public-private school funding policies of the Hawke socialist government between 1983 and 1986. In particular, he seeks to explain the implementation of several key policies which seem sharply at odds with the ideology and promises of that government. Why did an equity-oriented Labor government which had pledged to phase out federal aid to so-called 'wealthy private schools' reverse its policy and offer guarantees of continued aid to these same schools? Why did Hawke have extremely limited success in achieving a substantial reversal of the dramatic drift in the total proportion of federal aid being channelled from public to private schools under the conservative Fraser government? Smart explains Hawke's limited success to date in terms of: (i) the politically naive initial strategy used in the 1983 'partial phase-out' and the government's need to then 'back-off'; (ii) the unanticipated, yet perfectly predictable, powerful coalition of Catholic and non-Catholic private school forces which successfully fought the government's phase-out strategy; (iii) the difficulties, within a 'needs-based' aid framework of withdrawing or reducing Federal aid from the 'poor' Catholic schools which comprise the majority of private schools; and (iv) the inability, within the context of a large federal budget deficit, to massively increase the total federal cake for schools funding and channel it overwhelmingly to public schools — the basic approach which had been used by the Whitlam socialist government in the economically more buoyant early 1970s. Smart also seeks to explain how a socialist Labor government, traditionally committed to redistributionism and reform, was responsible for emasculating its own specially created and equity-oriented Schools Commission.

In chapter 8, 'Balancing public and private schools: The Australian experience and American implications', William Boyd discusses the significant and controversial implications of the Australian approach to public funding of private schools. As many critics point out, most democratic nations have not found it necessary to take the strict stand adopted by the US in barring the use of public funds by non-government schools. Among the nations that demonstrate this point, Australia in particular stands out. Indeed, it has been proposed as a success story, a model for the United States of how public dollars could be distributed beneficially to private schools without harming the public schools. However, Boyd argues that along with the successful features of the Australian approach go a number of disturbing features that suggest, at the very least, that Americans should be cautious about emulating this approach. In particular, Boyd warns of the potential risk of creating an undemocratic two-tiered education system in which the private schools educate the 'cream' of students and the public system becomes the second-class repository for those destined for lower-level callings in society.

In chapter 9, Berry Durston provides a thoughtful and incisive commentary on the chapters by Smart and by Boyd. Durston highlights the value-laden features of the public versus private school debate that often impede objective analysis of the issues that are involved. In response to criticism about the growing share of federal funds received by private schools in Australia, Durston presents figures supporting his view that this criticism is based upon an incomplete and misleading account of the facts.

In part 3, the influence of teachers unions on education policy in the US and Australia is examined. Randall Eberts and Joe Stone consider the effects of American public school teacher collective bargaining on educational practice and policy in a quantitative analysis of a large, national database linking unionized school districts to student performance. They argue that the impact of unionization on long-term institutional change has been positive in terms of student performance (as measured on standardized tests) and on the cost of provision of educational services. Eberts and Stone attribute this effect to the improved conditions in classrooms because unionized teachers receive higher salaries, teach smaller classes, spend less time in instructing students, and have more time for preparation. This makes unionized districts slightly more effective than nonunionized districts in educating average students. But, they conclude that the higher costs associated with union districts far exceed their small productivity advantage.

Jill Blackmore and Andrew Spaull argue that teacher unionism in Australia also has benefitted the state educational systems, and perceive two new directions that have led to unprecedented influence of unions in the formulation of state and local educational policy. The first trend, evident in Victoria, towards schools as the key units of decision-making and union activity, has meant that secondary, technical and primary teacher unions have influenced, and often intitiated, progressive and radical educational policies in Victoria on curriculum innovation, school organization, non-competitive assessment, non-sexist and Aboriginal education, peace education, and participation of students, teachers and parents on local and regional administrative bodies. This is against a backdrop of administrative decentralization and devolution, a trend counter to increased state centralism in other Australian states and in the American experience. The second direction is towards the development of federal teacher unionism through the newly-formed Australian Teachers Union, which has the potential to impact state teacher salaries and conditions and, by implication, educational policy and provision of services, due to a recent court decision that teaching, as an industry, lies within the federal conciliation and arbitration system of industrial relations.

One element common to the US and Australian experience is the impact of economic and demographic factors since the mid-1970s which has forced teacher unions to take a less militant stance. Since the 1960s, the National Education Association has joined with the American Federation of Teachers in the recognition of collective bargaining as a necessary strategy in order to maintain teachers' professional standing and economic well-being in difficult economic times. Now over 86 per cent of US teachers are unionized. This is remarkable considering the decline in unionism in the relatively less labor-intensive industrial and private sectors. A unique political partnership and industrial agreement in Victoria in a time of system contraction has also reduced militancy among teacher unionists, with a similar increase in membership. A second feature common to American and Australian teacher unionism has been the increased influence and control open to teachers in education policy-making through participative and localized decision making, as teachers increasingly perceive little distinction between unionism and professionalism.

While the final section, part 4, has obvious relevance for American policy, the three chapters report on important aspects of primarily Australian experience in relation to senior State education administrators and to some key issues of state administrative reorganization and co-ordination. In chapter 12, Fred Wirt, Grant Harman and Hedley Beare report on their interview study of the 'Changing roles of Australian education chief executives at state level'. What they find is consistent with similar interviews with American school superintendents — viz. that these key personnel in the process of state education policy have experienced substantial degradation in their roles in recent years as a result of the increasing political turbulence in their administrative environments. Essentially, the Directors-General, those formerly preeminent sources of policy advice to the Minister, have found themselves downgraded in influence and importance, as the channels of advice have become more plural and the players in the policy arena more numerous. The model of policy advice has altered from a tightly closed one dominated by the Director-General to a much more plural or open model. Among the causes of this change, the Directors-General repeatedly cited: the increasing politicization of the uppermost levels of the public service by suspicious politicians and powerful teachers union advisors; the increasing public disenchantment with education and the consequent resentment of professional advisors who had failed the community; and the intense and turbulent policy pressures created by a constricted economy.

In chapter 13, William Boyd and Judith Chapman reflect upon the successes and failures to date of Victoria's ambitious experiment in educational restructuring, the most far-reaching venture in decentralization and devolution of educational administration so far attempted in Australia. Given international interest in improving school effectiveness, the Victorian venture is of particular significance. Unlike most US state-wide reform efforts currently, it seeks school-level improvement through implementing democratic school-based management, with extensive community and staff involvement which necessitates a radically new role for school principals.

In chapter 14, 'Statewide arrangements for organizing Australian education', Grant Harman explores the current search across the Australian states for new and improved ways of coordinating the policy process at state level. Harman reports that the states have become increasingly dissatisfied with the capacity of their existing state departmental structures — largely unchanged since their creation in the late nineteenth century — to adequately cope with modern policy demands. Harman proposes some general principles and potential coordinating models for improved policy delivery. These principles and models also have some policy relevance for American policy-makers as the current push towards more powerful state-level education agencies gathers momentum in the US.

Finally, in chapter 15 Phillip Hughes presents a broad and thoughtful commentary on the chapters in parts 3 and 4. He stresses that, in assessing trends in education policy in Australia and the US, it is important not to oversimplify developments. As he notes, 'In both countries . . . we do not have unidirectional changes but rather more complex currents of change'.

Thus, we see movement toward both greater devolution and greater centralization. On balance, it is, as Hughes observes, a 'mixed balance-sheet'. Like a number of American commentators, Hughes concludes that 'the reforms so far put in place may not yet have reached the real focus for improvement — teacher, student and classroom, together with the factors that directly affect performance and response in that setting'. Consequently, the next wave of reforms must seek to reach more effectively into the classroom.

Conclusions

Let us attempt to pull together some of the main themes and conclusions that can be drawn from this set of comparative papers. Here we make no claim to an exhaustive or comprehensive analysis but rather seek simply to highlight some of those features which particularly strike us. Undoubtedly, other readers with different interests and agendas will want to emphasize different themes as they seek to grapple with the implications of this rich comparative data source for their own particular policy concerns.

Perhaps first and foremost, the papers generally confirm that the policy environment on both sides of the Pacific can be characterized by 'turbulence and change'. Confirming Toffler's (1970) prediction in *Future Shock*, everything about our education systems — their organizational structures, their leadership, their political and judicial environments, their teacher organizations and their financial underpinnings — is unquestionably in a state of flux and ferment. This, of course, adds immeasurably to the difficulty of the task of the policy-maker and manager who must operate in such an unstable environment with fewer constants.

In both countries, the present social and economic forces of decline are sources of turbulence and reform. Declining economic/budgetary circumstances, declining public confidence in schooling and declining legitimacy of administrative authority have become potent pressures for reform, indeed, for a fundamental reassessment of educational finance, policy and management (Boyd, 1983).

Furthermore, the processes of educational reform and the ideological perspectives of the political parties and other 'policy-players' produce efforts to readjust the balance among the interdependent and perpetually competing values of liberty, equality, efficiency and quality ('excellence') in each country's educational system (Boyd, 1984; Murphy, 1980). Particularly evident in these papers are the tensions and pendulum swings between the competing values of equality and excellence, between equality of provision and freedom of choice. Faced with a need to respond simultaneously to the diverse social and economic problems mentioned above, and to competing values, reforms that are proposed may seek both to tighten up the system — through measures to increase accountablility, performance and efficiency — and yet, at the same time, to loosen the system, through steps to increase participation and legitimacy via broader involvement in the policy-making process. These contradictory tensions are particularly evident in the chapters in part 4.

The increasing politicization of the policy-making environment is also striking. Politicians no longer seem content to leave the determination of most education policy issues to the professional educators. Thus, to take but one example, Reagan sought to destabilize national education advisory committees by stacking them with conservative appointees while Hawke sought to undercut the key advisory role of the Schools Commission by downgrading its functions and staffing levels. Both pursued such policies in order to promote their own policy preferences and dominance over the professionals. While education policy is becoming more 'politicized', at the same time it also is becoming more 'judicialized' and litigious, as the chapters of Levin and Birch demonstrate — and this is so even in the Australian context despite the absence of a Bill of Rights.

One does not have to search far to find the sources of the international trend toward a more politicized environment for education. Largely stimulated by the petro-dollar recession, in the past decade education, like most other areas of social policy, experienced a pendulum swing from more liberal to more conservative values. In both Australia and the US this process was assisted by the remarkably potent influences of 'neo-conservatism' and the 'New Right' agenda. Thus, equity issues and values in education, which shortly before had had paramount priority under Whitlam and Carter, were rapidly replaced with a focus on quality and excellence in education under Fraser and Reagan. Intent on reducing central power in Washington and Canberra, these two conservative leaders happily invoked the 'New Federalism' as a rubric to justify reduced federal expenditure on education. That this switch in dominant educational values was not solely attributable to the ideology of these conservative leaders, but rather to some larger international forces is perhaps borne out by the failure of the socialist Hawke government to achieve a return to more liberal policies and values in education between 1983 and 1986.

Here Wirt's analogy of the global village becomes particularly apt, for it applies not only to the papers upon which Wirt commented in part 1 but has generalizability to all the chapters in this volume. Wirt noted:

> Whether one studies these (education) systems as a summarizer of current events, a policy advocate, or a theory builder, comparative analysis of the politics [read also policy] of education has many benefits. A useful framework of analysis is the 'global village' concept of a highly interdependent world, one swept by currents of ideas and crises that have differential effects on the shores of many nations . . . Trans-national influences increasingly become a stimulus to . . . local policy ideas. Look at the parallel searches among nations for budget-cutting in education after the 1973 oil crisis. It is as if the currents surge through the global village, setting off eddies in each

hut. Each nation in a village seems a discrete unit in itself, with its own family and functions. But in the global village, these national huts must respond together in facing dangers that spring from the outside jungle.

Thus, it is very clear from the chapters in this volume that comparative analysis of educational policy provides extremely valuable insights. Furthermore, US and Australian education policy certainly appears to inhabit almost adjacent huts in the global village and so to experience many of the same surges of current and often to resonate in similar ways. However, we would contend that it is when our two countries resonate in opposite ways to the same current that policy-makers on opposite sides of the Pacific are provided with some of their most profound insights and feel most challenged to explore new and better ways of doing things.

Notes

1 See, for example, Peter West's (1983) thoughtful caveats concerning superficial comparisons of society and policy in Australia and America.
2 For a discussion of analytical methods in comparative education, see Kelly *et al.* (1982).

References

Boyd, W.L. (1984) 'Competing values in educational policy and governance: Australian and American developments', *Educational Administration Review*, 2, 2, spring, pp. 4–24.
Boyd, W.L. (1983) 'Rethinking educational policy and management: Political science and educational administration in the 1980s', *American Journal of Education*, 92, 1, November, pp. 1–29.
Butts, R.F. (1955) *Assumptions Underlying Australian Education,* Melbourne, Australian Council for Educational Research.
Grossman, D.L. (1983) 'Methodological observations' in Hancock, G., Kirst, M. and Grossman, D. (Eds) *Contemporary Issues in Educational Policy: Perspectives from Australia and USA*, Canberra, ACT Schools Authority and Curriculum Development Centre.
Hancock, G., Kirst, M.W. and Grossman, D.L. (Eds) (1983) *Contemporary Issues in Educational Policy: Perspectives from Australia and USA*, Canberra, ACT Schools Authority and Curriculum Development Centre (distributed in the USA by McCutchan Publishing Corp., Berkeley, CA.)
Kelly, G.P., Altbach, P.G. and Arnove, R.F. (1982) 'Trends in comparative education: A critical analysis' in Altbach, P.G., Arnove, R.F. and Kelly, G.P. (Eds), *Comparative Education*, New York, Macmillan.
Murphy, J. (1980) 'School administrators besieged: A look at Australian and American education', *American Journal of Education*, 89, 1, pp. 1–26 (also in Hancock, Kirst and Grossman, 1983).
Porter, P. (1983) 'Factors affecting the implementation of federal programs support-

ing educational change in the United States and Australia' in HANCOCK, G., KIRST, M. and GROSSMAN, D. (Eds) *Contemporary Issues in Educational Policy: Perspectives from Australia and USA*, Canberra, ACT Schools Authority and Curriculum Development Centre.

TOFFLER, A. (1970) *Future Shock*, New York, Random House.

WEST, P. (1983) 'Australia and the United States: Some differences', *Comparative Education Review*, 27, 3, October pp. 414–6.

Part 1
The National Picture

2 Reagan Conservatism and Hawke Socialism: Whither the Differences in the Education Policies of the US and Australian Federal Governments?

Don Smart

Overview

Under the radical reformist Whitlam Australian Labor Party Government (1972–1975), education was viewed as a central instrument for making society more equal and for promoting social reform. To a lesser extent this was also true of the Carter Administration. However, between the mid 1970s and early 1980s the western world underwent a severe economic recession and an accompanying pendulum swing from fairly liberal to much more conservative social, political and economic values and attitudes. The education policies of Reagan, Thatcher and Fraser reflected that pendulum swing and have been captured by the phrase the 'New Right Agenda'. When the Hawke Labor government came to power in 1983, whilst much of the educational rhetoric of the Whitlam era remained in Labor's platform, the reformist zeal and the determination to use education as an engine of social reform had largely evaporated. Under Hawke, Labor has moved right becoming a much more cautious party of the middle ground — the politics of electoral pragmatism and consensus have replaced the Whitlam politics of idealism and reform.

With Hawke, as with Reagan, anxiety about the budget deficit has dictated that 'sound economic management' overrides all other priorities. In both cases social and educational redistributionist policies have largely been crowded out — though in the case of Reagan, ideology provides an additional incentive for keeping such policies off the agenda.

The end result, in both the US and Australia, is that the key determinant of federal policy in education is economic not ideological — hence the greater degree of commonality in education policies than if ideology was allowed free rein.

Introduction

At the American Educational Research Association meeting in Chicago in 1985 I presented a paper entitled 'Fraser and Reagan "New Federalism": Politics of education in times of economic recession'. In that paper I noted some remarkable similarities in the broad general political philosophy and specific education policies of the conservative leaders (Fraser was Prime Minister of Australia's Liberal government from 1976–1983) of our two countries. In trying to set these two men and their 'New Federalism' policies in context I observed:

> In many respects, former Prime Minister Malcolm Fraser and President Ronald Reagan can be seen to be almost clone-like leadership products of the wave of conservative political and social forces which swept both countries (and much of the western world) from the mid-1970s — perhaps in large measure as a reaction to the more liberal and interventionist policies of their predecessors and to the accompanying severe economic recession which they both claimed to have inherited as a direct result. Whatever the merits of Fraser and Reagan's claims that their economic predicament was inherited from the policies of their liberal predecessors, there can be little argument that both men found a great deal of common ground in their diagnoses of the ailments besetting their respective economies and federal systems of government and in their prescription of policies to remedy those ills.
>
> Thus, Fraser in 1975 and Reagan in 1980, were swept into power arguing that their 'left-leaning' predecessors had let inflation get out of control, and the national deficit grow too large through their policies of 'welfare-statist' expenditure on public sector programs, especially in health, education, and social welfare. Further, they argued that their predecessors had, in general, encouraged the growth of centralized power in Washington and Canberra at the expense of the states and that public sector growth had been excessive and been fostered at the expense of the size and vitality of the private sector.
>
> Both men were elected to office on the promise of implementing solutions to these problems which included such common elements as: the need to reverse the centripetal forces in our respective federal systems by handing back more responsibilities (and the capacity to fund them) to the states; the need to reduce the federal government's deficit by substantially cutting back on its expenditure, primarily in social welfare and related areas; the need to simultaneously deregulate unnecessary federal restrictions on industry and the states, and to stimulate private sector investment and growth by 'supply-side' strategies such as major tax cuts and business incentives.

Amongst the common elements which I identified in Fraser and Reagan education policy were the following:

1   Disestablishment and De-emphasis

Efforts to *eliminate or reduce the role of the federal government in education* by:
  (i)   closing the Department of Education and/or related federal education agencies [for example, Department of Education (DE) and National Institute of Education (NIE) in US and Curriculum Development Centre (CDC) and Education Research and Development Committee (ERDC) in Australia];
  (ii) substantially *reducing federal funding for education* [for example, Education Consolidation and Improvement Act (ECIA) in US and Treasurer Lynch's 'Razor Gang' in Australia];
  (iii) weakening the credibility and influence of the federal education agencies by altering their agendas through the use of the *political appointment process* and/or by *ignoring or neutralizing their decisional output.*

2   The 'New Right' Educational Agenda

This agenda contained such elements as:
  (i)   promoting policies *supporting educational excellence* whilst simultaneously *squeezing equity issues into the background;*
  (ii) continually *denigrating the public schools* whilst emphasizing the right to *parental choice* in education and *promoting the interests of private schools* (through advocacy of tuition tax credits and vouchers in US and increasing aid to private schools via the Commonwealth Schools Commission in Australia);
  (iii) demanding a return to 'the basics' and 'discipline' in our schools;
  (iv) emphasizing the narrow competitive and vocational roles of schools and their links with the economy to the detriment of their broader social and integrative roles in society.

The accuracy of my observations so far as Reagan education policy is concerned, is largely borne out by the detailed research of scholars such as Clark and Amiot (1981), Schuster (1982), and Clark and Astuto (1984, 1985 and 1986). In chapter 3 Clark and Astuto provide a comprehensive analysis of Reagan's policies in education from 1980 to 1986 and thus permit me to focus in my chapter largely on Hawke's education policies and on attempted explanation of the similarities with and differences from Fraser and Reagan policies.

Predicting Hawke Socialist Education Policy

In a nutshell, my argument in the 'New Federalism' paper in 1985 was that in both countries the spectre of huge Federal deficits and increased central power in conjunction with the conservative ideologies of Fraser and Reagan, contributed to striking policy reversals designed to reduce the Federal role in education and to implement a 'New Right' educational agenda.

Given that Fraser's conservative Liberal government was replaced by the Hawke socialist Australian Labor Party (ALP) government in March 1983, it might be argued that in Australia, all of the above constraints to a revival of the long-term post-war trend of Federal expansion in education — with the vital exception of the continuing large (Aust $6b) Federal deficit — had been removed. Consequently, on the basis of Hawke's party's pre-election promises and the previous Whitlam ALP government's (1972–1975) education policies, we might reasonably have predicted a significant shift and altered emphasis in Australia's federal education policy away from the Fraser and Reagan model.

It is important to note that the ALP has a long democratic socialist tradition of social reform and redistributionist policies — deriving as its name suggests, from its origins as the party representing the workers as distinct from capitalists and employers. Despite its strong affiliations with the trade union movement (over 60 per cent of the Australian workforce is unionized) it has never been a doctrinaire party.

The party has an extremely democratic policy-making framework enabling policy proposals to filter up from local and state branches to the supreme policy-making body — the ALP Biennial Federal Conference. This broadly representative body which also contains strong representation from federal politicians including the leader (Hawke) debates and establishes official ALP policy — the so-called 'platform'. The policies enshrined in that platform are technically binding on ALP politicians — that is, in office, ALP leaders (unlike their conservative counterparts) are technically obliged to implement the policies. Any leader who implements policies contrary to or in conflict with the platform does so at his peril and may face the ultimate sanction of expulsion from the party.

Under the radical reformist (though still very moderate by international socialist standards) Whitlam ALP government from 1972–1975 — the first Labor government for a period of twenty-three years — education was viewed as a central instrument for making society more equal and for promoting social change and reform. Thus some of Whitlam's early measures included: the creation of a federal Schools Commission with a vast budget to be allocated to all schools on a basis of 'need' (positive discrimination); the abolition of tertiary tuition fees so as to remove economic barriers to access to higher education; the assumption of total federal responsibility (previously shared by state and federal governments) for funding all universities and colleges of advanced education, thus ensuring a nationally coordinated and equitably financed tertiary education system across the country; and the introduction of a means-tested non-repayable living allowance scheme Tertiary Education Assistance Scheme (TEAS) open to all students. All these policies were part of the ALP platform on which Whitlam was elected to office.

Given the Whitlam government's record of educational reform and the ALP's education platform and election promises at the time of the Hawke government's assumption of office in 1983, we might have reasonably predicted a significant shift away from the Reagan-Fraser education policy along the following lines:

1   Overall Federal Role in Education Policy and Funding

(a)   A renewed commitment to a strong federal presence at all levels of education, symbolized by substantial increases in federal expenditure — reversing the cut-backs of the Fraser years.

(b)   A return to a major federal role in curriculum innovation and diffusion and to educational research through reinstatement of the Federal Curriculum Development Centre and the Education Research and Development Committee — both of which had been axed under Fraser.

2   Equity and Excellence Issues

(a)   Less emphasis on issues of educational excellence and a greater emphasis on equity issues such as improved participation rates in upper secondary schools in post-compulsory education.

(b)   A greater emphasis on improved access for the disadvantaged (girls/women, migrants, aboriginals, the handicapped/disabled) at all levels of education.

(c)   A greater emphasis on affirmative action and equal opportunity in educational institutions.

(d)   Improved foreign aid in the form of expanding government funded educational provision in Australia for overseas students from neighbouring lesser developed countries.

3   School Funding and Policy

(a)   A reassertion in policy and practice of the federal government's 'primary obligation' to public schools before private schools.

(b)   A renewed emphasis on funding equity reflected in reinstatement of substantial needs-based (positive discrimination) differentials in funding within the private school sector — thus reversing the sharp drift back towards equal per capita funding under Fraser.

(c)   A de-emphasis of Fraser's focus on excellence and freedom of choice and a strong defence of the quality and standards in the public school system — including resistance to demands for national testing and monitoring of standards in numeracy and literacy.

(d)   In line with the above, implementation of policies to strengthen the federal Schools Commission which had been seriously weakened under Fraser — including efforts to restore the power and influence of the state offices of the Schools Commission as bodies guaranteeing compliance with federal policy.

4 Higher Education Policy

(a) A reversal of the harsh Fraser cut-backs in federal funds (the source of 95 per cent of all university and college funds) for higher education institutions. Increased funds to meet deteriorating provision of: buildings, maintenance, research equipment and personnel, libraries, academic staff and student places.

(b) Defiance of strong conservative party demands for the reintroduction of tertiary tuition fees (Australia has had a policy of free tertiary tuition since Whitlam government legislation in 1974).

(c) A reversal of some of the more draconian Fraser higher education accountability/economy measures such as: attacks on academic conditions of service (for example, tenure and sabbatical leave); 'rationalization' and forced amalgamations of tertiary institutions.

5 'Economistic' Approaches to Education

(a) A rejection of the strong Fraser focus on the economic and vocational functions of schooling at the expense of a more balanced view which acknowledged the importance of broad-based general education for all students as the basis for future flexibility and adaptability.

(b) Resistance to the growing pressures from Fraser's Liberal Party and from some influential 'free market' economic advisors urging the federal government to 'privatize' — to treat public education as any other marketable commodity by such measures as the introduction of vouchers and fees and to explore the scope for generating export income from marketing higher education to foreign students from neighbouring Pacific rim countries.

Hawke Policies in Practice: How Different?

How different, then, have the socialist Hawke government's education policies been in practice, from the Fraser-Reagan prototype during its period of office 1983–1986? In general, prediction has proved remarkably hazardous. Whilst some of the predicted policy reversals have occurred, in most of these cases the degree of change has been generally quite modest and in many policy areas little or no change from the Fraser policy has emerged in practice. Such has been the disgust of the Australian Teachers Federation with the ALP's education policies that it produced a paper in 1984 entitled 'Hawke in Fraser's clothing' (Marginson, 1984).

I will seek to explain the reasons for change or lack of change as I analyze particular Hawke education policies. However, there are a number of general factors operating which help to explain the relatively modest degree of change achieved by the Hawke government during its first three years in office. These factors and the unfolding of education policy are elaborated in greater detail in Smart *et al* (1986) 'The Hawke government and education 1983–1985'.

General Contextual Factors Contributing to the Hawke Government's Cautious and Incremental Approach to Change

1 *Preoccupation with the Deficit and Need to Demonstrate 'Sound Economic Management'*
From its earliest days, the Hawke government was preoccupied with the size of the deficit. From well before it achieved power, too, the ALP was extremely conscious of its need to establish its credentials in government as a 'sound and responsible economic manager'. It had the notorious legacy of the Whitlam years (1972–1975) to live down, during which time that socialist government had acquired a partly deserved reputation for poor economic management and profligate expenditure.

2 *The Hawke Style: 'Government by Consensus'*
In contrast to the 'crash through or crash' confrontationist style of leadership displayed by both his predecessors (Whitlam and Fraser), Hawke has carefully cultivated a consensual approach to government perhaps best characterized by one of his Party's election slogans 'Bringing Australia Together'. Hawke has built up elaborate mechanisms for ensuring broad consultation between unions, business and government on all major facets of economic policy. His so-called economic and tax summits received widespread national and international attention as examples of government by consensus.

3 *Hawke Pragmatism*
No doubt reflecting on the remarkable brevity of the spectacular radical-reformist Whitlam government, Hawke and his colleagues seem intent on retaining office in the long term. Eschewing much of the traditional left-wing rhetoric and ideology of Labor, Hawke and his Cabinet have adopted an extremely pragmatic approach to government. This approach is consistent both with the more conservative mood of the electorate and with Hawke's background. His lengthy formative training years — he only entered federal politics in 1980 — were spent in the trade union movement, where for years, as President of the Australian Council of Trade Unions, he honed his skills as a negotiator of compromises, a resolver of conflict. These experiences have left him distrustful and cynical of ideology. Many cynics in the left wing of the ALP see his approach as 'pure pragmatism' and doubt that he has any real commitment to the ALP's central principle of equality.

His fairly conservative Cabinet — perhaps significantly more right wing than the Federal Parliamentary Labor Party Caucus with which it not infrequently clashes — has read well the more conservative mood of the great mass of the Australian electorate, and has pragmatically tailored its policies accordingly. Thus the ALP government has, by and large, studiously avoided implementing left-oriented policies which might 'rock the boat'. Such an approach has led some ALP influentials to warn that long-held ALP socialist principles are in danger of being 'sold out' to Hawke-style policy pragmatism.

Hawke Education Policies 1983–1985

I will now briefly examine the Hawke government's actual education policies and achievements under the five headings and in relation to the predictions about change which I inferred earlier.

Overall Federal Role in Education Funding and Policy

The Hawke government has signalled its clear intention that the federal government will remain a strong partner with the states in formulating broad national policy and maintaining its financial commitment at about existing levels. This does not, of course, mean that the proportion of total federal outlays devoted to education will not continue to drift downwards (from their high of 9 per cent in 1976–77 they are currently around 7 per cent (see figure 1)). In fact, economists have been arguing that based on realistic figures of enrolment growth and growth in GDP, education could in the 1990s fare quite favourably even if the proportion of total federal outlays on education drifted a little below existing levels (Burke, 1985, p. 21). In each of its three budgets to date, the Hawke government has provided for real increases in Federal expenditure on education of the order of 5 per cent. Thus the Fraser cuts in federal education expenditure in real terms have been reversed. However, given the austerity of the Fraser years, the Hawke increases for education, although an improvement, have not been sufficient to prevent deterioration in provision, particularly in higher education. I will return to this later.

Curriculum and research role
So far as a reinstatement of the Federal role in curriculum development and educational research is concerned, achievement has been 'mixed'. The Hawke government has honoured its promise to re-establish the Curriculum Development Centre (CDC). However, to date, despite repeated assurances of interest by the Federal Minister for Education, Senator Susan Ryan, the federal government has not re-established the Education Research and De-

Figure 1: Australian Federal Government Expenditure on Education as a Proportion of Total Federal Expenditure: Actual 1976/77 to 1985/86: Estimated 1986/87.

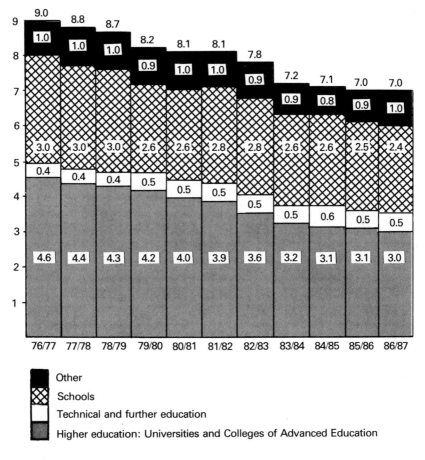

Other

Schools

Technical and further education

Higher education: Universities and Colleges of Advanced Education

Source: CTEC Triennial Report for 1985-87, Vol.1, Part 1, April 1984 Budget Papers No. 1. 1984-85 to 1986-87, Department of Finance

Table 1: Some Key Areas of Australian Federal Budget Outlays 1974–5 to 1986–7 in Constant 1979–80 Dollars ($b)

Outlays	Whitlam (ALP) 1974–75	Fraser (Liberal) 1975–76	1977–78	1978–79	1980–81	1982–83	Percentage increase of 1982–83 on 1973–74	Hawke (ALP) 1983–84	1984–85	1985–86	1986–87 (est)	Percentage increase of 1986–87 on 1974–75
Defence	2.684	2.627	2.794	2.868	3.218	3.496	+30.25	3.667	3.785	3.972	4.129	+53.84
Education	2.731	2.671	2.813	2.773	2.602	2.716	−0.55	2.783	2.880	2.925	2.898	+6.11
Health	2.108	4.165	3.160	3.181	3.305	2.504	+18.79	3.005	3.896	4.077	4.068	+92.98
Social security and welfare	6.095	7.096	8.695	8.876	8.994	10.316	+69.25	11.198	11.366	11.424	11.559	+89.65
Total budget outlays	29.261	30.792	31.285	31.789	32.728	35.771	+22.25	28.335	40.607	41.617	41.628	+42.26

Sources: Budget Papers, H.R. 21 August 1984, p. 369
Budget Papers, H.R. 19 August 1986, p. 380

velopment Committee which until 1981 allocated $2.5m annually in education research funds based on open refereed competition. Thus, a federal government which currently spends over $4b annually on education is still in the anomalous position where it does not currently foster a significant education research effort — apart from the narrow short-term policy-oriented research commissioned through its in-house education agency budgets.

Equity and Excellence Issues

Participation, access and equity in education

The Hawke government has given high priority to equity concerns and especially to those of promoting increased participation and enhanced access at all levels of education. Indeed, its very success in increasing secondary retention rates to year 12 and encouraging more Australians to seek entry to post-secondary education has produced a serious shortage of places in tertiary institutions (Smart *et al*, 1986).

One of the reasons for the Hawke government's focus on educational access and participation was the disturbingly high level of youth unemployment with which it was confronted on taking office — March 1983 being almost the nadir of Australia's economic recession. Partly as a response to this problem, and partly stemming from its long-standing ALP principles of equity and access, the Hawke government in 1983 launched its Participation and Equity Programme (PEP). PEP was to be the ambitious '... centrepiece of the overall framework of youth policies ... (with) the twin objectives of increasing participation in education and introducing greater equity in the Government's overall provision for young people' (Ryan, Senate, 25 August 1983, pp. 240–1). A central goal was to achieve, by 1990, a situation where the majority of young people were completing the equivalent of a full secondary education either in school or in Technical and Further Education (TAFE), or in some combination of work and education.

This has proven a remarkably successful strategy already. Between 1981 and 1984 national year 12 retention rates have risen from 35 per cent to 45 per cent (Quality and Equality, 1985, p. 199). In the first two years of the Hawke government, unemployment in the 15–24 year ago group fell by 76,000 whilst the number in the same age group participating in full-time post-secondary education rose by 56,000. In the words of the Chairman of the Commonwealth Tertiary Education Commission (CTEC), Hugh Hudson (1985) '... it is clear that the expansion in education has been a more important factor in reducing unemployment of young people than has improvement in economic activity' (p. 49). A recent federal government committee — Quality of Education Review — optimistically predicted that the bulk of youth unemployment might be eliminated by 1992 through the introduction of a new federal youth traineeship programme combined with continued expansion of full-time education opportunities at the same level as the past two years (1985). Perhaps the biggest problem with this scenario is that the 1983–85 post-secondary expansion occurred with very limited increases in funding so that tertiary institutions are now jammed tight with students and facing deteriorating academic and instructional conditions. Further expansion cannot occur without a much more generous infusion of recurrent and capital funds.

Enhanced educational access for the disadvantaged
In the area of enhanced access for the disadvantaged, the Hawke government has also achieved considerable success. The retention rates of girls in year 12 (48 per cent) continue to surpass those for boys (42 per cent) and total female enrolments in colleges of advanced education now exceed those of males whilst they are also fast approaching parity in universities. Through the federal government's tertiary PEP scheme money has been provided to tertiary institutions for such worthwhile purposes as: 'examining mathematics and sciences in primary teacher education courses; reviewing the provision of enclave programmes for Aboriginal people; evaluating teaching materials for 'marginal students' with inadequate language and numeracy skills; . . . and developing programmes to increase the participation of women in science, technology and management-based courses' (CTEC Report for 1985–87, Vol 2).

A variety of initiatives in Aboriginal education have been set in train but progress has been partly blunted by the complex division of responsibility for Aboriginals between state and federal governments and even within the federal bureaucracy, between the Departments of Aboriginal Affairs, Education and Employment and Industrial Relations. Following the report of a major parliamentary committee on *Aboriginal Education* (1985), the Minister for Education, Senator Ryan, announced in March 1986 the transfer of all Aboriginal education programmes from the Department of Aboriginal Affairs to the Department of Education. She also announced that the National Aboriginal Education Committee would become the government's principal advisor. She expected these two moves to enable her to ' . . . consolidate all the work done in Aboriginal education to streamline our administration and to build on the very solid gains . . . already made' (Ryan, Press Release, 5 March 1986).

Affirmative action and equal employment opportunity programs
Despite substantial initial resistance from the Australian Vice Chancellors Committee and other quarters, Senator Ryan has been largely personally responsible for ensuring the adoption of affirmative action and equal employment opportunities programs in most tertiary institutions since 1983.

Foreign student assistance
Undoubtedly in this area the ALP has surprised many of its supporters. During 1984 the government received the reports of the Jackson Committee

on Australia's Overseas Aid Programme and the Goldring Committee on Private Overseas Student Policy (Smart *et al*, 1986). Taking the very much in vogue 'privatization' line, the Jackson Committee viewed education as an export commodity. Emphasizing the 'user-pays' principle, it opted for full cost recovery through fees, together with a three-tiered scholarship system involving government to government scholarships, scholarships on merit and special scholarships. In contrast, the Goldring Committee recommended a continuation of the overseas student charge — a contribution to total costs — at a uniform rate for all undergraduates. In March 1985 the government announced its policy, essentially opting for the Goldring model with the overseas student charge to be increased to 35 per cent and then 45 per cent of the full cost of a place in 1986 and 1987 respectively. Overseas students unable to be accommodated within this government subsidized aid programme would be able to seek entry to courses at full cost. This is currently a very fluid policy area with tertiary institutions largely inexperienced in marketing education, jostling each other and competing for a share of the allegedly lucrative overseas student market. There are many within the ALP who are extremely uneasy about this tertiary education experiment with the 'free-market' and its potential for inequity, exploitation and damage to the traditional overseas student aid programme. Already there has been strong protest from subsidized overseas students who are nearing completion of their studies in Australia and who have suddenly been confronted with unpredicted fee hikes. Belatedly the Hawke government has agreed to 'hold the line' on fees for existing overseas students — but this only adds to the impression of ill-planned policy-making on the run.

School Funding and Policy

As demonstrated in chapter 7 this is a classic example of a policy area in which Hawke's pursuit of community consensus — together with the considerable lobbying clout of the Catholic hierarchy and the wealthy private school establishment — forced him to reject the ALP's official policy. That is to say, despite strong formal ALP policy platform commitments and election promises to phase out federal aid for wealthy private schools, the Hawke government, like the Whitlam Government before it, ultimately found it expedient to back away from this policy. Instead, Hawke chose the more expensive consensus option of maintaining aid for wealthy schools at existing levels whilst substantially increasing aid for the poorer Catholic private schools and for government schools.

Naturally this consensus solution was seen as the betrayal of long-term ALP principles for short-term electoral pragmatism by many ALP members and public school supporters. Thus an Australian Teachers Federation Research Paper described it in the following terms:

Don Smart

> It is hard to capture in words the sense of outrage and betrayal
> amongst government school teachers and parents following the re-
> lease of the Federal Government's Guidelines for Schools Funding on
> 14 August this year.
>
> In one stroke the Hawke government silenced the militant
> minority opposition of the private school supporters by giving them
> everything they wanted, stroked the captains of industry with a
> promise that education would be brought into line with their needs,
> guaranteed the fiscal 'rationalists' that there would be no Whitlamite
> expansion of education funding (except to private schools), soothed
> the 'back to basics' lobby by adopting their rhetoric and reassured all
> those who fear the teacher unions with a very public declaration of
> the government's intention to shut the unions out of any influence
> ove education policy.
>
> It was a spectacular conservative coup. Hawke had become
> Fraser, only this time there was no alternative waiting in the wings.
>
> Given the finely-tuned electoral pragmatism and neo-
> conservative economics of the Hawke government, these outcomes
> in retrospect look less surprising. (Marginson, 1984.)

Whilst the Hawke government was unable to 'deliver' on the issue of phasing
out aid to wealthy private schools and whilst this offended many left-wing
members of the ALP, it is fair to say that in most other respects the Hawke
government has implemented the spirit of its education policy. For example,
it has reaffirmed its 'primary obligation' to the public rather than the private
school system and backed up that reaffirmation with guarantees of a redres-
sing of the imbalance of federal funding (over 50 per cent of the $2b federal
aid bill goes to the 25 per cent of students in private schools) away from the
private and towards the public education sector (Ryan, 1984). Simultaneously, it confirmed its commitment to a more strongly needs-based approach to
funding private schools through the extension of Fraser's relatively undifferentiated three-category system of 'need' into a much refined twelve-
category system with differential funding for schools in each category. Thus
the wealthiest category of private schools will have its federal assistance more
or less permanently pegged at the existing level of $277 (elementary) and
$440 (secondary) per capita, whilst by contrast, the poorest non-government
schools (mostly Catholic) will be receiving $1034 (elementary) and $1526
(secondary) per capita by 1992. Perhaps the ALP is simply adopting a
longer-term time frame for the ultimate phase out of aid to the wealthiest
schools.

*De-emphasis of excellence and freedom of choice and strong defence of
quality and standards in public education?*
As predicted, there has been some down-playing of issues of excellence and
freedom of choice — though the decision not to phase out federal aid to the

wealthiest private schools was viewed by many as a victory for freedom of choice and an acknowledgement by the government of the right of all taxpayers to some assistance from the federal education budget.

Nevertheless, the public and symbolic affirmations of confidence in the quality and contribution of the public education system that many educators had expected from the Hawke government have been largely absent. Indeed, in the view of many educators the attitudes and approach of the Hawke government has been uncharacteristically unhelpful and unsupportive. Both Prime Minister Hawke and Education Minister Ryan have on several occasions seriously questioned the quality and direction of the education system as a whole and put on notice the federal government's intention to rigorously examine whether it gets value for money from its substantial financial outlays (Marginson, 1984).

The QERC report
No doubt the widespread community concern with standards and the quality of education — together with the enormity of the federal deficit — have been mutually reinforcing pressures which have obliged the federal government to look closely at issues of educational accountability and outcomes. The result has been several major Commonwealth inquiries — the Quality of Education Review committee (QERC) for the schools sector and the Efficiency and Effectiveness Review in the post-secondary sector. The QERC report appears to have been 'forced' on the Minister for Education as a result of intervention by senior bureaucrats in the Departments of Finance and Prime Minister and Cabinet. In their review of the Department of Education's 1984 pre-Budget submission, these bureaucrats asked what evidence there was to show that the massive increase in federal per pupil school expenditure (of some 50 per cent between 1973 and 1983) had improved the quality of education (Smart *et al*, 1986).

Two overriding concerns dominated the terms of reference of QERC — establishing 'value for money' and gearing the education system more closely to labour market needs. Unlike the Karmel Report of 1973 which was largely concerned with education *inputs*, QERC was required to establish that there were identifiable educational *outcomes* from Federal aid.

However, measurement of outcomes in education is a highly complex and difficult task which requires agreement on goals and often involves assumptions by clients that all outcomes are conveniently measurable. QERC's quest for output indicators such as achievement score progress from existing state department and private school records proved largely unsuccessful. Faced with conflicting evidence from measurement and anecdotal sources about whether there had been gains or losses in cognitive achievement over the decade, QERC was ultimately forced to offer its own impressionistic conclusion. It concluded that schools had by and large used the increase in federal aid to respond effectively to new challenges and demands and 'produced results superior to those which would otherwise have been the case'. On the basis of these QERC 'impressions', the Hawke government essentially re-committed itself to existing levels of federal aid for schools. However, undoubtedly the most important result of QERC has been its recommendations for future policy which Hawke has endorsed. These re-commendations largely focus on the need to develop and monitor measures of outcomes and to establish with fund recipients a firm commitment to progress in certain priority areas. Some of the key recommendations were:

(i) Recurrent grants should in future be premised on negotiated agreements between the Commonwealth and government and non-government school authorities with declared priority areas which should include: basic skills in primary; enhancing the competencies of disadvantaged students which would improve their likelihood of completing secondary schooling; more equal representation of girls in all major subject areas; and teacher development programmes appropriate to these priorities.

(ii) Greater accountability by recipients of Commonwealth funds in the form of three-yearly accountability statements describing changes in: levels of attainment in general skills; post-compulsory participation rates by socioeconomic class, by gender and by rural-urban location; statistics on post-compulsory subject choice of girls and the proportions sitting major exams in each major subject.

(iii) Reviews of most of the extant Schools Commission specific purpose programmes within the next few years.

(iv) The telescoping of the separate funds for many existing specific purpose programmes into the general recurrent funding vote and the key objective of these former programmes to become part of the formal negotiated agreements.

(v) For all remaining specific purpose programmes there was to be an effort to simplify the number of objectives and evaluation indicators and a requirement to regularly report progress towards the achievement of these objectives. *(ibid)*

Neither the state education departments, the private schools nor the Commonwealth's own Schools Commission have been very enthusiastic about these proposed 'negotiated agreements' and 'accountability statements' with their strong emphasis on evaluation of 'progress indicators'. It remains to be seen how much of QERC will ultimately be implemented. Nevertheless it is a clear demonstration of federal concern about standards and economy and in general, represents a body-blow to tthe Schools Commission (see the SC publications 'Discussion of Some Issues Raised in Quality of Education in Australia' (1985) and 'Quality and Equality' (1985)).

Efficiency and effectiveness review of tertiary education
The creation of this review is yet another policy decision which many educators would have considered more in keeping with the draconian Fraser

era of accountability, amalgamations and rationalization. The review which is due for release during 1986 was commissioned by Senator Ryan in mid-1985 and is chaired by the head of CTEC, Mr Hugh Hudson. It was initiated at a time when several federal politicians were calling for the creation of state 'Razor Gangs' to carve $200m of 'fat' from the budgets of tertiary institutions — all of which are totally funded by the federal government. For this reason it is unclear whether it is a friendly 'smokescreen' accountability device to protect higher education from the politicians, or whether the federal minister and her Cabinet colleagues are looking for more 'sacrifices' from the universities and colleges in order to reduce the deficit. Certainly, the rumours emanating from Canberra suggest that it will have some unwelcome news for many academics so far as research and postgraduate funding are concerned.

It is fair to say then, that the pressures for accountability and centralized coordination which ironically were honed into an 'art-form' under Fraser 'Federalism' have been kept alive and well under Hawke. The Reagan approach, by contrast, seems to have been to cut the budget at the centre but then deregulate and decentralize its expenditure by state and local authorities, giving them maximum freedom to determine their priorities. Interestingly, both Hawke and Reagan appear to be agreed on the value of national monitoring of achievement indicators.

Higher Education Policy

Funding

Between the mid 1960s and mid 1970s, higher education in Australia went through a halcyon period of unprecedented expansion and well-being. In 1974, just as the Australian economy began to deteriorate, the Whitlam government assumed total financial responsibility for universities and colleges. By 1975 it was clear that the Federal budget generally, including education, would have to be 'reined in'. From 1975 to 1983 under Fraser, the overall federal education budget remained virtually static in real terms and the higher education budget component suffered real cuts. Many colleges of advanced education were forced to amalgamate. University and college building programs virtually ground to a halt, and libraries and research equipment and facilities were further 'run-down'. Unfortunately, this deteriorating situation was 'masked' to some extent under Fraser by a downturn in student enrolments in the late 1970s. However, this situation was initially exacerbated under Hawke because of a lack of understanding of the seriousness of the problems and because the very high youth unemployment problem led to top priority being given to secondary school and TAFE PEP programs. These very programs have now further exacerbated the problem by increasing the demand for tertiary education well above the supply of available tertiary places.

In addition, the unnecessary political furore which developed between mid-1983 and mid-1984 over the possible cessation of federal aid to private schools forced the Hawke government to come up with an unnecessarily expensive funding package for the public and private schools sector which had already done extremely well compared to tertiary institutions. For example, in its March 1985 Report, the Commonwealth Tertiary Education Commission ruefully pointed out that whilst in the preceding decade per student expenditure in schools had increased by 50 per cent, per student expenditure in universities and colleges had decreased by 8 per cent.

Another serious barrier to the solving of this financial problem was (and perhaps still is) the widespread lack of sympathy and support for higher education amongst federal politicians. Up until very recently there has been a strong tendency for ALP government leaders to follow the Fraser economistic managerial line — viewing the tertiary institutions as organizations ripe for efficiency auditing and rationalization, of seeing them in narrow vocational terms and of blaming the high levels of unemployment on the quality and 'unsuitability' of their courses. In a very real sense, higher education has been a 'whipping boy' for a wide cross-section of those in the ALP government. Few politicians have had a sympathetic word for the institutions: from the Prime Minister (who personally sabotaged a duly-determined academic salary hike), to the Minister for Education (who attacked the universities as 'bastions of privilege'), to the Minister for Finance (pushing the reintroduction of tertiary tuition fees), to lowly backbenchers, who sought to establish state 'razor gangs' to trim $200m of 'fat' off the tertiary budget and carve up the tenure and salaries of senior academics. Such attitudes were, in part, attributable to a government which had been heavily influenced, if not totally coopted, by the heavy onslaught of neo-conservatism and free-market ideas circulating in Australia — a theme to which I will return shortly.

In a nutshell, whilst the Hawke government now seems more conscious of the serious financial plight of tertiary education, its response to date has been too little and too late. Institutions with any spare capacity have been encouraged to take additional students but have been funded by the federal government at well below marginal cost. The result has been deteriorating educational services and provision. Through such cheap money policies, between 1983 and 1987 the Hawke government will have 'packed' an additional 28,000 students into Australian higher education. The real problem is that such a cheap policy is a once-off opportunity and that further tertiary expansion — and the ALP's PEP policy in the schools will ensure continuing expansion of demand for tertiary places — will only be possible at considerably greater expense. There are presently increasing signs that state governments are feeling the grass-roots pressure for more tertiary places and may be gradually re-emerging as a new source of tertiary funds. In the past twelve months, the Northern Territory has created and will fund its own university, the Victorian government has funded an additional 1500 tertiary places, and the Western Australian government has spent $7m on a new tertiary campus at Bunbury. Such developments were unthinkable two years ago.

Tertiary tuition fees
It is undoubtedly something of a surprise that several senior Hawke Cabinet Ministers would seek to overturn existing ALP platform policy to reintroduce tertiary fees which had been abolished by the Whitlam government in the interests of equity only a decade earlier. Senator Peter Walsh, the Finance Minister, anxious to reduce the deficit has argued for the past eighteen months that free tertiary tuition is a 'rip-off' for the rich and that fees should be reintroduced. Walsh and others, including the Prime Minister, appear to have been influenced by the strong flowering of 'free-market' economic advice circulating in Canberra during 1984–1985. The concept of tertiary education purely as a financial investment in an individual's economic future appealed to the prevailing mood of 'privatization' and 'user pays' amongst some of the increasingly conservative financial managers in the Hawke Cabinet. This concept has acquired increased attractiveness as the enormity of the cost of fixing the backlog of neglected problems in tertiary education has dawned on the politicians.

Ultimately, in March 1985, following an overwhelming vote of opposition to fees in the Education Committee of Caucus, Walsh and Hawke withdrew their fees proposal from Cabinet. Despite several subsequent attempts by Walsh to revive the issue, the results of an ANOP opinion poll in April 1985 (showing that 74 per cent of Australians opposed fees) will probably ensure that the issue does not come up for reconsideration at the ALP Biennial Conference in July 1986. In fact, in March 1986, Senator Susan Ryan publicly announced to a conference of students that the fees issue was officially dead and would not be raised again by the Hawke government. Nevertheless, given the serious budgetary problems of the Hawke government and its pragmatic approach, I doubt that fees can be completely written out of the short-term agenda.

Reversal of Fraser-type draconian measures in higher education
Many educators, perhaps naively, believed that the Hawke government would end the period of harsh and seemingly malicious attacks on higher education which were widespread under Fraser. However, as I have already indicated, not a great deal has changed. Many ALP politicians and ministers have been unsympathetic to higher education and have advocated severe economy measures and greater accountability. Attempts to reintroduce tertiary fees, deny salary increases, undermine academic conditions and the initiation of the CTEC Efficiency and Effectiveness Review are seen by many academics as symbolic of the Hawke government's betrayal of higher education.

Don Smart

Economistic Approaches to Education

Over-emphasis on the economic and vocational goals of education
Many educators have been disappointed at the lack of apparent difference
between the stance of the Hawke and Fraser governments on this issue. The
government has placed great weight on increasing the numbers of science,
technology, business and computer students at the expense of the humanities
and social sciences. Hawke also raised some educational eyebrows in
September 1984 when he inferred that the schools were contributing to the
problem of youth unemployment: 'We must face up completely honestly to
questions whether the present-day education system is adequate to the task;
to whether it is of such quality that we can be confident of our children's
future? Frankly, I have my doubts.' (Marginson, 1984).

Privatization of higher education
It has also come as a surprise to many ALP supporters to find that the Hawke
government has been so willing to 'take on board' the 'commodity' view of
education and so accept many of the 'free-market' and 'privatization' proposals in circulation. Tertiary fees is one example. Another was the outrageous
Fane Report (1984) commissioned by the Prime Minister's Economic Planning and Advisory Council. Amongst its recommendations was a proposal
that all tertiary institutions be put on the market and sold off to the highest
bidder regardless of whether the bidder intended to use them for educational
purposes. Naturally the report was laughed out of court. Perhaps more
important though, is the Hawke government's decision to encourage institutions to earn export income through the marketing of higher education to the
neighbouring South-East Asian region. Following a joint Department of
Education and Trade 'Mission' to the region in September 1985, the government announced guidelines to institutions for the admission of full-fee paying
overseas students. A range of other options is also being encouraged, including off-shore delivery of courses via distance education or actual on-the-
ground delivery via the establishment of branch campuses in South-East
Asia. This is an extremely fluid area at the moment, with the government
seemingly making policy on-the-run. It remains to be seen how it will affect
tertiary institutions in the long-run, particularly if private or semi-private
separate campuses are established in Australia for overseas students. The
government undoubtedly hopes that it will reduce the current almost total
financial reliance of institutions on Canberra. Strong encouragement is also
being given to institutions to diversify their research funding away from
Canberra and towards industry.

Outcome of Analysis

How then, might we sum up our analysis of Reagan and Hawke education policies as reflected in the foregoing discussions and as illustrated in charts A and B.

Perhaps the first thing to be said is, that unlike the dramatic ideological sea-change of education policies and policy preferences reflected in the US switch from Carter to Reagan (see chapter 3) or the earlier Australian switch from McMahon to Whitlam (Smart, 1978) the switch from conservative Fraser (who had so much in common with Reagan) to socialist Hawke has been a significantly more gradual and less perceptible experience. That is not to say, however, that Hawke's policies have not been different in some vital areas. Thus on *some, but by no means all*, of the big ideological issues Hawke's socialist government has 'stood up and been counted':

(i)   Where Reagan and Fraser sought, respectively, to eliminate, and reduce the federal role, the Hawke government has sought to uphold a strong federal presence in education.

(ii) In the face of a mounting federal deficit, Fraser and Reagan cut education expenditure, whereas Hawke achieved modest growth; that is to say, where Reagan substituted exhortation for money, Hawke did not.

(iii) The real 'litmus test', presumably, is Hawke's performance on the 'conservative education agenda'. In this respect, Hawke possibly just survives the crucial 'equity-excellence pendulum test'.

Whereas Fraser and Reagan in a myriad of ways have emphasized excellence as a value in education and down-played equity issues, Hawke has, generally speaking, done exactly the opposite — though 'socialist purists' would point to notable 'faintnesses of heart' with respect to funding for wealthy schools and the tertiary fees 'flip-flop'. Where Fraser and Reagan have pushed freedom of choice and support for private schools, Hawke has emphasized the primary obligation of government to public schools. Reversing what the left sees as a Fraser-induced federal 'bias' in funding to private schools will not be achieved overnight but the Hawke government has begun to address the problem. Whilst Hawke has confirmed a continuation (and even increase) of federal aid to private schools he has insisted on a more sophisticated differentiation of 'need' and asserted that the wealthiest schools will not receive any increase in assistance. Nevertheless, the failure to end aid to wealthy schools will continue to be a 'sore point' with the left wing of the ALP and with public school parent and teacher organizations. Hawke has also vigorously promoted increased access to and participation in post-compulsory education by youth and by various disadvantaged groups in society. On at least two items of the 'conservative agenda' though, Hawke is in agreement with Fraser and Reagan. Both he and his Minister for Education have berated standards and the quality of education, and he and his government have in a

Chart A: *The Federal Role, Governance and Finance of Education*

Policy	Reagan	Fraser	Hawke
1 Commitment to a strong federal role in education	No (abolish federal role)	Reduced federal role	Yes
2 Committed to closure of:			
Education department	Yes	No	No
Other education agencies	Yes (closed NIE)	Yes (closed CDC, and ERDC)	No (reopened CDC)
3 Emasculation of agencies?			
Education department	Yes	N/A	N/A
National Institute for Education	Yes	N/A	N/A
Schools Commission	N/A	Yes	Yes
4 Decentralization of policy and control away from Washington/ Canberra	Yes	More centralization and coordination (eg, CTEC's college mergers)	No New CTEC Act strengthened D.E.
5 Deregulation	Yes	No	No • Contradictory policies • Negotiated agreements • Principles not detailed
6 Cut federal education expenditure	Yes (ECIA) substantial success	Yes marginal success	No Modest Growth of 5 per cent per annum
7 Promotion of greater efficiency and cost-effectiveness in expenditure of federal education budget	Yes via deregulation, decentralization and budget cuts	Yes thru regulation & coordination from Canberra • College mergers • Centres of research excellence • CTEC • Budget cuts	Yes • CTEC Act • QERC • Efficiency review

Chart B: The Conservative Education Agenda

Policy	Reagan	Fraser	Hawke
1 Promote excellence	• Commission on excellence • Bully pulpit • Promotion of competition	• Centres of research excellence • More aid for private schools	• Emphasis more on equity • Concerns about quality of education • Pegged aid to wealthy private schools
2 Downplay equity issues	• Yes, almost off agenda • IRS to 'lay off' non-compliant private schools • Deregulation policy allows • Reagan to put onus for equity issues on states	• Yes, reduced 'needs' categories to three • Resulted in more money for wealthy private schools	• No, re-emphasize equity issues: 1) Schools funding 2) PEP (schools & TAFE) 3) Tertiary PEP 4) Affirmative action & equal employment opportunity programs
3 Freedom of choice/support of private schools	• Tuition tax credits • Education vouchers • Fostering competition between public & private schools	• Increased aid to private schools • Explored voucher system • Decreased proportion of federal aid going to public schools	• Increased aid to poor private schools • More stringent conditions for establishing new private schools • Restrictions on new funded places in existing private schools
4 Attacks on public education system	• Criticism of standards, discipline, lack of parent control of curriculum and methods	• Criticism of public school standards • Frequent attendance at private school functions • Blamed education system for youth unemployment	• Blamed inadequacies of education system for youth unemployment • Universities attacked as 'bastions of privilege' • Attacks on academic salaries and conditions
5 Stress on economic and vocational function of the education system	• Strong emphasis on economic and productivity concerns • Stress on competition	• Transition from school to work program • Expand vocational education provision (TAFE) in preference to university & college • Established major inquiry (Williams) into education and training • Criticised mismatch between educational system output and needs of business and the economy • Blamed educational system for youth unemployment	• Strong focus on TAFE expansion and access • Establishment of youth training scheme • Criticized mismatch between educational system and needs of business and economy • Blamed education system for youth unemployment

variety of contexts shown themselves to have a peculiarly economistic and narrow view of education. Thus, Hawke publicly endorses a view of education which emphasizes its economic and vocational functions. Such values as productivity and competitiveness in education are given prominence and the broader social and integrative functions of education — not to mention the importance of providing broad general education at tertiary level — tend to be ignored.

Clearly, then, the Hawke socialist government has distinguished itself from the conservative governments of Fraser and Reagan in certain crucial respects. On the other hand the Hawke government is not nearly so distinct as we might have predicted, and in some major respects it is almost indistinguishable. For example, it has pursued policies of financial stringency, rationalization, coordination, accountability and efficiency in higher education which are distinguishable from Fraser's only in degree.

The Hawke government's generally cautious and pragmatic style and policies reflect the dominance of the right wing of the Party in the Cabinet and a commitment to capturing and retaining the centre ground of Australian politics. Much to the chagrin of the left wing of the ALP, Hawke has:

(i)   continued to provide federal aid to wealthy private schools despite official ALP policy to phase it out;
(ii) despite official party policy to the contrary, made several attempts to have Cabinet endorse the reintroduction of tertiary tuition fees;
(iii) promoted a degree of 'privatization' of the tertiary sector by encouraging the marketing (at 'cost plus') of courses to foreign students both within and outside Australia;
(iv) changed Australia's overseas aid approach by increasing substantially the tuition fees for private foreign students studying in Australian universities and colleges.

The Emasculation of the Schools Commission

Perhaps one of the greatest ironies of Hawke government education policy has been the emasculation during 1985–86 of the Schools Commission — a Commission originally established to promote Labor government policies of equity in the schools by the Whitlam government in 1973. Under Fraser, the Schools Commission came increasingly to be viewed by the ALP left as a creature of the private schools. This perception was reinforced by Fraser's appointment as Chairman, of Dr Peter Tannock, an educationalist closely identified with the Catholic education sector — and further reinforced when two representatives on the Commission of the public school teachers and parents dissented from the majority recommendations of the Commission in 1984 — largely on the grounds that the funding recommendations were biassed strongly in favour of the private schools sector (see chapter 7).

Although the ALP Government adopted the rather expensive recommendations of this Report (*Funding Policies for Australian Schools*, 1984) — including the continuation of aid to the wealthy schools — the dissatisfaction of the public schools sector at the seeming inability of the Hawke government to persuade the Commission to regard as its highest priority its 'primary obligation' to public schools, had not been lost on Hawke. Thus when opportunities arose in 1984–85, Hawke proceeded to emasculate the Commission. Fortuitously for the government, Tannock resigned and was ultimately replaced by Garth Boomer — a significantly lower profile and less experienced bureaucratic strategist. In the interim, the recommendations of the QERC Report and a Commonwealth Public Service Board review of the Commission led to decisions by Hawke and Ryan to transfer the administrative staff, responsibility and funds for the 'big ticket' Schools Commission programs into the Commonwealth Department of Education. In one fell swoop, the Schools Commission was effectively neutered — albeit under the pretext of enhancing its capacity to concentrate on its primary function of giving policy advice!! Departmental control of the programs and funds will give the Minister a much greater degree of influence and control than when they were in the hands of an independent statutory Commission. Following a review of the Schools Commission's remaining special purpose programs it is conceivable that a number of these will be terminated or phased out and the funds so released also transferred out of the Schools Commission's control.

Conclusions and Predictions

The education policies of the Hawke ALP socialist government have so far proven to be more akin to those of the conservative Reagan and Fraser governments than might have been expected. The Hawke government has essentially conformed to a well-defined international trend away from strong public support for education and welfare spending — a trend clearly manifest in Thatcher's Britain and Reagan's USA. The degree of conformity is partly attributable to such factors as: the common constraints imposed in both countries by huge federal deficits; the generally conservative social, economic and educational climates and contexts within which leaders are operating in the 1980s; the conservative historical lessons imbibed by Hawke from the brief radical reformist Whitlam era; the deliberate Hawke strategies of pursuing a highly consensual and pragmatic approach to policy development which implies eschewing left wing ideology; a willingness by Hawke to ignore party policy where pragmatism suggests it is prudent and possible to do so. Internationally, the trend away from education and welfare spending has had the effect of removing protection and support for groups disadvantaged by the current distribution of economic resources in relation to access to education and consequent social mobility.

In defence of the Hawke government, it can be said that certainly education funding has fared better than it did under Fraser and than it has under Reagan and Thatcher. Nevertheless, Hawke failed to halt the downward spiral in the proportion of total federal budget devoted to education which commenced under Fraser and, compounded by redistribution, the relative position of public schools and higher education has deteriorated. Again, in defence, it can be argued that, confronted with unprecedentedly high youth unemployment, Hawke was right to tackle that priority first. Furthermore, the PEP initiatives provided a countervailing force promoting educational access for some of the traditionally disadvantaged groups.

Despite these caveats, it seems quite possible that the legacy of the Hawke government may well be a set of educational policies which are destined, on balance, to increase rather than reduce inequalities in our society. For example, the Commonwealth's total financial contribution to public schools continues to lag behind that to private schools and in higher education the proportion of students eligible for TEAS continues to decline whilst the competition for increasingly scarce university and college places continues to grow.

Where, Then, Do the Policies of Reagan and Hawke Diverge?

Undoubtedly, the two most striking dimensions on which Reagan and Hawke differ are the predictable ones based on their different ideologies: Reagan's 'federalism' inclines him towards a minimalist position with regard to the federal role in education, whereas Hawke's socialist position inclines him towards a strong federal role; similarly, Reagan's conservative philosophy inclines him to emphasize excellence and freedom of choice whilst exorcizing equity issues, whereas Hawke's perspective inclines him to focus on equity issues and downplay excellence.

There is every likelihood that their respective policies will continue to diverge over time. Nevertheless, given the economic, political and other constraints on both men it is highly unlikely that Reagan will achieve his ultimate goals of closing down the Department of Education completely or introducing tuition tax credits — or that Hawke will implement ALP policy of phasing out aid to independent schools. Ironically, in the conservative 80s it is quite possible that Hawke might ultimately preside over the reintroduction of tertiary tuition fees — a policy strongly opposed by his party platform.

Perhaps the most striking feature of Hawke education policy is the lack of congruence between ALP platform and action or implementation. Whitlam implemented Party education policy whereas Hawke has done so to a much more limited degree. It is this preoccupation with economic policy and apparent lack of concern for redistributionist principles which concerns many ALP supporters.

One optimistic sign on the Australian horizon is the spate of speeches (during 1985–86) by ALP influentials including McLelland, Dawkins, Hayden and Whitlam — all of whom have urged the Hawke government to ensure that in its current preoccupation with 'sound economic management' it does not lose sight of the ALP's guiding objectives of social reform and redistribution.

So far as the US is concerned, the renewed interest in, and commitment to education flowing from the 'reform movement' provides greater optimism that necessary increases in expenditure will be achieved. However, Reagan's determined stance makes it likely that such increases, if they are to be sustained, will continue to come from the states and locals — not from the federal government.

References

Aboriginal Education (1985) Report of the House of Representatives Select Committee on Aboriginal Education, AGPS, September.
BURKE, G. (1985) 'Quantity and Quality in Education', Monash University, November.
CLARK, D.L. and AMIOT, M.A. (1981) 'The impact of the Reagan administration on federal education policy', *Phi Delta Kappan*, December.
CLARK, D.L. and ASTUTO, T.A. (1984).
CLARK, D.L. and ASTUTO, T.A. (1985) 'The Significance and Permanence of Changes in Federal Education Policy' draft, Indiana University, December.
CLARK, D.L. and ASTUTO, T.A. (1986) 'Federal education policy in the US: The conservative agenda and accomplishments', paper presented to the annual meeting of the American Educational Research Association, San Francisco, April. (see chapter 3 in this volume).
COMMONWEALTH TERTIARY EDUCATION COMMISSION (1985) *Report for 1985–7 Triennium*, Volume 2, Part 2, September Canberra AGPS.
Discussion of Some Issues Raised in Quality of Education in Australia (1985) Commonwealth Schools Commission, Canberra.
FANE, G. (1984) *Education Policy in Australia*, EPAC Discussion Paper.
Funding Policies for Australian Schools (1984) Commonwealth Schools Commission, Canberra.
GOLDRING, J. (1984) '*Mutual Advantage: Report of the Committee of Review of Private Overseas Student Policy*', Canberra AGPS.
HUDSON, H. (1985) 'Economic and political change: Its implications for tertiary education', *The Australian TAFE Teacher*, November.
JACKSON, R.G. (1984) *Report of the Committee to Review the Australian Overseas Aid Program*, Canberra AGPS.
MARGINSON, S. (1984) 'The schools guidelines: Hawke in Fraser's clothing', *ATF Research Notes*, 2, 6 September.
Quality and Equality (1985) Commonwealth Schools Commission, Canberra.
QUALITY OF EDUCATION REVIEW COMMITTEE, (Chairman P. KARMEL), *Quality of Education in Australia*, Canberra, AGPS.
RYAN, S. (1984) address to the National Press Club, Canberra, 15 August.
SCHUSTER, J.H. (1982) 'Out of the frying pan: The politics of education in a new era', *Phi Delta Kappan*, May.

Scott, A. (forthcoming) 'The quality of education review committee', in Smart, D. (Ed.) *Major National Reports in Australian Education.*

Smart, D. (1978) *Federal Aid to Australian Schools,* St Lucia, University of Queensland Press.

Smart, D. (1985) 'Fraser and Reagan "New Federalism": Politics of education in times of economic recession' paper presented at the annual meeting of the American Educational Research Association, Chicago, April.

Smart, D., Scott, R., Murphy, K. and Dudley, J. (1986) 'The Hawke government and education 1983–85', *Politics,* 21, 1, May, pp. 63–81.

Smart, D. (1987) 'The Hawke Labor government and public-private school funding policies in Australia, 1983–1986', see chapter 7 in this volume.

3 Federal Education Policy in the United States: The Conservative Agenda and Accomplishments[1]

David L. Clark and Terry A. Astuto

Introduction

Have the past six years produced a significant, enduring change in federal educational policy? Is there more to come? The answer to these questions depends upon the individual or group framing the criteria on the basis of which the questions are answered. Jack Jennings (1985), long time Counsel for education for the Committee on Education and Labor, House of Representatives, sees little change:

> The smoke of debate [over the federal role in education] should not obscure the reality that the prospects for the survival of federally funded education programs are greater today than at any time since Reagan took office. The President forcefully challenged the very existence of these programs during his first term. But he failed to achieve his goal. In the process of opposing the President's on-slaught, Carl Perkins was able to forge a new bipartisan consensus in Congress on the importance of these programs in the total effort to improve US education. (p. 567)

Denis Doyle and Terry Hartle (1985) maintained a view similar to Jennings arguing that:

> What the administration achieved was accomplished in the first six months of the term ... Many of its most important goals — tax credits, school prayer, regulatory reform, abolishing the department — are increasingly unlikely. By any score card it has lost more battles than it has won ... In basic outline the federal role in education looks very much as it did under Presidents Nixon, Ford, and Carter. (pp. 148–9)

Eileen Gardner (1984) in *Mandate for Leadership II: Continuing the Conservative Revolution* assigned mixed grades to the Administration's first term performance. While lamenting losses in Congress over tuition tax credits, vouchers, school prayer, and the reform of student financial aid, Gardner cited the beginning of a successful revolution, i.e.:

> The Commission on Excellence in Education rallied the nation which has begun the long, arduous journey back to world preeminence in education. Thanks to the Commission, far reaching reform has been generated without additional federal money or mandates. The response to the report on Excellence and the chapter 2 block grant is prophetic: Americans are proving themselves capable and willing to take on the responsibility for educating their children through state and local initiatives — initiatives that were stymied by the growing federal control. (p. 54)

Laurence Iannaccone (1985) viewed the changes as both of significance and duration:

> Whatever the political outcome of the 1986 mid-term and 1988 national elections may be, President Reagan and Secretary Bell have accomplished their goals for changing the locus of the educational policy making process, its value-driven policy premises and redefining the mission of the schools. These were (i) to return educational policy making to the states and local districts ('where it belongs' in the words of Secretary Bell, April, 1981); (ii) to establish this philosophy of government for a generation; and (iii) to emphasize basic skills and academic achievement as the central mission of the public schools. (p. 5)

However accurate or valid these assessments may be judged to be, they employed different criteria for change. Jennings used the continued existence of federal programs in education as the criterion. Doyle and Hartle addressed the question at a more global level; the basic outline of the federal educational role was the criterion. Gardner used a set of specific policy preferences in education espoused, in general, by political conservatives, for example, school prayer, tuition tax credits, increased standards. Iannaccone (1985) judged success against what he argued were the most important tools of President Reagan rooted in one overarching goal of domestic policy, i.e., 'to transfer many domestic programs to the states' (p. 4).

The thesis we will argue in this chapter differs markedly from the interpretation of Jennings and Doyle and Hartle; extends beyond the concerns covered by Gardner; is generally consistent with the interpretation of Iannaccone. The thesis is two-fold:

1   A major redirection of federal educational policy has occurred in the past six years. The essence of that policy has been altered in

basic ways. The bipartisan consensus noted by Jennings is a new consensus in support of a different federal role rather than a new consensus in favor of existing programs.

2   The scope of the redirection will be broadened over the next five to fifteen years and many of the changes will become institutionalized for a new era of federal educational policy. The change that has occurred had its roots in years preceding the Reagan Administration, although its lifeblood was furnished by that Administration, and will continue to dominate educational policy development for decades, not solely for Reagan's second term.[2]

So that you can fairly assess our thesis and the evidence we present in support of its validity, we should make our criteria clear. Firstly, the criteria should encompass the substantive content of the policy preferences in education being discussed and acted upon at federal, state, and local levels. These substantive criteria include both what education should be about, for example, concentration on basics and character education, and how education should be conducted, for example, parental control and choice, and individual and institutional competition. Secondly, the criteria should include procedural issues that deal with the role of governmental levels in policy development and administration, for example, disestablishment of the Department of Education, devolution and deregulation.

Accomplishments of the Reagan Administration in Federal Educational Policy: 1981–1984

Before turning to the changes in direction in educational policy over the past six years, we will offer a cursory retrospective (*c.*1980–81) of where the change began. Our argument is that some of the changes have been profound and dramatic. Since it is often easy to adjust over time to even dramatic changes, our cause is served by reminding you of the starting point.

Retrospective: 1980–81

Six years ago, under the heading, 'The teachers' coup', *The New Republic* commented:

> Veteran power brokers have been pushed aside by a relative newcomer to the hurly-burly of capital politics — the National Education Association. In the last four years the NEA has helped elect a President, single-handedly forced a Department of Education down Congress' throat, and lobbied successfully for dramatic increases in federal spending on education. (Chapman, 1980, p. 9)

Teacher training institutions were afraid that the new teacher centers (referred to routinely as NEA's proprietary legislation) would usurp the teacher education function of the university.

The new Department of Education (ED) under the leadership of Shirley Hufstedler was administering 150+ categorical programs with a staff of over 6000 employees and growing. Almost every one of those programs had:

— its own staff
— its own legislative authority
— its own budget
— its own advisory committee and consultants
— and regulations
— and system of evaluation
— and special constituencies of parents, businesses, and educators
— and protective legislative authors and sponsors in Congress.

ED was big business before the Department ever hit the ground and there was no reason to suspect that it would not become bigger.

If you were involved with ED at all, you remember the Teacher Corps, the State Capacity Building Program, the National Diffusion Network, the Joint Dissemination Review Panel. ED was out where the teachers were, involved vigorously in the dissemination and diffusion of new ideas.

The Department focused on equity for the handicapped, for ethnic minority groups, for women. If you submitted a proposal to ED for research, training, or technical assistance, equity concerns had to be reflected in both the content and staffing of the project. Perhaps that is an appropriate way to conclude the retrospective, i.e., by identifying the dominant lexicon of terms that controlled the discussion and emphases of the era:

1 Equity
2 Needs and access
3 Social and welfare concerns
4 The common school
5 Regulations, enforcement, and monitoring
6 Federal initiatives and interventions
7 Diffusion of innovations

These are foreign terms in Washington today and the new lexicon is especially interesting because an essentially conflictual set of terms has emerged that fits the new educational policy discussions in Washington, i.e.:

(i)   Excellence; standards of performance; individual competition
(ii) Ability; selectivity; minimum entrance standards
(iii) Economic and productivity concerns
(iv) Parental choice; institutional competition
(v)   Local initiative; deregulation, limited enforcement

(vi)   State and local interests and initiatives
(vii) Exhortation; information-sharing

Finally, to place the change in contemporary perspective, imagine substituting President Reagan's comments on education in his 1984 State of the Union Address in President Carter's address in 1980. The educational community would have imagined it had been struck by a thunderbolt. In fact, President Reagan's comments were barely newsworthy when he said:

> But we must do more to restore discipline to the schools; and we must encourage the teaching of new basics, reward teachers of merit, enforce standards, and put our parents back in charge. I will continue to press for tuition tax credits to expand opportunities for families, and to soften the double payment for those paying public school taxes and private school tuition. Our proposal would target assistance to low and middle income families. Just as more incentives are needed within our schools, greater competition is needed among our schools. Without standards and competition there can be no champions, no records broken, no excellence — in education or any other walk of life. And while I'm on the subject — each day your members observe a 200-year-old tradition meant to signify America is one nation under God. I must ask: If you can begin your day with a member of the clergy standing right here to lead you in prayer, then why can't freedom to acknowledge God be enjoyed again by children in every school room across this land. (p. 91)

Contrast this statement with the lexicon of federal educational policy terms numbered 1–7 above. Something big has happened. A major change has taken place. The significance of the change remains to be debated in later sections of this chapter.

1981 — Budgetary Reductions

In 1981, the educational policy of the Reagan Administration was dominated by procedural considerations. Washington insiders referred to the five Ds, i.e., disestablishment (elimination of the Department of Education), deregulation, decentralization, de-emphasis (reduction of the position of education as a priority on the federal agenda), and, most importantly, diminution (reduction of the federal budget in education). Although the Administration's education agenda was precise it lacked a substantive dimension. The components were (i) derivative from broader social policy preferences, for example, reduce the social program budget, eliminate regulations, foster the new federalism; and (ii) reflective of procedural concerns about the federal role in education, for example, stop throwing money at the problems of education,

get the feds off the backs of state and local policy makers who are better able
to deal with educational problems.

Unsurprisingly, then, as is obvious in table 1, the early achievements of
the Administration reflected these procedural emphases. Educationists were
jolted by the first significant reductions in the federal education budget in a
quarter century. There was, in fact, not even an interesting debate about the
cuts. The Administration insisted that reductions in the overall federal budget
were imperative, the cuts had to come from the social programs portion of
the budget, and education was required to take its share. That meant cutting
whenever and wherever it was possible. Before the dust settled the cumulative reductions in the fiscal year 1981 and 1982 budgets had amounted
to roughly 20 per cent.

The federal education budget turned out to be a more vulnerable target
than its defenders had anticipated. Educationists discovered anew that the
budget issue facing them was not simply the size of next year's increase. The
1981 budgetary losses created a mindset that has persisted, i.e., the expectation for less. In the intervening years, educationists have accepted the notion
that a program that does not lose money from year to year has been
successful in defending its position. If diminution is a policy preference, that
lesson is a necessary first step.

The big news in 1981 seemed to be only the budget. As it turned out
that was not quite the case. Secretary Bell also established the National
Commission on Excellence in Education and its Chairperson, David P.
Gardner, signaled a central theme that would persist and reappear two years
later when he commented, 'the absence of [such] a standard [of achievement]
tends to translate into a situation where there's less pressure [to achieve] and
lowered expectations on the part of students to take more difficult courses or
a wider range of them' (Ingalls, 1981, p. 11). The Administration asserted
less specific substantive goals in 1981 than its current policy preferences
reflect, but the affective response of the interviewees representing the Administration in 1981 was clear — and it sets the stage for many of the more
specific policy preferences of later years, to wit:

- Public education is failing; mediocre at best, wholly ineffective at
  worst.
- The federal presence in education has made a bad situation worse.
  Federal intervention has removed the action from the state and local
  levels where the problems must be solved.
- Federal regulations are an unnecessary burden on state and local
  educational officials. They are contributing to the mediocrity of the
  field.
- Federal involvement in education has been misdirected, i.e., emphasizing social and welfare concerns rather than educational performance.

Table 1: The Reagan First Term: Changes in Federal Educational Policy — 1981–84

Year	Hallmark	Actions	Effects
1981	Rescissions Reductions	• Cumulative education budget cuts of over twenty percent	• Establishing the expectations for less (diminution)
1982	Block grant Deregulation	• Implementation of ECIA • Revocation of regulations • Constraint of enforcement of regulations	• Dismantling the categorical programs (disestablishment, decentralization) • Constraining ED from the design of educational interventions (disestablishment, decentralization) • Moving accountability to the state level (deregulation, decentralization)
1983	Report of the National Commission on Excellence	• Publication of *A Nation at Risk* • Support for the design of career ladders for teachers and other forms of merit pay • Encouragement of upward adjustment of standards • National Forum on Education	• Moving from a focus on equity to excellence • Focusing improvement strategies on adjusting standards (decentralization) • Reducing the role of the educationist in school improvement • Increasing educational policy activity at the state level (decentralization)
1984	Awards and Recognition	• Secondary School Recognition Program • Academic Fitness Awards • Excellent Private Schools Program • National Distinguished Principals Program	• Developing consensus on direction of reform • Highlighting reform already underway (disestablishment, decentralization) • Recognizing established performance

David L. Clark and Terry A. Astuto

1982 — The Block Grant

If a successful thrust toward diminution was the achievement in 1981, the key event of 1982 was implementation of the Education Consolidation and Improvement Act (ECIA) — a thrust toward decentralization. The education block grant delivered on the statement in the 1980 Republican Platform Text calling for replacement of the 'crazy quilt of wasteful programs with a system of block grants that will restore decision making to local officials responsible to voters and parents' (p. 2034). The block grant was less than the Administration's aspirations. Vocational education and special education escaped inclusion in the block. But a vital change had been effected. The flow of federal involvement in educational policy had been reversed. The addition of new categorical programs was made significantly more difficult; the likelihood that existing programs would be added to the block grant was made more likely. From 1958 to 1982, the conservatives were fighting a vigorous, but losing battle, categorical proposal by categorical proposal, to thwart the extension of federal involvement in education. Now the liberals found themselves pressed to save existing categorical initiatives with little chance of adding new ones. The significance of the block grant is in reversing this trend which, simultaneously, removed ED fom the business of inventing and sponsoring federal-level interventions in education. The block grant can be viewed as an enabling step toward the President's concept of the new federalism as it might be applied to education.

Less dramatic, but complementary to the block grant, was the effort to disentangle the federal government from the web of regulatory requirements attached to the categorical programs. The disentanglement was based on revocation and non-enforcement. In the former category, for example, Secretary Bell announced the revocation of thirty sets of rules associated with nineteen of the categorical programs that had been included in the block grant. Enforcement was constrained, for example, by preventing the Department's Office of Civil Rights from using Title VI to require bilingual instruction in the public schools.

Halfway through the first Reagan Administration an unexpected realization dawned on the educationist community. The conventional wisdom held by previous administrations toward education had operated on the assumption that the education lobby, individually and collectively, was a force with which the executive branch needed to be concerned. But this Administration had almost entirely ignored that lobby. With the exception of Secretary Bell, leaders in ED were non-educationists — appointed without reference to or consultation with the educational community. The Administration went out of its way to snub the largest lobby of all, the National Education Association. Consultation with the education community about planned changes in education was replaced by press conferences to announce the changes. And the consequences to the Administration of this unorthodox behavior appeared to be minimal. In fact, the educationist lobby had begun to accommodate to the new rules of the game and had settled in for a rearguard action protecting critical elements of the federal role in education. Whatever else one could say about the first half of the Reagan Administration and however successful individual lobbies and lobbyists had been in protecting their interests, the initiative lay in the hands of an Administration that wanted to chart a new course in federal educational policy.

1983 — The Reform Reports

The kindest interpretation of the reason for the appearance of the plenitude of reform reports on education in 1983 and 1984 is that there was a groundswell of concern about education two to three years earlier. A more realistic explanation is probably that the reports were the fallout from a period of uncertainty about where education was headed at the national level. The reversal of the normal course of events that seemed likely from President Reagan's early statements about the field encouraged the establishment of a commission, committees, task forces and teams to examine where the field was and where it was headed. Surely that is an appropriate explanation for the National Commission on Excellence in Education. The Commission was one of the few steps the new Secretary of Education could take without conflicting directly with one or another of the Administration's positions about deemphasizing, diminishing, and decentralizing the federal role in education.

There were a number of curious effects. One of the original five Ds, i.e., deemphasis, suffered a setback. The President discovered that involvement in educational policy can be fun and rewarding. Most importantly from the Administrations's viewpoint, the involvement was possible without compromising seriously the criteria of diminution, decentralization, deregulation or, even, disestablishment. The follow-up on the Commission Report was centered in the state capitals. No major new federal initiatives were required. Exhortation and suasion actually worked as the keystone to the federal role in the field. The report itself and the follow through on the report had four effects that confirmed biases of the Adminstration:

1   By title and content, the report switched the attention of educational reformers and policy makers from equity to excellence. The argument of the report is essentially that excellence begets true equity.
2   *A Nation at Risk* baldly omitted the educationist community from most of the reform recommendations. No one reading the report would expect educationists to be the key actors in the reform movement.
3   The report suggested a school improvement strategy based on modified standards and requirements. This contrasted sharply with the complex school improvement efforts of ED built around such

technical assistance strategies as the National Diffusion Network or the Research and Development Exchange.

4 The locus of action for reform was switched from the national level to state and local levels. While recognizing a federal role in education, the recommendations focused on standards and requirements under the control of state and local policy makers.

1984 — Awards and Recognition

The President had a relatively busy 'education year', although expectations for education policy in an election year are always modest. The year was kicked off in December 1983 with a National Forum on Education in Indianapolis. The Forum was clearly an activity of consensus building to validate the Excellence Commission's report and to encourage the states to be about the business of educational reform. The primary activity of ED was to keep education visible through a variety of awards programs for teachers, principals, students and schools — awards to celebrate the existence of excellent performance in education wherever it existed. The strategy worked well to defuse education as a campaign issue but, equally importantly, its effects on educational policy were to:

1 Highlight reform moves already underway;
2 Imply that the tactics in education employed by the Administration to date were already bearing fruit;
3 Encourage state policy makers to press ahead with such popular reform topics as career ladders for teachers, increased graduation requirements, competency tests for teachers, and lengthened school calendar years and school days.

First Term Report Card

An assessment of the success of the Administration in educational policy during its first term should be made on the basis of its asserted policy preferences in 1980/81, not those that have developed during the past six years. How would they fare in their five subject areas? Here is our grading.

Table 2: First Term Report Card on Education
for the Reagan Administration

Policy Preference Area	Grade	
Diminution	B+	1
Deregulation	B	2
Decentralization	A	3
Disestablishment	C	4
Deemphasis	B−	5

Comments of Grader

1 Your biggest gains in pursuit of diminution occurred early. However, the continued decline in programs and positions in ED plus holding the line on expenditures for all programs except the guaranteed student loan entitlements were better than could have reasonably been expected. Most importantly, you established the expectation for less.

2 After the initial push to clear out regulations in ED, your gains have been made chiefly by allowing regulations to atrophy through non-enforcement. The block grant abetted this overall effort and you deserve a better than average grade.

3 Although the block grant has not been extended to vocational and special education, you should be proud of your achievement in your aim to decentralize. Educational policy activity at the state level has increased at an enormous rate. Most important of all, you have made it virtually impossible to generate and sustain interest in new categorical programs. The action agenda in policy is in the hands of the states. The flow of federal policy is toward additional decentralization rather than intervention.

4 Judged as a *de jure* issue you have failed. But there is no way to overlook the fact that the Department has been halved in size, that its programs have been reduced sharply, and its program initiatives have almost entirely disappeared.

5 The furore surrounding the National Commission on Excellence in Education report almost dropped this grade to a critically low level. However, a good recovery is underway. No one believes that you have a priority interest in education or education policy at the federal level. Your interests are now channeled to encouraging the states and exhorting them to push your substantive interests in achieving a good education.

As report cards go, this one covers a long time period, a time during which the Administration added educational policy interests of a substantive order to its earlier procedural emphases. The current list of preferences will be commented upon in the next section, but before leaving the earlier time period, we should add some affective changes that represent accomplishments outside the five Ds. By tying into predispositions of the American people prior to 1980 about education and by emphasizing the President's view of education in the media, the Administration has convinced or agrees with a large segment of the populace that[3]:

— the core problems of the schools are discipline, drugs, standards, and teachers;
— school improvement can be achieved by establishing and adhering to higher standards and requirements for admission to educational curricula, progress through the schools, and exit from the schools;
— problems of education cannot be solved at the federal level. Efforts to do so have failed;

— parents should control the choice of schools their children attend and should be involved in their children's education;
— localities should be in control of their own schools;
— moral values, prayer, and character education need to be returned to the schools;
— a cabinet-level department of education is not needed;
— the federal government should be less rather than more involved in education;
— schools would be better if they were not a public monopoly;
— achievement levels in public schools should be made public and compared across school systems, within and across states;
— teachers would be better if they earned salary increases by merit;
— most students do not work hard enough in school;
— most students graduate from high school with insufficient preparation to earn a living or go on to college;
— school curricula should concentrate on the basics, include more 'hard' subjects and fewer electives.

The most interesting feature of these opinions about education is not whether they were latent in the sixties and seventies or whether they have grown in the eighties but that they now fit the present agenda being advocated by the President and the Secretary of Education. As one looks ahead at the possible policy changes in education in 1986–1988 and beyond there is, at least currently, substantial support among the American people for the Administration's policy preferences.

Current Progress on the Administration's Policy Agenda

Federal policy changes are difficult to portray. On the one hand, specific policy actions or speeches generate a sense of crisis that too much is happening too quickly. Conversely, policy shifts move at such a glacial pace that the movement is barely noticeable. However, consistency between the policy actions and assertions and the policy preferences of the Reagan Administration provides evidence of progress on the Administration's educational policy agenda. That is the level of analysis that will be pursued in this section. Actions and assertions will be used to illustrate policy preferences — the commitment to them and progress toward their achievement.

Table 3 lists the current policy preferences of the Reagan Administration and illustrates contemplated and completed actions that support those preferences. The agenda was not hard to compile. Whether one analyzes a radio address on education by the President, State of the Union messages, or Secretary Bennett's testimony at his confirmation hearing, the same issues are discussed and the same positions are advocated. This agenda is consistent with the 5 Ds but extends into the substantive dimensions of education in which the President has a strong personal interest.

Table 3: Educational Policy Preferences of the Reagan Administration 1985—1988

Policy Preference	Supportive Actions and Emphases
1 *Disestablishment of ED*: (a reduced federal role in education)	Reduction of ED staff size Intra-agency reorganization and consolidation Budgetary reductions Program elimination Alternative agency forms
2 *Institutional Competition*: (breaking the monopoly of the public school to stimulate excellent performance)	Tuition Tax credits Vouchers School awards programs 'Wall chart': monitoring state educational achievements
3 *Individual Competition*: (recognizing excellence to stimulate excellence)	Merit pay, career ladders for teachers Academic fitness program Awards to teachers and principals Eligibility for post secondary scholarships, fellowships, and loans
4 *Performance Standards*: (increasing minimum standards for teachers and students)	Increased credit requirements for high school graduation Proficiency examinations in addition to course requirements Competency tests for teachers Modified admission and certification standards for teachers
5 *Focus on Content*: (emphasis on basics to insure performance in critical instructional areas)	Concentration on: • traditional basics, the 3 Rs • new basics, science, mathematics, computer skills Scholarships for science and mathematics teachers More required courses for college and vocational preparation Funds for NSF and ED for science and mathematics education
6 *Parental Choice*: (parental control over what, where, and how their children will learn)	Tuition tax credits Vouchers Parental involvement in the schooling process Parental involvement in determining curricular content
7 *Character*: (strengthening traditional values in schools)	Discipline in the schools Character education School prayer Work ethic
8 *Devolution*: (continued transfer of educational authority to state and local levels)	Extension of the block grant Deregulation and limited regulatory enforcement Elimination of unnecessary programs Reduction in educational expenditures Federal role of support, encouragement, and exhortation

Before turning to the preferences, however, we want to comment on two frequent assertions relevant to the analysis, i.e., that this Administration (i) is disinterested in education, and (ii) has had no policy agenda for education. These are not simply charges from political antagonists but observations of scholarly analysts, some of whom favor the general positions of the Administration. For example, Denis Doyle and Terry Hartle contended that in the first Administration Reagan had no overarching educational policy; that, 'the real nature of the Reagan Administration's interest in education . . . was not great. In truth, beyond the battle of the budget the Administration cared little — it cared not enough to do much, up or down' (p. 149). If we believed the Doyle and Hartle assertion to be true we would be more casual about where educational policy is headed and what its effects are likely to be on American schools.

Such comments, however, need to be considered in a relative context, i.e., compared to what. This President talks about education at the drop of a hat. He lectures about it in his State of the Union messages. He comments on it in his weekly radio show. And he says the same things — basic themes with modest variations. His predecessors, courted by the educationist community, seldom fitted in a word about education in State of the Union messages. If they thought about education at all it was a well guarded secret. In relative terms, this Administration, from the White House, exhibits more interest in education than its predecessors but it gives off ambiguous signals by its actions, for example:

- ED was ignored for most of the first Reagan Administration. Staff and programs were cut. Positions in ED were used as a dumping ground for political appointments.
- The professional education community was disregarded by the President and by ED.
- No substantive program initiatives were mounted by the Administration and forwarded for Congressional action.
- The Administration cut the ED budget arbitrarily without regard for program consequences.
- When the going got tough on the Administration's proposals, i.e., further budget cuts, eliminating ED, tuition tax credits, school prayer, the Administration used up few political chips in the battle.

All these assertions are true. Collectively they may indicate that education is not the high priority item on the federal agenda that many of its advocates would wish. Of course it is not and it never has been. Education is a small-scale item in Washington. Everyone simply assumes that it is overwhelmed as a policy concern by the budget deficit, defense, the strength of the social security system, health, and agriculture. However, this President has exhibited an almost avocational interest in the field. He cares about educational issues in a way uncharacteristic of his predecessors. The issues he cares about *are* an agenda and they reflect the position of a large political constituency. Actions advocated by and taken by the Administration that are labeled anti-education by the educationist community are, instead, actions that fit the policy preferences and relatively stable agenda of the Administration, to wit:

- ED was dumped on because it was an unwanted department populated by long-time liberals. The Department is being set up for disestablishment.
- The professional education community opposed the President in the 1980 election and advocated a federal role in education repugnant to him. They were ignored to weaken their influence.
- The lack of program initiatives at the federal level is appropriate to encourage state and local initiatives and to reduce the federal involvement in education.
- The budget cuts were part of a broader fiscal strategy. If the federal budget is healthy, economic growth will allow education to flourish with state and local tax dollars. And, of course, federal dollars pumped into education have had a pernicious rather than an efficacious impact on education.
- One may not be able to argue that the Administration has risked its life on education issues. But session after session the Administration has proposed the same actions, i.e., budget cuts, tuition tax credits, school prayer, disestablishment. The Administration has not been foolhardy in support of its goals, but it has been assiduous.

Lest we move too far in the opposite direction we should summarize our observations about educational policy in the Reagan Administration. Education is a weak and sporadic policy concern at the federal level. This President is more interested in educational issues than most of his predecessors. His interests range from structure, i.e., advocating devolution, to how to run a classroom, i.e., concentrate on basics, traditional values, and discipline. The Administration projects a more consistent policy agenda in education than any Administration since Lyndon Johnson. This consistency added to the constancy of the pursuit of its preferences has, is and will accomplish more change than the Administration has been credited with to date.

Now, back to table 3 and the current policy preferences.

Disestablishment

None of the Administration's preferences has attracted less Congressional support than the elimination of the Department of Education. Prior to Secretary Bennett's nomination hearings, the President defused the issue of the *de jure* elimination of the Department by assuring Senator Hatch by letter that he would not propose to abolish the Department *at this time* because of lack of support in Congress. So that this position would not be misunderstood, the President added, 'I still feel ... that federal education programs could be administered effectively without a Cabinet level agency' (*Education Week*, 6 February 1986, p. 9).

The White House and the Office of Management and Budget have pursued a program designed to substitute *de facto* abolition of ED for the failure of the *de jure* action. The staff of the Department has been reduced from roughly 7400 employees in 1980 to 5000 in 1985. The activities of the Department have been reduced sharply by:

(i)   eliminating categorical programs now covered by the block grant;
(ii) removing sets of regulations;
(iii) reducing in status and scope such programs as Women's Educational Equity, migrant education, desegregation assistance;
(iv) constraining, in most cases eliminating, new program initiatives;
(v)   reducing the Department's budget.

The current actions of the Administration are consistent with its past efforts. The President charged Secretary Bennett with responsibility for reorganizing the agency. To date this has resulted in a consolidation of the research and school improvement programs of the Department under a newly-appointed Assistant Secretary for Education. The consolidation merged the National Institute of Education with the National Center for Educational Statistics. This simplifies the internal structure of the Department and effectively eliminates the free-standing National Institute of Education.

The President's budget for the 1986 fiscal year called for a $3 billion decrease for ED. The Gramm-Rudman-Hollings legislation (Balanced Budget and Emergency Control Act of 1985, PL 99–177) will further decrease the federal investment in educational programs. The 87 budget request was $15.2 billion — $3.2 billion less than the current appropriation and $2.5 billion below the 86 Gramm-Rudman requirements. Secretary Bennett has asserted, '"I'm a strong advocate for education, but I'm not an advocate for increased" spending' (*Education Week*, 16 April 1986, p. 11). And he has emphasized his belief that the most powerful tool available to the Department is to lead the revitalization of education through the use of the bully pulpit provided by his office.

The position asserted by the Heritage Foundation in *Mandate for Leadership II* (1984) reflected the basic position of the Administration:

The establishment of a Cabinet-level Department of Education was an historic blunder, a combination of overweening federal ambition and pandering to interest groups. Still, the Department exists. The question now becomes: How can it be turned into an agency of minimum nuisance, modest scope and yet positive moral influence on the nature and quality of American education. (p. 54)

The author of that report proposed a three-function agency, i.e., a check-writing machine, a statistical bureau, and a pulpit to project 'a vision of what citizens might reasonably expect from their children's schools, teachers, textbooks, and colleges' (p. 55). That author, Eileen M. Gardner, was chosen by Secretary Bennett for a post in the Secretary's office but ran a cropper in her confirmation hearings. Her view of the Department, however, seems to reflect that of the Secretary and probably signals continued efforts to reduce enforcement and regulation, consolidate programs through intra-departmental mergers, and emphasize the role of the Secretary in moral and educational suasion.

There is an important point to be noted in regard to this policy arena. If you were to imagine a continuum of actions in support of the policy preference for disestablishment you might imagine it ranging from *de jure* elimination (the most extreme action) to, perhaps, continued reduction in ED staff size or constraints on enforcement (as illustrations of more modest vigor in pursuit of the preference of disestablishment). However, if you imagined the continuum of actions that might be considered on the policy issue of the appropriateness, role, and scope of a department of education you would include an expanded department, more federal level responsibility for education, and added areas of needed federal enforcement. The policy debate over the establishment of ED in the first place considered the full range of possibilities from the necessity for a department to a reduction in the influence of the then-existing Office of Education. The current Administration, of course, has no responsibility for representing the full continuum of actions. However, it is obvious that there are those who not only favor saving the Department in some form but also would advocate building on its current role. In Washington today they are invisible. The debate over ED covers its survival and how constrained its role will become. There is no effective force advocating its expansion. As we move through the policy preferences, you should keep this in mind. The policy debate over education is constrained by a truncated continuum of preferences and actions in the areas that the Administration has laid out for consideration. Individual actions are opposed or thwarted effectively, for example, *de jure* disestablishment of the Department of Education, but the overarching policy preference is not challenged by a counter-preference, for example, an expanded federal role in education to be administered by an enhanced cabinet-level department.

Institutional Competition

President Reagan has no doubt about the efficacy of institutional competition as a route to excellence in education. In his State of the Union Message in 1984 he noted 'without standards and competition, there can be no champions, no records broken, no excellence in education or any other walk of life' (p. 91). Implementing a policy of institutional competition has been both easy and difficult. The easy parts are the awards and recognition programs and the dissemination of comparative levels of school achievement. Awards programs have blossomed, for example, Secondary School Recognition Program, Excellent Private Schools Program, special honors to school boards that adopted the recommendations of the National Commission on Excellence in Education, awards for vocational education programs, and exemplary chapter 1 programs. Secretary Bennett proclaimed 1985–1986 as the 'Year of the Elementary School' and added an awards program for exemplary elementary schools. The Secretary's 'wallchart', initiated by former Secretary Bell, contrasted educational indicators of input and attainment by states and institutionalized interest in comparative achievement. Having initially criticized the utility of the wallchart, the Council of Chief State School Officers voted to conduct cross-state assessments of student achievement. Findings from these assessments will be reported each year beginning in 1987.

The difficult part has turned out to be gaining support for either tuition tax credits or vouchers that would set up competition between public and private schools and among public schools for potential students. The Administration's commitment to push on this front has not wavered. In an address to the National Association of Independent Schools, the President asserted that 'these proposals have the support of the American people. Make no mistake. Secretary Bennett and I intend to see them through to their enactment'. He argued, as he has in the past, that, 'tuition tax credits and education vouchers would foster greater diversity and, hence, higher standards throughout our system of education' (Bridgman, 1985b, p. 1). Tuition tax credits and vouchers for students eligible for chapter 1 funds were included in the Administration's 1986 budget proposal. In November 1985, following the *Felton* decision, ED drafted a new voucher bill, The Equity and Choice Act of 1985 (TEACH); Undersecretary Bauer noted that it would be one of the Department's top priorities. The Secretary has been active in supporting and encouraging state level initiatives for voucher plans.

The general policy preference of institutional competition and the more specific program proposal for tuition tax credits illustrate this President's personal response to some educational policy issues. One ED administrator compared the President's commitment to tuition tax credits to his support for tax reform, that is, as items of concern personally and directly to him. As the notation from the State of the Union Address indicated, the President assumes that the relationship between competition and achievement is an aphorism. This may lead him to the conclusion that the American people are also committed to tax credits and vouchers and the evidence from national polls indicates that although the public does not favor tax support for parochial schools, it does favor vouchers.

A committed Administration with public support suggests that the movement toward some form of tax credits and vouchers to supplement institutional awards programs is likely in a number of states, if not at the federal level.

Individual Competition

The Administration's interest in competition as a route to educational excellence includes teachers, students, and administrators. The primary action involving teachers has been the advocacy of merit pay. This was one of the few initiatives by Secretary Bell that was embraced unequivocally by the White House. Secretary Bell used discretionary fund grants to the states to encourage planning and experimentation with career ladder plans and other forms of merit pay. The President cheered him on. In his presentation to the National Association of Independent Schools, he said in support of merit pay, 'hard earned tax dollars have no business rewarding mediocrity. They must be used to encourage excellence' (Bridgman, 1985b, p. 29). By 1985, thirty-eight states had some form of merit pay legislation, typically career ladders, enacted, endorsed, or under consideration by the legislature (Bridgman, 1985a, p. 31). Of that group, two had state-wide plans in operation and five had adopted trial policies. This is an interesting policy preference to examine because it has been opposed openly by the National Education Association, opposed — except under controlled conditions — by the American Federation of Teachers, noteworthy by its absence in the current personnel policies of over 95 per cent of the local education agencies in the country, but supported regularly in public opinion polls.

The emphasis on competition among students and principals has been more benign. The latter group has received recognition through the school awards programs and elementary school principals have been honored under the National Distinguished Principals Program. The basic national program for students has been the Academic Fitness Awards. One can argue, however, that the modification of academic standards is a form of individual competition that may, over the long haul, have a greater impact on student's educational opportunities than would any student-to-student competition. To date, the direct competition has been limited to a press for higher academic standards to qualify for student loans and fellowship programs in higher education.

The environment for stimulating individual competition can be generated by (i) granting awards to achievers; or (ii) limiting salary increments or promotion or admission to institutions or programs to those who reach specified levels of performance. Awards programs highlight achievement and introduce minimal tension. Merit pay or career ladders or standards for access to extra-curricular activities or eligibility for student aid are quite different matters. They provoke tension. Teachers' organizations walk a fine line between opposition to a popular policy and evidence from the organizational literature that the effect of merit pay may be deleterious to the interests of their membership and to educational productivity. This battle will be waged in different forms in the fifty states with continued vocal and incentive support from the Administration. The issue of student competition for scholarship and fellowship funds in higher education is a battleground on which concerns for excellence and equity will be fought directly. Each side will attempt to mute the conflict by insisting on its concern for both. The Administration is more concerned about excellence.

Performance Standards

No emphasis in the report of the National Commission on Excellence in Education was more clear than the Commission's dissatisfaction with the achievements of the American educational system. Equally clear was its confidence that a key route to modifying that condition is through increasing minimum performance standards for students and teachers. This use of standards to effect school improvement stands in contrast to the previous efforts of the Department of Education to create and support such sophisticated diffusion and dissemination programs as the National Diffusion Network, The Research and Development Exchange, Teacher Corps, and Teacher Centers. This change has turned the attention of federal and state level educational policy makers away from concern with the stimulation and support of local school improvement efforts to standard setting for local performance; away from process to product.

Although there are instances of modified performance standards for students at other than the high school level, the initial emphasis has been on high school graduation. By 1985, over 80 per cent of the states raised graduation requirements, ten states established special honors diplomas, and fifteen states required exit proficiency examinations beyond the completion of course work to qualify for graduation (Bridgman, 1985a, p. 31). Thirteen state legislatures have manipulated the time of students in school by extending the school day or the school year and seven others had such a move under consideration (*ibid*).

Teachers have attracted more scrutiny in regard to the adjustment of standards than might have been predicted. Twenty-nine states have adopted various forms of proficiency examinations for teachers at both the points of admission to, and completion of, teacher training programs. The professional associations of teachers and teacher educators have responded to the obvious public support for higher standards. The American Association of Colleges for Teacher Education has endorsed a national professional examination for teachers. The National Council for the Accreditation of Teacher Education has adopted higher standards for program accreditation of schools of education. And both the NEA and AFT have announced support of entrance standards to the teaching profession that involve some form of competency testing for teachers.

Enthusiasm for adjusting standards by fiat is easy to muster. The policy maker is doing something about the problem. The solution is quick and visible. The cost is low. The responsibility for implementation is elsewhere. The counter points are obvious but hard to argue, i.e., the effect on equity, the inability to meet the new standards with current resources, the complexity of effecting improvement-oriented change in organizations. The adjustment of standards for admission to teaching may not solve the enduring problem of attracting top college graduates to a low paying job with few opportunities for advancement. But it does express, at least symbolically, the concern of the policy maker for teacher quality. Some states have already added, and others soon will, school improvement programs that provide additional resources at the local level to support the press for higher achievement standards. But the emphasis on minimum standards reflects the feeling by the public that the schools have been underachieving, that educationists cannot or will not effect reform on their own, that teachers and administrators are not as capable as they ought to be, that students are not working hard enough, and that expectations for performance by students and teachers have been deteriorating not increasing. The federal level policy makers in education will employ their bully pulpit to advocate higher standards. The states will adopt higher standards. The local education agencies will implement the standards. Predicting the effects may be ambiguous, but predicting the vigorous pursuit of this policy preference seems clear.

The vexatious policy issue surrounding the adjustment of standards is the impact of the modified standards on equity for minority groups and the poor. Secretary Bennett has stated the Administration's position, i.e., higher standards will benefit the poor. He argues that although there may be an initial increase in the dropout rate, the ultimate benefit will accrue to the economically disadvantaged through the acquisition of the skills and knowledge that will open up the economic system to them. That position will be debated.

Focus on Content

Secretary Bennett introduced the phrase '3Cs' to describe the special emphasis of his term of office. The first of these is content. The Reagan Administration has pushed this preference earlier under slightly different labels — concentration on basics and on the new basics, i.e., science, mathematics, and computer skills. State legislatures have picked up the theme by requiring more high school graduation credits in science and mathematics, subjects where enrollment in advanced courses had declined. Half of the states have established scholarship and forgiveable loan programs to encourage high school students to enter teaching; most of these programs are concentrated on mathematics and science.

The only federal educational policy initiative of the past six years that smacks of the old categorical programs was PL 98–377 — the act to support pre-collegiate mathematics and science education. The bill was signed into law by President Reagan on 11 August 1984. That legislation responded to the alleged dismal state of mathematics and science instruction in the schools by authorizing and appropriating funds to both the National Science Foundation and the Department of Education for activities ranging from teacher institutes, to merit scholarships, to Presidential awards for teaching excellence, the development of instructional materials, and grants to colleges and universities and local and state education agencies.

The content focus on 'hard subjects', whether old or new basics, has not ignored vocational education. However, the Administration's emphasis in vocational education is the direct link between education and employability. Similarly, the Secretary's attack on bilingual education was grounded in his concern for opening up opportunities for employment and advanced education to bilingual students who need English proficiency.

The Secretary has indicated his desire to expand the focus on content beyond the basics to a dialogue about what is to be taught. In his early statements he criticized the lack of a coherent design in the curricula of many schools and offered the advice that schools should alter their programs to emphasize the 'core studies [that] constitute the nucleus of our schools' common curricula', stressing mathematics, science, English, and history (Hertling, 1985a, p. 10). *What Works*, the Department's recent dissemination effort, emphasizes findings on basic skills, reading, writing, mathematics, science, study skills and homework (pp. 21–42). In *First Lessons: A Report on Elementary Education in America* (1986), Bennett wrote, 'it is imperative that elementary educators focus first on the acquisition of basic skills and good habits through which children will be able to extend the reach of their learning in later years' (*Education Week*, 10 September 1986, p. 34).

Beyond a focus on the basics, the Secretary has noted his intention to finance activities to upgrade textbooks and teaching materials. And, 'he also seeks the development of projects that would allow the public to identify essential knowledge — literary works or historical events that should be familiar to every child' (Hertling, 1985b, p. 10).

When this policy was focused on the basics or the new basics, it seemed to be one of the Administration's least controversial preferences. The negative concerns expressed have been gentle reminders that the new basics may ignore the humanities or that the basics provided insufficient emphasis on foreign languages, the arts, and physical education. The recent additions to the agenda by Secretary Bennett may elevate the level of opposition confronted by the Administration. Past efforts to upgrade textbooks and teaching materials have often triggered ideological debates. A truly national debate over essential knowledge will stimulate dissension if the consequence appears to have practical implications for local schools. The better guess, however, is that the focus on content will be contained within areas of public consensus or indifference and that ED will support individuals and groups at state and local levels who share the general concern for an emphasis on traditionally defined basic courses of study.

Parental Choice

The second of the Secretary's three Cs is choice. Choice actually covers three distinct interests of the Administration: (i) parental control over where their children attend school; (ii) parental influence on what is to be taught, by whom, and how; and (iii) parental involvement in the schooling process for their children. However, the cornerstone of this policy preference is the creation of conditions under which parents can choose their child's school. Secretary Bennett argues that this is extending to the poor the privilege held by the more affluent who exercise the privilege by choice of neighborhood or choice of a private school. In *First Lessons*, Bennett wrote:

> I propose that we acknowledge parents' right to choose their children's schools as the norm, not the exception, and that we extend it to as many parents as possible — not just to those fortunate enough to live in particular communities or wealthy enough to change their place of residence. (*Education Week*, 10 September 1986, p. 34)

The necessary condition for parental choice of schools has been defined by the Administration as some form of educational vouchers. As was noted in the earlier section on institutional competition, the tactics to achieve this end now include both supporting state initiatives to establish voucher plans and a national plan targeted to children eligible for assistance under chapter 1.

Parental influence on what is to be taught, by whom, and how and parental involvement in the schooling process has, to this point, been primarily an issue of advocacy by the Secretary. *What Works* emphasizes the Administration's interest in parental control and involvement in their children's education, for example: 'parents are their children's first and most influential teachers' (p. 7); 'parental involvement helps children learn more effectively' (p. 19).

For so long as the issue of parental choice is presented exhortatively, the national controversy surrounding it will be minimal. No one argues that parents should not control their child's education. The controversy arises when the choice exercised by the parent clashes with community or societal norms. The choice of some parents will conflict with social values about topics as diverse as creationism, right-to-life, segregation, sexism, faith healing, and AIDS. Reconciling parental control with social, philosophical, or religious 'goods' is problematic. Ultimately, the home schooling movement is the only solution to non-conflicting parental choice. The bias of liberal and conservative parents in this country toward alternative choices among 'good' schools, subjects, and methods in education would result in conflicts that would involve this Administration in assuming substantive positions, for example, supporting prayer in the schools. That is the prospective concern of many liberals and the hope of many conservatives.

Character

Secretary Bennett's third C is character. In describing the use of the Secretary's discretionary funds to foster this goal, Bennett indicated that he wanted to fund projects that foster 'wholesome' student character. Schools should encourage 'such qualities as thoughtfulness, kindness, honesty, respect for the law, knowing right from wrong, respect for parents and teachers, diligence, self-sacrifice, hard work, fairness, self-discipline and love of country' (Hertling, 1985b, p. 10). Illustrating the types of character-related projects that could receive funds he mentioned: (i) use of history, literature, and other academic subjects to promote character development; (ii) establishment of clear goals and policies that 'respect and support values from the students' homes', and encourage attendance, academic excellence and an orderly, drug-free environment (*ibid*). The President is usually more direct in his definition emphasizing 'good old-fashioned discipline' and 'organized school prayer'. Bennett refers to the 'common culture' which he defines as composed of the democratic ethic, the work ethic, and the Judeo-Christian ethic (*Education Week*, 28 May 1986, p. 10). In the broadest sense, then, the Administration's position defines traditional American values as derivative from the work ethic and the country's Judeo-Christian heritage.

The implementation of this policy preference will continue to include advocacy of the school prayer amendment. Additionally, the Administration has funded a center on school discipline and violence. Reagan and Bennett have launched an anti-drug campaign. Two additional volumes of *What Works* concentrate on discipline and drug education. And the Secretary has used his discretionary funds to encourage projects on character development in the schools (Hertling, 1986, pp. 1 and 13).

This is a policy preference territory broad enough to cover areas of general agreement, for example, maintenance of a drug-free environment in schools, and topics of sharp disagreement, for example, sanctioned school prayer. Overall however, the Administration can expect broad public support for its position on character education since few of the proposals for action, except the school prayer amendment, infringe directly on local school practices.

Devolution

The Administration's definition of an appropriate role for the federal government in education is inherent in this policy preference, i.e., a visible presence without operational responsibilities that offers advice, counsel, support, encouragement, and exhortation to those who have operational responsibility — parents, local communities, and state governments. Some of the analysts who feel that the Administration has been thwarted in its goals to modify educational policy support their view by pointing to the stagnation of progress in the transfer of responsibility to the states following the early success with the block grant, deregulation, and the reduction in educational expenditures. We argue the reverse. The failure of the Administration's opponents to reassert a growing federal role has left the territory open to the states and they are claiming the territory. The level of state activity is increasing.[4] State level political leaders are benefiting from their increased involvement in educational improvement activities.

The continuing expansion of the state role in education is obvious in the activity of the state legislatures. Pipho (1985) noted, for example:

Georgia's reform law includes a full-day kindergarten program by 1987–88, a statewide core curriculum, a 10 per cent salary increase for teachers, a career ladder program for teachers.

Illinois passed a comprehensive reform act that includes forty-four education reforms and two tax increase measures. Elements include preschool programs, a mathematics/science academy, report cards for schools, performance-based pay programs, regional centers for computer education and gifted children, and $211 million in new money for education in 1986.

Missouri passed the Excellence in Education Act of 1985 that includes student competency testing in all basic skill areas, an incentive program to recruit teachers, district-based professional development committees, an incentive program to encourage the adoption of career ladders for teachers, and a unique legislative oversight provision that convenes a joint committee of the general assembly in 1988 and every fourth year after to study the public schools and make recommendations for legislative action.

Massachusetts approved a reform bill increasing expenditures for education by $210 million — targeted on school programs, student performance, and teacher and administrator performance. (pp. 101 and 175–6)

Further evidence of an expanded state role is the release by the National Govenors Association of *Time for Results: The Governors' 1991 Report on Education*. This report includes recommendations about leadership and the management of schools, use and maintenance of school facilities, improvement of the teaching workforce, increasing college quality, using technology, fostering parent involvement and choice, and strategies for addressing the needs of 'at risk' students. In describing the governors' interest in education, Governor Kean said: 'Education is good politics. Nobody is able to run for governor this year without an education agenda in either party' (Olson, 1986, p. 36).

The federal role in education has always been marginal in a quantitative sense (roughly 8 per cent of elementary and secondary school expenditures; about 20 per cent of higher education cost because of the student aid programs). Qualitatively one can argue that the investment, though small, has been critical to achievements in the areas of equity and access for minority groups and women. Education is lost in the midst of the federal budget. But it is a big ticket item at the state level, amounting frequently to from one-third to one-half of a state's budget. With an expanding state interest in educational policy, that up to five years ago was restricted almost entirely to the state aid formula in each state, and an accompanying leveling off and decline of federal initiatives and involvement, we would conclude that devolution is alive and well in Washington. The Administration is likely to win this battle by default.

Summary

The Administration's educational policy agenda is accompanied by a deemphasis on or disappearance of policy preferences in education held by the federal government prior to 1980. The federal role that emerged from 1955–1980 was the creation and adoption of interventions to improve the American educational system by opening it up to least well served clientele, establishing school improvement strategies and tactics, funding areas in which states and localities were deemed laggard or fiscally incapable of response, and monitoring and evaluating the success of those endeavors after they had been undertaken.

At the least, one can argue that this pre-1980 role has been contained by the Reagan Administration. The only exception of consequence that has emerged in the past five years is the mathematics and science legislation and its funding was halved after one year of operation. The national reports on the condition of education in 1983 and 1984 set the stage for a response of the magnitude of the National Defense Education Act of 1958 or the Elementary and Secondary Education Act of 1965. And the response occurred — *at the state level*. The federal response was, appropriately for this Administration, exhortation and encouragement.

The driving wheel behind the categorical programs of the 1960s and 1970s was equity of minorities, the poor, the handicapped, and women. That is no longer the case. Social and welfare concerns, including equity, are not major forces in national level decision making about education. This is not intended to be an argument that they are ignored — simply that they are no longer pivotal considerations. For the present, a different set of priorities are in place in Washington that places emphasis on excellence in performance, competition, selectivity, economic concerns, choice, local initiatives, and the support of traditional values. That is a different direction.

Likely Progress on the Administration's Policy Agenda

We think there are a variety of contextual conditions that suggest the Administration will make solid progress in its educational policy agenda over the next three years and that this trend toward devolution is likely to continue under successor administrations — Republican or Democratic. The conditions for change are more promising for the Administration now than they were in 1981, to wit:

1 *Consensus gentium* — The Administration is working with the 'agreement of the people'. Analyses of opinion polls indicate broad support for central elements of the Administration's program including (a) increasing standards; (b) concentrating on basics; (c) reasserting traditional values in schools; (d) reducing the federal role; (e) rewarding merit; (f) increasing parental choice; (g) increasing competition; (h) keeping schools close to the people. We find it hard to believe that a tenacious administration with a consistent policy agenda will be unable to continue to show progress in areas in which its policy preferences have a popular base of support.

2 *Decentralized activity* — The states are already making inroads on the interventionist role in school improvement that had characterized the federal categorical programs of pre-1980. What's more, this encroachment is paying positive political results at the state level. A new decentralized bureaucracy of educational policy analysts and specialists is appearing in state legislatures and governors' offices. There is no reason to believe that the states would look kindly on an effort to diminish the expanding role they are assuming. The movement toward devolution is already underway. To modify the movement will require the reversal of the current flow of activity.

3 *Truncated policy continuum* — The range of policy options in education being debated seriously in Washington today is narrow. In most areas, the options are from the status quo to the Administration's asserted position. The American Defense Education Act, for example, is not a weighty matter for discussion. Expansion of ED is not imaginable. Significant budgetary increases for education are out of the question. The Administration is sitting comfortably in a position where it can experience movement toward its preferences while defeats are simply break-even situations. To some extent this is

always true of the administration in office. However, in the case of the current Administration, the opposition is so muted that there are no live alternatives.

4 *Muffled buffers* — Both Congress and the professional associations find themselves in a difficult position to protect past educational policies and programs and in a nearly impossible position to initiate new directions. Neither of these natural buffers against executive preferences can move effectively against public opinion. The associations are labeled quickly as special interest groups and congresspersons are left vulnerable to attack at home. Congressional initiatives are made even less likely by the fact that state-level politicians are enjoying their new-found prominence in educational policy making and are not likely to look favorably, as they once did, on 'education senators or representatives'. Today, the most effective buffers against federal educational policy changes are those that maintain a low profile and fight battles of containment. Their ultimate success would be more likely if there were some reason to believe that the current policy preferences of the Reagan Administration have a narrow base of popular support. That is not so.

5 *New management team* — For the first time, the President has a management team in place at the Department of Education that is (a) committed to all aspects of the Administration's platform for education; (b) free of commitment to any previous administration's positions and to the professional associations in education; and (c) able to articulate the Administration's position to the media in a fashion that capitalizes on the concept of the bully pulpit. There is no reason to suspect that the vigor in pursuit of the Administration's objectives will wane even if the White House devotes little time to them. There is every reason to guess that the White House is more supportive of and open to the current management team in ED than to its predecessor.

Our intent is not to guess about specific actions that will occur in educational policy from 1986 to 1988 or beyond. We have those guesses and they are tempting to offer because they attract controversy and attention. But they distract from the central focus of our argument. The educational policy preferences of the Reagan Administration will all show progress over the next two years; and the cumulative effect will be to modify further the basic federal role in education, to stimulate continued growth and independence of the state governments in educational policy development, and to foster the substantive interests of the Administration in competition, increased performance standards, traditional values, parental choice, and a focus on the basics in education. To answer the questions with which we began:

1 Yes, the past six years have produced a significant, enduring change in federal educational policy.

2   Yes, there is more to come, in the remaining years of the Reagan Administration and beyond.

Notes

1 An abbreviated version of this chapter, entitled 'The significance and permanence of changes in federal education policy, appeared in *Educational Researcher*, 15, 8 October 1986, pp. 4–13.
2 Data for this chapter were gathered between January 1981 and October 1986. Interviews were conducted with more than fifty Administration officials, congressional staff members, representatives of professional education associations, and other informed observers of the Washington education scene. The interviews were complemented by a continuing analysis of documents and reports from and about the federal education establishment, in and outside of government. Support for this research was provided by the Maris M. and Mary Higgins Proffitt Foundation, School of Education, Indiana University.
3 A separate study was conducted that dealt solely with the popular support for the Administration's views on education prior to and after 1980. The report of that study summarized the major public opinion polls about education and general polls that included education questions from 1979 to 1986.
4 A separate study was conducted that dealt solely with the effects of federal educational policy changes on policy and program development at the state and local levels. The report of that study summarized and interpreted current educational policy activities at the state and local levels.

References

Bennett defines elements of 'common culture'. (28 May 1986) *Education Week*, p. 10.
BRIDGMAN, A. (1985a) 'State launching barrage of initiatives, survey finds', *Education Week*, 6 February, pp. 1 and 31.
BRIDGMAN, A. (1985b) 'Reagan pledges administration focus on choice', *Education Week*, 6 March, pp. 1 and 29.
BUDGET WATCH (1986) 'Legislators reject ED budget; Magnet school reform planned', *Education Week*, 16 April, p. 11.
CHAPMAN, S. (1980) 'The teachers' coup', *The New Republic*, 11 October, p. 9.
DOYLE, D.P. and HARTLE, T.W. (1985) 'Ideology, pragmatic politics, and the education budget', in WEICHER, J.C. (Ed.), *Maintaining the Safety Net: Income Redistribution Programs in the Reagan Administration*, Washington, DC, American Enterprise Institute for Public Policy Research, pp. 119–53.
Excerpts from Bennett's 'First Lessons'. (10 September 1986) *Education Week*, pp. 34–5.
GARDNER, E.M. (1984 'The Department of Education', in BUTLER, S.M., SANERA, M. and WEINROD W.B. (Eds), *Mandate for Leadership II: Continuing the Conservative Revolution*, Washington, DC, The Heritage Foundation, pp. 49–62.
HERTLING, J. (1985a) 'Bennett to spend discretionary funds on content, character, and choice', *Education Week*, 12 June, p. 10.
HERTLING, J. (1985b) '"Coherent design" missing in curricula, says Bennett in call for common core', *Education Week*, 20 March p. 10.
HERTLING, J. (1986) 'Secretary's grants finance efforts to boost '3C's', *Education Week*, 19 March pp. 1 and 13.

David L. Clark and Terry A. Astuto

IANNACCONE, L. (1985) 'Excellence: An emergent educational issue', *Politics of Education Bulletin*, 23, 3, pp. 1 and 3–8.

INGALLS, Z. (1981) 'Gardner brings a "traditional view" to new federal review of education', *Chronicle of Higher Education*, 9 September, p. 11.

JENNINGS, J. (1985) 'Will Carl Perkins' legacy survive Ronald Reagan's policies?', *Phi Delta Kappan*, 66 April, pp. 565–7.

NATIONAL COMMISSION ON EXCELLENCE IN EDUCATION (1983) *A Nation At Risk: The Imperative for Educational Reform*. Washington, DC, US Government Printing Office.

NATIONAL GOVERNORS ASSOCIATION (1986) *Time for Results: The Governors' 1991 Report on Education*.

1980 Republican platform text (1980) *Congressional Quarterly Weekly Report*, 19 July pp. 2030–56.

OLSON, L (1986) 'Governors draft 5-year blueprint to press reforms', *Education Week*, 10 September, pp. 1 and 36.

PIPHO, C. (1985) 'Education reform continues to command attention', *Phi·Delta Kappan*, 67, October, pp. 101 and 175–6.

Reagan, citing opposition, pledges not to abolish ED 'at this time' (1985) *Education Week*, 6 February, p. 9.

State of the union address (1984) *Weekly compilation of presidential documents*, 30 January, pp. 87–94.

US DEPARTMENT OF EDUCATION (1986) *What Works: Research About Teaching and Learning*. Washington, DC, US Department of Education.

4   The Courts as Education Policy-makers in Australia

Ian K.F. Birch

Introduction

Only by way of over-statement would educators or jurists in Australia lay claim to the fact that the courts in that country might be designated as significant education policy-makers. No one in Australia has had the temerity to suggest that the High Court of Australia or any other court could be seen to be assuming the mantle of 'Education Department of Australia'. However, it would be equally inappropriate totally to discount the role of the judiciary in the Australian education system.

School law has become established as a matter of interest and concern amongst Australian educationists in recent years. A literature on school law is being accumulated as cases have been tried and their decisions applied to participants in school systems and the administrators of schools. Teaching institutions have introduced courses in school law as school administrators and teachers have seen the futility of entering their professions without an adequate legal base. Public demand, particularly from parents and students, has fuelled this growth industry. Schools, too, have adapted curricula or introduced new courses to accommodate teaching in general law, which, in turn, has increased the focus on school law. This co-mixture of law and education indicates an extension of the application of law to a clientele previously peripherally affected rather than the emergence of a corpus of school law as a separate branch of law. But this is not to diminish the importance for education of some of the decisions which have been arrived at.

The post-1950 surge in the number of school law cases cannot detract from the fact that where there has been schooling there has been school law. Prior to the comparatively modern press for and the introduction of compulsory schooling, the law operated with respect to schools. The celebrated English case, *R v. Hopley*,[1] for example, reiterated the common law rule with respect to the administration of corporal punishment as applied to parents and schoolmasters (acting *in loco parentis*). But the advent of the free, compulsory and secular education era ushered in a new age for school law. From that point in time provisions for schooling were entrenched in legislation which was open to challenge whether it be on an issue of statutory interpretation, or of the jurisdictional competence of the legislature (particularly in federal systems of government) or a matter of the validity of the legislation *vis-à-vis* guaranteed rights, whether of common law or statute.

The Australian literature on school law is concerned predominantly with the role of the courts and is concentrated particularly on studies of particular cases and issues. Some attention has also been given to the legislatures' role in school law both in terms of analyzing statute law but not to the same degree as with the study of judicial decisions. In general terms, school law has been perceived as the application of legal norms to education and their impact on persons and systems.

The judicial role in policy-making in education in Australia is of two sorts. It is, in its own right, a maker of policy in the application of the law of torts in education. It is also effective in policy-making in its activities either in legitimizing and enforcing policy already determined by legislative or executive action, or in its checking that action and protecting those affected by its unlawful impact. Whilst the latter role predominates and provides the major index of law, the former is not without its importance.

In common law jurisdictions, the courts have established themselves as lawmakers in several areas notably in the law of torts. They have extended the scope of that law to education. In Australia, for example, the High Court has determined that a duty of care is owed by teachers to students, what the standard of care is, what the liability of the employer is when an employee is in breach of his duty of care, and what rules with respect to contributory negligence will operate. The courts have been instrumental in enabling parents to sue in a situation in which their children are compulsorily removed from their care. Further, it has been resolved for Australia that the teacher-student relationship of itself invokes the operation of the law of torts regardless of the capacity of schools to provide adequate care. Such decisions have important policy repercussions for school systems and focus on one aspect of the judicial policy-makers, which is treated at greater length in case study number two, which appears below.

The major role of the courts in policy-making in Australian education is in its legitimizing/checking mode. This role may be invoked either insofar as courts are required to determine the meaning of acts and regulations or in determining the validity of such law. As to the former the normal rules of statutory interpretation are applied or determinations are made as to meaning. In New South Wales, for example, the Supreme Court was required to determine whether the words 'secular instruction' should be interpreted to mean teaching only in the Christian religion or required the teaching of all religions.[2] The court resolved that the legislation required teaching in the Christian religion and, in so doing, legitimated the policy of the Education

Department whose curriculum for religious instruction was so limited, against the long-standing opposition of opponents of such instruction.

Although the number of Australian cases involving the participants of education before Australian courts is not large, there has been a considerable variety in the type of action which the courts have heard. Ministers for Education, Directors-General of Education and other educational administrators have had their actions scrutinized in the courts. Cases have been decided involving teachers, students and parents. Most of those involving teachers have embraced matters relating to the teachers' role particularly with respect to the administration of corporal punishment, the issue of negligence and industrial matters affecting teachers. Students have been involved in cases related to their compulsory attendance at school and in particular schools not necessarily of their choice. In recent times, students have been party to actions in which teachers have sued in defamation or assault. Parents have also fallen foul of the courts in like matters.

Almost all Australian school law is of a kind which might suggest that it is unlikely that the courts will play a role in educational policy-making other than a reactive one. But this is not alone the case. Indeed, quite important decisions of a proactive kind have been taken by the courts affecting the policy process of more than a merely cosmetic kind. Although few in number — the lack of provisions for rights may account for their paucity — these cases have impacted directly on educational policy-making. The two case studies which follow are illustrative of this point. The first is concerned with constitutional interpretation which is the area in which most impact on educational policy has been made by the Australian judicial system. In addition to the particular instance discussed there, the High Court has impacted upon education by way of its interpretation of several constitutional provisions including that related to the external affairs power of the Commonwealth[3] and its recent decision to distinguish an early case which effectively ruled teachers' unions out of contention for invoking federal jurisdiction in respect of industrial matters.[4] The second case study also highlights the judicial impact on education. As part of the development of the common law doctrine in respect of the duty owed by citizens to others, the courts have been required to apply that law to particular educational situations.

Case Study 1: The Courts and Educational Management

Australian courts have made a singular impression on the management of education in that country by way of a line of decisions by the High Court of Australia in respect of the constitutional power under which the Commonwealth government is able to make grants to the states. The particular power in question is section 96 of the Commonwealth Constitution (the grants power) which reads:

> During a period of ten years after the establishment of the Common-
> wealth and thereafter until the Parliament otherwise provides, the
> Parliament may grant financial assistance to any State on such terms
> and conditions as the Parliament thinks fit.

The grants power appears in the Commonwealth Constitution despite
the decision of the 1898 Federal Convention in Melbourne that such a
provision should not be included.[5] The matter was raised in 1898 in an
attempt to resolve the issue as to how the Commonwealth might distribute
the surplus revenue which was expected with the operation of section 87 of
the Constitution.[6] Under that provision, the Commonwealth government
was empowered to apply one-quarter of the net revenue raised from the
imposition of customs and excise duties — an exclusive domain of federal
power — towards its own expenditure. The problem remained as to determining a formula for the distribution of the remainder and whether additional constitutional means for effecting this distribution were required
besides the agreed-upon clauses in the draft constitution.

The proposition put to the 1898 Convention was that a power should
be included in the Constitution whereby the Commonwealth could render
financial assistance to any state in any manner it saw fit. Objections were
quick in coming to this proposal. Notable among them was the claim that
the states could be cast in the demeaning role of mendicants. This, along
with the problem of how to distribute the surplus, put paid to the proposal
which was easily defeated when put to the vote. The upshot was that when
the draft Constitution went to the people, it had only the section 87 provision.

The premiers of the colonies met in 1899 to iron out the differences
which had emerged on the constitutional provisions following the conventions. The question of the proposed Commonwealth control over customs
and excise and the allocation of the surplus revenue received attention. As no
satisfactory alternative emerged to the provisions of section 87, a compromise was reached whereby a complementary distribution power was agreed
upon. That provision, as finally drafted, passed into the Commonwealth
Constitution as section 96.

The 1899 intention of complementarity between sections 87 and 96 came
adrift within the first decade of the Commonwealth parliament. The operation of the section 87 was phased out with the passing into law of Surplus
Revenue legislation in 1910[7], in that the Commonwealth 'decided otherwise'.
However, section 96 remained in force since no provision was made nor has
since been made by the federal parliament to vary its force and effect.

This set of circumstances has had the important consequence that the
premiers have ended up with a rod for their backs and one of their own
making. For, standing alone, section 96 has provided the constitutional
mechanism by which Commonwealth governments have been able to in-

fluence a variety of matters which the states might be excused for considering their domain. Education legislation of this type is discussed more fully below.

Judicial Opinion and the Grants Power

The cases

In an opinion without peer among decisions of the High Court in terms of both the alacrity and brevity with which the scope of a constitutional provision was first decided, the Court announced, in 1926, that:

> The Court is of opinion that the *Federal Aid Roads Act* No 46 of 1926 is a valid enactment.
>
> It is plainly warranted by the provisions of section 96 of the Constitution, and not affected by those of section 99 or any other provisions of the Constitution, so that exposition is unnecessary. The action is dismissed.[8]

The grants at issue were ones in which the Commonwealth made funds available through the responsible Minister to the States from a trust account for the construction of roads specified in an agreement. The Commonwealth's contribution amounted to about one-quarter of the costs and conditions were imposed such as to place virtual control of the programme in its hands. Three years after the programme began, the State of Victoria challenged the validity of the legislation concentrating particularly on the executive administration of the grants by the Commonwealth and the conditions imposed by it.

Two other cases which go to provide the basis for arriving at a general statement on the scope of section 96 deal with the general question of grants to the states rather than the particularity of the grant as in the *Roads case*. Both cases are related in that the taxation power of the Commonwealth was centrally at issue. But the scope of section 96 formed part of the constitutional interest in each case.

The *First Uniform Tax case*[9] resulted from a challenge by four states to a programme of legislation introduced by the Commonwealth in 1942, whereby the federal government became the income taxing authority in Australia. Three of the four pieces of legislation enabled the Commonwealth to levy income tax, to have priority over the states in collecting that tax and to assume control of the states' resources for income by having their offices transferred to the Commonwealth. The fourth statute, the *Income Tax Reimbursement Act 1942*, established the means whereby the federal government could reimburse the states for the revenue lost because of the Commonwealth 'takeover' of income tax. The grants power came into contention with the passing of this Act in that it provided the constitutional base for the payment of moneys to the states and in that such payment was only to be made on the express condition that the federal treasurer was satisfied that a state had not raised revenue by means of personal income tax.

In a 4:1 decision, the High Court upheld the validity of the Income Tax Reimbursement Act as being within power. The war-time nature of the programme which played some importance in the decision related to the War-Time Arrangements legislation, in particular, played no part in the discussion of section 96. Some of the points raised and the dissenting opinion, in particular, will form part of the general exploration which follows of the established scope of section 96. Before turning to that discussion, mention needs to be made of the *Second Uniform Tax case*.[10] For reasons not readily discernible, except, perhaps, their own disarray, no state challenged the post-war revamped taxation scheme until 1957 when two pieces of legislation were attacked by Victoria and New South Wales. The successful challenge, on a 4:3 decision, was to that section of the Income Tax Act which required taxpayers first to meet any tax imposed by the Commonwealth before paying a state-levied income tax.[11] The unsuccessful bid was against the validity of the reimbursement legislation which continued to be the means by which the Commonwealth made payments to the states from the revenue received from income tax. The protection afforded that legislation, including its conditions for making grants, by section 96 was roundly affirmed in the unanimous decision of seven judges. The *Second Uniform Tax case* provides, therefore, a third example of an exposition of the scope of the grants power in which the judges were generally agreed as to the broad scope of the grants power. Their conclusions remain to be discussed.

The broad interpretation
The general conclusion to be drawn from the dicta in the cases explored thus far is that the grants power is capable of a very wide construction. In the words of Chief Justice Dixon in the *Second Uniform Tax case*:

> ... it is apparent that the power to grant financial assistance to any State upon such terms and conditions as the Parliament thinks fit is susceptible of a very wide construction in which few if any restrictions can be implied ...
>
> There has been what amounts to a course of decisions upon s.96 all amplifying the power and tendency to a denial of any restrictions upon the purpose of the appropriation on the character of the condition.[12]

In the face of such intepretation, it is difficult to conceive of circumstances in which grants may fall outside the power. This is highlighted further in that the general statement of breadth has been reinforced by a number of assertions about the force of the power in the light of the particular legislation which has come under challenge. They are:

  (i) that a law may make grants available for a purpose for which the Commonwealth otherwise has no constitutional mandate;
 (ii) that the Parliament may authorize the disposition of grants by executive action;
(iii) that grants may be made for a purpose to which a state is or is not making a contribution;
 (iv) that grants are valid even when there is discrimination as between states;
  (v) that in the process of the Commonwealth government making grants available, state governments may have no other function than that of conduit;
 (vi) that states may be induced to refrain from exercising sovereign powers;
(vii) that the concept of 'assistance' may be very broadly defined; and
(viii) that section 96 is not subject to other constitutional provisions.

Several of these propositions warrant further exploration given the attack mounted on the section by the plaintiffs in the *DOGS case*.

Purpose of a grant
The States Grants (Schools) legislation provided funds for a purpose, which, it may be argued, is beyond the power of the Commonwealth. There is certainly no specific grant of power to the Commonwealth in respect of schooling or education except insofar as it has a mandate to make laws for peace, order and good government in territories under its control. There is, however, the 'benefits to students' provision in section 51 (xxiiiA) of the Constitution, which was added in 1946, under which a wide range of educational benefits may be provided for students as Mr Justice Dixon observed in the *British Medical Association case*:

> The general sense of the word 'benefit' covers anything tending to the profit advantage gain or good of man and is very indefinite. But it is used in a rather more specialized application in reference to what are now called social services; it is used as a word covering provisions made to meet needs arising from special conditions with a recognized incidence in communities or from particular situations or pursuits such as that of a student, whether the provision takes the form of money payments or the supply of things or services.[13]

That form of direct assistance is, however, constrained as judges in the same case made clear. The constitutional permission was limited only to the provision of such benefits (not their regulation) and, in line with other social service provisions, no one could be compelled to accept the benefits offered. As a power, therefore, in respect of education, section 51 (xxiiiA) is limited.

A more major intrusion by the Commonwealth into education can flow from its making laws for peace order and good government in respect of other matters such as defence or persons such as migrants or aborigines.

Education may clearly be seen to be a part of the exercise of the constitutional mandate in these areas and this position has been reinforced by the High Court:

> Section 107 of the Constitution so far from reserving anything to the States leaves them the then residue of power after full effect is given to the powers granted to the Commonwealth ... The question in relation to the validity of a Commonwealth Act is whether it fairly falls within the scope of the subject matter granted to the Commonwealth by the Constitution. What subject matter will be determined by construing the words of the Constitution by which legislative power is given to the Commonwealth irrespective of what effect the construction may have upon the residue of power which the States may enjoy.[14]

Thus, in the exercise of its constitutional prerogatives the Commonwealth may become freely involved in such educational matters as pertain to that purpose. This in turn limits the extent to which one may freely argue that the Commonwealth has no power in education.

In the long run, however, it is unnecessary for a conclusion to be reached on the question as to the extent to which education is or is not a Commonwealth power. The decision in the *Roads case* makes the question almost redundant. For in that situation Commonwealth aid was for roads a matter over which the national government had no direct control. Nor, as the defendant, was the Commonwealth forced into the position of arguing for an indirect mandate over roads as, for example, in the exercise of the defence power. The Court determined the matter in terms of the scope of section 96, although the impugned legislation claimed no authority from that section. In so doing, it made possible the drawing of the conclusion that under that section the federal government may make grants to the states for purposes which are beyond the immediate power of the Commonwealth.

The Court's position was reinforced in the *First Uniform Tax case* with comments such as that of Chief Justice Latham who affirmed the principle that 'even though an indirect consequence of an Act, which consequence could not be directly achieved by the legislature, is contemplated and desired by Parliament, the fact is not relevant to the validity of the Act'.[15] With such judicial backing it is not difficult to assert with confidence that legislation providing grants to the States for educational purposes would be found to be within power.

The 'conduit' principle: In the cases so far mentioned the operation of the conduit principle is not immediately evident. For in the programmes under challenge, the Commonwealth proposed making payments to the states' treasuries. In the *Roads case*, payment was authorized on the condition it be used for prescribed roadworks; in the *Tax cases* payments were made to the states without any purposes attached.

Chief Justice Dixon commented on the 'conduit' principle in the *Second Uniform Tax case* and expressed considerable doubt as to whether section 96 — on his reading — permitted the Commonwealth in effect to circumvent state policy and support particular purposes. However, he deferred to the run of decisions in the High Court and the principle remains intact. This is of importance to the education sector of public spending in that the Commonwealth has, since 1964, made grants to non-government schools and school systems which the states could not interfere with after their acceptance but only merely pass them on.

Sovereign powers of the states: The *Tax cases* raised most pertinently the question of the extent to which the grants power might be used to impinge upon the sovereign powers of the states — in the cases in point, their power to impose income tax. The means by which states might be affected was the effective case of the words in section 96 'on such terms and conditions as the Parliament thinks fit'.

Although there was no discussion of these words in the *Roads case*, the decision clearly supported the right of the Commonwealth to impose the conditions it had, which designated not only the types of roads upon which funds were to be spent but also required that the states acknowledge that formal control of all the expenditure was vested in the Commonwealth. But it was in the *Tax cases* that the imposition of conditions assumed greater proportions in that no reimbursement was to be made to a state in any instance where it had levied an income-tax. Yet in these instances, too, most of the judges declared the validity of the imposition of conditions and their wide-ranging nature. Their position might best be summed up in the words of Mr Justice Williams in the *Second Uniform Tax case*:

> The grant is made out of Commonwealth moneys and it is for the Commonwealth Parliament to say on what terms and conditions such moneys shall be made available. Nothing could be wider than the words 'on such terms and conditions as the Parliament thinks fit' and they must include at the very least any terms or conditions with which a State may lawfully comply.[16]

Opposition to the broad interpretation was consistently maintained by Chief Justice Dixon in the same case. On his view terms and conditions imposed could have been expected to be those immediately relevant to the given situation which has required particular assistance. However, also consistently, the Chief Justice declined to do other than accept the cumulative effect of previous court decisions and join with the broader interpretation. In so doing, he, too, could see no tenable interpretation of the term aspect of the grants power other than in like language to that expressed by his colleagues.

Given the right of the Commonwealth to impose terms such as was found in the *Tax Reimbursement Act* of 1942 and succeeding legislation, the question of sovereignty loomed large. For it was argued for the states that their sovereignty was at issue not only in the denial of the right to impose a tax on income but also in the possible limit to the financial resources imposed on the states. In the *First Uniform Tax case*, the Chief Justice, Sir John Latham, held that the Commonwealth would not make laws in respect of the composition and functions of state governments simply because it had no power to do so.

Further, the grants power could not be claimed to be a means of doing so. But he did allow that Commonwealth legislation might validly weaken or destroy some activity of a state. Mr Justice Starke agreed with the first principle expressed by the Chief Justice in the case but found that section 96 was being used to deprive the states of a taxing power which deprivation was an infringement of their sovereignty. Where his brothers found themselves in contention with Starke J. was that they declined to interpret section 96 as a law compelling the states to surrender their interest in raising taxes on incomes. Mr Justice Williams observed, for example, that 'There is no illegal interference with the sovereignty of the States, because the matter of levying or not levying their own income tax is left entirely to the discretion of their own Parliaments'.[17] The run of opinion in the *Second Uniform Tax case* was similar with that of the 1942 decision with most judges supporting the contention that the law at issue did not compel a surrender of state power. Chief Justice Dixon responded to the plaintiffs' claim in this respect by commenting:

> If s.96 came before us for the first time for interpretation, the contention might be supported on the ground that the true scope and purpose of the power which s.96 confers upon the Parliament of granting money and imposing terms and conditions did not admit of any attempt to influence the direction of the exercise by the State of its legislative or executive powers.[18]

But, again, the Chief Justice deferred to the decisions of the High Court and allowed the possibility of an 'attempt' he would have preferred to debar.

'Assistance': The type of assistance rendered in the *Roads case* and the *Tax cases* was very different. In the former case, the assistance approved of was financial aid as part of the overall expenditure for a purpose of which the states were supportive. Assistance in the latter instance was of the most general kind in that moneys were simply paid to the states without any strings attached as to the purposes on which the grants should be expended. Yet both forms of assistance were of a narrow kind. The maintenance of roads was, no doubt, a function of the states and, to the extent to which additional funds were made available by the Commonwealth, assistance was provided. From the states' perspective, however, apart from the infusion of funds, the assistance apparently appeared to be dysfunctional in that the freedom of the states to determine priorities in road construction and repair

was impaired. If their preferences varied from the determination of the national government no assistance was forthcoming. The assistance was not, therefore, unequivocal. In the tax cases, the assistance comprised only the return to the states of what they would have expected to obtain from income tax had they levied it themselves. This assistance became a static amount in the sense that it became a politically unpalatable and, therefore, impossible option for the states to levy an additional income tax, thus affecting likely future state expenditure. That this was a somewhat broad definition of 'financial assistance' was intimated by the Chief Justice in the *Second Uniform Tax case* when he observed:

> That any enactment is valid if it can be brought within the literal meaning of the words of the section and as to the words 'financial assistance' even that is unnecessary. For it may be said that a very extended meaning has been given to the words 'grant financial assistance to any State' and that they have received an application beyond that suggested by a literal interpretation.[19]

But he accepted it as determinative of the issue.

The unfettered power: The judgment of the High Court in the *Roads case* was that section 96 was not affected by section 99 'or any other provision of the Constitution'.[20] The immediate effect of that decision was to enable the Commonwealth to make grants to any one or all states and in differing amounts. But whether the words could be taken at face value to mean that the grants power was unaffected by any other constitutional provision remained a matter not widely canvassed in the *Tax cases*. In the *First Uniform Tax case*, Mr Justice Starke hinted strongly at his concern that an unfettered section 96 could disturb the federal balance if not destroy it and he would deny that force to the section.[21]

Judicial restraint on the grants power: One consistent restraint on the scope of section 96 imposed by the judges in the cases mentioned thus far was that the grants power did not give rise to coercive legislation. The common refrain of the benches in both the *Tax cases* may be summed up in the words of the Chief Justice Dixon in his 1957 judgment: 'But in s.96 there is nothing coercive'.[22] Any law, therefore, which attempted to compel a state to act in a certain manner would be beyond power if section 96 were invoked as the constitutional authority.

Two implications flow from this non-coercive notion. The first is that the Commonwealth is prevented from making laws on the subject matter for which the grant is made. States Grants (Schools) legislation, for example, may not be used as a vehicle for the Commonwealth legislating on schools, unless, of course, that is possible under another head of power. That was the case in respect of taxation as section 51(ii) of the Constitution provides the federal government with a concurrent lawmaking power in taxation. Combining the exercise of that power with the inconsistency provision in section 109[23] of the Constitution enables the Commonwealth a dominant voice legislating on taxation in a way which would not be possible in education, given the limited, if any, federal power in that subject matter. Thus the non-coercive principle prevents the use of section 96 for direct (as opposed to the indirect means available by imposing terms and conditions) legislative intervention in matters otherwise beyond power.

The second implication of non-coercion advanced in the cases was that there was no power in the Commonwealth to compel acceptance of a grant. Section 96 'is but a power to make grants of money and to impose conditions on the grant, there being no power of course to compel acceptance of the grant and with it the accompanying term or condition'.[24] The decision to accept or not accept a grant was regarded as pivotal in the opinion of the judiciary. Were a state, for whatever reason, to accept a grant, it was deemed to surrender any right to escape the implications of its terms and conditions. Thus the Chief Justice in the *First Uniform Tax case* was not prepared to differentiate between the political and legal implications of accepting a grant.[25] Were a state induced politically to surrender some power in fulfilling the condition for obtaining Commonwealth largesse, there was no remedy to be found in the courts. For, on the cases canvassed, the judicial retort to state governments would be that they have the solution to the problem within their own reach.

Conclusion: The conclusion to be drawn from the cases so far discussed is that the broad scope of the grants power was well settled by 1957. Whether section 96 was subject to other constitutional provisions was open to question and the narrow view of the section might have encouraged further challenge. But even the main exponent of that position, Sir Owen Dixon, could only conclude of the earlier decisions considered by him that:

> They combine to give to s.96 a consistent and coherent interpretation and they each involve the entire exclusion of the limited operation which might have been assigned to the power as an alternative.[26]

Nevertheless the plaintiffs in the *DOGS case*[27] proceeded to launch an attack on the Commonwealth's use of section 96 to provide grants to the States in aid of non-government sectarian schools. Their efforts were in vain, however, and the High Court was unanimous in its view that the scope of section 96 was well established in the run of cases on this question. The court did, however, limit the view of the operation of section 96 being unfettered and asserted that that section was subject to the Constitution.

The grants power and education
Aid to the states' educational institutions has embraced all sectors of education from the pre-school to the tertiary level and both government and non-government undertakings. The universities and their constituent colleges

have been receiving grants via the states since 1951 while colleges of advanced education, teachers and pre-school teachers' colleges were the comparative late-comers in this field. At the school level both private and public institutions have been receiving aid since 1964 for both general and specific programmes. The tertiary sector is the subject of concentration in this discussion in that it better demonstrates how the grants power has been utilized to give the Commonwealth almost total control of an education sector and how, on one occasion, that use was successfully resisted by the states.

During the estimates debate in 1951, Prime Minister Menzies claimed that his government's proposal to provide funds for universities was 'designed to put every Australian university in a position of solvency'. 'This will be the most dramatic contribution' Menzies said, 'that has ever been made by the Commonwealth in my life-time to public education in Australia'.[28] The first States Grants (University) Act, which came into effect for the 1951 academic year, provided for Commonwealth assistance for recurring expenditure at universities and university colleges on the condition that the contribution from state governments and fees were three times the basic Commonwealth grant. Other conditions were imposed on the grants made. In the first place the states were required to pay the amounts specified to the university named and to ensure that it was applied for university purposes. Secondly, the states were put under an obligation to see that the amount stipulated in the schedule was applied by a university towards the teaching and administrative costs of that university's residential colleges and to return money not used.[29]

This watershed piece of legislation was in the form of a grant to the states for a given purpose and conditions were imposed on the use of the grant. In commenting on it, Prime Minister Menzies said:

> Therefore we have conditioned this new departure accordingly — because it is a new, almost a revolutionary, departure for the Commonwealth, which has neither power nor responsibility, if I may put it in that way, in the educational field, to say that irrespective of repatriation or any other matter with respect to which it has constitutional power to legislate, it will make grants to the States to assist those universities to be kept effectively operating and profitably developing.[30]

The 1953 States Grants (Universities) Act repealed the 1951 legislation and was itself repealed in 1955.[31] Further Acts were passed in each of the succeeding years to 1958 and parts of the Act in that year were amended in 1960. The legislation until 1957 varied little from that of 1951. The 1958 States Grants (Universities) Act incorporated the recommendations of the Murray Committee on government expenditure for the years 1958–60. The £22m to which the government was committed involved grants for recurrent and capital costs for universities and colleges and included the suggested emergency grants. The conditions applied were similar to those in earlier

Acts.[32] After tabling the first report of the Australian Universities Commission in Parliament in November 1960, Menzies introduced the States Grants (Universities) Bill implementing its recommendations. The resultant Act provided for financial payments to the states of almost £50m for the 1961–63 triennium. Included in this figure were subsidies for capital expenditure on a pound for pound basis while the proportion of recurrent expenditure was 1: 1.85, Commonwealth to State.[33] Similar conditions prevailed as in the previous legislation of this type.

Amendments were made to the 1960 legislation in later years. By a 1962 Act, for example, grants were made payable to universities for recurrent expenditure following an accepted increase in the salaries of academics and capital grants were provided for teaching hospitals.[34] In 1963, the Universities (Financial Assistance) Act was passed.[35] This legislation followed upon the reception of the second report of the Australian Universities Commission and provided for an expenditure of nearly £60m in the 1964–66 triennium.

Following the 1964 report of the Eggleston Committee on university salaries, bills were introduced into the House of Representatives to amend the *Universities (Financial Assistance) Act 1963* and the *States Grants (Universities) Act 1960–1963* to increase the Commonwealth's assistance to match the level of the salaries recommended. Menzies indicated that the states did not have to implement the salaries suggested.[36] It was made clear, however, that if the states paid lower salaries the recurrent grant would be less and, if higher salaries were allowed, there would be no matching Commonwealth contribution.

In March 1965, Senator Gorton, as Minister in Charge of Commonwealth Activities in Education and Research, presented to Parliament the Report of the Committee on the Future of Tertiary Education in Australia — the Martin Committee. The government indicated its agreement with recommendations related to the funding of certain new universities but declined to accept the Committee's suggestions that no new universities other than those mentioned should be established before 1975, and that part-time and external studies should be reduced or eliminated. The legislative implementation of the recommendation on funding came in the Universities (Financial Assistance) Bill 1965 which passed through both Houses.[37] Following the third report of the Australian Universities Commission, Senator Gorton announced that the government would pay its proportion of a universities' programme for the 1967–69 triennium costing $512m, some $56m less than the Committee recommended. The Universities (Financial Assistance) Act which implemented this decision provided for grants to the states totalling $175m.[38] In arriving at this figure for recurring expenditure, the government set salary standards without the aid of an independent tribunal compared with its 1964 approach.

In 1969, the Minister for Education, Malcolm Fraser, indicated that the government would accept financial responsibility for universities in the states to a total of $227m. Legislation to effect this decision was introduced a month later and passed through the Parliament.[39] Apart from the increase in the support for universities, the only significant difference in this Act from previous legislation of this type was a provision enabling institutions to obtain single items of capital equipment which cost more than $40,000. (Such items had previously been required to be part of a capital project.) Also in 1969 two Financial Assistance Acts were passed which enabled variations to be made in the building programmes of some universities and in the time periods during which payments could be made.

In its last budget before being removed from office in 1972 the Liberal-Country Party government allocated $344m for expenditure on universities. Its successor in government continued the high level of funding of university education but in 1973 some particularly Labor emphases became evident in the three States Grants (Universities) Acts.[40] One of these Acts provided grants for social service training at Sydney and Melbourne universities; the second made provision for the payment of grants totalling more than $2m to the states to be paid to needy university students, that is a student 'experiencing hardship by reason of his financial circumstances'; the third Act amended Act No 126 of 1972 by adding the provision that payment to the states was conditional upon the assurance from each that 'no University situated in that state charges fees in respect of that year [1974 or 1975] or any part of that year'. Thus, the Labor government achieved one of its goals with regard to education, namely, the abolition of fees at universities.

One matter not covered in the foregoing was the demonstration of the capacity referred to by the judges in the cases mentioned, to refuse to accept the attempted control of the Commonwealth by their declining a grant under section 96. In 1965 the Parliament passed the States Grants (Research) legislation which provided for grants to be paid to the states for use, if matched by the states, on special research projects. The government established the Australian Research Grants Committee to process applications for assistance and make recommendations to the Minister. The Committee was limited to apportioning $2m which was the balance of a sum of $5m which the Australian Universities Commission had recommended should be spent in the 1964–66 triennium. The legislation was supported by the opposition and passed into law without amendment.[41] Prior to the passing of this Act and Act No 5 of 1963 which provided for a special grant of $1m for research as part of the financial assistance to universities, Commonwealth governments had included money for research as part of their general assistance to universities. The provision of funds to the states for special research projects on a matching basis was the one 'education' occasion on which several of the states — New South Wales, Victoria and Queensland — decided that they would resist the imposition of the matching requirement. The Commonwealth responded by declaring, in 1966, that although it was ready to meet half the cost of the research projects recommended by both the Universities Commission and the Research Grants Committee, it would reduce its contribution to the former by the amount the states failed to match the latter.

Legislation was also introduced and passed by which the matching require-ment in the 1965 States Grants (Research) Act was no longer mandatory before a Commonwealth grant would be made.[42] The national government proceeded to meet the cost of the Research Grants Committee's recom-mendations in full.

This resumé of grants to university education, which extends only a little beyond the period between the *Second Uniform Tax case* (1957) and the most recent challenge to section 96 raised by the plaintiffs in the *DOGS case*, provides a convenient base for seeing the control which may be exercised by a Commonwealth government by means of section 96. Overtly it controlled the finance available to the universities and, therefore, covertly the expansion and development rate. It virtually controlled academic salaries by fixing recurrent grants to account for salaries at a given level. It fixed item expendi-ture on certain aspects of capital costs ranging from research equipment to the size of rooms in residential colleges. Finally, in 1973, the 'terms and conditions' phrase was used to ensure that funding for universities became the prerogative of the federal government, although the universities in the states remained statutory institutions under state legislature. Were this review of grants to universities continued to the present, it would show a downturn in federal support for universities and a control which has led to closure, collaboration and amalgamation all exercised constitutionally by means of the grants power. But sufficient has been covered to indicate that along with the judicial opinion discussed above, the practical use to which section 96 has been put has been deeply entrenched in Australian education.

Case Study 2: The Courts and Educational Misfeasance

The High Court of Australia has been significantly involved in determining policy affecting the management of schools in terms of the duty of care owed by school systems and their employees to their students. The role of the High Court in this area has been fairly recent and passes most participants in the education system by largely unnoticed. But it is the case that the courts in Australia determine the issue of negligence and, although the impact upon the actual administration of education may seem to be slight, it is the case that the courts have laid down the ground rules in this matter.

Seminal cases were decided by the High Court of Australia in 1964 in relation to the question of the responsibility of teachers and parents in negligence. The cases were *Ramsay v. Larsen* ((1964) 111 CLR 16) and *McHale v. Watson* ((1964) 111 CLR 384). The former of these covered a fact situation involving teachers, and the latter an episode in which parents play a key role. Each of these sets the stage for the respective responsibility of teachers and parents when their children are involved in accidents which are shown to result from negligence.

In *Ramsay v. Larsen*, the High Court sat to determine an appeal on two points of law. The first related to contributory negligence and requires a review of the salient facts. Larsen was found by a teacher up a tree trying to recover a set of keys which had lodged in the tree, despite previous warnings for him not to climb the tree. The teacher decided, however, that as Larsen was already in the tree, he should go about the business of recovering the keys and it was decided as a matter of fact that it was as he was in the process of doing what the teacher required that he slipped and fell. The court decided that there was no contributory negligence on the part of the student.

The more interesting feature of the decision in *Ramsay v. Larsen* as far as apportioning responsibility in negligence is concerned is the fact that, for the first time in Australia, the High Court established the rules for the responsibility of teachers in negligence. In its unanimous decision, the High Court affirmed that, given the requirements of the compulsory Education Act, children attended school in compliance with the law. Teachers were employed by the Crown to teach those students or, in the case of the private sector, parents were permitted to send their children to schools which were approved by the state. So it followed in the court's opinion that teachers' authority was derived from their employment by the Crown and not from the parent. In other words, in overturning an earlier New South Wales decision, the court affirmed that teachers did not act *in loco parentis* in the course of fulfilling their duties. Whilst the court did not dismiss entirely the notion *in loco parentis* in terms of discussing teachers' responsibility in negligence, it did assert that teachers' authority was clearly obtained from their employment by the Crown and was not delegated by parents. The following extract which is a quote by Mr Justice Taylor from a judge in the New South Wales Full Court presents the appropriate legal picture for teachers, at least in Australian government schools:

> Pupils of the prescribed school age attending public schools have, during school hours, been compulsorily removed, by the authority of the Crown, from the protection and control of their parents. In view of that compulsion, by the establishment of public schools for the reception of such pupils, and the provision of teachers to impart instruction and maintain discipline, the Crown must be regarded as having taken over, in respect of the pupils, those obligations of which their parents have been deprived, including the obligation to take reasonable care for their safety — an obligation which is to be measured by that care which a careful father would take of his own children. It does not seem to me to be right to say, as was said in *Hole v. Williams*, that a teacher in maintaining discipline and imparting instruction, is exercising an authority delegated to him by the parents of a pupil ... (*Ramsay v. Larsen*, pp. 37–8)

Having asserted the law for Australia on the responsibility evolving from the introduction of compulsory education laws, the court went on to assert that the Crown, as with any other employer, was vicariously liable for the negligent acts of its employees — in this case teachers. In 1964, therefore, we have the situation where the High Court sheeted home the responsibility for negligent acts involving teachers to those teachers and their employers such that the Crown was placed in the position of being liable to be sued for the negligent acts of its teacher employees. It remained open for employers in that situation to sue employees for the recovery of damages awarded them on account of the negligence of an employee.

This significant policy change was a very appropriate one. The law to 1964 appeared to have enabled the employer of teachers under the compulsory education requirements to avoid responsibility for the negligent acts of the teachers it employed. That, of course, must have had considerable impact on the number of cases which came to the courts prior to 1964 and explains in part the greater number since. For prior to *Ramsay v. Larsen*, it was simply the case that unless the negligence complained of had been done by a teacher with means, there was, of course, little or no practical point in suing a teacher in negligence. Not only does one usually hope to obtain damages in such a case, but also, of course, clearly to cover one's costs. The 1964 policy opened the door to parents to sue a source which did have the where-with-all to meet the damages decided upon in the courts. At the same time, that policy lifted the total responsibility in negligence from teachers and whilst not removing that responsibility in principle, it certainly transferred its base from the teacher to the employer. One can only assume that subject to employers not seeking to recover damages awarded against them for the negligent acts of their employees, the teaching profession should have very much welcomed this policy switch as should have parents who now had a means for obtaining redress not previously available to them.

McHale v. Watson

This case also affirmed policy in respect of responsibility in negligence as far as parents were concerned. McHale, who was a minor at the time of the incident, sued Watson, also a minor, in trespass and for negligence. McHale had been hit in the eye by a sharpened piece of metal described as a dart which Watson threw. (This episode occurred completely independent of any school situation. Had this event happened in the school context, the substantive decision as to parents' responsibility in such cases would not have been different. The separate question of negligence on the part of teachers would of course have become an issue in the school situation.) So upset were Watson's parents over the incident that they paid some of McHale's hospital bills. The action came to court several years later.

The aspect of the case which is of particular interest in the context of responsibility in negligence is, of course, the negligence claim. In that regard, Mr Justice Windeyer sitting as a single judge (this case was heard in the High

Court because it involved parties from different states) determined two matters, namely:

(i) that in deciding a case of negligence involving a child, the court would determine what a child of that age might be expected to do when behaving responsibly in such a situation. (This issue was appealed to the full bench of the High Court a year later but that court decided in a 3:1 decision that Mr Justice Windeyer was right in his interpretation.); and

(ii) that a parent does not incur liability for a misuse which his child makes of some thing which the parent knows the child possesses and which the parent expects the child could reasonably use safely.

The policy emanating from *McHale v. Watson* might be one applauded by a parent being sued but might be less favourably regarded by a parent whose child has been injured negligently. For what this decision does is to cut off one avenue of redress which might otherwise have been available and leaves to a negligently injured child only the option of suing the other child. And children, like teachers, with few exceptions, are not noted for their possessing riches.

Directions Post-1964

The High Court of Australia broadened the scope of the responsibility of school authorities as far as negligence is concerned in *Geyer v. Downs* ((1977) 52 ALR 142). Again, in a unanimous decision, the High Court reiterated the points made above in terms of the baseline policy on the question of the duty of care owed by teachers. But something further was added in this case in which a concerned principal opened the gates of his lock-up school to provide a place of refuge principally for latch-key children. He was unable to provide supervision for those children, since teachers were not required to be at school under the New South Wales regulations until some time after the school was opened for this purpose. The significant policy advance asserted by the court in this situation was that a teacher-pupil relationship was established by the principal, that therefore there was a requirement for care to be exercised over those pupils and the fact that the principal was not at law able to provide such supervision was no defence in an action for negligence. In other words, in any school situation a duty of care does apply although it is claimed that it is not possible to provide supervision.

The policy implications for school systems of the decision in *Geyer v. Downs* are best exemplified by mentioning the decision in an unreported case in Queensland which was decided interestingly one year after *Geyer v. Downs*. In the Queensland case, a student lost his left eye following a playground accident in a one-teacher school. The judge in the case is reported to have roundly criticized the claim by the plaintiffs that the teacher should have been on duty all through his lunchtime.

> Such a proposition seems to me to be somewhat unreal as would a suggestion that a teacher in sole charge of such a school could go to the lavatory only at his peril between the time of the arrival of any children at the school and their departure. (*Courier Mail*, 22 July 1978. p. 20)

But, as a matter of fact, *Geyer v. Downs* is saying that supervision must be made available whenever students are required to be 'at school' no matter what the circumstances or the cost and that, where the lack of such supervision can be shown to be that causal connection required as between a breach of duty and the injury which follows, there is a clear liability in negligence.

The decision in *Geyer v. Downs* adds nothing to teachers' responsibility in negligence. The law described above applies in this case and the episode is one in which clearly it is a matter for educational administrators to decide what may or may not be done. The decision may have the effect of restraining initiatives in either school practice itself or the use of school resources. But it is the case that provided such initiatives are clearly school initiatives, that is they have an appropriate approval, it follows that the employer remains vicariously liable, if negligence flows from the exercise of such initiatives.

The final High Court case which attracts attention in terms of the responsibility issue in negligence is *Commonwealth v. Introvigne* ((1982) 41 ALR 577). The principal finding of the High Court which is of relevance to this discussion is that an education system can be liable in negligence. In this case, the principal of the school had died early on the morning of the day of the accident and the teaching staff had been gathered together to be told of that occurrence and of the arrangement attaching to such an occurrence. Only one teacher had been left on duty in the playground in this high school in the Australian Capital Territory and in the few minutes he was alone on duty, students swinging on the ropes of a flagpole managed to dislodge the metal capping of the pole, which hit Introvigne on the head. The plaintiff sued the Commonwealth as the system authority in negligence and the High Court supported the claim that such a system could be held to be negligent. In the words of Mr Justice Mason:

> There are strong reasons for saying that it is appropriate that a school authority comes under a duty to ensure that reasonable care is taken of pupils attending the school. This was a view expressed by Kitto J. in *Ramsay v. Larsen* (at p. 28). The immaturity and inexperience of the pupils and their propensity for mischief suggest that there should be a special responsibility on a school authority to care for their safety, one that goes beyond a mere vicarious liability for the acts and omissions of its servants. (at p. 587)

This case does not, of course, remove any of the responsibility resting on teachers as described above. What it may do is to establish the responsibility of school authorities in negligence. In this particular case, the authority was the Commonwealth of Australia and it was held liable even though it had in fact contracted with the New South Wales Government to provide the educational service for which the Commonwealth paid. Thus the court clearly suggested extending the capacity of persons injured and their parents to sue educational authorities *per se* in negligence.

The conclusion which may be drawn from the run of cases decided in the High Court is that teachers do have obligations in terms of the duty of care to be exercised with students but that where their acts or omissions can be shown to be negligent, they are protected by that law which requires their employers to bear the cost of any damages — the employers being vicariously liable. Further, the court has addressed the responsibility of educational systems in terms of negligence and has indicated that a system *qua* system may be liable in negligence.

Insofar as the question of indemnity is concerned, if one takes into account the decision of the courts and the regulatory provisions regarding indemnity, teachers are unlikely to suffer personal monetary loss in respect of school activities which result in negligence being proven. That of course may be some solace but is certainly not the end of the matter. Some aberrations, however, confuse the issue. One such aberration is an unreported Queensland case in which a teacher was sued alone in negligence and successfully so. The case involved a private school but, as it is unreported, it is difficult to determine why the teacher alone was sued. The teacher's school and the Queensland Association of Teachers in Independent Schools met the costs of an appeal by the teacher to the full court of Supreme Court. That appeal was unsuccessful. The damages awarded in the lower court were $6400 and although that amount was not high when one considers the damages which have been awarded in school negligence cases in Australia, nevertheless, the case reminds teachers of the fact that they alone can be sued and successfully so.

Conclusion

Courts in Australia will play an increasing role in education in the areas discussed above. Further, there is a growing awareness amongst Australia's education public of the judicial system as a mechanism for obtaining redress of different sorts. Interestingly enough, the future role of the courts is more likely to be constrained by legislative *fiat* rather than by that conservatism usually associated with the Australian judicial system. The case in point which supports such an assertion is the decision of the national parliament to put in place a Bill of Rights type provision, but one which will apply only to its own laws. That legislative restraint is one imposed by government itself,

Ian K.F. Birch

since the High Court has clearly demonstrated in the *Koowarta case* that
Commonwealth legislation implementing international agreements in the
states is within power. However, the government's decision will likely
restrain a more major judicial role in educational policy-making given that
rights in general are certainly not going to be implemented in the states by
way of national legislation.

Other factors may of course alter this situation. Included amongst these
is the possibility of state governments implementing rights' legislation. To
some extent this has already occurred and impinged on education by way
of equal opportunity legislation, for example. But, despite such sorties, the
overall impact of courts on Australian education is likely to remain somewhat subdued.

Notes

1 (1860) 2 F. & F. 202. Hopley beat a child in his care to death and on being
   convicted of manslaughter, his punishment of the boy here being found to be
   'excessive chastisement', he was sentenced to four years' penal servitude.
2 *Benjamin v. Downs* (1976) 2 NSW LR 199.
3 *Koowarta v. Bjelke-Petersen and others* (1982) 39 ALR 417.
4 *R v. Coldham and others, Ex parte The Australian Social Welfare Union* (1983) 153
   CLR 297. The case being distinguished was *Federated State School Teachers' Association of Australia v. Victoria and others* (1929) 41 CLR 569, in which the High Court
   decided that teaching in public schools was not an industry and that, therefore,
   government school teachers could not invoke federal power in respect of resolving
   a dispute with their state government employers.
5 *Official Record of the Debates of the Australasian Federal Convention*, third session, Vol
   II, Melbourne, no date, pp. 1100 ff.
6 Section 87 reads:

   > During a period ten years after the establishment of the Commonwealth
   > and thereafter until the Parliament otherwise provides, of the net revenue
   > of the Commonwealth from duties of customs and of excise not more
   > than one-fourth shall be applied annually by the Commonwealth towards
   > its expenditure. The balance shall, in accordance with this Constitution,
   > be paid to the several States, or applied towards the payment of interest
   > on debts of the several States taken over by the Commonwealth.

7 Section 3 of Act No. 8 of 1910.
8 *Victoria v. Commonwealth* (1926) 38 CLR 399. After hearing counsel for Victoria,
   R.G. Menzies, the Court interrupted the Solicitor- General for the Commonwealth and announced its decision without hearing him out. Menzies later commented on the outcome of this case, 'I had gout badly, I had five judges before me
   equally badly and I failed completely'.
9 *South Australia v. The Commonwealth* (1942) 65 CLR 373.
10 *Victoria v. The Commonwealth* (1957) 99 CLR 575.
11 Section 221 of the *Income Tax and Social Services Contribution Assessment Act
   1936–1956.*
12 *Second Uniform Tax case*, p. 605.
13 *Federal Council of the British Medical Association and others v. The Commonwealth*
   (1949) 79 CLR 201, pp. 259–60.

14 Per Barwick CJ in *Strickland v. Rocla Concrete Pipes Ltd* (1971) 124 CLR 468. Section 107 of the Constituion reads:

> Every power of the Parliament of a Colony which has become or becomes a State, shall, unless it is by this Constitution exclusively vested in the Parliament of the Commonwealth or withdrawn from the Commonwealth, or as at the admission or establishment of the State, as the case may be.

15 *First Uniform Tax case*, pp. 424–5.
16 *Second Uniform Tax case*, p. 630.
17 *First Uniform Tax case*, p. 463.
18 *Second Uniform Tax case*, p. 609.
19 *Ibid.*, p. 611.
20 Secion 99 of the Constitution reads:

> The Commonwealth shall not, by any law or regulation of trade, commerce, or revenue, give preference to one State or any part thereof over another State or any part thereof.

21 *First Uniform Tax case*, pp. 442–4.
22 *Second Uniform Tax case*, p. 605.
23 See note 7 for the wording of section 109.
24 Per Dixon CJ in the *Second Uniform Tax case*, p. 605.
25 *First Uniform Tax case*, p. 417.
26 *Second Uniform Tax case*, p. 605.
27 Attorney-General for Victoria (ex rel Black) v. Commonwealth of Australia (1981) 33 ALR 321.
28 *Parliamentary Debates (Commonwealth)*, 6 November 1951, p. 1573.
29 Act No. 81 of 1951.
30 *Parliamentary Debates (Commonwealth)*, 27 November 1951, p. 2786.
31 The Acts referred to in this paragraph are No. 75 of 1953, No. 28 of 1955, No. 37 of 1956, No. 7 of 1957, No. 27 of 1958 and No. 106 of 1960.
32 Sections 7 to 10 of Act No. 27 of 1958 and the Schedules to the Act.
33 Act No. 106 of 1960.
34 Act No. 51 of 1962.
35 Act No. 68 of 1963.
36 *Parliamentary Debates (Commonwealth)* HR44 11 November 1964, pp. 2790–1. The resultant Acts were Nos. 129 and 130 of 1964.
37 Passed into law as Act No. 40 of 1965.
38 Act No. 90 of 1966.
39 *States Grants (Universities) Act*, 1969, No. 76.
40 Acts No. 60 of 1973, 97 of 1973, and 176 of 1973.
41 Act No. 93 of 1965.
42 Act No. 92 of 1966.

5   The Courts as Education Policy-makers in the USA

Betsy Levin

Introduction

In discussing the role of courts as educational policy-makers in the United States, and contrasting this role with the very limited involvement of courts in educational issues in Australia, it is necessary to understand both the similarities and differences between the political-legal systems of the two countries. Both the US and Australia are federations with written constitutions and judicial review; the US Constitution was actually the model for the drafters of the Australian Constitution.[1] In both countries, the federal or commonwealth government was granted limited national powers; residual powers remain with the states. In both countries, then, the principal responsibility for education is lodged with state governments. Finally, both countries have experienced an *increase* in the federal role in education in the second half of this century.

Among the differences, however, are the fact that Australia has no locally organized educational system and has a less diverse population. It has a less ideological constitution, often explained by the fact that Australia did not have to fight for its independence. Thus the Constitution plays a much greater role in the minds of the populace in the United States, casting a sacred aura on everything we do and embodying, in some sense, *moral* principles. There is less concern in Australia for abuse of governmental power, since there was never a revolutionary government. More importantly, there are no guarantees of individual liberties and rights in the Australian Constitution similar to our Bill of Rights and the Fourteenth Amendment. Incorporation of these guarantees in the Australian Constitution was deliberately rejected by its drafters.

Thus, the traditions and political/legal cultures of the two countries help to explain the differences in the role their courts play in education. In Australia, there is much more deference to the professional. The culture in the United States, fostered by our Bill of Rights, means that parents are more ready to assert what they believe to be their legal rights against the professionals, and courts are more ready to enforce these rights. Also, since our society is more diverse, there is more disagreement over *who* is to decide *which* values to inculcate in our youth than there is in the more uniform society of Australia. These disputes have often ended up in the courts in the guise of disputes over constitutional principles.

Education in the United States is primarily a state function. As is true in Australia, there is no direct federal constitutional responsibility for education. Nevertheless, Congress has enacted laws providing federal grants-in-aid of various kinds to state and local educational agencies, as well as laws protecting the civil rights of various categories of students. The constitutional authority for these statutes and their implementing regulations lies in Article I, Section 8, Clause 1 of the Constitution — the Taxing and Spending Clause — which has been interpreted by the courts as permitting various conditions and mandates to be attached to the receipt of federal funds.[2] Constitutional authority for the many civil rights mandates enacted by Congress my also lie in Section 5 of the Fourteenth Amendment, which provides that Congress may 'enforce, by appropriate legislation, the provisions' of that Amendment (primarily the equal protection and due process clauses). Australia has a constitutional provision, Section 96, similar to Article I, Section 8 of the US Constitution, which would also seem to permit conditions to be attached to the receipt of Commonwealth funds, and the Australian High Court, in several cases, has so held.[3] However, there has been little use of this section by Parliament compared to Congress' extensive use of the Taxing and Spending Clause.

Thus, in the United States, the courts have played an important role in *interpreting* federal laws passed by Congress and the implementing regulations promulgated by the Executive Branch. The courts are also involved in applying general law in the context of the schools — for example, labor issues and issues of employment discrimination can arise in the context of public schools as it can in the context of any other state institution or agency.

Beyond interpreting and applying laws and regulations adopted by the political bodies, however, the courts have been active in interpreting and applying the Constitution. Courts are not really involved in education per se or acting as educational policy-makers, but are fulfilling their function as protectors of the constitutional rights of students, teachers and other employees of the school systems and parents. The principal issues in which the courts have been involved include the establishment clause and the free exercise of religion clause, individual rights of free expression, liberty, privacy, and due process, and group rights to equal protection which, in the context of education, means equal access and treatment, regardless of race, national origin, gender, or handicap.

The constitutional questions in the context of schools are as follows: Are there constitutional constraints on the extent to which school authorities can control and regulate the lives of students and teachers? And, conversely, do students and teachers have the same constitutional rights as all citizens in our society, or are these rights limited within the school environment? These broader questions encompass such issues as: What are the bounds of permissible government socialization of students? What 'academic freedoms' does the school teacher bring to the classroom? When are officials constitutionally required to permit students and teachers to express contrary viewpoints? With regard to fair procedures, are students and teachers constitutionally protected against arbitrary official actions? And finally, to what extent do equity-based claims constitutionally constrain or impose obligations on school officials? Thus, the constitutional claims made on the courts with regard to schooling have been principally directed toward the protection of individual freedom and the attainment of equality. In the first instance, the countervailing factor is concern for the stability and order of the educational enterprise; in the second instance, it is the differing conceptions of equality and the extent to which the educational enterprise is constitutionally obligated to respond to the equity-based claims of various groups absent a showing of intentional discrimination.

The remainder of this chapter attempts to show, on the one hand, the extent to which the educational enterprise is constrained by various constitutional rights and, on the other hand, the extent to which these constitutional rights are circumscribed by the special characteristics of the school environment.

With this as background, then, we find that the courts in the United States have, since the second half of this century, been involved in almost every conceivable area of educational policy. The federal courts in the United States began to assume a significant policy making role in the field of education beginning with *Brown v. Board of Education.*[4] For the remainder of the 1950s, the courts were primarily concerned with implementing the constitutional requirement that no student be denied an equal educational opportunity because of his or her race. In attempting to remedy the constitutional violation of intentionally segregated schools, courts became enmeshed in such areas as student and teacher assignments and compensatory and remedial programs (to undo the educational effects of unconstitutional segregation), long the sole prerogative of educators.

While this concern has continued, the federal courts have also become involved in other areas which also had traditionally been the prerogative of school authorities:

- school curriculum issues;[5]
- student and teacher rights of free expression and of non-disruptive protest;[6]
- exemptions from state compulsory school attendance laws;[7]
- school financing issues;[8]
- gender discrimination;[9]
- discrimination against handicapped students;[10]

- bilingual or English language instruction for those with limited English skills;[11]
- school personnel policies;[12]
- student discipline;[13]
- liability of school officials for violating the civil rights of students;[14]
- tracking and classification of students;[15] and
- minimum competency testing.[16]

As I have noted, there is no tradition of court involvement in education in Australia and, even if Australia had such a tradition, the results would be very different — constitutional claims involving the First, Fourth, and Fourteenth Amendments in the United States would not arise in Australia, since equivalent provisions are not found in the Australian Constitution. Moreover, the lower federal courts were not established in Australia until 1976 and they do not have a general 'arising under' jurisdiction as do such courts in the United States, as provided for in Article III of the US Constitution: 'The judicial power shall extend to all cases, in law and equity, arising under this Constitution, the laws of the United States, and treaties made ... under their authority'. Instead, the Australian federal courts are limited to specific areas such as bankruptcy and restrictive trade practices.[17]

The initial question, whether states may constitutionally compel all children to be educated in staterun schools, was resolved by the US Supreme Court in *Pierce v. Society of Sisters*,[18] which held that while the state may compel all children to attend school, parents have a constitutional right to choose between public and private schools. The balance struck between the interests of the state and the parents thus appears to be as follows: the state may inculcate its values in the public schools, but parents are free to choose for their children private schools which teach somewhat different values — although the state may regulate those schools to some extent.[19] However, while the state must permit private education in the interest of allowing parents a choice, it need not fund it and, in fact, may not fund it.[20]

Nearly fifty years after *Pierce*, the Supreme Court confronted the question whether there are constitutional interests of parents and children that outweigh the state's interests in compelling all youngsters to attend some school (whether public or private). The Court, in *Wisconsin v. Yoder*,[21] emphasized that parental direction of the *religious* upbringing of their children is an important interest to be protected. The Court also noted, however, the importance of education to our democratic society. Since, in this case, the Amish parents had satisfied the state's interest in educating its future citizens through the eighth grade, the Court found that the interest of the state in compelling two more years of education was outweighed by the burden on the religious freedom of the parents. Only the dissent discussed the possibility of the child's interest being different from that of the parent.[22] Indeed, the case seems really to be about who has the right to inculcate which values — parent or state — and not one about individual rights.

Thus, students may be required to be in some school for the purpose of learning. If parents elect to send their children to public schools, the state has a much greater role to play in selecting the curriculum and regulating what is taught than it does in private schools. Education necessarily involves the process of selection; it also requires some degree of order to carry out the educational mission. On the other hand, students have some rights protected by the Constitution. Thus, the courts have indicated that students (and teachers) do not 'shed their constitutional rights ... at the schoolhouse gate'.[23] Nevertheless, these rights are often circumscribed because of the 'special characteristics of the school environment'.[24]

Constitutional Limits on the Inculcation of Religious and Political Values

Religious Socialization

The principal cases resolving the question of the proper place of religion in the curriculum of the public schools — that is, the extent to which school authorities can socialize their students to religious values — were decided in the early 1960s. In *Engel v. Vitale*, the Court struck down a non-denominational prayer written by the New York Board of Regents for use in the public schools.[25] A year later, in *Abington School District v. Schempp*, the Supreme Court reviewed the practice of reading verses from the Bible and the recitation of the Lord's Prayer in public schools.[26] The Court pointed out that the state must be neutral with regard to religion, which means that a state may not require a religious service even with the consent of the majority of those affected.[27] Justice Clark was careful, however, to distinguish between the study of religion or of the Bible 'when presented objectively as part of a secular program of education', and religious exercises.[28] Not until 1980 did the Supreme Court deal with another school prayer case. In *Stone v. Graham*, the Court held unconstitutional, as violative of the Establishment Clause, a Kentucky law that required the posting of the Ten Commandments on the walls of public school classrooms,[29] since the law had 'no secular legislative purpose'.[30] The Court again indicated, however, that the case would be different if the Ten Commandments were integrated into the school's curriculum, where the Bible could be studied as history, ethics, or comparative religion.[31]

These cases pose a difficult dilemma. On the one hand is the concern whether the school — a government agency — should be conducting a religious program when the Constitution left that to parents and religious organizations. On the other hand, the total omission of religion from the schools may itself teach children something about the role of religion that is contrary to the message their parents want taught.

The Supreme Court, in interpreting the Establishment Clause has, however, taken a very restrictive view toward any attempt on the part of school authorities to inculcate religious values. The totality of the Court's opinions indicates that religious worship or religious doctrines, no matter how generalized or ecumenical, cannot be part of the curriculum.

The other side of the Establishment Clause is the Free Exercise of Religion Clause. There have been no Supreme Court cases dealing with interference by public school officials with the free exercise of religion of children attending those schools,[32] although the issue was raised in *Abington School District v. Schempp*[33] by Justice Stewart in his dissenting opinion in that case. He argued that 'a doctrinaire reading of the Establishment Clause leads to irreconcilable conflict with the Free Exercise Clause', noting that there was a 'substantial free exercise claim on the part of those who affirmatively desire that their children's school day open with the reading of passages from the Bible'.[34] The majority, however, gave little weight to this argument in the face of the strong Establishment Clause claim.

Following *Wisconsin v. Yoder*, which dealt with the issue of exemptions from compulsory schooling in the context of a claim of an undue burden on the free exercise of religion,[35] lower court cases have involved the extent to which private, sectarian schools can be regulated by the state[36] or the federal government[37] without impermissibly burdening the free exercise of religion.

A type of free exercise claim has been made by some who have argued that public support of private education is a constitutional entitlement, meaning that the government, to be truly neutral, must subsidize religious education. This reading of the Free Exercise Clause says not only that the State cannot interfere with the exercise of one's religion, including the choice of a religious school, but that there is an affirmative requirement to provide sufficient resources to enable parents to choose a religious education for their children.[38] The question of constitutionally compelled subsidization of non-public education has rarely been adjudicated by the courts, but in those few cases that have reached the courts, the response has been a negative one.[39] In *P.E.R.L. v. Nyquist*, the state had argued that the purpose of the tuition reimbursements and tax credits adopted by the legislature was to promote the free exercise of religion on the part of low-income parents who otherwise might not be able to afford a religious education for their children.[40] The majority dismissed this argument, noting that it might often be impossible to promote the free exercise of religion without violating the Establishment Clause. 'In its attempt to enhance the opportunities of the poor to choose between public and non-public education, the state has taken a step which can only be regarded as one of advancing religion'.[41] The Supreme Court has failed, however, to suggest the basis for resolving the tension between the two clauses. It may be that the two clauses can never be reconciled — that is, the effect of 'neutrality' under one clause may necessarily be to violate the other clause.

Lower courts have considered a variety of free exercise claims in the context of public schools: parents have asserted that the subject matter of the courses taught, the books and the materials assigned, the manner in which such courses are taught, or the imposition of certain school rules and regulations unconstitutionally burdens the practice of their religion. In these cases, courts have attempted to strike an accommodation between the rights of parents to determine the religious upbringing of their own children and the power of school authorities to decide which values are to be imparted and to which norms students are to be socialized.

It should be noted that while the Australian Constitution does have an Establishment Clause as well as a Free Exercise Clause, since there is no equivalent of our Fourteenth Amendment, these constitutional principles do not apply to the states. Moreover, there is less diversity of religions in Australia than in the United States so the frequency with which free exercise claims against various activities of the schools arise in the United States may be quite different than in Australia.

Political and Moral Socialization

While the extent to which religious socialization can be undertaken in schools has been sharply limited by the courts,[42] less clear is the extent to which the Constitution limits political and moral socialization. *West Virginia v. Barnette* acknowledges the right of school authorities to attempt to foster patriotism in the schools, but limits the means by which they can do so, holding that the Constitution protects the right of non-participation in a patriotic ritual that, in effect, coerces an expression of belief.[43] So too, the plurality of opinion in *Board of Education, Island Trees Union Free School District v. Pico* suggests that the First Amendment prohibits the editing out of particular ideas with a view to 'prescrib[ing] what shall be orthodox in politics, nationalism, religion, or other matters of opinion,'[44] but otherwise the removal of certain books and curricular materials from the school library may be permitted.[45] The justices of the plurality opinion found that the First Amendment protected the 'students' right to receive information',[46] at least in the context of a school library. Does a student's right to know include the right of access to books or curricula that reflect racial, religious, or gender bias? The tension between the First Amendment's prohibition of censorship and the desire to transmit other constitutional values such as non-discrimination thus becomes clear. Dicta in the plurality opinion in *Pico*, however, suggest that school officials may, with regard to the classroom at least, remove books for *any* reason,[47] unhampered by any mandate of the First Amendment.

The reverse side of the coin is the extent to which parents have a constitutional right to exempt their children from being socialized to values held by the majority. Absent a clear Establishment Clause claim, it is unlikely that parents can demand that certain books or courses be excluded from the public school curriculum approved by school authorities.[48] And absent a clear Free Exercise claim — that is, that a fundamental tenet of their religion is being unduly burdened[49] — it is also unlikely that parents can exempt their children from certain courses to which they may object on moral or other grounds,[50] particularly since *Pierce* protects the option of sending their children to private schools if they disagree with the values being taught in the public school.[51] If the Constitution protects the right of parents to bring up their children as they wish,[52] that right may be given short shrift in the public schools as long as the Constitution requires the state to permit parents to send their children to private schools with somewhat different messages.[53]

Freedom of Expression for Teachers and Students in the School Environment

Complete freedom of expression on the part of students — or of teachers — is inconsistent with the schooling enterprise, which requires order and control. Thus, while there are constitutionally protected rights of speech, press, and association, these rights are limited where their exercise would disrupt the educational enterprise.

Speech or Symbolic Speech

Tinker v. Des Moines Independent Community School District, the leading case on the First Amendment rights of public school students, involved several high school students who had violated the school's regulation prohibiting the wearing of black armbands (as a symbol to protest the Vietnam War) while on school premises.[54] The school authorities had argued that the wearing of armbands was banned because those with opposing viewpoints might become upset, resulting in a disruptive atmosphere. The Court stated, however, that an 'undifferentiated fear or apprehension of disturbance is not enough to overcome the right to freedom of expression'.[55] In order for school officials to be able to limit such expression, they must show 'that engaging in the forbidden conduct would "materially and substantially interfere with the requirements of appropriate discipline in the operation of the school"'.[56] The *Tinker* standard thus clearly provides less protection for free expression in the special environment of the schools than is available to the ordinary citizen. The Court did not articulate any clear standards for determining what showing is required in order to find 'material and substantial interference'. Thus, lower courts have developed varying standards as they have applied the *Tinker* principles to cases involving newspapers, leaflets, buttons, and after-school political clubs or organizations.[57]

Student Newspapers

The law with regard to the dissemination of student newspapers, including 'underground' newspapers, is that school authorities can control and regulate the time, place and manner of dissemination as long as the regulations are not used to stifle the student's First Amendment rights. School authorities have frequently required that before any literature is disseminated, it must be submitted to them for approval. Most courts take a restrictive view toward such prior restraint requirements, requiring them to be accompanied by adequate procedural safeguards,[58] although the standard is less restrictive than that applied in the case of society at large.[59] And the courts have taken as restrictive a view of sanctions imposed after publication as they have of prior restraints. The Supreme Court found the actions of a state university in expelling a college student for distributing an underground newspaper, said by the university to be 'indecent', to be unconstitutional. 'The mere dissemination of ideas — no matter how offensive to good taste — on a state university campus may not be shut off in the name alone of "conventions of decency".'[60]

In summary, there has been an increase in judicial protection of the First Amendment rights of students to express themselves through student newspapers, whether underground or school-sponsored, or through symbols such as armbands and buttons. As long as the material being disseminated does not substantially disrupt or materially interfere with school activities or is not obscene, the power of school authorities to control the content of what is being disseminated is slight. Some lower courts, however, have required relatively little of school authorities for a showing of substantial disruption, thus significantly reducing the extent to which First Amendment rights are protected in the school environment.

Student Organizations

The extent to which the First Amendment protects the right of individuals to associate to further their beliefs in the environment of a school or university was dealt with by the Supreme Court in *Healy v. James*.[61] The Court noted that the 'special characteristics of the school environment' pemitted government to prohibit 'lawless action' that went beyond those actions that were crimes.[62] The *Tinker* standard applies, meaning that 'associational activities need not be tolerated where they infringe reasonable campus rules, interrupt classes, or substantially interfere with the opportunity of other students to obtain an education'.[63] Nevertheless, since the effect of the denial of recognition of the student organization is a form of prior restraint, school authorities have the burden of proving the likelihood of disruption.

Although the college in the *Healy* case refused to recognize a 'local chapter' of Students for a Democratic Society (SDS), denying it the use of campus facilities, various other student organizations were permitted access. Thus, *Healy* might be seen as concerned with equal treatment — that is, *if* a college permits student organizations access to its facilities, it cannot exclude one based on the political or social views the organization espouses. But can a high school or college deny *all* student organizations access to its facilities or is there a constitutional obligation to provide a forum? In *Widmar v. Vincent*,[64] the Supreme Court held that once a university permits its facilities to be used by student groups, it may not exclude from the forum any speech activity — including religious speech — based on content, absent a compelling state interest. Moreover, the Court interpreted *Healy v. James* as holding that a state university is an open forum *per se* for students so that any attempt to restrict students' access to buildings, facilities, and other forms of communication 'must be subjected to the level of scrutiny appropriate to any form of prior restraint'.[65] And does the answer depend on whether it is a college or a high school? The Third Circuit in *Bender v. Williamsport Area School District*, in ruling that the use of high school classrooms for religious student group meetings violates the Establishment Clause, also noted — contrary to *Widmar* — that '[t]he [school district] would have been justified in refusing to reserve high school property for use as a public forum for expression, and would violate no constitutional constraints in doing so'.[66]

Personal Appearance

Other issues of constitutionally protected student expression have arisen in the context of lawsuits challenging hair and dress code regulations. Does a student have a constitutional right to govern his own appearance? (And if so, is it the First Amendment's freedom of symbolic expression, the right of privacy found in the penumbras of the First, Fourth, Fifth and Fourteenth Amendments, or even the Equal Protection and Due Process Clauses that are being asserted?) The issue of whether a male student attending a public school has a constitutionally protected right to wear his hair in any manner that he pleases has thoroughly divided the federal circuit courts,[67] and the Supreme Court contributed to the stalemate by its repeated refusals to review such cases.[68] Thus it is unclear to what extent there is such a constitutional right.

Teacher Rights of Expression

To what extent does a teacher, within the special demands of the school environment, have certain rights of expression? These questions have arisen in a variety of contexts. One is the extent to which the right of the teacher as citizen to express himself or herself is circumscribed by being an employee of the school system. The other area concerns the teacher as a professional and his or her right to determine course content, selection of books, and the ideas and values to be presented. Is there an independent right of academic freedom,[69] or is it a corollary of the 'students' right to know'?[70] These issues have not been clearly resolved by the Supreme Court.

With regard to the question of academic freedom in the classroom, the Supreme Court has never decided a case that squarely dealt with this issue. *Keyishian v. Board of Regents* notes that academic freedom is 'a special concern of the First Amendment' and that protecting the free exchange of ideas within our schools is fundamentally important in promoting an open society.[71] *Keyishian* also noted that 'the classroom is peculiarly the "marketplace of ideas"' in our society.[72] However, *Keyishian* did not deal with the classroom and the teacher's right to choose the curriculum or to teach the curriculum in any particular way, nor did *Keyishian* deal with public elementary and secondary school teachers.[73] The case was primarily concerned with New York's attempt to bar communists from the teaching profession.

Epperson v. Arkansas comments on 'arbitrary' restrictions upon the freedom of teachers to teach and students to learn, but resolved the case on the basis of the Establishment Clause. The majority opinion noted that the state's 'undoubted right to prescribe curriculum for its public schools does not carry with it the right to prohibit, on pain of criminal penalty, teaching of a scientific theory or doctrine where that prohibition is based upon reasons that violate the First Amendment'.[74] Justice Black, in his concurring opinion, sharply narrowed the idea that some notion of 'academic freedom' is protected by the First Amendment.

> I am ... not ready to hold that a person hired to teach school children takes with him into the classroom a constitutional right to teach sociological, economic, political, or religious subjects that the school's managers do not want discussed ... I question whether ... 'academic freedom' permits a teacher to breach his contractual agreement to teach only the subjects designated by the school authorities that hired him.[75]

On the other hand, while Justice Stewart would allow the state to determine whether a particular subject should or should not be included in a public school curriculum, in his view, the state should not be constitutionally permitted to punish a teacher for mentioning that there are other approaches to a particular subject.[76] Finally, if there *is* some aspect of 'academic freedom' that has independent constitutional protection,[77] it may be only at the college or university level and not in public schools.

While lower court cases vary significantly as to whether 'academic freedom' in a classroom with regard to subject and content selection is constitutionally protected,[78] dicta in Justice Brennan's plurality opinion in the *Pico* case suggest that school authorities have unfettered discretion to inculcate community values in students through the curriculum.[79] Thus, if this view prevails, the teacher would appear to have no unilateral right to dictate the lessons (especially value lessons) to which the student will be exposed. If the classroom is the vehicle for imparting values, perhaps it cannot also be an open 'marketplace of ideas'.

Other issues that have often been grouped under the rubric 'academic freedom' really are concerned more with the freedom of expression of teachers as citizens outside the classroom and the extent to which such expression must be balanced against the interest of the state as employer. For example, in *Pickering v. Board of Education*, a teacher had written a letter to the local newspaper critical of the school board. The *Pickering* holding is that 'absent proof of false statements knowingly or recklessly made by him, a teacher's exercise of his right to speak on issues of public importance may not furnish the basis for his dismissal from public employment'.[80] However, if the teacher's statements have been shown to have impeded his or her performance in the classroom or otherwise interfered with the regular operation of the schools, as might be the case if he or she had 'the kind of close working relationships ... which ... [require] personal loyalty and confidence', the speech might not be protected.

In *Mt. Healthy City School District v. Doyle*, a teacher claimed that his dismissal was in retaliation for activities protected by the First Amendment. The school board, however, insisted that his dismissal was due to his incompetence. The Court held that the teacher has the burden of establishing that his conduct was constitutionally protected, *and* that his conduct was a motivating factor in the board's decision not to rehire or to dismiss him. However, even if the teacher meets this burden, the school board may still show, by a preponderance of the evidence, that it would have reached the same decision as to the teacher's reappointment even in the absence of the impermissible factor.[81]

While the *Pickering* doctrine may protect a teacher's public criticism or criticism voiced privately to an administrator or to his or her fellow teachers,[82] it is not clear whether it would extend to teachers who voice their criticisms in the classroom or before a student audience.[83]

The Requirements of Fair Procedures in the School Environment

Institutional rules and regulations may be as important to the socialization of students as the formal educational process. Much litigation has revolved around the extent to which the Constitution constrains school authorities in the manner in which these rules are applied to students and teachers. Are there certain requirements of fair procedures, even in the special environment of the school and regardless of the age of the student, that must be provided before a student's person or property can be searched for evidence of the commission of a crime or a violation of a school rule, or before disciplinary action can be taken for failure to comply with institutional rules and norms?

Fourth Amendment Requirements

New Jersey v. T.L.O. dealt with questions of what procedural protections are available to students in obtaining evidence to prove an infraction of a school rule or of a crime.[84] When may the special environment of the school permit a lesser standard to be applied to students that would not be constitutionally permitted if applied to citizens in society at large? What actions, if any, may school officials undertake that would be barred by the Constitution if the actions were those of the police?

Generally, a search made of private property is 'unreasonable' under the Fourth Amendment if made without a valid search warrant.[85] Even when the circumstances are such that courts have permitted warrantless searches, however (for example, where necessary to prevent concealment or destruction of evidence),[86] such searches usually require a showing of a 'probable cause' belief that the law has been violated.[87] In *New Jersey v. T.L.O*, however, the Court, in balancing school authorities' 'substantial' interest in maintaining discipline in the classroom and on school grounds against students' legitimate expectations of privacy,[88] fashioned a less protective standard for searching students. The search must be 'justified at its inception' and the scope of the search 'reasonably related' to the circumstances which originally justified the search.[89] A search by school authorities is 'justified at its inception' when there are *reasonable* grounds for suspecting that the search will turn up evidence that the student has violated either the law or rules of the school. The search is of permissible scope when 'the measures adopted are reasonably related to the objectives of the search and not excessively intrusive in light of the age and sex of the student and the nature of the infraction'.[90] Moreover, there is no warrant requirement for inschool searches.[91]

Due Process Requirements

Important constitutional values are incorporated in our notions of fairness that underlie the due process clause. To what extent does the nature of the school environment and its special demands affect the traditional requirements of due process that apply to citizens in our society?

Goss v. Lopez, in a five-to-four opinion, holds that there can be state-created entitlements to a public education that are protected by the due process clause. In other words, the right to an education may not be withdrawn on the grounds of misconduct, absent some procedures for determining whether the misconduct has occurred.[92] *Goss* also holds that arbitrary deprivations of liberty are prohibited.[93] However, having decided that some process is due, it appears that the requirements of due process can be quite minimal in the school environment. In the case of a ten-day suspension of a student for disciplinary reasons, *Goss* requires only that the student be given notice of the charges against him, an explanation of the evidence against him, and an opportunity to explain his version of the story. Immediate removal from school may be justified in some cases even before the hearing. The hearing itself may simply be a brief meeting between the student and the disciplinarian minutes after the alleged transgression.[94] More stringent safeguards, however, may be required for deprivations of education that might be significantly longer than the ten-day period involved in *Goss*.[95]

Just two years after *Goss*, also in a five-to-four opinion, the Court held that although the administration of corporal punishment for allegedly violating school rules implicated a constitutionally protected liberty interest, 'the traditional common law remedies were fully adequate to afford due process'.[96] Thus, no advance procedural safeguards were constitutionally required for the administration of corporal punishment.[97]

Since academic grades and evaluations were said by the Supreme Court to involve more subjective and evaluative judgments than the typical factual questions presented in the average disciplinary decision, such evaluations were not readily adapted to procedural tools.[98] Thus, the determination of how much process is required turns on whether the classification is one for 'academic' or for disciplinary reasons. The Court, however, did not necessarily say that no process is due when the dispute is 'academic' in nature, although it would appear to be minimal.[99]

The Supreme Court has held that a teacher has a right to procedural due process before being terminated from his position, depending on whether the teacher can show a liberty or property interest at stake which warrants Fourteenth Amendment protection. In 1972 the Court articulated standards for finding such interests in *Board of Regents v. Roth*[100] and *Perry v. Sinderman*.[101]

The Obligation to Provide Equal Educational Opportunity

Problems of Definition

The Equal Protection Clause of the Fourteenth Amendment also imposes some constraints on the ways in which public schools may operate. One of the difficulties, however, is determining what is the nature of the entitlements to equal educational opportunity that are embodied in the federal Constitution. Demands upon public schools can be affirmative, asserting an entitlement to a minimum educational opportunity, to equal access to the schooling process, or to a specified educational outcome. Or they may be framed negatively, asserting a right to be free of discrimination on the basis of race, sex, handicap, or class in the operation of the public schools.

Race

The most fully matured and litigated definition of equal educational opportunity is the right of minority students to be free of racial discrimination. The principal issues have concerned (i) the requirements for finding that the constitution has been violated; and (ii) the scope of the remedy once a constitutional violation has been established. Under the first category, the following questions have been raised: Can intentional actions of school authorities that lead to segregated schooling, even when there has been no law mandating segregation, constitute de jure segregation?[102] Can intent be inferred from actions that have the foreseeable effect of fostering segregation?[103] Are actions not motivated by intent to segregate, but that result in segregated patterns of schooling, unconstitutional? What is a 'continuing' violation?[104] Does the lapse of time between past segregative acts and present segregation eliminate the presumption of causation and hence intent?[105] The second category has included such questions as: Are quotas or affirmative action to assist minorities who have been handicapped by past discrimination unconstitutional?[106] What are permissible techniques for remedying unconstitutional segregation and are there limits to their use by the judiciary?[107] When is a system-wide remedy permissible, and what proof is required before a system-wide remedy can be ordered?[108] Can school district boundaries be reorganized in order to devise an effective remedy?[109]

Gender

As with minority students, equal educational opportunity with regard to gender is an assertion of the right to be free of discrimination on the basis of gender. However, most of the case law has developed under Title IX of the 1972 Education Amendments and its implementing regulations.[110] Thus, there has been limited constitutional development in this area. Early cases, prior to the passage of the Act and its subsequent regulations, were litigated primarily in the lower courts. Many of those cases indicated that a 'separate but equal' program would be permissible because it did not connote 'a stigmatizing inferiority', as did race.[111] Thus in gender cases, courts often treated differently the complete denial of access to a particular curriculum, course, or athletic activity and 'separate but equal' educational offerings.[112] 'Separate but equal' in the case of gender differentiation may *not* be 'inherently unequal'.[113]

The Supreme Court has viewed race as a suspect class, triggering the 'strict scrutiny' equal protection standard of judicial review of state actions resulting in unequal treatment on the basis of race. This means that the state has the heavy burden of showing that there is a compelling interest justifying its action and that its compelling objective could not be accomplished by less restrictive means. However, in *Craig v. Boren*, a gender discrimination case (not involving education), the Court indicated that gender would not be treated as a suspect class, as is race, but as a category requiring intermediate level scrutiny. Thus, a gender classification must serve important governmental objectives and must be substantially related to the achievement of those objectives before it can be upheld.[114] It is unclear whether, if a case involving gender segregated elite public high schools[115] were before the Supreme Court today, separate but equal schools would be upheld under the *Craig v. Boren* standard. *Mississippi University for Women v. Hogan* does not resolve that issue.[116] That case involved the exclusion of males from Mississippi University for Women's School of Nursing. Justice O' Connor, writing for the majority, held that the state failed to meet its burden under the *Craig v. Boren* standard. Mississippi had argued that its single-sex admissions policy was designed to compensate for discrimination against women. The state was unable, however, to show that women were discriminated against in the field of nursing. Indeed, Justice O'Connor found that the policy of excluding males from the School of Nursing 'tends to perpetuate the stereotyped view of nursing as an exclusively women's job'.[117] The state also failed to show that the gender-based classification was substantially related to its purported compensatory objective since MUW permitted males to audit nursing courses. The opinion does not indicate whether the same result would have been reached if men were excluded from an engineering curriculum or if there were either an all male or a coed nursing school nearby.

Resources

In addition to equal educational opportunity issues raised in the context of denial of access to programs or of 'separate but equal' programs, equal educational opportunity has been defined in terms of resources — dollars per pupil or the educational resources those dollars buy. The school finance reform movement of the 1970s concerned inequalities in educational opportunity (resources) among school districts.[118] The issue in those cases was when, as a constitutional matter, inequalities among districts in the amount of money spent per pupil were impermissible. A variety of standards for assessing whether a school financing system provided students with an equal educational opportunity were developed.[119]

When *San Antonio Independent School District v. Rodriguez*[120] came before the Supreme Court, in order to trigger the 'strict scrutiny' equal protection standard of judicial review of the state's school financing scheme, the plaintiffs sought to persuade the Supreme Court that the Texas school financing legislation, which resulted in inequalities in per pupil expenditures among school districts, discriminated on the basis of wealth, which they argued was a 'suspect' classification like race. The Court, however, held that Texas' system of financing schools did not discriminate against any class of persons considered suspect.[121] A class, the Court said, is suspect if it is 'saddled with such disabilities, or subjected to such a history of purposeful unequal treatment, or relegated to such a position of political powerlessness as to command extraordinary protection from the majoritarian political process'.[122]

The *Rodriguez* plaintiffs also argued that education was a fundamental right, attempting to tie education to rights already declared fundamental, such as free speech and voting. This argument met with no success, however. The Court saw the connection as no more compelling than the connection between housing, food, or other subsistence needs and the right to vote. It refused 'to create substantive constitutional rights in the name of guaranteeing equal protection of the laws', stating that for a right to be fundamental it must be 'explicitly or implicitly guaranteed by the Constitution'.[123]

Since, according to the *Rodriguez* majority, the finance system neither discriminated against a suspect class nor touched on a fundamental interest, the financing scheme must be assessed in terms of the rational basis standard of review. The Court found that the existing system was rationally related to the purpose of promoting local school district control.[124]

The Supreme Court's opinion in *Rodriguez* distinguished relative differences among school districts in per pupil expenditures from a state 'financing system that occasioned an absolute denial of educational opportunities to any of its children'.[125] The Court noted that a tuition assessment plan that 'absolutely precluded [poor children] from receiving an education ... would present a far more compelling set of circumstances for judicial assistance than the case before us today'.[126] Those statements raise two related constitutional questions: (i) Under what circumstances, if any, is exclusion of a class of children from public schools constitutionally justifiable; and (ii) if absolute deprivation of an education is unconstitutional, can this principle be extended to certain children who, although attending public schools, are 'functionally excluded'? *Doe v. Plyler* raised the first question and *Lau v. Nichols* the second question. These cases are discussed below.

Physically, mentally, and linguistically handicapped students: While handicapped students and limited English proficient students have, like minorities or women, sought to be free of discrimination — i.e., to be treated equally with respect to educational offerings — in some circumstances these groups have sought to impose an affirmative duty on the government to remove a barrrier not necessarily of the government's making, such as limited English language ability. Under this interpretation of the equal educational opportunity that is protected by the Constitution, the government has a duty to treat people *differently*. For example, children who speak only Chinese may be constitutionally entitled to special educational programs even though they have the *same* access to teachers, books, etc. as other children, since they cannot understand what goes on in the regular classroom where only English is spoken. If they do not receive special treatment, the argument goes, they do not have an opportunity equal to that of others to take advantage of the education the government offers to all. The denial of equal protection of the laws then arises because the government fails to classify them and treat them differently than all other school children.

The issue is further complicated by the question whether the constitutional violation occurs only when the failure of the government affirmatively to provide such children with extra resources or special treatment has amounted to the functional equivalent of an absolute deprivation of education,[127] or whether the violation occurs merely when school authorities have failed to take action to overcome barriers of language or handicap that impede a child from learning equally with those without such barriers.[128] This approach to equal educational opportunity — the focus on an affirmative duty to provide special, additional services for certain groups — has not yet been held by the Supreme Court to be constitutionally dictated.

The only cases involving handicapped students to reach the Supreme Court involved the interpretation of federal statutes and regulations.[129] The Court has not resolved a constitutional case involving either total or functional exclusion of the handicapped from education or inappropriate education for such students. It seems evident, after *Cleburne*,[130] however, that the handicapped are not to be treated as a suspect class. Indeed, *Cleburne* indicates that the handicapped are entitled only to the application of the rational relationship standard on equal protection claims.[131] However, now that *Doe v. Plyler*, discussed below, has held that education is an important interest, would the handicapped receive some special protection under the Constitution with regard to education? Or if the handicapped are not even to be considered as of intermediate status, do they receive even less protection than illegal aliens? On the other hand, *Doe v. Plyler* involved the total exclusion of illegal alien children from public schooling and we have seen that even in *Rodriguez* the total deprivation of education might be constitutionally impermissible. Thus, arguably, the total exclusion — or perhaps even the functional exclusion — of handicapped children from education would be deemed unconstitutional, but the failure to provide an appropriate or equal education (if 'equal' were interpreted as special treatment and additional resources to bring the handicapped child to the same starting line as other children) would not be constitutionally impermissible.

Similarly, the 'functional exclusion' of language minority children has been struck down by the Supreme Court in *Lau v. Nichols* solely on statutory grounds and not on constitutional grounds.[132] The question has been raised whether there is an affirmative duty on the part of school officials to provide special educational programs for limited English proficient children in the absence of any prior discrimination by the state. The Supreme Court has not dealt with this issue on constitutional grounds and lower court decisions suggest that if the question were presented to the Supreme Court, it would be unlikely that the Court would find such a duty on the part of school officials absent intentional and deliberate discrimination.[133]

Illegal aliens: In *Doe v. Plyler*, the Court was faced with total deprivation of the education of illegal alien children.[134] The Court indicated that education was an important, although not a fundamental, interest and that the classification of illegal alien children was of an intermediate, not suspect, status. Thus Texas' statute which permitted school districts in that state to bar illegal alien children from public schooling was held unconstitutional. Whether placing these children in separate schools, or giving them fewer educational resources, although not denying them access to all education, would withstand intermediate level scrutiny is not clear.

Conclusion

Unlike a citizen in US society, whose First Amendment rights of free expression and of the free exercise of religion can be circumscribed only when the state has shown a compelling justification, and its objective can be accomplished by no less restrictive means, the courts appear to balance First Amendment rights of students and teachers against the interest of the school authorities in inculcating community values and in maintaining order and control so that the educational mission can be accomplished. The same appears to be true of Fourth Amendment protections and the procedural due process requirements of the Fourteenth Amendment. Moreover, in many instances, these constitutional rights appear to be given greater weight when the environment is that of a college or university than when it is a high school.[135] This appears to be attributable to two factors. One is that the university is a place for inquiry, the 'marketplace of ideas', and less a place for inculcating community values or for socializing students than is the public high school. The other factor is the age of the students, who in a college or university are thought to be more mature and thus better able to evaluate ideas for themselves.

In addition to these individual rights, there are also questions of the extent to which the Constitution protects the right of various pupil populations not to be denied equal educational opportunity on the basis of impermissible classifications. Here there has been less of a balancing of interests because of the 'special circumstances of the school environment'. Rather, the constitutional requirements, developed in other areas of the law, seem to be applied: that an affirmative duty may not be imposed on school officials unless there is proof of intent to discriminate or the classification is a stigmatizing one, or there has been a total deprivation of education based on an impermissible classification.

The struggle to determine the extent to which individual constitutional rights of students are to be protected as against the need of the educational enterprise for order and control, and the obligation of school authorities to provide equal access and treatment for all categories of students will undoubtedly continue in the courts. I would argue that in determining the extent to which school authorities should be constrained by constitutional requirements, courts should bear in mind the fact that the school is no longer the extension of the parent, but of the government. Among our most important democratic values is preventing abuses of governmental authority and disabling government from acting arbitrarily, from suppressing alternative viewpoints and ideas, and from treating various groups unequally. These values and concerns, so deeply rooted in our constitution, and particularly in our Bill of Rights, perhaps justify judicial intrusion on behalf of the rights of students and teachers, and explain the greater degree of judicial involvement than is the case in Australia.

Acknowledgements

The author wishes to acknowledge the very able research assistance of Stephen A. Hess, a law student at the University of Colorado School of Law.

Notes

1 See generally, LEVIN, B. (1985) *Equal Educational Opportunity for Children with Special Needs: The Federal Role in Australia*, 48 LAW & CONTEMP. PROBS. p. 213.
2 See Fullilove v. Klutznick, 448 US 448 (1980); Lau v. Nichols, 414 US 563 (1974); Oklahoma v. United States Civil Serv. Comm'n, 330 US 127 (1947).
3 See LEVIN, B. (1985) *Equal Educational Opportunity for Children with Special Needs: The Federal Role in Australia*, 48 LAW & CONTEMP. PROBS. pp. 213 and 253–6.
4 347 US 483 (1954).
5 Epperson v. Arkansas, 393 US 97 (1968).
6 Tinker v. Des Moines Independent School District, 393 US 503 (1969); Papish v. Board of Curators of the University of Missouri, 410 US 667 (1973); Pickering v. Board of Education, 391 US 563 (1968); Mt. Healthy City Board of Education v. Doyle, 429 US 274 (1977).
7 Wisconsin v. Yoder, 406 US 205 (1972).
8 San Antonio Independent School District v. Rodriguez, 411 US 1 (1973).
9 Mississippi University for Women v. Hogan, 458 US 718 (1982); Vorchheimer v. School District of Pennsylvania, 430 US 730 (1977), *affirming by an equally divided Court*, 532 F.2d 880 (3d Cir. 1976).
10 Board of Education v. Rowley, 458 US 176 (1982); Irving Indep. Sch. Dist. v. Tatro, 468 US 883 (1984).
11 Lau v. Nichols, 414 US 563 (1974).
12 Cleveland Board of Education v. LaFleur, 414 US 632 (1974).
13 Goss v. Lopez, 419 US 565 (1975); Ingraham v. Wright, 430 US 651 (1977); Board of Curators of the University of Missouri v. Horowitz, 435 US 78 (1978).
14 Wood v. Strickland, 420 US 308 (1975); Carey v. Piphus, 435 US 247 (1978).
15 Hobson v. Hansen, 267 F. Supp. 401 (D. D.C. 1967), *aff'd sub nom.* Smuck v. Hobson, 408 F.2d 175 (D.C. Cir. 1969) (*en banc*).
16 Debra P. v. Turlington, 644 F.2d 397 (5th Cir. 1981).
17 LEVIN, B. (1985) *Equal Educational Opportunity for Children with Special Needs:*

The Federal Role in Australia, 48 LAW & CONTEMP. PROBS. pp. 213 and 220 n. 39.

18 268 US 510 (1925).

19 In holding in *Pierce* that while the state may make education compulsory, it may not compel all children to attend its own schools, the Court indicated that the State could 'reasonably' regulate private schools.

> No question is raised concerning the power of the state reasonably to regulate all schools, to inspect, to supervise and examine them, their teachers and pupils; to require that all children of proper age attend some school, that teachers shall be of good moral character and patriotic disposition, that certain studies claiming essential good citzenship must be taught, that nothing be taught which is manifestly inimical to the public welfare. 268 US at 534.

> Two other Supreme Court cases decided at about the same time as *Pierce* dealt with the extent to which government can regulate non-public education. *See* Farrington v. Tokushige, 273 US 284 (1927); Meyer v. Nebraska, 262 US 390 (1923). Other than these cases, the extent to which states may regulate private schools has been litigated only since the mid-1970s and primarily in state courts. *Compare* Ohio v. Whisner, 47 Ohio St. 2d 181, 351 N.E.2d 750 (1976) (striking down state regulations), *with* State ex rel. Douglas v. Faith Baptist Church, 207 Neb. 802, 301 N.W.2d 371, *app. dismissed,* 454 US 803 (1981) (upholding regulations). *Cf.,* Runyon v. McCrary, 427 US 160 (1976).

20 Under the Establishment Clause, the state is not permitted to fund nonpublic sectarian schools. Any aid will violate the Establishment Clause which either has a 'principal or primary effect' of advancing religion or whose administration will excessively entangle the government with the state. Lemon v. Kurtzman, 403 US 602 (1971). A long line of cases since *Lemon* has articulated those standards and refined their application, culminating in Grand Rapids School District v. Ball, 473 US 373 (1985) (unconstitutional primary effect) and Aguilar v. Felton, 473 US 402 (1985) (unconstitutional entanglement).

21 Wisconsin v. Yoder, 406 US 205 (1972).

22 *Ibid.* at 241 (Douglas, J., dissenting in part).

23 Tinker v. Des Moines Independent School Dist., 393 US 503, 506 (1969).

24 *Ibid.*

25 370 US 421 (1962). In an often-quoted statement, Justice Black said that the Establishment Clause 'must at least mean that [it] is no part of the business of government to compose official prayers for any group of the American people to recite as a part of a religious program carried on by government'. *Ibid.* at 425.

26 Abington School Dist. v. Schempp, 374 US 203 (1963).

27 *Ibid.* at 225.

28 *Ibid.*

29 449 US 39 (1981) (per curiam).

30 *Ibid.* at 41.

31 *Ibid.* at 42. In the most recent school prayer case, Wallace v. Jaffree, 472 US 38 (1985). The Court struck down an Alabama statute authorizing a period of 'meditation or voluntary prayer' as not reflecting a clear secular purpose, and thus violating the first *Lemon* test. It should be noted that most of the Establishment Clause cases arose in the context of public aid to parochial schools. See, for example, Grand Rapids School District v. Ball, 473 US 373 (1985); Aguilar v. Felton, 473 US 402 (1985); Mueller v. Allen, 463 US 388 (1983); Wolman v. Walter, 433 US 229 (1977); Roemer v. Maryland Public Works Board, 426 US 736 (1976); Meek v. Pittenger, 421 US 349 (1975); Sloan v. Lemon, 413 US 825

(1973); Committee for Public Education v. Nyquist, 413 US 756 (1973); Hunt v. McNair, 413 US 734 (1973); Levitt v. Committee for Public Education, 413 US 472 (1973); Lemon v. Kurtzman, 403 US 602 (1971).

32 Lower courts have considered a variety of free exercise problems. See, for example, Menora v. Illinois High School Association, 683 F.2d 1030 (7th Cir. 1982), *cert. denied*, 459 US 1156 (1983) (prohibition against headgear in basketball games not unconstitutional in excluding yarmulkes); Walsh v. Louisiana High School Athletic Association, 616 F.2d 152, *rehearing denied*, 621 F.2d 440 (5th Cir. 1980), *cert. denied*, 449 US 1124 (1980) (transfer rule not unconstitutional as applied to prevent student from playing for religious high school); Moody v. Cronin, 484 F. Supp. 270 (C.D. Ill. 1979) (requirement of 'immodest' clothing in physical education classes violated free exercise rights of some students); Roman v. Appleby, 558 F. Supp. 449 (E.D. Pa 1983) (counseling sessions with student on matters of religion, sex, family relationships, etc. violated neither parents' nor students' free exercise rights).

33 374 US 203 (1963).

34 *Ibid.* at 309, 312. (Stewart, J., dissenting).

35 406 US 205 (1972).

36 *Compare* Ohio v. Whisner, 47 Ohio St. 2d 181, 351 N.E.2d 750 (1976) *with* State ex rel. Douglas v. Faith Baptist Church, 207 Neb. 802, 301 N.W.2d 371, *app. dismissed*, 454 US 803 (1981).

37 See, Brown v. Dade Christian Schools, 356 F.2d 310 (5th Cir. 1977) (*en banc*), *cert. denied*, 434 US 1063 (1978). The plurality opinion declined to reach the question of the constitutionality of S1981 as applied to a religious school, holding that there was substantial evidence to support the findings of the trial judge that 'defendants' policy of segregation was not the exercise of religion'. 556 F.2d at 312.

38 ARONS (1976) *The Separation of School and State: Pierce Reconsidered*, 46 HARV. EDUC. REV. 76.

39 See, for example, Brusca v. State of Missouri, 332 F. Supp. 275 (E.D. Mo. 1971), *aff'd mem.* 405 US 1050 (1972). The plaintiffs in the *Brusca* case argued that the failure of the state to subsidize religious schools violated the neutrality that the state must follow in the Establishment Clause.

40 Committee for Public Education and Religious Liberty v. Nyquist, 413 US 756, 764–65 (1973).

41 *Ibid.* at 788.

42 See, for example, Abington School District v. Schempp, 374 US 203 (1963); Engel v. Vitale, 370 US 421 (1962); Epperson v. Arkansas, 393 US 97 (1968); Stone v. Graham, 449 US 39 (1981) (per curiam); Wallace v. Jaffree, 472 US 38 (1985).

43 319 US 624 (1943).

44 457 US 853, 872 (1982), *quoting* West Virginia Bd. of Educ. v. Barnette, 319 US at 642.

45 School officials may remove books from the school library that are 'pervasively vulgar' or educationally unsuitable. *Pico*, 457 US at 871 (plurality opinion). *Pico* does not, however, impose a requirement on the part of school officials to *add* certain books to their school libraries. *Ibid.* at 871–72.

46 457 US at 868. The right to receive information and ideas is 'an inherent corollary of the rights of free speech ... explicitly guaranteed by the Constitution ...' *Pico*, 457 US 853, 867 (plurality opinion), and students too have these First Amendment rights. Access to ideas 'prepares students for active and effective participation in the pluralistic, often contentious society in which they will soon be adult members'. *Ibid.*

47 'Petitioners might well defend their claim of absolute discretion in matters of *curriculum* by reliance upon their duty to inculcate community values'. *Pico*, 457 US at 869 (plurality opinion) (emphasis in original).
48 See, for example, Hopkins v. Hamden Board of Education, 29 Conn. Supp. 397, 289 A.2d 914 (1971).
49 See, for example, Davis v. Page, 385 F. Supp. 395 (D.N.H. 1974).
50 See generally, HIRSCHOFF (1977) *Parents and the Public School Curriculum: Is There a Right to Have One's Child Excused from Public Instruction?*, 50 SO. CAL. L. REV. 871.
51 Note Justice Brennan's comments in the context of the First Amendment's religion clauses:

> Attendance at the public schools has never been compulsory; parents remain morally and constitutionally free to choose the academic environment in which they wish their children to be educated. The relationship of the Establishment Clause of the First Amendment to the public school system is preeminently that of reserving such a choice to the individual parent, rather than vesting it in the majority of votes of each State or school district. The choice which is thus preserved is between a public secular education with its uniquely democratic values, and some form of private or sectarian education, which offers values of its own. In my judgment the First Amendment forbids the State to inhibit that freedom of choice by diminishing the attractiveness of either alternative — either by restricting the liberty of the private schools to inculcate whatever values they wish, or by jeopardizing the freedom of the public schools from private or sectarian pressures.

Abington School Dist. v. Schempp, 374 US 203, 242 (1963) (Brennan, J., concurring).
52 See, for example, Pierce v. Society of Sisters, 268 US 510 (1925); Meyer v. Nebraska, 262 US 390 (1923).
53 The *Pierce* Court identified the interest at stake as 'the liberty of parents ... to direct the upbringing and education of children under their control', and noted 'those who nurture [the child] and direct his destiny have the right, coupled with the high duty, to recognize and prepare him for additional obligations'. 268 US at 534–35. A later Supreme Court case identified that right as 'cardinal', but cautioned that 'neither the rights of religion nor rights of parenthood are beyond limitation ... [T]he state has a wide range of power for limiting parental freedom and authority in things affecting the child's welfare'. Prince v. Massachusetts, 321 US 158 (1944) (upholding state law applied to prevent child from passing out religious literature on streets). The extent of the state's power in education was held to be quite broad in Baker v. Owen, 398 F. Supp. 294 (M.D.N.C.), *aff'd mem.* 423 US 907 (1975), which held that the parent's right was not 'fundamental'. 395 F. Supp. at 299.
54 393 US 503 (1969).
55 *Ibid.* at 508.
56 *Ibid.*
57 See, for example, Pliscou v. Holtville Unified School District, 411 F. Supp 842 (S.D. Cal. 1976) (students' right to publish and solicit advertising for unofficial school newspaper is protected); Hatter v. Los Angeles City High School District, 310 F. Supp. 1309 (C.D. Cal. 1970) (distribution of leaflets and wearing of tags urging boycott of school candy sale to protest dress code is not protected activity); Dixon v.Beresh, 361 F. Supp. 253 (E.D. Mich. 1973) (school must recognize eligible student groups absent showing of disruption or impairment of school operation); Guzick v. Drebus, 431 F.2d 594 (6th Cir.), *cert. denied*, 401 US

948 (1970) (regulation against wearing of button announcing anti-war demonstration upheld in light of potential disruptive effect).
58 See, for example, Baughman v. Freienmuth, 478 F.2d 1345 (4th Cir. 1973).
59 A few courts have held that school officials cannot require prior approval under *any* circumstances without violating the First Amendment's prohibition of censorship. See, for example, Fujishima v. Board of Ed., 460 F.2d 1355 (7th Cir. 1972).
60 Papish v. Board of Curators of University of Missouri, 410 US 667, 670 (1973) (*per curiam*).
61 408 US 169 (1972).
62 408 US at 190.
63 *Ibid.*
64 454 US 263 (1981).
65 454 US at 268, n. 5.
66 741 F.2d 538, 546 (3rd Cir. 1984), *rev'd on other grounds*, 475 US 534 (1986).
67 Four circuits voted affirmatively on this issue. Richards v. Thurston, 424 F.2d 1281 (1st Cir. 1970); Massie v. Henry, 455 F.2d 779 (4th Cir. 1972); Holsapple v. Woods, 500 F.2d 49 (7th Cir.) (per curiam), *cert. denied*, 419 US 901 (1974); Bishop v. Colaw, 450 F.2d 1069 (8th Cir. 1971); *cf.* Dwen v. Barry, 483 F.2d 1126 (2d Cir. 1973), *rev'd sub nom.* Kelley v. Johnson, 425 US 238 (1975). Five other circuits rejected these constitutional claims. Zeller v. Donegel School District, 517 F.2d 600 (3rd Cir. 1975); Karr v. Schmidt, 460 F.2d 609 (5th Cir.) (*en banc*), *cert. denied*, 409 US 989 (1972); Gfell v. Rickelman, 441 F.2d 444 (6th Cir. 1971); Hatch v. Goerke, 502 F.2d 1189 (10th Cir. 1974); Olff v. East Side Union High School Dist., 45 F.2d 932 (9th Cir. 1971), *cert. denied*, 404 US 1042 (1972).
    The courts have also divided on the issue with regard to whether the plaintiff's rights were protected if he were a college student, even though not protected if a high school student. Although the Fifth Circuit had struck down a student's claim in *Karr v. Schmidt*, in Lansdale v. Tyler Junior College, 470 F.2d 659 (5th Cir. 1972) (*en banc*), *cert. denied*, 411 US 986 (1973), the court held that because of a college student's maturity and thus the educational institution's diminished role, the balance is in favor of the individual. The adult's constitutional right to wear his hair as he chooses supersedes the state's right to intrude. By contrast the Ninth Circuit stood firm against both college and high school students, seeing no distinction. See King v. Saddleback Junior College Dist., 445 F.2d 932 (9th Cir.), *cert. denied*, 404 US 979 (1971); *Olff, supra.*
68 The Supreme Court, however, decided a case concerning a policeman who claimed that a hair length regulation violated his First Amendment freedom of expression, as well as the Fourteenth Amendment's guarantee of due process and equal protection. Kelley v. Johnson, 425 US 238 (1976). The majority held that the burden was on the plaintiff to show that the regulation was irrational or arbitrary and this he could not do since either a 'desire to make a police officer readily recognizable to the members of the public, or a desire for the esprit de corps which such similarity is felt to inculcate within the police force itself', was held to be a rational justification for the regulation. 425 US at 248. Whether and to what extent the *Kelley* decision is applicable to teachers and students in schools remains a better of speculation. Teachers are not employees in a state military organization, although they are supposed to be role models for students. Students, on the other hand, are neither analogous to policemen nor to teachers.
69 The majority in *Epperson v. Arkansas* cites Meyer v. Nebraska, 262 US 390 (1923), as holding that the Due Process Clause prohibits arbitrary restrictions upon the freedom of teachers to teach. 393 US 97, 105 (1968).

70 See Board of Education, Island Trees Union Free Sch. Dist. v. Pico, 457 US 853 (1982).

71 385 US 589, 603 (1967).

72 *Ibid.*

73 In *Keyishian,* faculty members of a state university had refused to sign a certificate that required them to declare that they were not Communists, or that if they had been Communists, that they had communicated that fact to the president of the state university in New York. Thus, the case involved the attempt of a state to exclude subversives from the teaching profession. However, *Keyishian* does not suggest that the holding might be limited to college professors. The Court declared the entire law unconstitutional and not merely the amendment covering higher education employees.

74 393 US 97, 107 (1968).

75 *Ibid.* at 113–14 (Black, J., concurring).

76 *Ibid.* at 115–16 (Stewart, J., concurring). In Minnesota State Board of Community Colleges v. Knight, 465 US 271 (1984), Justice Brennan, in a dissenting opinion, seems to suggest that *Epperson* was decided on grounds of academic freedom rather than the Establishment Clause, 465 US at 296.

77 For contrasting views of the extent to which 'academic freedom' is protected by the Constitution, see VAN ALSTYNE, *The Constitutional Rights of Teachers and Professors,* 1970 DUKE L.J. 841, and GOLDSTEIN, *The Asserted Constitutional Right of Public School Teachers to Determine What They Teach,* 124 U. PA. L. REV. 1293 (1976).

78 *Compare* Parducci v. Rutland, 316 F. Supp. 352 (M.D. Ala. 1970) (teacher has right to determine use of appropriate classroom materials which are not obscene or disruptive) *with* Cary v. Board of Education, 598 F.2d 535 (10th Cir. 1979) (teachers have no right to choose books which school board bans).

79 457 US at 869.

80 Pickering v. Board of Education, 391 US 563, 573 (1968).

81 Mt. Healthy City School District v. Doyle, 429 US 274, 286–88 (1977).

82 See, for example, Givhan v. Western Line Consolidated School District, 439 US 410, 415 n. 4 (1979).

83 See, for example, Nigorian v. Weiss, 343 F. Supp. 757 (E.D. Mich. 1971); Clark v. Holmes, 474 F.2d 928 (7th Cir. 1972), *cert, denied,* 411 US 972 (1973).

84 New Jersey v. T.L.O., 469 US 325 (1985).

85 Camara v. Municipal Court, 387 US 523, 528–29 (1967).

86 Chimel v. California, 395 US 752 (1969).

87 Almeida-Sanchez v. United States, 413 US 266, 270 (1973).

88 469 US at 339.

89 *Ibid.* at 340.

90 *Ibid.*

91 *Ibid.* In the course of its opinion, the Court identified — but did not rule on — a variety of related questions. While the petition for certiorari only questioned the applicability of the exclusionary rule to evidence in criminal juvenile delinquency proceedings obtained illegally by school authorities, the Court's finding that the search was legal obviated the need to address the exclusionary rule. Consequently, the Court expressly reserved judgment on that issue after noting a split in lower court authority, 469 US at 330–33 and n. 2, 3. Since there was no ruling on this matter, the Court also did not address whether, even if it should find that the exclusionary rule applied to illegally obtained evidence used in criminal proceedings, the same evidence could be used by school officials in a disciplinary proceeding.

    Several more unanswered questions concern police involvement in school searches. The Court limited its holding to searches made by school authorities acting on their own and, while raising the issue, did not intimate its opinion about searches in which the police and school authorities act together or where one acts on the request of the other. 469 US at 337, n. 5 and at 341, n. 7. Furthermore, the standard articulated in *T.L.O.* turned on the Court's acknowledgment of the student's legitimate expectation of privacy in her personal property. The Court noted that it is an open question whether or not the same expectation of privacy in school storage space (lockers, desks, etc.) is in fact legitimate and thus entitled to Fourth Amendment protection. While the Court did not answer the question, it noted that lower courts are divided on the issue. 469 US at 337, n. 5.

92 419 US 565 (1975).
93 *Ibid.* at 575–75. The Court found that the students had a liberty interest in their 'good name, reputation, honor, or integrity' and noted that the charges — if sustained — could damage the students' standing among classmates and teachers as well as 'interfere with later opportunities for higher education and employment'. *Ibid.* at 575.
94 *Cf.* Goldberg v. Kelly, 397 US 254 (1970); Bell v. Burson, 402 US 535 (1971).
95 For example, more formal hearings could be required at which the student may be represented by counsel, confront witnesses against him and cross-examine them, and call his own witnesses. *Goss*, 419 US at 583–84.
96 Ingraham v. Wright, 430 US 651, 672 (1977).
97 *Ibid.* at 676–80. *Ingraham* also held that Eighth Amendment protection is inappropriate and thus inapplicable in corporal punishment cases. 'The openness of the public school and its supervision by the community', state laws prohibiting excessive punishment, and recourse against school officials in civil or criminal actions provide adequate protection for the student. 430 US at 671. Thus, in the Court's view, the child is quite unlike a sequestered criminal who may need constitutional redress for beatings by a jailer. The Court concluded that there was neither justification in case law nor in the history of the Eighth Amendment to extend its protection beyond criminals.
    Justice White argued in a strong dissent that the existence of various safeguards or state authorized redress is irrelevant to the Constitution's prohibition against excessive punishment. 430 US at 683 (White, J., dissenting). So long as there are any excessive beatings in schools, those beatings are 'punishments' within the meaning of the Eighth Amendment and subject to judicial scrutiny. It is absurd, he argued, to hold that 'corporal punishment in public schools, no matter how barbaric, inhumane, or severe is never limited by the Eighth Amendment'. *Ibid.* at 692.
98 Board of Curators of the University of Missouri v. Horowitz, 435 US 78 (1978).
99 *Ibid.* at 85–86. The Court referred to the requirements of *Goss v. Lopez, supra,* for school conduct rule violations and held that for a failure to meet academic standards 'far less stringent procedural requirements' are necessary. Since Horowitz — a medical student — had been warned several times that her progress was not satisfactory and was even examined by seven independent physicians prior to her dismissal, those minimal requirements were met in her case.
100 408 US 564 (1972). *Roth* found that a property interest in the professor's continued employment must be based on 'a legitimate claim of entitlement' to the position. Since Roth was merely serving a one year, non-tenure-track appointment, he had no legitimate claim of entitlement and the Board was not constitutionally required to inform him of the reasons for their decision not to rehire him. Moreover, because the decision was not accompanied by any 'charge against him that might seriously damage his standing and association' in the

professional community, Roth could not claim injury to any liberty interest he might have had in his reputation. *Ibid.* at 574.

101 408 US 593 (1972). *Perry* emphasized that a teacher need not have tenure to have a property interest in his position. Instead, the Court held the requisite 'legitimate claim of entitlement' could be based on an 'understanding fostered by the college administration' amounting to a '*de facto* tenure program' *Ibid.* at 600–01. Thus Sinderman — a veteran of ten one-year appointments with the Texas college system including four in his last position — was entitled to show at trial 'such rules (of the Texas college system) or mutually explicit understandings' which supported his claim to a property interest. *Ibid.* at 601. If Sinderman could establish that interest at trial, then he would be entitled to a hearing at which the Board would have to inform him of the grounds for its decision and allow him to challenge the sufficiency of those grounds. *Ibid.* at 605.

102 Keyes v. School Dist. No. 1, 413 US 189 (1973).

103 *Compare* Johnson v. San Francisco Unified Sch. Dis., 500 F.2d 349 (9th Cir. 1974) *with* Oliver v. Kalamazoo Bd. of Educ., 368 F. Supp. 143, 161 (W.D. Mich. 1973), *aff'd*, 508 F.2d 178, 181–82 (6th Cir. 1974), *cert. denied*, 421 US 963 (1975). *See also* Arthur v. Nyquist, 573 F.2d 134 (2d Cir. 1978), *cert. denied*, 439 US 860 (1978).

104 Columbus Board of Educ. v. Penick, 443 US 449 (1979).

105 See, for example, *Keyes, supra* at n. 102; *Columbus II, supra*, at n. 104; Swann v. Charlotte-Mecklenberg Board of Education, 402 US 1 (1971); Pasadena City Board of Education v. Spangler, 427 US 424 (1976).

106 Regents of the University of California v. Bakke, 438 US 265 (1978).

107 Swann v. Charlotte-Mecklenburg Board of Educ., 402 US 1 (1971).

108 *Keyes, supra*, at n. 102; *Columbus II, supra*, at n. 104.

109 Milliken v. Bradley, 418 US 717 (1974).

110 20 U.S.C. Secs. 1681–1682; 34 C.F.R. pt. 86.

111 The case of Vorchheimer v. School District of Philadelphia, 532 F.2d 880 (3rd Cir. 1976), reached the Supreme Court, but the Third Circuit decision denying a woman student access to an all male academically elite public high school because there was a similiar academically elite high school for women was affirmed by an equally divided Court. 430 US 703 (1977).

112 Lower courts have held that schools must provide equal opportunities to males and females for the chance to participate in athletic competition. For example, if the school does not offer a particular women's team sport offered to men, then it must allow women the chance to compete on the men's team. See Brenden v. Independent School District No. 742, 477 F.2d 1292 (8th Cir. 1973) (tennis and skiing), Hoover v. Mieklejohn, 430 F. Supp. 164 (D. Colo. 1977) (basketball). *Hoover* noted that separate, but comparable, teams for men and women would provide the constitutionally required equality of opportunity since the mere separation of teams by gender would not involve the 'stigmatizing inferiority' for one group which race divisions involve. 430 F. Supp. at 170. However true that may be, there is still a problem in assessing which 'separate' sports programs are in fact, 'equal'. *Compare* Dodson v. Arkansas Activities Association, 468 F. Supp. 394 (D. Ark. 1979) (difference in boys' and girls' basketball rules had no rational basis since founded merely on tradition (*with* Cape v. Tennessee Secondary School Athletic Association, 563 F.2d 793 (6th Cir. 1977) (state had rational basis for providing different rules for boys' and girls' basketball).

113 Brown v. Board of Education, 347 US 483, 495 (1954).

114 Craig v. Boren, 429 US 190, 197 (1976).

115 Vorchheimer v. School dist. of Philadelphia, 430 US 703 (1977), *aff'd by an equally divided Court*, 532 F.2d 880 (3rd Cir. 1976).

116 458 US 718 (1982).

117 *Ibid.* at 730.
118 See generally LEVIN, B. *Current Trends in School Finance Reform Litigation: A Commentary*, 1977 DUKE L.J. 1099.
119 After San Antonio Independent School District v. Rodriguez, 411 US 1 (1973), was decided, most standards were developed under state constitutional provisions rather than under the Equal Protection Clause of the Fourteenth Amendment of the US Constitution. See, for example, Serrano v. Priest, 5 Cal. 3d 584, 487 P.2d 1241, 96 Cal. Rptr. 601 (1971) (*Serrano I*) (fiscal neutrality standard under Fourteenth Amendment's equal protection clause); Serrano v. Priest, 18 Cal. 3d 728, 557 P.2d 929, 135 Cal Rptr. 345 (1977) (*Serrano II*) (fiscal neutrality standard under state constitution's equivalent of equal protection clause); Robinson v. Cahill, 62 N.J. 473 303 A.2d 273, *reargument*, 63 N.J. 196, 306 A.2d 65, *cert. denied sub nom.* Dicey v. Robinson, 414 US 976 (1973); Seattle School District No. 1 of King County v. State, 90 Wash. 2d 476, 585 P.2d 71 (1978); Board of Education v. Nyquist, 94 Misc. 2d 466, 408 N.Y.S.2d 606 (1978), *modified*, 83 A.D.2d 217, 443. N.Y.S.2d 843 (1981), *modified*, 453 N.Y.2d 27, 453 N.Y.S.2d 843, 439 N.E.2d 359 (1982).
120 411 US 1 (1973).
121 In the *Rodriguez* Court's view, the subject of the classification was property-poor *districts*, not poor persons. The injured class was said to be comprised of all students who lived in low-property wealth school districts, rather than indigent students who might live in either low- or high-property wealth districts or indigent students who lived in property-poor school districts. Justice Powell, who wrote the majority opinion, noted that the precedents involving wealth discrimination had been confined to discrimination on the basis of *personal* wealth. 411 US at 20.
122 411 US at 28.
123 *Ibid.* at 33–34. The Court also noted that the cases in which it had held the strict standard applicable involved legislation that infringed or interfered with the free exercise of a fundamental right. In *Rodriguez*, by contrast, the state of Texas was not interfering with or restricting the ability of school districts to provide education. Instead, by allocating some state funds to school districts, rather than relying solely on local revenues to finance education, the state was attempting to expand, not restrict, the available educational offerings. *Ibid.* at 37–39.
124 411 US at 56.
125 411 US at 38.
126 *Ibid.* at 25, n.60.
127 Fialkowski v. Shapp, 405 F. Supp. 946 (E.D. Pa 1975); *cf.*, Lau v. Nichols, 414 US 563 (1974).
128 *Cf.* Board of Education v. Rowley, 458 US 176 (1982); Equal Educational Opportunity Act of 1974, 20 U.S.C. Sec. 1703(f).
129 Board of Education v. Rowley, 458 US 176 (1982); Irving Indep. Sch. Dist. v. Tatro, 468 US 883 (1984).
130 City of Cleburne v. Cleburne Living Centre, Inc., 473 US 432 (1985).
131 473 US at 440.
132 Lau v. Nichols, 414 US 563 (1974).
133 *Cf.*, Washington v. Davis, 426 US 229 (1976).
134 457 US 202 (1982).
135 See, for example Establishment Clause cases which emphasize college students' maturity and scepticism, versus high school students' impressionability in assessing the 'primary effect' of state aid programs. *Compare* Widmar v. Vincent, 454 US 263 (1981) (religious student groups may use university facilities for meetings) *with* Bender v. Williamsport Area School Dist., 741 F.2d 538 (3rd Cir. 1984), *rev'd on other grounds*, 475 US 534 (1986) (religious student groups may not

use high school facilities for meetings); and *compare* Tilton v. Richardson, 403 US 672 (1971), and Roemer v. Board of Public Works, 426 US 736 (1976) (permitting public aid to sectarian colleges), *with* Lemon v. Kurtzman, 403 US 602 (1971), and Grand Rapids School Dist. v. Ball, 473 US 373 (1985) (prohibiting public aid to sectarian elementary and secondary schools). See also treatment of other First Amendment interests. *Compare* Karr v. Schmidt, 460 F.2d 609 (5th Cir.) (*en banc*), *cert. denied*, 409 US 989 (1972) (high school hair regulations are appropriate given the schools' mission and relative immaturity of high school students), *with* Lansdale v. Tyler Junior College, 470 F.2d 659 (5th Cir. 1972) (*en banc*), *cert. denied*, 411 US 986 (1973) (college student's right to wear hair any length he wishes is protected).

6   National Australia–United States Education: A Commentary

Frederick M. Wirt

Chapters 2–5 need to be seen in a comparative framework because each contributes to understanding what has occurred across national systems of education. Whether one studies these systems as a summarizer of current events, a policy advocate, or a theory-builder, comparative analysis of the politics of education has many benefits. A useful framework of analysis in that regard is the 'global village' concept of a highly interdependent world, one swept by currents of ideas and crises that have differential effects on the shores of most nations. In this chapter, implications of that framework are applied to the four chapters, although Smart's chapter does so on its own.

How Can We Compare?

Any comparison must first start with units that have something comparable about them. Wilkins (1986) has suggested a sequence of organizations neces- sary to do such comparison. What is the policy problem in a unit of govern- ment, what change causes that problem, can this change be related to a larger scale pattern of change, can the problem be compared with a similar scale in another unit, what elements of the first unit contribute uniquely to the problem, and what aspects of another unit's problem enable one to use study derived from the first unit?

I believe this 'catechism' of comparative method can be deduced from the panel papers. No matter how the governance of education is arranged, they all possess in common a set of *values,* respond to social *change,* and have political *institutions* to make and administer policy services.

First, values are both explicit (manifest) and implicit (latent) in all policy. In education, there is agreement across nations that the major values to be sought are quality (recently called 'excellence'), equity (sometimes called 'equal educational opportunities'), efficiency (recently tied to 'cost-benefit' considerations), and choice (always tied to political control). That is because, despite differences in political and economic systems, education seeks to

129

improve certain qualities of individuals, to apply resources in a roughly equitable manner to accomplish that, and to administer the service as efficiently as possible.

Second, nations are always undergoing some social change, and that process provides a common basis for comparison. An even more common element of that change process is the presence of trans-national events which are generated by the spread of an idea or a crisis, events which have intra-national effects. The search for literacy among most nations over the last century or more typify the influence of an idea; the grave effects of world wars in this century show how transnational events cost lives of the educable and drain schooling resources gone to war.

Third, the variety in national political systems should not cause us to lose sight of its primacy in each nation in educational policy making. Nor should we ignore the fact that all governments finance or administer education. In that process, there are some common questions which all nations must address. Namely, should government do anything about a particular schooling problem (a philosophical query)? What should be done about the problem (a programmatic query)? How should it be administered, at what level and by which office (the implementation query)? Who will pay for it (the finance query)? And finally, did it work (the evaluation query)?

These queries underly the four chapters of this section, thereby providing common elements that permit comparative study, which I will only illuminate in this commentary. This analysis applies a basic causal framework to the two nations, namely: *transnational social changes have had effects upon the three major values in educational policy decisions, as mediated by national culture and institutions.* Implicit in this framework is the metaphor of a global village in which these nations' education system must operate.

Transnational Changes in the Global Village

Three transnational events intersect in these chapters, although they are implied in most cases.

The Trauma of International Recession

Since the mid-1970s, all nations except the energy-sufficient have suffered traumatic consequences from the 1973 oil embargo. The major consequence was a common recession that led to national deficits, which led to a budget-cutting response, which led to a politics of reallocations, which in turn affected all education systems (Wirt and Harman, 1986).

The chapters of both Clark-Astuto and Smart pinpoint precisely the end results of this international trauma, namely negative externalities which reached into educational policy making. Their chapters show how governments under different political parties, whether motivated by Keynesian fiscalism or Friedmanite monetarism, sought to cope with the petro-dollar crunch. Clark and Astuto more generally, but Smart more in detail, show how this fiscal response necessarily caught up education. At the state-local level in the United States, even graver budgetary cuts, absolute or relative, hit all but the most thriving region of the south-west (although it, too, is now slowing down). Formal government at all levels might repond to the recession in ways comfortable to their resources and values, but all had to recognize and adjust to this transnational event.

Basic Educational Values

There is a striking parallelism in these two nations (and others as well) about the priority given educational values in recent decades. All four chapters refer to the priority given to equity in the 1960s and 1970s and to quality and efficiency thereafter. In this shift among values, the Levin and Birch chapters point out the judicial dimension of the legislative events portrayed in the Clark-Astuto and Smart chapters. Relative prosperity of the earlier period enabled national leaders to think about redistributive policy, but the post-1973 recession trauma raised questions about efficiency, that is, what nations got for what they spent. And dissatisfaction with the effects of equity policies set off a later cry over the threat to quality that redistribution had created.

Even the same groups, under different names, also appeared. Teacher organizations and defenders of minorities and the poor, and their party agents, dominated the school agenda until the late 1970s. Thereafter, business groups and defenders of traditional societal values, and different party agents, were heard more clearly and effectively. Through this latter period in the United States, however, the Supreme Court has continued its defense of redistributive policies involving race and gender, in education and other policy domains.

The Education of the West

Implicit in all four chapters has been another transnational event which has altered the way that citizens think about society. That event was the increasing education of the West; more — maybe all — nations have given more money and instruction for more students than ever before in world history. This transnational event has created a generation better educated than their parents, and more inclined to do what champions of education always said it would do. They widen their perspectives on the possible, and they challenge what has been in order to fulfill their manifest capacities. As one political result, they question traditional values in every institution, evaluate the very utility of institutions themselves, staff the agencies of governance at all levels, and, in short, seek new policy directions.

As a result of this difference in generations, there is now a new world outlook in Western nations (Inglehart, 1977), a 'silent revolution' that has transformed basic perceptions of what is possible in social life; note that this change took place after the burgeoning schooling of post-war generations. Look at the consequences developed in these chapters for just two nations. National government had to do more both programmatically and financially; the concept of 'rights' surrounding the child in school expanded by tort or constitutional law; there was no professionally-determined definition of 'one best system' nor were school professionals 'managers of virtue'; political parties became carriers of education policy, and so on. Very little, maybe none of this, were dominant ideas when World War II ended. But today the veterans and baby-boom generation accept such ideas as societal givens, which they inspired.

The Mediating Effects of National Political Institutions

All four chapters make an important point: transnational events do not have a homogenous affect across nations because national culture and institutions act to shape the influence of such events. These national factors prismatically filter singular events into differentiated patterns. Note the differentiating impact reported in these chapters even for two nations.

Executive Leadership and Differentiation

A major role is played by national leadership in shaping transnational in-fluences. Even in the United States, where presidents had no educational policy before Lyndon Johnson and the Great Society two decades ago, now presidents do proclaim it, albeit differing in their stances. In this regard, Clark and Astuto show how two presidents took sharply different stances, moving from a basic concern for equity to one for quality and efficiency, from more concern for nationalizing such policy to devolving it. In Australia, as Smart shows, executive leadership by the prime minister has been high on the national agenda in the 1960s expansion of secondary education, the Whitlam federal expansion in the 1970s, the reduction of Canberra's role by Fraser, and the moderate change of Hawke currently.

Not only did the executive expand to meet challenges to education, but the distinctive presidential and parliamentary systems, and the accompanying ideologies, produced different school policy results. Private education could benefit in Australia but not in the US because of ideology and its repository — the constitution. Centrally funding of higher (tertiary) education on a full basis was accepted in the first but not the latter, a gain because of an ideology about proper objects of taxation — even though bashing the national capital is a prime political sport in both nations. The role of trade unions in government differed strongly, a constituent element formally placed in the Labor party and only an affiliated group in the Democratic party. The result was that this group's interests were not formally part of public policy programs in the latter — although teachers did well under both parties when in power.

The Judiciary and Differentiation

The role of the judiciary in these two nations is differentiated mightily by a central fact, the presence of two elements in the jurisprudence of the US not found in Australia. These are the constitutional Bill of Rights and the role of a definitive Supreme Court. These differences had consequences for how school policy was devised and administered in the two places.

The Levin chapter is an extraordinarily thorough summary of an extremely complex flood of litigation over schools and student roles. At the core of the spate of cases she summarizes and organizes is the existence of a Bill of Rights which generates a constitutional law on the basis of which individuals can make claims to advance or protect their rights to schooling. In speech, due process of law, and equal protection of the law, the American student today is protected against constraints from a range of actions once deemed legitimate. Not least, removing the idea of the school professional as standing *in loco parentis* (which meant in practice *in loco Deo*) led to the new legal concept of the student as an individual surrounded by certain rights that no school official could abridge. Similarly the enormous Federal efforts to provide desegration, special education, and procedural guarantees against local and state official tyranny all stem from the presence of a constitution. As a result, schools have been made to do more to meet these standards of equality, freedom, and justice.

In Australia, however, as Birch clearly points out, the absence of such a Bill of Rights creates no such body of judicial decisions from which to shape the meaning of education law. There are some cases, he notes, which have had lasting effects on the financing of schools; also, we see the dimunition of the authority *in loco parentis*. But because Australian political history has eschewed a body of rights which over-reach a state's authority — and Canberra's as well — there is no recourse for constituents of schooling when they seek change. Rather, they must turn to legislation for that purpose; there is great elasticity in how legislation determines rights in this system.

A second judicial factor, closely linked to the first, is the presence of a national court whose decisions are binding upon all governments. The Constitution-makers foresaw the need for a final arbiter when disputes among states, or of states with Washington, would arise — the umpire function. But the Supreme Court as early as 1803 took on another role, interpreting national legislation against the Constitution. While there was great potential for national involvement in schooling, that lay dormant until the 1960s. Since then, the Court has generated the hundreds of decisions over schooling summarized in Levin's chapter. While Australia also has a high court, its primacy in interpreting the Constitution and national legislation is not that of America's. But it has had important consequences at a few points in defining educational policy, as Birch carefully demonstrates.

The point is that the prismatic quality of national institutions when set across transnational events means that any comparative study must look for both similar and uncommon events. These four chapters clearly demonstrate just such differentiation.

Transnational Impacts of Educational Values

We have noted that all educational systems seek some combination of four values — equity, efficiency, quality and choice. But a latent problem, arising in both nations and implied in these four chapters, is that these values contain inherent contradictions — which generates one torrent in the politics of education. For example, to achieve equity for some may well mean redistributively taking resources that might have gone instead for a higher quality education for others. Also, efficiency is highly desirable for some, but choice — which can confound efficient means — is desirable for yet others. Choice-based policy that seeks to optimize rewards in a system can dilute the quality sought by a few.

As Smart noted, nations engaged in a 'pendulum swing' between the values of equity and quality; Clark and Astuto address this alternation between Presidents Carter and Reagan in detail. This pendulum effect is also seen fully in Levin's chapter, where equity concerns have driven much litigation recently. Even Birch's treatment of the change over in *in loco parentis* notes this conflict. Recent efforts to increase citizen participation through administrative devolution in Australian states raises the same choice-efficiency conflict that energizes much local politics of education in the US. These examples illustrate, without exhausting, the inherent contradictions of values, which underlie the politics of government, the 'authoritative allocating of values and resources'. Incidentally, much the same picture is evident in the United Kingdom, to judge from recent analysis of the shift under the Thatcher government from equity to quality at the national level, and the shift from efficiency to choice under Labour governments in local school authorities.

The Virtues of Comparison

As we all know from the wisdom of 'Sesame Street', 'Some things are not like other things.' But there are virtues in comparing seemingly unlike 'things'. These virtues are to provide: a check on parochialism in thinking about policy and theory; and an awareness of how differences in political systems differentiate what policies result. Nevertheless, comparative studies also show us how differences can be overcome by non-parochial events, so that 'Some things are truly like other things.' All these truisms are made manifest in these four chapters; Smart even approached his writing from a comparative perspective. But from the chapters we can illuminate these virtues of comparison.

A Check on Parochialism

Parochialism explains what may be general only in terms of the local. It is like the sign outside a small college town in Ohio that read, 'The center of everything.' But what comparison provides are reasons for being very modest on giving credit for policy change and effects to local agencies.

Comparison will show, for example, that one's national leaders, no matter how exalted by their partisans and parties, are actually caught up in international forces about which they can do little but play around the margins. Smart demonstrates how Australian Hawke had to modify that holy of holies — party ideology's control over the Labor party — in order to deal with budget constraints traceable to an international recession. Might not Hawke's backing down from party ideology hint at what the next American president from either party's center may end up doing, namely, taking some parts of both parties' programs? The point is that when we get caught up in only a national focus on national leaders and education, we presume that the results reflect what the leaders did. Such a judgment is defective for lack of an international perspective and a sense of what other nations may be doing that is similar.

Another check on parochialism that comparative analysis provides is seen in the important role of the political party — especially one's own. The Democratic party in the 1960s may have been expanding the national role in schooling services and finances, but that was also being done by Labour and Conservative parties in the UK, and the Liberal (conservative) party in Australia even earlier (although much expanded also under Labor's Whitlam government in the mid-1970s). The Republican party of the US had many supporters happy with devolving the federal role under Reagan (detailed by Clark and Astuto), but the same was being done by a Liberal party in Australia (see Smart) which is not ideologically compatible with all policy ideas of the GOP.

In short, seeing what others elsewhere are doing in policy terms is remarkable chastening in claiming that policy change is driven by local factors.

Awareness of the Importance of Constitutional Differences

Another virtue of comparison lies in understanding that seeming similarities in political systems exist alongside vast differences which affect the policy world. Both the nations studied by this panel seem much alike in their political systems, as Levin has noted elsewhere — federal, constitutional, democratic, highly educated citizenry. But each of these attributes also differs significantly between the two nations. There is no local authority in Australian federalism to speak of, and Canberra is far more constrained in authority than is Washington. The difference made by a Bill of Rights in their constitutional systems has already been noted. Democracy in Australia means a dominant role given to party government at all levels, citizens must vote or else be fined, elections can be called at any time, one votes much more for a prime ministerial candidate than the local parliamentary member, and so on.

These differences make for policy differences that need be analyzed in comparative studies. Returning again to the Bill of Rights difference, and as Levin shows clearly, we see the variety of freedom and justice in education that it provides. Birch shows how the high court's reluctance to amplify the meaning of freedom fitted its constitutional founders' basic political judgment of how little the states wanted a strong Canberra. The American case has a great potential for nationalizing the protection of freedom and justice, while the Australian case has a potential for devolving such protection to where political power has always rested — the states.

The Eddies of International and National Forces

Such differences must nevertheless respond to new ideas and conditions arising among local elites and the general public, as well as to transnational factors. Transnational influences increasingly become a stimulus to those local policy ideas. Look at the parallel searches among nations for budget-cutting in education after the 1973 oil crisis. It is as if the currents surge through the global village, setting off eddies in each hut. Each nation in a village seems a discrete unit in itself, with its own family and functions. But in the global village, these national huts must respond together in facing dangers that spring from the outside jungle.

In summary, the chapters in this section all touch on common elements of this global village concept. Each nation seems a hut, feeling separate but actually responsive to outside forces sharing common ideas and strategies in their separate responses, and — quite often — thinking that only their hut is under attack. Together the chapters remind us of the continuing wisdom of

John Donne's insight: 'No man is an Island, entire of itself; every man is a piece of the Continent.' And 'a piece' of the global village.

References

INGLEHART, R. (1977). *The Silent Revolution.* Princeton, N.J. Princeton University Press.

WILKINS, R. (1986) 'Gaining insights from foreign studies: A catechism for review', *Educational Management and Administration*, 4, pp. 49–59.

WIRT, F. and HARMAN, G. (Eds) (1986). *Education, Recession, and the World Village,* Lewes, England, Falmer Press.

Part 2
Public and Private Schools

7 The Hawke Labor Government and Public-Private School Funding Policies in Australia, 1983–1986

Don Smart

Undoubtedly two of the most unexpected education policy shifts attributable to the Hawke Labor government have been its somersaulting to a position of support for Federal aid to the so-called 'wealthy private schools' and its significant downgrading of the role of the Labor-created (and equity-inspired) Commonwealth Schools Commission.[1] How could a socialist Labor government traditionally committed to a redistributionist and reformist platform adopt such policies? This chapter explores the often conservative and pragmatic policies adopted in the schools area by the Hawke government and seeks to explain the economic, social and political factors underlying them.

Introduction: The Political Context of Hawke

Education policy under the Hawke Labor (ALP) government from 1983–1986 has frequently been characterized by paradox and contradiction. The strong reformist commitment to education and equality of opportunity usually associated with Labor governments has been put under severe test by economic and electoral considerations. In the process, ALP platform and principles have, in the view of some within the party, often taken a battering at the hands of pragmatism and pressures for privatization. Characteristically, in the pursuit of a broad-based community consensus settlement on education issues — as with other major issues such as uranium, American nuclear ships and Aboriginal land rights — Hawke has been prepared to confront the ALP Caucus and challenge established party policy. In the process, he sometimes seems to be supporting policies more appropriate to his predecessor, Malcolm Fraser, and the conservative Liberal government than to a party supposedly committed to reform. For a fuller account of Hawke education policy including higher education see Smart *et al* (1986).

Such contradictions should come as no surprise to students of public policy, for education, like other areas of government policy, is locked in a complex historical web of political, economic and social relationships and understandings. This pre-existing web heavily constrains the degree of freedom which policy-makers have in seeking to reshape the amorphous and slow-moving education enterprise in new directions.

A key constraint on Hawke — as on his conservative counterparts in the UK and US — has been serious concern about the state of the economy and in particular, worry about the massive federal budget deficit (currently estimated at about US $9b). In fact, concern about the twin economic problems of the deficit and historically high youth unemployment have been dominant forces shaping (some would say distorting) the education and other policies of the Hawke government. 'Sound economic management' has been an understandable preoccupation of the Hawke government, particularly given the widespread popular perception of the previous Whitlam Government as notoriously spendthrift and economically profligate.

Internalizing the history lesson inherent in the brevity of the radical reformist Whitlam government's occupancy of the Treasury benches, Hawke's approach has been to go cautiously and occupy the middle-ground of Australian politics. Thus Hawke's inclination is generally to eschew traditional left-wing Labor ideology in favour of pragmatism and to show a strong preference for a consensual approach to decision-making. Nowhere has this been more evident than in the sensitive policy areas of funding for 'wealthy' private schools and the proposed reintroduction of tertiary tuition fees. On both these issues, having initially argued for a policy preference consistent with its ideological opposition to social and financial privilege, the government (or in the case of fees, more correctly Hawke, Finance Minister Peter Walsh, and several other powerful Cabinet members) pragmatically sized up the mounting political costs of pursuing such policies and then — at least temporarily — deferred to well-organized vested interests.

This chapter will focus its attention on four key related schools policy developments which have occurred under Hawke: the so-called 'historic schools funding settlement' of 1984, the Participation and Equity Program, the highly political Quality of Education Review Committee Report, and the downgrading of the Schools Commission.

Before examining these four issues, however, let me briefly spell out the major value orientations evident in Hawke's education policy.

Value Orientations Evident in Hawke Education Policy

First, the ALP government has shown itself to be more committed to maintaining a strong federal role in education than its Fraser predecessor.

Second, this commitment is reflected in a willingness, so far, to improve or maintain levels of Federal funding in education and in a centralist approach to coordination and policy-making in relation to that Federal expenditure.

Third, the Hawke government has sought to reverse the swing of the excellence-equity pendulum. In contrast to Fraser, equity issues in education are with some notable exceptions, being given greater attention — though cynics would argue that this has been done more at the level of rhetoric than at the level of practical implementation.

Fourth, the Hawke government has adopted a more economistic view and approach to education than might have been expected. There has been a tendency to stress the vocational/competitive/technological role of education and even, on occasions, to resort to the old Fraser routine of blaming education for youth unemployment. In addition, there has been a growing Federal emphasis on accountability for the educational dollar — not just in financial input terms but a much greater insistence on evidence of educational outcomes in terms of progress and efficiency indicators.

Pressing School Issues Confronting the Hawke Government in 1983

There were two pressing school issues confronting the Hawke government when it came to power in 1983. One was the long-standing and divisive 'state aid' (aid to private schools) problem. This problem had been temporarily submerged since the creation of the generously funded Commonwealth Schools Commission under Whitlam in 1973. However, it had re-emerged during Fraser's conservative government (1975–1983) and the Hawke-led ALP opposition, in its pre-election statements in 1983 had promised to tackle the problem if elected to government. The other problem was the disturbingly low national level of student retention to Year 12 (in 1982, 64 per cent of students were leaving school without completing grade 12). This problem had a special salience for Hawke because of the potential which increasing school retention had for reducing the alarming levels of youth unemployment (25 per cent in the 16-19 age group). On assuming power in 1983, the ALP government tackled both the state aid and the school retention problems.

State Aid

The Whitlam and Fraser Legacy

In 1969, Malcolm Fraser as Federal Minister for Education in the conservative Liberal-Country Party government introduced a novel system of recurrent grants to private schools based on a standard per capita grant. By 1972, the Liberal-Country Party government had formalized this Commonwealth grant at 20 per cent of the per-pupil recurrent costs in government schools (the so-called 'nexus'). As one of its first acts on coming to power in 1972 the Whitlam government implemented ALP policy by establishing an Interim Committee of the Schools Commission (Karmel Committee) to propose a more equitable system of funding schools based on the actual financial 'needs' of individual schools (Smart, 1978). The Karmel Committee classified private schools into eight categories of need (A-H, A being the wealthiest or least 'needy') and proposed different levels of per capita funding for each category. It proposed a massive increase of almost a half billion dollars for government and private schools in 1974–75. Sympathetic to ALP redistributionist ideology, it also proposed that federal aid to the two wealthiest categories of private school (A and B) be phased out altogether over the two years 1974–75. This latter proposal was rejected by the Whitlam Cabinet in favour of immediate cessation of aid to such schools.

Naturally, this course of action was strenuously opposed by the parents and supporters of all private schools (Weller, 1977). Surprisingly, perhaps, some of the strongest opposition came from the Catholic Bishops and Catholic education hierarchy which argued forcefully that no student should be denied a basic per capita grant by virtue of parental wealth. Ultimately, when the legislation became bogged down over this issue in the Opposition-controlled Senate, the Country Party achieved a compromise with the government, part of which conceded that all students were entitled to a basic per capita grant. In retrospect, it is clear that the conflict generated during 1973 by this ALP attempt to enforce the principle of removing aid from the few very wealthy schools was counterproductive. The amount of money to be saved was relatively small and the bad feeling, media publicity and conflict generated was disproportionate to the potential gains to be achieved. Apparently lacking a sense of history in relation to this issue, the Hawke government was to duplicate this bitter episode a decade later with essentially the same outcome!

Under Fraser between 1975 and 1983, a less sympathetic attitude to the 'needs' approach saw a collapsing of the Schools Commission's eight categories of need into just three, a re-establishing of a generous 'nexus' with government school costs for even the wealthiest category of private schools, and a consequent acceleration of the total proportion of Schools Commission funds going to private schools. (The dramatic extent of the increase in private school funding is illustrated in figure 1.) By the end of the Fraser era the 24 per cent of students in private schools were receiving 56 per cent of the Schools Commission's recurrent grant budget. The explanations for this drift of Schools Commission resources to the private schools sector are complex. They are in large measure attributable to: the failure of the Schools Commission to impose maintenance-of-effort conditions on recipient private schools; to more and more lenient categorization of private schools; to the dramatic growth of new private schools and of enrolments in existing private schools as a result of sympathetic Schools Commission policies. The Catholic

Figure 1: Changes in Selected Commonwealth Budget Aggregates Between 1975-76 and 1982-83 (Real Terms)

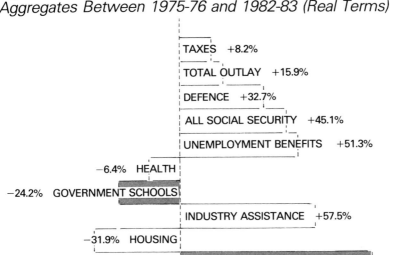

Source: Commonwealth of Australia, 1983-84 Budget Paper Number 1, p.358-63.

system, in particular, which was near collapse in 1973, underwent significant renewal and growth as a result of Schools Commission policies and support (Ryan, 1984 *Commonwealth Record,* p. 207; Praetz, 1983, p. 39; Marginson, 1985).

Initially the creation of the 'needs' oriented Schools Commission in 1973 'defused' the state aid conflict by creating a bigger cake and by promoting a consensual settlement which effectively coopted or disarmed those in public schooling who were later to oppose its implications. Initially there was more money for all. However, by the early 1980s as a result of policies which transferred a growing proportion of Schools Commission funds to the private sector, dissatisfaction amongst state school supporters re-emerged. This dissatisfaction was further fuelled by the change of Chairmanship of the Schools Commission in 1981. When the term of the original Labor-appointed Chairman, Dr Ken McKinnon, expired, Fraser did not renew his contract and instead replaced him with Dr Peter Tannock who was closely identified with the Catholic schools sector. Public school parent and teacher groups were outraged and openly referred to Tannock as the 'Commissioner for Private Schools'. In 1981 the state school parent and teacher representatives on the Schools Commission prepared a minority report condemning the Fraser government's interference with Schools Commission policy and the continued funding drift to the private schools. Opposition hardened, and in January 1982 the Australian Teachers Federation moved to a 'no state aid' position and when its member's term expired on the Schools Commission at the end of 1982 it refused to nominate a replacement.

The ALP Opposition Hardens Its Attitude to State Aid

This growing dissatisfaction amongst state school supporters was reflected in a hardening of ALP education policy. The revised 1982 Platform required 'that Commonwealth funds be available only to those non-government schools whose total private and public resources do not exceed the resources of comparable government schools'.

As the March 1983 election approached, the ALP articulated its concerns and fleshed out the specifics of its schools funding policy. In an official statement, Shadow Minister for Education, Chris Hurford, declared:

> Labor will end the unfairness of the Fraser Government's policies. They have rekindled the wasteful state aid debate by cruelly unjust appropriations of the education dollar. This has caused the resentments which are so divisive ... Labor believes that the national government should be ensuring that the scarce education dollar must go in preference to those schools with less rather than to those schools which are already above a *community standard*.

Hurford indicated, and Hawke in his policy speech confirmed, that the fifty wealthiest private schools would have their grants (then 20 per cent of government school running costs) reduced to 15 per cent in 1984 and 10 per cent in 1985. Thus, at the end of Labor's first term, whilst all private schools would still be receiving a Commonwealth grant, the wealthiest schools would be receiving considerably less and there was an implicit assumption that the grants to these schools would be phased out.

As Dawkins and Costello noted, Labor had determined 'to make a decisive move to break the log-jam' on the 'divisive state aid issue' and this was to be done by abandoning the 'nexus' and having the Schools Commission develop a community standard, 'a level of resources which the community at large will accept as necessary for children in various settings to get a high standard of schooling' (*Schools Commission,* 1983, p. 2). Once the 'community standard' was defined, wealthy schools which chose to remain outside it would be denied any aid at all (Dawkins and Costello, 1983 pp. 73–9).

The Hawke Government's 'Hit List' of Forty-one Private Schools

In July 1983, just a few months after taking office, Senator Ryan, Minister for Education, took the first decisive (though historically and strategically naive) step towards implementing this ALP policy. She announced in her guidelines to the Schools Commission that the nexus was to be abandoned and the recurrent grants of the forty-one wealthiest private schools were to be reduced by 25 per cent. The remainder of the schools in the wealthiest category (1) were to receive no increase in their grant for 1984, whereas category 2 and 3 schools were to receive increases of 1 per cent and 3 per cent respectively.) In a predictable response — almost a rerun of the 1973 conflict — the private schools sector sprang to the defence of its wealthiest members. As in 1973, the Catholic sector staunchly defended the right of wealthy non-Catholic private schools to retain their grants at existing levels and argued for the retention of the percentage-link or nexus (Hogan, 1984). As Jane Kenway (1984) has pointed out, the media fixated on this most sensational aspect of the guidelines and the wealthy schools were quickly dubbed 'victims' of Susan Ryan's 'hit list'. The fact that 90 per cent of private schools were to share an increase of $9.5m in grants for 1984 and that government schools were to receive an extra $31.4m was largely lost as attention focused on the plight of the forty-one wealthy schools.

The predictable and inevitable result, however, was that Ryan found herself in deep trouble during the latter months of 1983 as she was obliged almost daily to address large and frequently hostile gatherings of anxious private school parents across the country. For the second time in a decade, the ALP in government discovered that the wealthy private school lobby and the Catholic Bishops in combination are a formidable opposition (Kitney, 1982, p. 3). In retrospect, the $4m to be 'saved' from these forty-one 'elite' schools and redistributed was so miniscule in a Schools Commission recurrent budget of $1221.8m that it was almost laughable. Ultimately, Hawke was obliged to intervene himself. Amidst rumours that Ryan would be moved to another portfolio, Hawke joined her in the task of addressing meetings and lobby groups to reassure them that this decision was not the 'thin end of the wedge' and there was no intention to phase out aid to private schools.

Hawke Becomes More Conciliatory to Private Schools

In a further measure to quell the panic in the private schools, Ryan and her Department prepared a widely distributed booklet, reassuringly titled *Commonwealth Support for Non-Government Schools,* providing information about the government's 'policies for non-government schools in 1984 and beyond'. It explained the decision to 'break the percentage link' (nexus) and move to a 'community standard' as the only way to overcome the continuing inequalities in school resources by a more redistributive approach. However, it reassured schools that because there would be more money available, redistribution would harm few and 90 per cent of private schools would receive increased grants in 1984. That year was to be an interim year whilst the Schools Commission carefully researched and devised the 'community standard'. Hawke's intervention and the booklet were, of course, counter measures designed to restore the badly shaken confidence of the significant private school electorate and, as Ryan put it, to 'lay(ing) to rest some of the mistaken and sometimes outrageous claims which have been made about the policies of the government I represent' (*Schools Commission*, 1983, pp. 2–3).

Clearly the Government had been rocked by the extent of the reaction to its policy and by early 1984 the signs were obvious that the cautious and pragmatic government would not pursue its declared intention to 'phase out' aid to the wealthiest schools. In a speech at Geelong College in March 1984 Ryan hinted as much when she declared:

> Insofar as change may be thought desirable in the national education system, under the Hawke Government *it will be gradual and reformist, rather than abrupt and radical.* Indeed, it could hardly be otherwise, given the complexity of the questions which must be asked and answered and given our commitment to *consultation and consensus* (emphasis mine). (*Commonwealth Record*, 1984, pp. 379–81).

The Schools Commission's Report on Funding Policies

In March 1984 the Schools Commission's eagerly awaited report, *Funding Policies for Australian Schools* was released. It was later dubbed an 'historic settlement' by the *Sydney Morning Herald* (14 August 1984). This controversial document of 140 pages contained minority reports from two commissioners representing government school interests. The report detailed the 'community standard' and spelled out recurrent funding options for the Commonwealth to be examined in the context of the forthcoming 1984–85 budget deliberations.

The Report acknowledged various ministerial guidelines and objectives including: the need 'to restore the community's confidence in the government's determination to give all children access to properly staffed and equipped schools'; the desire to give 'greater weighting' to the principle of 'need'; and the need to 'have particular regard to the deep concern of the government about the extent of inequality in Australian schooling'.

At the outset too, the Report acknowledged the Commission's obligations under its Act, both to have regard to 'government's primary obligation to provide and maintain public schooling of the highest standard', and to 'have regard to the prior right of parents to choose government or non-government schools for their children'. As to the former obligation, it acknowledged that 'significant modification to present funding arrangements' would be necessary to ensure that the Commonwealth more directly supported the role of public education. As to the latter, it acknowledged the continuing public debate about the *extent* to which private schools should receive public support but asserted rather forcefully:

What cannot be denied is the entitlement of all children to resources for schooling consistent with their educational needs. This is an entitlement children enjoy in their own right, and has nothing to do with their parents' financial capacities or tax contributions.

Amongst its key recommendations, the Report proposed a 'community standard' of $2195 per primary student and $3240 per secondary student with an additional loading for government schools because of their 'different circumstances' and obligations. The report also stressed the vital need for 'a period of stability and agreement about the future direction of Commonwealth and State general resources funding'. The Hawke government was well aware of this need after the turbulent debate of the preceding eight or nine months!

Urging the government to boost confidence by providing guaranteed levels of funding for the four years 1985–1988, the Commission proposed three options for the recurrent funding of government schools. Each option was premised on an annual increase in the federal contribution and the options ranged in cost over four years from an additional $140m to $240m.[2]

For private schools, the Commission recommended a new eight- or twelve-category system of need based on the percentage of the community standard or government school standard derived from private sources by 1988. The Commission expressed its preference for a twelve-category scheme linked to the community standard. This scheme would cost the federal government an additional $106m over the four years. (The ATF has disputed the Schools Commission's estimates of costs, arguing that they are much too conservative and the real costs could be much higher.) Perhaps partly sensing the weakened resolve of the government on the issue of 'phasing out' aid to the wealthiest schools and certainly, partly reflecting the views of the commissioners representing the private sector, the report gently recommended that *all schools* be eligible for a category 1 grant.

Key Public School Commissioners Dissent from Report

Two of the key public school representatives on the Commission, Joan Brown (national parent body) and Van Davy (ATF), refused to endorse the report and submitted their own separate and highly critical minority reports. Both raised the by-now familiar accusation (in relation to the Schools Commission) that the document focused excessively on the funding needs of private schools in derogation of the Commission's 'primary obligation' to government schools (*Schools Commission,* 1984, pp. 115 and 121). They asserted that the annual increases recommended for private schools alone would put such a financial burden on the Commonwealth that it would seriously compete with the much-needed increases for government schools. Both were also highly critical of the enormous financial drain which the

Commission's recommended continuing provision for new places in private schools would incur (from $80–$100m extra over four years). They argued that this inevitably reduced the scope for government school funding and that the provision itself reflected the Commission's priority for the principle of access and choice over other key priorities including 'primary obligation to government schools' and the 'promotion of greater equality of outcomes'. Both were also critical of the concept and methodology behind the community standard and Brown urged retention instead of government school standard costs as the only appropriate yardstick.

In a departure from ATF official policy of 'no state aid', Davy proposed a compromise — a moratorium on *additional* Federal expenditure for private schools, with no new places to be funded and maintenance of private effort to be conditions for continued funding. In the final section of his minority report, Davy condemned the flimsiness of the methodology underlying the 'community (target) standard' and severely criticized the nature of the Commission's inquiry process:

> The procedures and the time-line have been most unsatisfactory resulting in a report that will do nothing to generate confidence in and support for the Schools Commission from those serving the government schools.

In spite of this, however, the majority view in the report gave the Hawke Government the justification for reversing or halting the 'phase-out' to wealthy schools should it decide that pragmatism and consensus argued for such an approach.

The 1984 ALP Conference Confirms 'Phase-Out' Policy

With only a month to go before the government was to announce its decisions on school funding, the July 1984 ALP Biennial Conference — the supreme policy-making body of the ALP whose decisions are technically binding on ALP politicians — in Canberra threw an obstacle (albeit not insurmountable) in the path of what might otherwise have been a smooth policy reversal. At that conference, a series of reformist resolutions were moved and passed which reflected the prevailing 'pro-government school' mood of the party. The most salient of these resolutions called upon the Federal Government 'to continue to phase out all funding support for the most wealthy private schools ... and redirect these funds to government and non-government schools on the basis of need'. The conference also recommended that an additional $260m of recurrent funds be provided by the federal government for government schools by 1986. Ironically, the Federal Minister for Education, Susan Ryan, was one of the prime movers in the adoption of these policies at the conference (ALP Biennial Conference, Canberra, July 1984, Education Resolution No 3 — see Ramsay, 1984).

Hawke and Ryan Reject 'Phase-Out' and Opt for Consensus

On 14 August 1984 the Government announced its new funding policy for schools. Both Hawke and Ryan took great pains to describe it as an historic settlement designed to 'take off the political agenda of the 1980s the tired old state aid rhetoric of the 1960s' (Ryan, 1984a). On close analysis, it is revealed to be an extremely generous funding policy, pragmatically designed to defuse the state aid debate and ensure consensus by making more money available for virtually all schools and simultaneously giving long-term stability by promising legislation guaranteeing levels of funding for four years (see tables 1 and 2).

The Schools Commission's 'twelve-category option' and 'community standard' was endorsed as was the recommendation that all schools receive aid. The wealthiest schools categories (1 and 2) were guaranteed their existing money grants would be maintained *in real terms* though without the real increases applying to schools in all other categories. Government schools were to be given a real increase in Commonwealth funds of 50 per cent

Table 1: Commonwealth General Recurrent Grants for Non-Government Schools 1985–1992

Category	1985 $	1986 $	1987 $	1988 $	1989 $	1990 $	1991 $	1992 $
Primary								
1	277	277	277	277	277	277	277	277
2	370	370	370	370	370	370	370	370
3	378	387	398	414	431	449	455	460
4	559	559	559	559	559	559	559	559
5	565	574	584	603	619	631	640	644
6	571	586	606	631	661	692	704	712
7	576	598	627	666	708	752	772	781
8	768	779	792	811	828	843	848	850
9	771	786	808	834	859	880	890	896
10	774	796	824	857	892	919	935	942
11	777	804	840	881	923	960	980	988
12	781	812	855	906	956	999	1024	1034
Secondary								
1	440	440	440	440	440	440	440	440
2	586	586	586	586	586	586	586	586
3	594	602	613	631	649	667	674	678
4	889	889	889	889	889	889	889	889
5	893	898	906	918	930	940	946	950
6	901	917	938	968	1001	1032	1046	1051
7	909	936	973	1021	1070	1120	1143	1154
8	1211	1218	1226	1234	1243	1249	1253	1255
9	1216	1231	1251	1272	1294	1312	1319	1323
10	1222	1246	1277	1311	1345	1372	1385	1390
11	1227	1258	1297	1344	1392	1429	1450	1458
12	1232	1269	1319	1379	1436	1482	1514	1526

Source: Commonwealth Schools Commission Report for 1986, pp. 9–10.

over eight years — as contrasted with a real decrease of 1.9 per cent during the seven years of the Fraser government.

Many ALP Supporters Feel 'Betrayed'

Naturally this consensus solution was seen as the sacrificing of long-term ALP principles for short-term electoral pragmatism by many ALP members and public school supporters. Thus an ATF Research Paper described it in the following terms:

> It is hard to capture in words the sense of outrage and betrayal amongst government school teachers and parents following the release of the federal govenment's guidelines for schools funding on 14 August this year.
>
> In one stroke the Hawke government silenced the militant minority opposition of the private school supporters by giving them everything they wanted, stroked the captains of industry with a promise that education would be brought into line with their needs, guaranteed the fiscal 'rationalists' that there would be no Whitlamite expansion of education funding (except to private schools), soothed the 'back to basics' lobby by adopting their rhetoric and reassured all

Table 2: Commonwealth Allocations for Schools, 1986

1986 National Allocations
Commonwealth General Resource Programs for Schools
(expressed in estimated December 1984 prices)

	1985 ($'000)	1986 ($'000)
GOVERNMENT PROGRAMS		
General Recurrent (a)	354 414	373 740
Capital	165 501	150 890
NON-GOVERNMENT PROGRAMS		
General Recurrent (b)	660 947	671 074
Short Term Emergency Assistance	643	643
Capital (c)	59 727	54 406
TOTAL	1 241 232	1 250 753

(a) As this program operates on a per capita basis, final costs will be subject to actual enrolments each year.

(b) Based on latest available year's actual enrolments (1984); final payments are dependent on actual enrolments for 1985 and 1986, the distribution of increased enrolments among the funding categories, the outcome of appeals by schools against their funding categories and the number of new schools to quality for Commonwealth per capita and establishment grants; based on projected enrolments, total costs are estimated at an additional $13m–$15m in 1985 and $25m–$27m in 1986.

(c) Includes amount to be transferred from Department of Community Services in 1986. An amount has also been included in 1985 for reasons of comparison.

National Allocations 1986
Commonwealth General Resource Programs for Schools
(expressed in estimated December 1984 prices)

	1985 ($'000)	1986 ($'000)
GOVERNMENT PROGRAMS		
Primary Basic Learning	5 549	5 549
Participation & Equity	40 698	20 349
Computer Education	5 251	5 251
English as a Second Language		
— General Support	42 458	40 855
— New Arrivals (a)	10 004	10 004
Disadvantaged Schools	30 034	30 034
Special Education		
— Recurrent	18 845	18 072
— Integration	1 419	1 361
Early Special Education	1 668	1 668
NON-GOVERNMENT PROGRAMS		
Primary Basic Learning	1 466	1 466
Participation & Equity	4 768	2 384
Computer Education	1 313	1 313
English as a Second Language		
— General Support	17 958	17 084
— New Arrivals (a)	1 070	1 070
Disadvantaged Schools	5 833	5 833
Special Education		
— Recurrent	4 819	4 621
— Integration	407	390
— Support Services (b)	13 000	12 467
Early Special Education	426	426
JOINT PROGRAMS		
Participation & Equity	1 701	850
Early Special Education	1 780	1 780
Multicultural Education	4 975	4 771
Ethnic Schools (a)	5 037	5 037
Country Areas	10 228	9 809
Children in Residential Institutions	2 289	2 289
Severely Handicapped Children	3 738	3 738
Professional Development	11 301	11 301
Education Centres	2 393	2 393
Projects of National Significance	1 818	1 818
TOTAL	252 246	223 983

(a) As these programs operate on a per capita basis, final costs will be subject to actual enrolments each year.

(b) Amount to be transferred from Department of Community Services in 1986. An amount has also been included in 1985 for reasons of comparison.

Source: Commonwealth Schools Commission Report for 1986, p. 57.

those who fear the teacher unions with a very public declaration of
the government's intention to shut the unions out of any influence
over education policy.

It was a spectacular conservative coup. Hawke had become
Fraser, only this time there was no alternative waiting in the wings.

Given the finely-tuned electoral pragmatism and neo-
conservative economics of the Hawke Government, these outcomes
in retrospect look less surprising. (Marginson, 1984).

Ryan's speech to the National Press Club of 15 August 1984 confirms the
impression of a Minister and a government extremely anxious to find a
compromise and willing to spend their way out of trouble.

... This package of decisions means that there is no legitimate way
in which the State aid debate can be pursued, and that a real basis for
consensus in schools funding has been achieved... Too much of the
government's time has been taken up with arguments about dollars.

It was not only the ALP ideologues who felt this solution smacked of
expediency. For example, the widely respected political commentator, Alan
Ramsay (1984) was cutting in his criticism of Ryan's speech and the turnabout:

Thus the government that seventeen months ago pledged its primary
obligation to the state school system, and built its education policy
on the priority of money for the neediest, will now enshrine financial
support for even the wealthiest private schools in the statutes.

Participation and Equity in Schools

The sense of betrayal felt by some public school supporters over the Hawke
'historic settlement' in the school funding arena should not be permitted to
obscure the efforts made by the mildly reformist Hawke government to
implement ALP platform in relation to enhancing access to and participation
in education at all levels.

Perhaps the single education program which best captures the long-term
educational goals and ideals of the ALP is the so-called PEP program. During
1983, Ryan said of PEP:

The new program ... will be the centrepiece of the overall
framework of youth policies ... The program will have the twin
objectives of increasing participation in education and introducing
greater equity in the government's overall provision for young
people ...

Government wishes to achieve a situation where, by the end of
this decade, most young people complete the equivalent of a full

secondary education, either in school or in a TAFE institution, or in some combination of work and education. (CPD, Senate, 25 August · 1983, pp. 240–1).

However, it would be wrong to see this program as a unique ALP innovation, evolving neatly from pre-existing ALP education policy which, rooted in the Walker (1944) and Karmel Reports (1973), has had a long-standing concern with the issue of equality of educational opportunity. Rather, it is an amalgam of ALP educational idealism with elements of existing Fraser government policies[3] and the pragmatism of Hawke, responding swiftly to the unprecedentedly high levels of youth unemployment confronting the incoming government. This was linked to a desire to 'correct' simultaneously Australia's remarkably low secondary school retention and completion rates (only 36 per cent of students were completing grade 12 in 1982) and increase participation in post-compulsory education.

However, the largely instrumental nature of the catalyst for PEP should not detract from the government's clear commitment to placing a high priority on the educational and employment needs of young people and its 'recognition of their significance in national recovery and reconstruction'. Right from day one, the Hawke government set in train a number of initiatives to promote a more coordinated approach to the area of youth policy. The recent Priority One and Youth Traineeships programs and the Kirby Report on Labour Market Programs are all testament to a strong concern for youth.

The government allocated $74m for PEP in 1984, all but $4m of which was for government educational institutions including TAFE and the universities and colleges. Most of it was to be targeted at the approximately 40 per cent of schools with the lowest retention rates and to be used to reduce the number of students who leave school prematurely by seeking to stimulate broadly based changes in secondary education (Commonwealth Schools Commission, 1984, p. 1).

The Apparent Success of PEP

Probably through a combination of fortuitous circumstances and sound policy the outcome for the Hawke Government has been remarkably satisfying. Partly through a firming trend in school retention rates which preceded PEP and partly through the PEP strategy, national retention rates through grade 12 have climbed dramatically from around 35 per cent in 1982 to 45 per cent in 1984 and probably around 50 per cent in 1985 (Schools Commission, 1985). The apparent combined effects of Hawke economic strategy as well as secondary and tertiary PEP were also gratifying. In the first two years of the Hawke government, unemployment in the 15–24 age group fell by 76,000 whilst the number in the same age cohort participating in full-time post-compulsory (age 16+) education rose by 56,000. According to the Chairman of the Commonwealth Tertiary Education Commission: 'it is clear that the expansion in education has been a more important factor in reducing unemployment of young people than has improvement in economic activity' (Hudson, 1985, p. 49). A recent federal government committee optimistically predicted that the bulk of Australia's youth unemployment might be eliminated by 1992 through a combination of continued expansion of full-time education opportunities and the introduction of a new federal youth traineeship scheme (QERC, 1985).

Criticisms of PEP

Despite these statistics, PEP is not without its critics. This is partly, no doubt, because PEP highlights a central dilemma for Australian secondary schools in the 1980s — how to balance the demand for a uniform academic curriculum against the need to provide for new types of non-tertiary-bound students. The NSW Teachers Federation has criticized PEP for lacking direction and failing to analyze the needs of students. As a consequence, it argues, schools are taking the 'soft options' approach and providing non-academic students with 'bread and circuses' whilst they spend their final school years avoiding the dole queues (Dawson, 1985). Max Charlesworth, the Liberal Catholic philosopher summed up the growing anxieties about PEP in other quarters:

> Paradoxically, in the name of helping under-privileged youth, a dual system of education is being set up, which in effect perpetuates the structure of privilege in our society, a structure in which knowledge and power remain in the hands of the few (quoted in Smart *et al*, 1986).

In a surprise move too, in the May 1985 mini-budget, the Hawke government provided a further source of disenchantment to its reformists when it slashed the schools PEP budget by $23m — or 50 per cent (*Schools Commission Report for 1986*, Canberra, September 1985).

Quality of Education Review Committee

The emergence of the Quality of Education Review Committee (QERC) was consistent with the trend in other western countries including the US and UK. As Scott (1986) has noted, economic difficulties have increasingly led western governments of both the left and the right to 'perceive their education systems as predominantly aimed towards producing an internationally competitive workforce'. Two overriding concerns were responsible for the emergence of QERC and dominated its terms of reference — establishing 'value for money' from federal expenditure (whilst simultaneously 'putting the lid' on federal spending on schools) and gearing the education system more closely to labour market needs (Smart *et al*, 1986).

Undoubtedly, widespread community concern about educational standards and the enormity of the Federal deficit were mutually reinforcing pressures which pushed the Hawke Cabinet in what might have been considered an unusual direction for a Labor government. QERC appears to have been 'forced' on the Minister for Education as a result of 'intervention' by senior econocrats in the Departments of Finance and Prime Minister and Cabinet. In their review of the Education Department's 1984 pre-Budget submission, the bureaucrats demanded evidence that the massive increase in federal per pupil expenditure (50 per cent between 1973 and 1983) had improved the quality of education. Thus, unlike the Karmel Report of 1973 which was primarily concerned with financial and educational *inputs,* QERC was required to establish that there were identifiable educational *outcomes* from federal aid. It appears likely that the Minister for Education was virtually obliged by Cabinet to agree to this inquiry as a precondition to Cabinet approving the expensive 'historic settlement' schools funding package (Smart *et al*, 1986).

Given that it was to enquire only into the schools sector, the membership of the Committee raised some eyebrows. The members were Professor Peter Karmel (Vice-Chancellor of the Australian National University) as Chairman, Hugh Hudson (Chairman of Commonwealth Tertiary Education Commission), Dr Barry McGaw (Director of Australian Council for Educational Research, recently resigned as Professor of Education at Murdoch University), Mr Peter Kirby (Assistant Director General of Employment and Training in Victoria) and (later) Ms Helen Williams (then Deputy Secretary of the Commonwealth Department of Education, later Secretary). The ATF and State Directors-General of Education unsuccessfully sought membership of the Committee, arguing that it was dominated by unsympathetic tertiary educators and Commonwealth bureaucrats. It is also noteworthy that no member of the Schools Commission was appointed, for implicit in QERC's establishment was the government's concern to evaluate the role of the Schools Commission itself. As we shall see, QERC's creation may well have been from the outset part of a wider strategy to downgrade the role of the Schools Commission. Even if no such strategy existed, certainly QERC was to have that effect.

Predictably, perhaps, QERC was unable to come up with conclusive measures or evidence of the beneficial effects of massive Federal aid between 1973–1984. However, its 'impressions' were that schools had 'produced results superior to those which would otherwise have been the case'. Whilst essentially supportive of continued federal aid to schools, QERC's major recommendations emphasized the need in future to devise better means for agreeing on the goals to be achieved and monitoring and gauging the educational outcomes. Thus it recommended:

- future recurrent grants should be based on 'negotiated agreements' between the Commonwealth and the other parties (state governments and non-government education authorities) which declared priority areas (for example, basic skills, disadvantaged students, etc);
- triennial accountability statements describing changes in prescribed educational indicators relating to the priority areas (for example, levels of attainment in general skills, post-compulsory education participation rates by socioeconomic class/gender/rural-urban location, etc);
- reducing the number of existing specific purpose (categorical) programs and tightening up the reporting requirements associated with these.

Whilst the federal government was quick to endorse QERC, there has been limited progress towards implementation — for neither the State Education Departments, nor the private schools, nor the Commonwealth's own Schools Commission have been very enthusiastic about the proposed 'negotiated agreements' and 'accountability statements' with their heavy emphasis on evaluation indicators. The state departments, in particular, have expressed unwillingness to jump through inconvenient 'Commonwealth hoops' for the sake of relatively minor funds which constitute only 7 per cent of their total recurrent schools expenditure.

The views of the NSW Education Minister are probably fairly representative:

> QERC is less concerned with quality and standards of attainment than with justifying a transfer of funds from schools which cater for all comers (public) to schools which cater for particular sections of the population (private) and to tertiary institutions. It is also an attempt to dictate to the states what their priorities and policies for education should be ... I regard this as a direct attack on the constitutional responsibilities of the states. (quoted in Scott, 1986)

In the final analysis, I find myself very much in agreement with Scott's (1986) assessment of QERC:

> The origins of QERC, arising as it did out of Cabinet discord over education spending, the 'value for money' thrust of the Committee's terms of reference, and the extraordinary speed with which it operated, all tend to lend credence to the view that the intention behind establishing the Committee was the result more of financial than educational considerations.

Just one month after the release of the QERC Report, the Treasurer's May mini-budget carved $48.2m off the Schools Commission's total $1,474b budget for 1986 — a net reduction in real terms of 1.3 per cent on 1985.

Ironically, public schools suffered the brunt of the cuts (2.7 per cent reduction) whilst private schools achieved a 1 per cent increase (Schools Commission Report for 1986).

QERC was clearly a highly political exercise which was as much about keeping the lid on future schools spending and justifying a shift in emphasis to the funding needs of the tertiary education sector as it was about educational standards. Furthermore, it became a vehicle for assisting in the downgrading of the Schools Commission's previously central role in school funding and policy determination.

Shifting Priorities and Power in Canberra: The Emasculation of the Schools Commission

During the Hawke government's first three years of office a significant shift of bureaucratic power and influence has been occurring. Gradually, a somewhat vulnerable and relatively uninfluential Department of Education has been strengthening its power and influence with the Minister — partly through changes in its leadership and partly through expansion of personnel and budget at the expense of the Schools Commission and Department of Aboriginal Affairs. Simultaneously, the Commonwealth Tertiary Education Commission — partly through the political skills of its new Chairman, Hugh Hudson, and partly through the increasingly obvious signs of neglect in the tertiary sector — has climbed to prominence as a key advisor to the Federal Education Minister and Cabinet.

The ascendancy of the Department was undoubtedly assisted by the rising prominence of its new Permanent Head, Helen Williams, during a period of hiatus and vulnerability in the Schools Commission's leadership. Dr Peter Tannock resigned at the end of 1984, leaving the Commission's leadership in limbo. Despite being a Fraser appointee and being labelled by many public school supporters as primarily a private school sympathizer, Tannock was an able bureaucrat who competently defended the Schools Commission's turf. Once he left, the knives were out. During the first half of 1985, whilst a new Chairman was being sought, QERC and a Public Service Board Review were instrumental in ensuring that Cabinet would agree to the transferring of the Schools Commission's two key programs — together with their billion dollar budget — and almost half of its staff to the Department of Education. By the time the new Chairman, Garth Boomer — a curriculum, rather than policy, specialist — was in place, the Schools Commission was clearly destined for a significantly downgraded role. Ostensibly freed from major program administration so that it could play an 'enhanced policy advice' role, the Commission is looking increasingly as though its main function will, in fact, be to run a Curriculum Development Centre.

The Shadow Minister for Education, Senator Peter Baume, alleged that Senator Ryan had been single-minded in her determination to 'gut' the Commission and predicted that, deprived of its database, it will become a powerless advisory body whose advice will be ignored as irrelevant to the implementation process (*Canberra Times,* 10 July 1985).

In July 1985, a union survey revealed massive alienation among Schools Commission staff as a result of chronic understaffing and organizational uncertainty:

> The constant movement of people out of the Commission, the internal changes necessary to meet workloads ... has resulted in staffing instability for the programs administered by the Commission. There is a serious morale problem as staff at all levels attempt to carry out complex administrative tasks ... while under pressure to provide policy advice as well (*Sydney Morning Herald,* 17 July 1985).

It is difficult to avoid the conclusion that the Labor government has deliberately emasculated the Schools Commission. Perhaps concluding that the Commission had become too oriented towards the private schools and too difficult to control, Cabinet decided to pull more financial and policy responsibility back into the hands of the ministerially-controlled Department — a decision which coincided nicely with the territorial imperatives of a Department striving to justify its own continued existence.

Conclusion

Under the radical reformist Whitlam ALP government from 1972–1975, education was viewed as a central instrument for making society more equal and for promoting social reform. However, between the early 1970s and the early 1980s the western world underwent a severe economic recession and an accompanying pendulum swing from fairly liberal to much more conservative social, political and economic values and attitudes. The education policies of Reagan, Thatcher and Fraser reflected that pendulum swing. When the Hawke Labor government came to power in 1983, whilst some of the educational rhetoric of the Whitlam era remained in Labor's platform, the reformist zeal and the determination to use education as an engine of social reform had largely evaporated. Under Hawke, Labor has become a much more cautious party of the middle ground. The politics of electoral pragmatism and consensus have largely replaced the politics of idealism and reform. Anxiety about the budget deficit has ensured that 'sound economic management' has remained the predominant priority and largely pushed social and educational redistributionist policies into the background. As a result, the major determinants of education policy have been economic rather than ideological.

During the latter half of 1985 a number of respected and influential ALP elder statesmen dating from the Whitlam era (including Hayden, McLelland and Whitlam) began warning the Hawke Government about the dangers of losing sight of its traditional Labor goals and philosophy in its desperation to win acceptance by big business and the advocates of privatization. McLelland warned the Party:

> If the only reason you're in politics is to stay in office you're not going to be making much difference to the obvious inequities in society (*Weekend Australian*, 13–14 July 1985).

The Hawke 'scoreboard' in educational reform to date suggests that the Party is pre-occupied with staying in office. Nevertheless, its reading of the conservatism of the electorate is an essentially accurate one and its pragmatic and consensual policies are totally understandable, if not acceptable to the ideologically pure within the ALP.

Notes

1 For the benefit of American readers the following Australian terminology needs explanation: the federal government and the Commonwealth (government) are synonymous; private schools are also commonly referred to as independent or non-government schools.
2 Option 1 would result in the Commonwealth reaching a target of contributing 10 per cent of the community standard by 1988. Option 2 would result in the Commonwealth meeting a constant 8 per cent of the community standard. Option 3 would involve an annual 10 per cent increase in Commonwealth contribution over the four years.
3 See for example Commonwealth Tertiary Education Commission (1982) *Learning and Earning: A Study of Education and Employment Opportunities for Young People*, Canberra, AGPS. This report was prepared for the Fraser government and recommended PEP-type solutions.

References

COMMONWEALTH SCHOOLS COMMISSION (1984) *Participation and Equity in Australian Schools — The Goal of Full Secondary Education*, Canberra, Commonwealth Schools Commission.

COMMONWEALTH TERTIARY EDUCATION COMMISSION (1982) *Learning and Earning: A Study of Education and Employment Opportunities for Young People*, Canberra, Commonwealth Tertiary Education Commission, AGPS.

DAWKINS, J. and COSTELLO, R. (1983) 'Education progress and equality' in REEVES, J. and THOMPSON, K. (Eds), *Labor Essays 1983: Policies and Programs for the Labor Government*, Melbourne, Drummond.

DAWSON, C. (1985) 'Government under fire as PEP starts to flag', *The Australian*, 6 February.

HOGAN, M. (1984) *Public Versus Private Schools*, Ringwood, Penguin.

HUDSON, H. (1985) 'Economic and political change — Its implications for tertiary education', *The Australian TAFE Teacher*, November.

KENWAY, J. (1984) 'Ideology, the media and private schooling — The year of the "Hit List"', paper delivered at the Australian Association for Research in Education conference, Perth, November.

KITNEY, G. (1982) 'Dawkins stakes future on rolling private schools', *National Times*, 7–13 November.

MARGINSON, S. (1984) 'The schools guidelines: Hawke in Fraser's clothing', *ATF Research Notes*, 2, 6 September.

MARGINSON, S. (1985) 'The collapse of the 1973 Karmel consensus', *AFT Research Papers*, 9, 15, December.

PRAETZ, H. (1983) 'The non-government schools' in BROWN, R.K. and FOSTER, L.E. (Eds), *Sociology of Education,* Melbourne.

QERC (1985) *Report of the Quality of Education Review Committee,* (Chairman Prof P.H. Karmel), Canberra, AGPS.

RAMSAY, A. (1984) 'The turnabout of a state-aid advocate', *National Times*, 24 August.

RYAN, S. (1984a) Statement by the Minister of Education to Parliament, 14 August.

RYAN, S. (1984b) Address to the National Press Club, 15 August 1984.

SCHOOLS COMMISSION (1983) *Commonwealth Support for Non-Government Schools* Canberra, Schools Commission.

SCHOOLS COMMISSION (1984) *Funding Policies for Australian Schools* Canberra, Schools Commission.

SCHOOLS COMMISSION (1985) *Quality and Equality* Canberra, Schools Commission.

SMART, D. (1978) *Federal Aid to Australian Schools,* St Lucia, University of Queensland Press.

SMART, D. *et al* (1986) 'The Hawke government and education 1983–1985', *Politics,* 21, 1, May, pp. 63–81.

WELLER, P. (1977) 'The establishment of the Schools Commission: A case study of the politics of education' in BIRCH, I.K.F. and SMART, D. (Eds), *The Commonwealth Government and Education 1964–1976*, Drummond, Melbourne.

8 Balancing Public and Private Schools: The Australian Experience and American Implications

William Lowe Boyd

The growing demands for excellence, diversity, and choice in American education have raised with renewed vigor a perennial issue of educational policy: Should private schools receive public funds and, if so, on what basis? The American tradition, bolstered by our Supreme Court's interpretation of the Constitution's provision on the separation of church and state, has been to bar the use of public funds by non-government schools. But, as many critics point out, most democratic nations have not found it necessary to take such a strict stand on this issue.

Among the nations that demonstrate this point, Australia in particular stands out. Indeed, it has been proposed as a success story, a model for how the United States might undertake public funding of private schools (Doyle, 1984; Finn, 1985; Sherman, 1982 and 1983). Unfortunately, the reporting on this subject has glossed over some significant problems. Along with the successful features of the Australian approach go some disturbing features that constitute the subject of this chapter. A consideration of both sets of features suggests, at the least, that Americans should be cautious about emulating the Australian model. More broadly, cross-national research shows that a delicate balance in public policy must be struck if there is to be parity of esteem between public and private schools and equality of opportunity as well as excellence and choice in education.

The Australian Experience

As an example for Americans, Australia stands out because, beyond being an English-speaking democracy with numerous cultural similarities to the United States (like Canada), it even has a Constitution consciously patterned in many respects after the American model. Yet, in a dramatic departure from the American experience, Australia's nearly identical constitutional language on the separation of church and state has been interpreted to permit state aid to sectarian schools. In the celebrated DOGS (Defenders of Government Schools) case the nation's High Court ruled, in 1981, that so long as public monies are distributed even-handedly, rather than for the purpose of creating one state-sponsored religion, there is no breach of the Australian Constitution (Sherman, 1983). This ruling, along with the breadth, minimal regulations, and apparent social acceptance of federal aid to private schools in Australia, has made it a favorite example for American proponents of educational choice, tuition tax credits, and educational voucher plans (for example, Doyle, 1984; Finn, 1985).

Although there are many similarities between Australia and the United States there also are striking differences (West, 1983). For instance, the educational traditions of the two nations are quite different. American visitors are struck by the legacy in Australia of the British dual-system of education: elite private schools for a few and government schools for the masses. Although this British legacy has been tempered by Australia's commitment to equality of opportunity, restrictive arrangements for entry into higher (tertiary) education — combined with free tuition upon admission — reinforce the perceived advantages of the grooming provided by elite private schools. However, the fundamental political basis for public funding of private schools comes not from the elite school sector but from a third important sector: the Catholic schools, most of which are not elite in admissions, fees, or resources.

In 1971, Catholics constituted 27 per cent of Australia's population, a segment of the electorate that politicians must respect.[1] The distribution of students among the three sectors of schools in 1970 was 17.8 per cent in Catholic schools, 4.1 per cent in non-Catholic private schools, and 78.2 per cent in government schools. Since the level of state aid increased in the mid-1970s, the trend has been for the non-government school enrolment to increase. Thus, by 1982 the figures were 18.3 per cent in Catholic schools, 5.5 per cent in non-Catholic private schools, and 76.2 per cent in government schools.[2]

Like many countries, Australia initially relied on schools provided by church groups.[3] In 1872, however, the Colonial parliaments passed legislation making education 'free, compulsory, and secular' and, at the same time, abolishing the financing of religious schools. This arrangement continued until 1952, when a law was passed allowing small tax deductions for schools fees. Then, in 1964, at a time when the Catholic schools were in severe financial straits, Prime Minister Menzies introduced a program of more substantial state aid. Initially, it consisted of a modest federal program of grants to public and private schools for science buildings and equipment.

Sherman (1982), who sees in the Australian experience a recipe for how to introduce state aid for private schools in the US, glosses over the controversy which ensued in Australia.[4] He reports that, 'With the initiation of aid ... public hostility to government aid gradually dissipated. Once in place, aid programs tended to be accepted by the community at large, if not by the established educational interest groups' (p. 397). West (1983, p. 414) sharply disagrees with Sherman's assessment, noting that the Defense of Government Schools lobbying group was formed as a result of the initiation of aid. Similarly, Hogan (1984, p. 3) reports that, 'For the rest of the 1960s the conflict over education funding at the Commonwealth and state levels was the most important domestic issue in Australian politics. Only Vietnam rivalled the issue of "state aid" for media attention and in its divisive social effects.'

Sherman is correct, though, about the general acceptance of state aid in the long run. As time went on, the government began to contribute substantially to the recurrent (operating) costs as well as capital costs of private schools. The expansion of state aid continued in the 1970s under both the Whitlam Labor government and the succeeding Fraser Liberal government. This trend was less controversial while the economy was strong, budgets were expanding, and support appeared to be concentrated on impoverished (mainly Catholic) private schools. To the dismay of public educators in Australia, however, by the end of the 1970s the private school share of federal aid exceeded the government school share and was increasingly available to elite 'establishment' schools (Sherman, 1982). Moreover, there was some perception that federal aid was helping non-government schools expand and increase their enrollments at a time when government schools were confronted with a shrinking total pool of students.[5] It was no coincidence, therefore, that the legal challenge to the constitutionality of this arrangement was brought at this time, and that in 1981 'for the first time in the history of the [Commonwealth] Schools Commission, the parent and teacher representatives on the commission filed a minority report, dissenting from the commission's recommendations on aid to the two school sectors' (Sherman, 1982, pp. 400-1).

The Commonwealth Schools Commission had been established in 1973 by the Whitlam government to provide a mechanism for forging national education policy. That same year the Karmel Report defined the terms for the Commission's initial effort at financing non-government schools on the basis of their *wealth* and *needs*. As Hogan (1984) observes:

> The terms of the modern debate were set by the Karmel Report in 1973. It is not whether there is to be aid for private schools, but how much, in what kinds of ways, according to what principles, and for what purposes? Consequently the main protagonists can be redefined according to their attitude to the Karmel values. Defenders of public schools tend to accept the needs principle whereby some schools get more government money while others get less or even none. Sup-

porters of private schools tend to see the needs principle as a threat and consequently they argue for a stricter equality of treatment by governments in their funding decisions. (p. 24)

The great success of the Australian approach to funding private schools thus is the establishment of principles for the financial maintenance of educational choice combined with a concern for equalizing educational opportunity via a needs-based funding approach. This approach ensures alternatives to the government schools for those who desire a particular religious education or who object to the educational philosophy, methods, or secularism of government schools. In the latter regard, for instance, many non-Catholic immigrant groups tend to prefer the Catholic schools to the government schools.

The great defect of the Australian approach is that, despite the needs-based principle, in practice significant portions of state aid nevertheless continue to subsidize and encourage an elitist sorting dynamic. This dynamic creams off upper-middle class students and weakens the government schools which still must serve three-quarters of the student population. Thus, at the heart of the continuing tensions over state aid to private schools in Australia are divisive issues of social class, privilege, and elitism versus social justice and the maintenance of quality schools for the masses (Hogan, 1984; West, 1983).

Visitors from North America are surprised by the robust and remarkably extensive array of elite private schools in Australia and even more by the fact that these schools, despite their frequent wealth and 'posh' facilities, receive generous amounts of federal funding. Indeed, not a few Australians also are surprised and perplexed by this established, but still controversial, fact. Even though there is wide acceptance of the principle of state aid for private schools, many Australians wonder why wealthy private schools should receive substantial aid so long as numerous government schools have less than ideal educational arrangements and facilities (Hogan, 1984; West, 1983). What compelling public purposes justify this policy? The answer seems to be that there are no compelling public purposes, only compelling political reasons for this policy.

In 1983, when a new Labor government in Canberra proposed to end recurrent funding for forty-one wealthy private schools around the nation, this triggered a major and successful protest from the upper-middle class patrons of elite schools (Hogan, 1984). For example, over 5000 attended a protest meeting held at Sydney Town Hall. Though no Catholic schools were on the government's 'hit list', Catholic leaders, fearing that their schools might be next to be hit, joined forces with those demanding a continuation of recurrent funding for the elite schools. Commenting on the influence of the upper-middle class, Hogan (1984) observes that:

In the matter of school funding the case for the schools of the poor is argued (not very well) by the public school teachers' unions and, more disinterestedly, by the [Commonwealth] Schools Commission.

Neither, however, has been as effective in the politics of school funding of the last twenty years as have been the organizations supporting middle class independent schools. (p. 2)

That government schools indeed have unmet needs and suffer from the creaming-off process is made clear by one of the most knowledgable Australian educational experts, Professor Grant Harman. Speaking of Victorian high schools, he says they are:

undoubtedly inferior compared to the better non-government secondary schools. They are also seen to be inferior by parents who send their children to non-government schools, and often too by many parents and students who support public education. I know of no other high school system in the world where so many of those who run the system, from senior officials to school principals and to classroom teachers, send their own children to non-government schools. It is no wonder then that morale and aspirations in high schools are low, especially when so many high school buildings confirm the message of inferiority or mediocrity. (Harman, 1983, p. 31)

In a similar vein, Davidson (1984), commenting on the growing exodus from government schools, remarks that, 'If present trends continue, the middle classes will cease to be represented in Australia's [state] secondary schools except in front of the blackboard.'[6]

Although the dominance of non-government schools over state secondary schools is said to be especially pronounced in Victoria, I heard much the same message that Davidson and Harman articulate from people all around Australia.[7] At the least, it is clear from conversations I had in all six states that academics and leaders in state education systems rarely send their own children to government secondary schools. This is something less than a resounding vote of confidence for government schools. Indeed, the upper-middle class abandonment of government secondary schools (with the exception of a few that are selective and, hence, elite) is such that among intellectuals even committed socialists usually send their children to private schools, being unwilling to disadvantage them by subjecting them to the impoverished academic atmosphere of the depleted student bodies of state schools.

I experienced this problem first-hand when two of my children attended what was described as one of the best government high schools in Geelong, the second largest city in Victoria. By contrast with their experience in the United States, they found that very few of their peers at the school, which was in a middle-class neighborhood, had any academic orientation or any plans to go on to higher education. Some people told us that we had made a mistake, that we should have sent our children to one of the elite private schools in the city.

Our experience gave us a clear perception of how Australian youth are divided and labeled according to whether they belong to the prestige and elite networks of the 'old school tie'. The stark differences are apparent at a glance, as Harman (1983) notes, in the contrast between the frequently inferior quality of state school buildings and grounds and the elegant facilities and grounds typical of the elite schools. But the differences go far beyond such cosmetic considerations; they affect the life chances of Australian youth. For just one poignant example, parents of students at our school lamented that local employers would hire the graduates of local private schools who had *failed* the Higher Schooling Certificate exam in preference to graduates of even middle-class state schools who had *passed* the same important, culminating exam.

In sum, Australian education, like American education, has obvious weaknesses as well as strengths. Both societies desire not only quality and liberty in education, but also equality. This requires a balancing of competing values, which in turn requires a delicate balance between public and private schooling. Clearly, neither society has achieved an ideal balance (*cf.* Boyd, 1984; Murphy, 1980). In the United States, our approach has given the public schools a near monopoly on schooling in many locales. Frequently, this has produced monopoly pathologies, including insensitivity to consumers' desires and a coercive restriction of choice and diversity. Our judicially enforced neutrality toward religion often borders on outright hostility. Local control of schooling via local school districts permits some choice, diversity, and responsiveness to local consumers, but also produces great inequalities due to disparities in local wealth and *de facto* segregation by race and social class.

In Australia, by contrast, the highly centralized state-wide school systems provide a high level of equality in educational services within states, but generally little opportunity for local control or discretion.[8] The tendency toward highly bureaucratized and standardized state schooling is offset by the options provided by non-government schools subsidized by government funds. But the vast majority of Australian youth do not benefit by these options and must rely on the state schools, which are hurt both by the creaming-off process fostered by government support of the elite private schools and by invidious comparisons with them.

If private schools are disadvantaged by the American approach, the opposite is the case in Australia. Indeed, many Australians feel the balance has tipped too much in the direction of non-government schools (Aitkin, 1986; Davidson, 1984 and 1985; Randell, 1984). They fear that this trend could lead to such a decline in support for state schools that there could be a reduction in 'the standard of public education available to the more disadvantaged sections of the community' who cannot afford private school fees (Randell, 1984, p. 7). As Don Aitkin (1986), professor of political science at the Australian National University, observes:

> I am still looking for the hard evidence that supports a view that private schools should be preferred now, where public schools

would have served a generation ago. What I can see without difficulty is the continual erosion of support for our public school system, which is the single most important institution in the building of Australian society.

Similarly, Kenneth Davidson (1985) notes that:

Under Mr Whitlam, the objective of state aid was equality of educational opportunity by bringing Catholic schools up to the standards of the state schools. We have since moved a long way from that ideal as the rich vie for relative advantage for their children in an increasingly competitive market for jobs and tertiary places, while demanding public funding for their private ambition as of right.

Rather than reducing elitism and social class distinctions, the present scheme of funding Australian schools tends to reinforce these problems. It seems to reflect Aitkin's (1986) comment that:

In my more cynical moments I come to the view that Australia is a reluctant democracy with hundreds of thousands of would be aristocrats screaming to be let out. That perception always seems most accurate when schools and education are in the field of vision.

These issues of elitism and class conflict are what make state aid remain controversial despite acceptance of the principle of funding sectarian schools. Indeed, the tension between public and private schools in Australia seems to be increasing, as witnessed by the fact that the Australian edition of *Time* magazine featured a ten-page cover story on the problem in May 1987 (Ashenden, 1987).

Because of the high level of state-aid now received by non-government schools in Australia, there really are *two* publicly-funded systems, one *inclusive* (the state schools) and one *exclusive* (the private schools) in student admission policies.[9] The exclusive system is also remarkably free of regulation by the government. Indeed, state-aid comes with so few strings attached that Davidson (1985) contends that private schools escape accountability for the funds they receive. On the other hand, defenders of private schools contend that government regulation has increased greatly and has become not only a burden but a serious threat to their autonomy.

Finally, a point that seems to go unnoticed is that present policies in Australia actually provide the wealthy with a *double subsidy* in education. They not only have their elite private schools subsidized, but also benefit disproportionately from the absence of significant fees at the universities, where, because of their educational advantages, they qualify for more than their proportional share of the inadequate supply of places available.[10] Thus, higher education for the privileged is substantially subsidized by the less well-off.[11] While the policy of free tuition at universities is attractive because it facilitates attendance by the poor, it also encourages the affluent to spend

on expensive and exclusive private schools and rewards them disproportionately for doing so.

Implications for America: Dilemmas of Choice and Elitism

The question for Americans is, would public funding of private schools lead
to the same kind of problems here that are experienced in Australia, not to
mention many other countries? There is a real danger that it could. What
most likely would occur, however, would depend a great deal on the details
of the policy adopted and whether sufficient safeguards could be built in and
maintained despite political lobbying to relax them. In the Australian case, an
influential segment of the population favors elite private schools and even
Labor governments committed to needs-based funding have been unwilling
(or unable) to cut off, or substantially reduce, aid to wealthy private schools.
Thus, they have continued subsidizing a dynamic that tends to undermine
the public schools. However, there is some evidence from other nations that
aid to private schools can be provided without necessarily undercutting the
public schools or promoting excessive elitism. But while the idea of enhancing liberty and choice in education is most appealing, it is critical to recognize
that the dynamics fostering negative outcomes are all too easily set in
motion.

Since the Australian experience includes many distinctive features that
have promoted a preference for private schools, it is hazardous to project
from it to what might occur with state-aid in the United States. These
features include such considerations as: (i) a British colonial/aristocratic
legacy (undisturbed, as in the American case, by a revolution); (ii) a British
tradition of dual school systems accentuated by convict colony origins; (iii)
highly centralized, bureaucratized statewide school systems and, concomitantly, generally strong statewide teachers unions; (iv) a large Catholic
population; (v) a much smaller total population and economy than the
United States, perhaps increasing the perception of career advantages to be
gained via private schooling; (vi) a very large immigrant population in
government schools since World War II, which may reduce their attractiveness to the advantaged and upwardly mobile; and (vii) free tuition for tertiary
education, making the cost of private schools somewhat equivalent to American families' investment in higher education.

Despite these distinctive features, it is possible to put the Australian
experience into perspective by referring to the comparative international
research on public and private schools conducted by Estelle James (1984a,
1984b, 1985 and 1986). Her findings demonstrate the delicate balance that
must be struck in funding and regulating public and private schools if parity
of esteem between them is to be maintained. To begin with, she finds that
the greater the cultural heterogeneity in a society, the more people seem to
desire homogeneity in their schools and the larger is the private sector of

schooling. The frequently superior school climate and student achievement in private schools are associated with their tendency toward homogeneity of values, purpose, and student bodies compared with the more heterogeneous situation usually found in public schools, since they have the responsibility to serve society generally (James, 1986).

Noting that one of the most significant types of heterogeneity involves academic ability, James (1986) comments on the consequences of the sorting of students that is likely to occur between public and private schools:[12]

> Suppose the amount learned by each student depends positively on the ability and prior achievement of other students in the classroom. Then, each student will prefer to be in an environment where the average level of ability is high and, in a mixed group, education can be said to be 'redistributed' from the more to the less bright. In a public school monopoly [involving heterogeneous schools], bright students have no recourse against this redistribution ... [However,] once private schools are permitted and particularly if they are facilitated by public subsidy, high ability students may opt out of the public system, thereby preventing educational redistribution. Some private institutions will announce that they admit only superior students and superior students will be attracted, even if these schools spend less per student than the public schools, because the superior student input enhances the educational climate and produces greater learning at lower cost. Of course, learning will be similarly hurt in public schools as average student quality falls there (pp. 5–6).

There is an alternative to this outcome, however. Public schools can adopt policies making them more like private schools. As James (1986) puts it:

> If we allowed competition among public schools, many of them would become differentiated according to academic criteria, with students seeking the best school and schools seeking the best students within a large catchment area. Each school would then be more academically homogeneous than the typical public school is today. This is the system used in Holland, where public and private secondary schools are equally subsidized, equally selective and equally preferred. It is also used in most Japanese high schools and universities. There, the private sector is very large and not heavily subsidized, but the public institutions compete for students, are highly selective and (consequently) are considered the elite first-choice institutions. Similarly, the few competitive public high schools we have in the US ... are relatively homogeneous academically and are on top of the educational hierarchy (pp. 6–7).

One of the problems in both Australia and America is that too many public high schools seem to have erred in the direction of excessive egalitarianism, thereby undercutting their academic standards and reputations (*cf.* Boyd, 1984; Cusick, 1983; Powell, Farrar and Cohen, 1985). On the other hand, educational systems organized according to highly competitive, meritocratic principles can easily err in the direction of excessive elitism. James (1986) observes that American high schools usually have tried to strike a balance by offering a variety of courses and academic tracks within a single school, which necessitates a large facility, staff, and student body. But what frequently results is the 'shopping mall high school' (Powell, Farrar and Cohen, 1985) in which many students are lost in a confusing melange of offerings, purposes, permissiveness, and people.

Unfortunately, there are no simple solutions to the tension between elitism and egalitarianism. Unless restrained in some way, the 'sorting and creaming' dynamic set in motion by selective, competitive schools quickly creates a number of vexing problems. For one thing, what is to become of the less able and less motivated students who are difficult to teach? As Murnane (1983, p. 406) notes, 'since the population of students is fixed, it is impossible for all students to attend schools with the most desirable student bodies'. Because of compulsory education laws and students' rights to a free public education, 'students who are not sorted into private schools must be educated in public schools' (*ibid*). This ensures that some public schools must bear the burden (and reputation) of educating the less attractive, lower achieving students. Even where public school systems successfully create selective 'magnet' schools that are attractive to middle and upper-middle class families, as in New York City, there is the problem of those left behind in the regular, 'unspecial' public schools.[13] The experience in places such as New York City and Buffalo, New York makes clear what is obvious on the face of it: the morale and character of the regular schools are likely to suffer by comparison with the 'special' schools. If the average or 'unspecial' student is neglected in the comprehensive high school, as Powell, Farrar, and Cohen (1985) show is the case, can we hope they will be better served in an 'unspecial' school?

On the other hand, if the public schools do not create some attractive (and, hence, usually selective) schools, there is the likelihood that their more affluent and ambitious clients will abandon them whenever acceptable private school alternatives are available. By lowering the cost of private school alternatives, state aid to private schools will greatly increase the rate of middle class abandonment of public schools. And, as the economist, A.O. Hirschman (1970) clearly demonstrates, contrary to the popular expectation that competition will spur public sector monopolies to improve their performance, there is a good chance the *opposite* will happen. While competition ordinarily may spark higher levels of performance, when the organization in question is a tax-funded, public quasi-monopoly, such as public school systems, the reverse may be the case. Under these circumstances, the gradual exit from the organization of dissatisfied clients 'is ineffective as a recuperative mechanism, but does succeed in draining from the firm or organization [many of] its more quality-conscious, alert, and potentially activist customers or members' (*ibid*, p. 55). Moreover, as Albert Shanker (1983), President of the American Federation of Teachers, has noted, even a small percentage loss of such clients can be quite serious: 'These are the parents who are active in the PTA, who campaign for adoption of the school budget and who lobby for state and federal aid. [These are the] parents [who] provide a disproportionately large share of the parental participation and political support for public schools.' (p. 475).

Indeed, it would be naive to think that a small percentage loss of the more advantaged and articulate clients would be of little political significance to the public schools. Yet Secretary of Education William Bennett went well beyond this position in advocating tuition tax credits (*Education Week*, 1985). He said that they would not undercut public schools because no more than 20 to 30 per cent of our students would end up in private schools, a mere 10 to 20 per cent increase over the 10 per cent now in private schools. By contrast, Shanker worries about the political clout that would go with an increasing pool of private school patrons. Wouldn't they desire to increase the amount of state-aid they received? Shanker (1983) observes:

> At the present time, the private schools have only 10 per cent of the students, yet the political influence of this single-issue constituency was strong enough to win passage of tax credits in the House and fail only narrowly in the Senate in 1978. In 1980 it succeeded in getting the Republican Party to adopt a platform plank in favor of tax credits — and it won the support of Ronald Reagan. If the 10 per cent now in private schools have so much political power, what can we expect if the public school/private school balance shifts modestly from 90/10 to 80/20 — doubling the private school constituency? (p. 475)

Shanker also underscores the unfair nature of the competition that will occur between public and private schools if the latter receive state-aid but, as the proponents of aid (including Secretary Bennett) desire (*Education Week*, 1985), few state regulations along with the aid. Public schools still would have to meet their diverse obligations to racially integrate students and staff, to educate the handicapped, to retain disruptive students, to employ only certified personnel, and to bargain collectively with their employees. 'What meaning', asks Shanker (1983), 'can competition have when the government compels [public] schools to live with policies which are largely unpopular, exempts private schools from these same policies — and then offers tax credits to help parents take their children from schools which comply to those which do not?' (p. 476).

What easily can develop under these circumstances, and what Shanker (1983) fears, is that the public schools can get caught in a downward spiral of decay, disillusionment, and abandonment, ending up as schools of last resort, populated by those who cannot escape: the disadvantaged of society. What many observers fear has been well stated by Stephen Bailey (1981):

Looking ahead, it is easy to become increasingly pessimistic about public support for the common schools. Major signs, especially continuing inflation, . . . an aging population, and an increased interest in voucher schemes and federal tuition tax credits all point to a reprivatization of educational services and to fewer public resources for education generally. The logical result of these trends is unsettling, to say the least. At the end of this road may well be ghettoized schools for the urban poor, non-English-language schools for Hispanics, racially pure schools for the bigoted, religious schools for the devout, and for the well-off, a wholesale reversion to the private academies of the nineteenth century. It is difficult to see how any coherent value consensus in the society at large could possibly survive such fragmentation of educational programs, institutions, and support services. (p. 38)

In regard to these fears, the Australian experience, at least with respect to the well-off, is not very reassuring. We must not forget that at the heart of the success that American public schools have enjoyed historically has been their ability to attract and retain the support of the middle and upper middle classes. As Paul Peterson (1985b), concludes, from his study of the evolution of schooling in Atlanta, Chicago, and San Francisco, the 'common' public school in America:

did not develop automatically; it had to compete with alternative models of providing education. Its chief competitor was [the European] two-class, dual system of schooling . . . If public schools were defined as charity schools for the poor [as under the dual system], they would acquire the ignominious image reserved for almshouses and homes for the incurable. If they were to depend solely on the eleemosynary instincts of the public, they would have limited scope and be starved for resources. The drive for common schooling . . . was thus not simply or even primarily a campaign to bring schooling to the masses. On the contrary, the campaign focused on making public schooling sufficiently attractive so that middle-class parents would choose these schools over private forms of education. (p. 11)

As many now recognize, demographic trends in the United States suggest that, even without aid for private schools, it may be increasingly difficult for the public schools to retain the support of non-minority middle and upper-middle class parents. Particularly in urban areas, the public school population is increasingly composed of racial, ethnic, and language minority groups (Garms and Kirst, 1980). These groups tend to be less active and influential politically, and have a higher incidence of learning and physical disabilities and of single-parent families. As minority groups increasingly characterize the population of public schools, majority groups may become less willing to finance these schools and to send their children to them.

Already there is some evidence that the affluent segment of the baby-boom generation is less committed to support of the public schools than their counterparts in earlier generations (Odden, 1985). They desire quality and choice in schooling and can generally pay to get it since they tend to be double-wage earner families.

If government aid subsidizes educational choice and encourages abandonment of public schools, within a policy framework that places few restrictions or obligations upon private schools, what real assurances do we have, particularly in the present demographic situation, that the societal outcome will be as desirable as the advocates of unrestricted state-aid claim? Will Adam Smith's 'invisible hand' really cause innumerable private choices to cumulate into a desirable 'public good'? Will we be able to celebrate both pluralism and social cohesion, relying on the tender ministrations of the mass media to supply the glue that holds together our diverse society? Or will the absence of more constructive shared socialization erode the fabric that binds us together? One thing is clear: There is a whole body of theory and research on collective choice that abundantly demonstrates that rational private choices frequently produce irrational societal outcomes, the proverbial 'tragedy of the [overgrazed] commons' (see example, Barry and Hardin, 1982).

Unfortunately, there is an inescapable trade-off between, on the one hand, promoting social democracy and social cohesion and, on the other hand, maximizing educational choice and achievement via selective and socially segregated schooling. Estelle James is sensitive to this problem and it is worth quoting at some length her conclusions regarding the experience in Holland, since they make clear the delicate balance that must be struck in regulating the balance between public and private schools:

> The extensive reliance on private schools in Holland has reinforced the religious segmentation within society. If all groups prefer such segmentation, it is Pareto-efficient; but a social dilemma exists if one group prefers segmentation while another group prefers integration. Then, a choice between the two policies also implies a choice about the distribution of utility between the two groups. In Holland, the separatists won a clear victory in this struggle.
>
> The separatist-integrationist division did not, however, correspond to a class division; nor has the private school system contributed to class segmentation. This is partially because specific mechanisms, such as restrictions on tuition charges and teacher salaries, have been adopted to maintain equality, and partially because class stratification is, instead, provided by other structures within the educational system. The Dutch system has probably strengthened ... public education, since private school budgets are directly tied to public school budgets, and nongovernmental financing sources are limited. This suggest that privatization does not

necessarily contribute to elitism, perpetuation of class differences, and weak public schools — but elaborate structural differences between the Dutch and American educational systems and their role in society preclude easy transferability of this result. (James, 1984a, pp. 623–4)

The American tradition has been to resist promoting separatism in schooling, but to preserve the independence of non–government schools. Private schools understandably prize their autonomy, for it is central to their ability to create their distinctive character (*cf.* Rodman, 1985). Thus, present day proponents of aid for private schools want to have things both ways; they want aid but with few or no strings attached. Yet research on many countries, from Australia to Zimbabwe, consistently shows — despite what Milton Friedman says (Friedman and Friedman, 1980) — that if a society desires to subsidize educational choice but retain equality of opportunity, private as well as public schools must be regulated by the government. This is why Richard Bates (see Andrews, 1984) contends that much of the debate over state aid in Australia has been misguided; instead of arguing about the levels of aid that public and private schools should receive, the focus should be on the *principles* underlying the aid and the regulations necessary to support these principles.

Of course, regulating private schools as the price they pay for the aid they receive always is unpopular. Moreover, it produces an irony that often is noted: As state aid increases, state regulation of private schools tends to increase and in time the differences between public and private schools begin to disappear.[14] James (1984a) notes that:

[P]rivate schools in the Netherlands are heavily regulated by government with respect to inputs. Also, but to a lesser extent we find regulations over output characteristics ... These are partially designed to achieve equality, but they come at the expense of choice which the system was designed to ensure... [A]s the private sector grows, through governmental subsidies, it becomes more like the public sector. (p. 624)

An alternative to increasing the regulation of private schools, of course, is to deregulate the public schools and make them more responsive to market forces. But this is controversial and problematic for all the reasons already discussed. The fact that introducing either *more or less* regulation of public and private schools is controversial shows just how difficult it is to close the gap between public and private schools. Ideally, we should seek a desirable middle ground in regulation that avoids the problems associated with the extremes of regulative and laissez-faire approaches. Clearly, it is the excessive bureaucratization and impersonality of many public schools that makes private schools attractive to many parents. The responsiveness of public schools to their clients is greatly diminished by their bureaucratic (non-market) governance system and employee unionization, both of which feed on each other (Boyd, 1982; Michaelsen, 1977). Indeed, a major recent survey of the attitudes of public and private school teachers and administrators shows that the political/bureaucratic ethos of public schools, unlike the market ethos of private schools, tends to foster attitudes that are inconsistent with the attributes of effective schools (Chubb and Moe, 1986). Consequently, there is a substantial case for efforts to introduce some aspects of the market dynamic into public schools through some measure of deregulation.

Thus, both public and private schools can benefit by emulating each others' strengths (Powell, 1986; Powell, Farrar and Cohen, 1985). And, the end of the road for public and private schools, when both are government funded and regulated — at least to some degree — need not necessarily be bland bureaucracy, mediocrity, and a loss of freedom. Depending upon what a society desires, and what is politically feasible, there is evidence that it is possible to achieve a balance between the extremes of regulative and laissez-faire approaches (James, 1984a, 1984b and 1986). In turn, this will involve striking a balance between elitism and egalitarianism in schooling arrangements, one that provides for excellence and choice, but also equal opportunity, dignity, and respect for the worth, contributions, and rights of all (*cf.* Gardner, 1961).[15] The competition between excellence and equity in American education today, as Strike (1985) observes, is too often cast in terms that pit the need for human capital and economic competitiveness against the Jeffersonian ideal of human dignity and participation (see also Bastian *et al,* 1985; Katznelson and Weir, 1985). In debating and shaping educational policy for public and private schools in Australia, America, and elsewhere, we need more attention to thoughtful discussions of the full range of issues involved, such as those found in *Schools for the A.C.T.* (1983) and in the works of Michael Hogan (1984) and Estelle James (1984a, 1984b, and 1986). Otherwise, we may find ourselves embarked on a dangerous course. In a pluralistic and unequal society, private choice in a subsidized, but unregulated education market easily can lead to divisive societal outcomes that few would desire.

To reiterate, this does not mean that we cannot strike a desirable balance between equity and choice, only that to do so requires a *regulated* education market including private as well as public schools. Besides the options for achieving this suggested by the lessons from Holland and Japan, another alternative lies in some sort of *regulated* educational voucher plan, one with adequate safeguards against racial, ethnic, religious, and social class discrimination.[16] But as attractive as such plans seem to many people, they nevertheless elicit opposition. This was vividly demonstrated in California in 1979–80, when one of the most eloquent advocates of vouchers, John Coons, led an ill-fated campaign to place a voucher proposal on the state ballot (Catterall, 1982). Coons' voucher proposal represented a very sophisticated attempt to balance the values of choice and equity. However, the degree of regulation of private schools embodied in Coons' proposal was unacceptable to the parochial school lobby in California:

Despite a wealth of state and national publicity, and despite a year-long campaign by Coons to secure the support of organized private school interests, including the Catholic schools' associations, the petition drive did not come close to attracting the needed number of signatures to have it placed on the ballot. In fact, it garnered only a handful of active volunteers and failed to win the endorsement of a *single* organized interest group in the state, including those of private schools, during the campaign. (Catterall, 1984, p. 438, emphasis added)

Significantly, as van Geel (1978) has shown, the uncertainty and complexity introduced by voucher proposals, and especially those that attempt to build in safeguards against what might happen under unregulated plans, become an obstacle to public understanding and political success.

In the final analysis, then, Americans are left with this question: Is it politically feasible and socially desirable to undertake public funding of private schools if it can work constructively only through changes in the system of regulations that are sure to provoke strong political opposition from *both* public and private school supporters? If policy were made solely on rational grounds, and if the advocates of public and private schools were willing to accept regulatory changes that would modify the character of *both* sectors, we might easily achieve and maintain the delicate balance necessary for parity in this arena. But in the rough and tumble world of American politics, with committed lobbies on both sides of the issue, it is far more likely that the balance will shift substantially one way or another. This is what happened historically with the ascendance of the 'common' public schools. We may agree that a more equal balance between public and private schools is needed now, but do we have the political wisdom and ability to achieve and maintain it?

One possible scenario is that public discontent with the status quo in American education will continue to grow, eventually providing enough political support for the forging of a new balance between public and private schools. For instance, mounting national concern about the need for policies that will promote US economic 'competitiveness' — coupled with revelations about such matters as the continuing poor math performance of American students when compared to students from other nations — is likely to bolster the view that improved educational achievement is necessary for better economic performance in this technological age. Suppose, then, that the 'excellence' movement falters, public school performance lags, and there is growing acceptance of of research claiming to document the inefficiency of public schools as compared to private schools (for example, Coleman and Hoffer, forthcoming; Chubb & Moe, 1986, forthcoming). If this happens, we then could witness the political sea change necessary for the creation of a new balance between public and private schools (Boyd, forthcoming).

What is more likely, though, is that we will eschew not only variants on the Australian approach of directly funding private schools, but also tax credits and vouchers as well. Two other scenarios seem more likely. First, the public schools may well be able to maintain the status quo, essentially, through a combination of habituated loyalty, public apathy, gradually improving performance as a result of the excellence movement, and massive institutional strength (see Peterson, 1985a). On the other hand, a middle-ground scenario is quite possible, one that would increase parental choice but still leave private schools without public funds. An important component of the 'second wave' of reform now underway (see, for example, Pipho, 1986) is the increasing recognition of the need for measures to enhance parental choice among public schools and thereby to ameliorate the monopoly performance problems of our public schools.[17] Similarly, as part of the 'second wave' effort to revitalize the performance and career and incentive structures for teachers and school administrators, it is necessary to break up the complacent, consumer-insensitive monopoly relationship that public schools enjoy in relation to most of their clients. All of these goals can be advanced by fostering curriculum variety and differentiation among public schools and then competition among them for clients (Clark, 1985a, 1985b). To be sure, this still leaves private schools out of the picture and liberty still would be inhibited, particularly in terms of family preference for religous education. Consequently, we may look forward to a possible improvement in the balance of choice and equity in education, but the precarious balance necessary for *full choice with equity* between public and private schools is likely to remain elusive.

Notes

1 See table 15 in *Schools for the A.C.T.*, Vol 2, 1983, p. 67.
2 Figures from table 1.6 in *Australian School Statistics*, 1984, pp. 8–9.
3 For an overview of the history of funding of public and private schools in Australia, see *Schools for the A.C.T.*, Vol. 1, pp. 10–19.
4 Sherman's (1982) analysis is sophisticated, informative, and insightful, but even within the limitations of what he reports about the Australian experience his data could almost as easily be used to make a case *against* the Australian approach to public funding of private schools.
5 This tension particularly comes to fore when there are proposals to expand existing private schools or build new ones in areas where existing government schools are underutilized or are facing the prospects of declining enrollments. In Canberra, this situation led the Minister for Education and Youth Affairs, Senator Susan Ryan, to appoint a 'Committee of Review' to study and report on the potential impact of Radford College, a proposed new Anglican private school (*Schools for the A.C.T.*, 1983). Similarly, *The Australian* reports that, 'The NSW [New South Wales] Teachers Federation has applied under FOI [Freedom of Information] legislation for documents on the [government's] decision to fund years 11 and 12 extensions to [a Catholic systemic senior high school in Dubbo], despite claims by three nearby public high schools that the subsequent drop in their student numbers would affect curriculums in all schools' (Houghton, 1986).

William Lowe Boyd

6 Davidson (1984) cites figures drawn from a Commonwealth Schools Commission report showing that the state schools' share of all Australian secondary students declined from 76 per cent in 1975 to 72 per cent in 1982, and that a further decline to 68 per cent is projected by 1987.

7 The author was a Visiting Fulbright Scholar at Monash and Deakin universities during the first half of 1984.

8 The state of Victoria is in the midst of a major effort at decentralization and devolution in its state school system. See Boyd (1984) and Chapman and Boyd (1986), and chapter 13 in this volume.

9 According to Lawton (1985), Australian private schools currently 'receive grants that average about 60 per cent of the expenditure levels of government schools' (p. 82). Less affluent private schools receive substantially more.

10 Underfunding of university-based education in Australia in recent years has produced an annual outcry and debate about the number of additional student places that are needed.

11 For an economic analysis of this problem in the case of free tuition for higher education in California, see Hanson and Weisbrod (1969). For a discussion of the scholarly controversy this research prompted, see Garms, Guthrie and Pierce (1978, pp. 436–40)

12 On this sorting dynamic, see also the similar analysis by Murnane (1983).

13 See the discussion by Metz (1984) of the organizational and political dynamics set in motion by magnet schools.

14 Erickson's (1982) research in Canada suggests that the special qualities of private schools are indeed fragile and easily upset by the addition of government financial aid and regulations.

15 Resnick (1986) reports that recent cognitive research shows that features of the higher order thinking skills associated with elite education are implicit in the basic skills emphasized in mass education. If, as Resnick thinks, there is some promise that mass schooling might be restructured to make explicit and enhance these thinking skills, then some of the achievement gap might be closed that now makes elite education attractive. See also Berman's (1985) discussion of the Minnesota Plan for school reform, which delays student tracking and specialized programs until the last two years of secondary education.

16 For discussions of the merits of various kinds of educational voucher plans, see Coons and Sugarman (1978); Jencks *et al,* (1970); Levin (1980); West (1982).

17 On this increasing recognition, see *Time for Results* (1986); Clark (1985a and 1985b); Chubb and Moe (1986).

References

AITKIN, D. (1986) 'Public education needs disinterested champion,' *The Age*, Melbourne, 16 January.

ANDREWS, N. (1984) 'Private schools promote elitism,' *The Mercury*, Hobart, 18 May.

ASUENDEN, D. (1987) 'Private or state? A collapse of confidence, drives parents from government school systems,' *Time* (Australian edition), 4 May, pp. 56–65.

BAILEY, S.K. (1981) 'Political coalitions for public education,' *Daedalus*, 110, 3, summer, pp. 27–43.

BARRY, B. and HARDIN, R. (Eds) (1982) *Rational Man and Irrational Society? An Introduction and Sourcebook.* Beverly Hills, CA, Sage.

BASTIEN, A., FRUCHTER, N., GITTELL, M., GREER, C. and HASKINS, K. (1985) *Choos-*

ing Equality: The Case for Democratic Schooling, a report of the New World Foundation, New York, The New World Foundation.

BERMAN, P. (1985) 'The next step: The Minnesota plan,' *Phi Delta Kappan*, November, pp. 188–93.

BOYD, W.L. (1982) 'The political economy of public schools,' *Educational Administration Quarterly*, 18, 3 summer, pp. 111–30.

BOYD, W.L. (1984) 'Competing values in educational policy and governance: Australian and American developments,' *Educational Administration Review*, 2, 2 spring, pp. 4–24.

BOYD, W.L. (forthcoming) 'Public education's last hurrah? Schizophrenia, amnesia and ignorance in school politics, *Educational Evaluation and Policy Analysis*.

CATTERALL, J.S. (1982) 'The politics of education vouchers,' unpublished doctoral dissertation, Stanford University.

CATTERALL, J.S. (1984) 'Politics and aid to private schools,' *Educational Evaluation and Policy Analysis*, 6, 4, winter, pp. 435–40.

CHAPMAN, J. and BOYD, W.L. (1986) 'Decentralization, devolution and the school principal: Australian lessons on statewide educational reform,' *Educational Administration Quarterly*, 22, 4, fall, pp. 28–58.

CHUBB, J.E. and MOE, T.M. (1986) 'No school is an island: Politics, markets, and education.' *The Brookings Review*, 4, 4 (fall), pp. 21–8.

CHUBB, JOHN E. and MOE, TERRY M. (forthcoming) *Politics, Markets, and School Performance* Washington, DC: The Brookings Institution.

CLARK, B.R. (1985a) 'The high school and the university: What went wrong in America, part 1,' *Phi Delta Kappan*, February, pp. 391–7.

CLARK, B.R. (1985b) 'The high school and the university: What went wrong in America, part 2,' *Phi Delta Kappan*, March, pp. 472–5.

COLEMAN, J.S. and HOFFER, T. (forthcoming) *Public and Private High Schools: The Impact of Communities*, New York, Basic Books.

COMMONWEALTH SCHOOLS COMMISSION (1984) *Australian School Statistics*, 1 st ed. Canberra, Commonwealth Schools Commission.

COONS, J.E. and SUGARMAN, S.D. (1978) *Education By Choice: The Case for Family Control*, Berkeley, CA, University of California Press.

CUSICK, P.A. (1983) *The Egalitarian Ideal and the American High School: Studies of Three Schools* New York, Longman.

DAVIDSON, K. (1984) 'Hidden asset of private schools,' *The Age*, Melbourne, 26 April.

DAVIDSON, K. (1985) 'State aid: Time for an accounting,' *The Age*, Melbourne, 28 November.

DOYLE, D.P. (1984) *Family Choice in Education: The Case of Denmark, Holland, and Australia.* Washington, D.C., American Enterprise Institute.

Education Week (1985) 'Bennett opposed to increased private-school regulation,' 27 March p. 9.

ERICKSON, D.A. (1982) 'Disturbing evidence about the "one best system"' in EVERHART, R.B. (Ed.), *The Public School Monopoly*. Cambridge, MA, Ballinger.

FINN, C.E. JR. (1985) 'Education choice, theory, practice, and research,' testimony before the Senate Subcommittee on Intergovernmental Relations, Committee on Governmental Affairs. Washington, D.C.: US Department of Education 22 October.

FRIEDMAN, M. and FRIEDMAN, R. (1980) *Free to Choose: A Personal Statement*, New York, Harcourt, Brace and Jovanovich.

GARDNER, W. (1961) *Excellence: Can we be Equal and Excellent too?* New York, Harper and Row.

GARMS, W.I., GUTHRIE, J.W., and PIERCE, L.C. (1978) *School Finance: The Economics and Politics of Public Education* Englewood Cliffs, NJ, Prentice-Hall.

William Lowe Boyd

GARMS, W.I. and KIRST, M.W. (1980) 'The political environment of school finance politics in the 1980s,' in GUTHRIE, J.W., (Ed.), *School Finance Policies and Practices, The 1980s: A Decade of Conflict* Cambridge, MA, Ballinger.

HANSON, W. and WEISBROD, B.A. (1969) 'Distribution of costs and direct benefits of public higher education: The case of California,' *The Journal of Human Resources*, 4, 2, spring, pp. 176–91.

HARMAN, G. (1983) 'The White Paper and planned change for education in Victorian government schools.' *Research working paper no. 83.10* Parkville, Centre for the Study of Higher Education, University of Melbourne.

HIRSCHMAN, A.O. (1970). *Exit, Voice, and Loyalty: Responses to Decline in Firms, Organizations, and States,* Cambridge, MA, Harvard University Press.

HOGAN, M. (1984) *Public Versus Private Schools: Funding and Directions in Australia* Ringwood, Penguin Books.

HOUGHTON, K. (1986) 'Teachers plan FOI "guerilla war" on school funding,' *The Australian*, 10 January.

JAMES, E. (1984a) 'Benefits and costs of privatized public services: Lessons from the Dutch educational system,' *Comparative Education Review*, 28, 4 November, pp. 605–24.

JAMES, E. (1984b) 'The public/private division of responsibility for education: An international comparison,' paper presented at Conference on Comparing Public and Private Schools, Stanford University, 25–26 October.

JAMES, E. (1985) 'Public versus private education: The Japanese experiment,' unpublished paper, State University of New York at Stony Brook.

JAMES, E. (1986) 'Comment on public-private school research and policy,' paper presented at conference on Research on Private Education: Private Schools and Public Concerns, What We Know and What We Need to Know, Washington D.C. Catholic University of America, 24 February.

JENCKS, C. *et al* (1970) *Education Vouchers: A Report on Financing Elementary Education By Grants to Parents*, Cambridge, MA, Center for the Study of Public Policy.

KATZNELSON, I. and WEIR, M. (1985) *Schooling for All: Class, Race, and the Decline of the Democratic Ideal*, New York, Basic Books.

LAWTON, S.B. (1985) *A Survey of the Governance of Roman Catholic and Denominational Education in Canada, the United Kingdom Ireland, Australia and New Zealand* study prepared for the Ontario Planning and Implementation Commission, 30 September.

LEVIN, H.M. (1980) 'Education vouchers and social policy' in GUTHRIE, J.W. (Ed.) *School Finance Policies and Practices: The 1980s: A Decade of Conflict,* Cambridge, MA, Ballinger Publishing Co.

METZ, M.H. (1984) 'The life course of magnet schools: Organizational and political influences,' *Teachers College Record*, 85, 3, spring, pp. 411-30.

MICHAELSEN, J.B. (1977) 'Revision, bureaucracy, and school reform,' *School Review*, 85, February, pp. 229–46.

MURNANE, R.J. (1983) 'How clients' characteristics affect organization performance: Lessons from education,' *Journal of Policy Analysis and Management*, 2, 3, pp. 403–17.

MURPHY, J. (1980) 'School administrators beseiged: A look at Australian and American education,' *American Journal of Education*, 89, 1, pp. 1–26.

ODDEN, A. (1985) 'Education finance 1985: A rising tide or steady fiscal state?,' *Educational Evaluation and Policy Analysis*, 7, 4, winter, pp. 395–407.

PETERSON, PAUL E. (1985a) Economic and political trends affecting education. Unpublished paper. Washington, DC: The Brookings Institution.

PETERSON, PAUL E. (1985b) *The Politics of School Reform, 1870–1940*. Chicago: University of Chicago Press.

PIPHO, C. (1986) 'Restructuring the schools: States take on the challenge,' *Education Week*, 26 November, p. 19.

POWELL, A.G. (1986) 'School complacency and the future of research on private education,' paper presented at conference on 'Research on Private Education,' Washington, DC: Catholic University of America, February 24.

POWELL, A.G., FARRAR, E. and COHEN, D.K. (1985) *The Shopping Mall High School: Winners and Losers in the Educational Marketplace*. Boston, MA, Houghton Mifflin Co.

RANDELL, S.K. (1984) 'Challenges facing educators in the 80s in Australia,' *Unicorn*, 10, 1, pp. 6–15.

RESNICK, L.B. (1986) 'Instruction and the cultivation of thinking,' paper available through the Educational Research Forum, an AERA sponsored computer network and database operating on CompuServe, 4 March.

RODMAN, B. (1985) 'Independent schools fear reforms threaten their autonomy,' *Education Week*, 13 March, pp. 1 and 14.

Schools for the A.C.T.: How Public, How Private? (1983) Report of the Committee of Review into the Impact of Radford College. Volume 1: Report Volume 2: Appendixes. Canberra, Australian Government Publishing House.

SHANKER, A. (1983) 'The first real crisis,' In SHULMAN, L.S. and SYKES, G. (Eds), *Handbook of Teaching and Policy*, New York, Longman.

SHERMAN, J.D. (1982) 'Government finance of private education in Australia: Implications for American policy,' *Comparative Education Review*, 26, 3 October, pp. 391–405.

SHERMAN, J.D. (1983) 'A new perspective on aid to private education: The Australian experience,' *Phi Delta Kappan*, May, pp. 654–5.

STRIKE, K.A. (1985) 'Is there a conflict between equity and excellence?,' *Educational Evaluation and Policy Analysis*, 7, 4, winter, pp. 409–6.

Time for Results: The Governors' 1991 Report on Education (1986) Washington, DC: National Governors Association.

VAN GEEL, T. (1978) 'Parental preferences and the politics of spending public educational funds,' *Teachers College Record*, 79, 3, February, pp. 339–63.

WEST, E.G. (1982) 'The prospects for education vouchers: An economic analysis' in EVERHART, R.B. (Ed.) *The Public School Monopoly*, Cambridge, MA, Ballinger Publishing Co.

WEST, P. (1983) 'Australia and the United States: Some Differences', *Comparative Education Review*, 27, 3, October, pp. 414–6.

9 Public and Private Schools: A Commentary

Berry H. Durston

Smart and Boyd provide two very useful and scholarly additions to the literature on public and private schools in Australia and America. In his chapter Smart outlines the position taken by the Hawke Labor government in adverse economic circumstances in tempering party policy with political expediency to maintain a system of public funding for private schools in Australia. Boyd describes the Australian experience largely through the published observations of a number of Australian and American commentators and points to some possible implications of public funding for private schools in America.

It is sometimes difficult to get past the rhetoric associated with emotive terms such as 'private education', 'education of the elite', 'elitism', 'elite private schools', 'wealthy schools' and 'posh facilities' in order to set aside the entrenched prejudices and stereotypes that persist. For example, there is a tendency to equate private education with elitism despite the fact that private schools in Australia generally cater for a very broad spectrum of society in terms of social class, intellectual ability and wealth. Though they have no particular cost advantages in that they employ qualified teachers and pay them award rates, many private schools in Australia operate at below average public school costs. There is a similar tendency to focus on the so-called elite schools while avoiding any obligation to identify these schools and to place them in the broader context of the total provision of education in Australia. Certainly it is a gross exaggeration to claim that in Australia generous amounts of public funds are being directed to elite private schools, that public funding promotes excessive elitism and that private schools escape accountability for the public funds they receive.

For some, the very existence of private schools threatens the quality of public education. They express concern about the effect on the morale of the public schools of the drift of students towards the private schools and about public perceptions of the parity of esteem between the two sectors. The apparent abandonment of public schools by certain social groups in the community is seen as an erosion of support for public schools, particularly on the part of some of the more affluent, articulate and politically aware members of society, which could adversely affect the level of resources that public schools are able to command. The withdrawal of their children, it is claimed, leaves public schools as the providers of education for those who cannot or choose not to attend private schools and weakens the representative nature of public education.

In seeking to blame the private schools for the shortcomings in the public schools, they fail to address the legitimate reasons why people prefer private schools. It is simplistic in the extreme to brand the supporters of private schools as anti-social and self-interested, or to assert that somehow it is undemocratic to sustain a range of schools both public and private, with different aims and philosophies. Some commentators have a regrettable habit of comparing the worst schools in the public sector with the best in the private sector. This practice overlooks the considerable diversity of schools in the private sector and assumes that all schools in the public sector are much the same, which is demonstrably not the case.

There are those, on the other hand, who believe that a democratic society gives citizens choices and obligations. They argue that education policy should not be predicated on the deliberate restriction of freedom of choice but rather on permitting maximum choice consistent with a free society. The prior right of parents to choose the kind of schooling that they wish their children to receive is inalienable. For them, a truly democratic society can afford a pluralism of schools including those which are entirely publicly funded, free and secular and those with a particular religious or philosophical ethos which are privately funded in full or in part. They contend that it is in the best interests of the harmonious development of children for the school to be an extension of the home. The reinforcing influences of school and home will be diminished greatly if the child experiences a conflict of values between them. In fact, it is argued, choice in education is a virtue: It breeds commitment characterized by willing involvement and eager participation. Rather than being assigned, students and teachers are involved in a voluntary association which produces powerful educational dynamics. They further contend that the crucial ingredient in successful schools is the school ethos: the sense of common purpose and reciprocal expectation which schools and their communities have for each other. Public funding for private schools creates and facilitates that choice.

Forms of Public Funding

Public funding for private schools can take a number of different forms. It can be indirect or direct. Indirect financial support may range from concessions on local, state or federal government charges, to sales tax exemptions and the free supply by government of consumable items or services for use in private schools. Parents may receive tax deductions, rebates or credits for schools fees and expenses, free public transport for their children attending private schools or payments in the form of allowances or subsidies towards school fees, books, accommodation and clothing. Gifts to private schools may be tax deductible in certain circumstances. Direct funding may take the form of payments to private schools from public sources for capital or recurrent purposes, grants in connection with specific purpose programs (for example, targetting disadvantaged groups for additional support or encouraging particular initiatives in schools) or interest subsidies on long term loans for capital works. Payments may be made at a flat-rate per capita or based on an assessment of the financial need of the school or the family.

Private Education in Australia

Boyd highlights the fact that Australia and America make two very interesting case studies. In the United States there is no direct public investment in private schools; the opposite is the case in Australia. It is noteworthy that despite similarities in the constitutional and legal frameworks of America and Australia, the courts have arrived at quite different interpretations of the legitimacy of public funding for private schools. Whereas in Australia the courts have confirmed the legality of payments to private schools under certain conditions, in the United States the interpretation has been much more restrictive on the grounds of the separation of church and state.

   As Boyd points out:

> The great success of the Australian approach to state aid ... is the establishment of principles for the financial maintenance of educational choice combined with a concern for equalizing educational opportunity via a needs-based funding approach.

This has been achieved by the introduction of a system of Commonwealth recurrent grants paid to schools on a per capita basis according to their enrolments with every school approved for funding receiving at least category 1 grants and schools allocated to a funding category ranging from 1 (lowest) to 12 (highest) according to an assessment of its private income. Schools in certain categories (1, 2 and 4) receive a base grant only (which is indexed) while the other schools also receive a betterment component designed to improve the resources to assist the school towards reaching a nominated percentage of the notional 'community standard' which is intended to be reached by 1992. In addition, the states (and territories) make per capita grants to private schools but the level of grant differs considerably from one state to another and for the vast majority of schools is well below the value of the Commonwealth grant.

   There is no doubt that public funding has been a successful means of improving access to private schools in Australia giving more parents an opportunity to exercise choice. In the period 1975 to 1985 the proportion of students enrolled in private schools rose from 21.3 per cent to 25.8 per cent.[1] In 1985 there was an overall reduction in the number of students attending schools in Australia compared with 1984 (from 3,017,720 to 3,006,169). In one year, primary enrolments fell by 37,130 from 1,739,986 to 1,702,856 while secondary numbers rose by 26,117 from 1,253,425 to 1,279,542. However, the fall in enrolments occurred in the public sector which decreased by 1.3 per cent (29,718) whilst students in the private schools increased by 2.4 per cent (18,167). But the fact that 25.8 per cent of Australian children attended private schools is not the full measure of demand for private schooling. The exercise of choice is still constrained by the lack of available places in private schools.

Reference to the fact that the private school share of federal recurrent grants exceeds the public school share conveniently focuses on Commonwealth tied grants which are the only direct source of federal funding to private schools but a minor avenue of federal funding for the states, which receive the bulk of their funds from the Commonwealth in the form of untied tax sharing grants which are available for a wide range of public expenditure including education.

Estimates provided by the Commonwealth Department of Education based on an analysis of Commonwealth and state budget papers indicate that about $A7,233.7 million of public funds were expended on public and private schools in 1984/85.[2] Of these funds $A5,767.7 million (79.7 per cent) were provided by state governments and $A1,466 million (20.3 per cent) by the Commonwealth. According to these estimates, some $A6,106.2 million of public funds were spent on 2,230,833 students in public schools, an average of $A2737 per student. In contrast $A1,127.5 million of public funds were spent on 775,336 students in private schools, on average of $A1454 a head.

In 1984/85 the 74.2 per cent of Australian children attending public schools received 84.4 per cent of the public expenditure on schools, whereas 25.8 per cent of Australian children enrolled at private schools received only 15.6 per cent of the public funds. Commonwealth grants accounted for about 11 per cent of spending on public schools (the states meeting the balance) and about 36 per cent on private schools. Of the total cost of running private schools about 19 per cent is met by state governments and the remaining 45 per cent from private sources. However, this is an average position and many private schools receive less than 20 per cent of their income from public sources, Commonwealth and state combined.

The claim that generous amounts of public funding are being directed to elite private schools warrants close analysis. In 1986 private schools at the lowest level of per capita grant (category 1) received $A298 per primary student and $A472 per secondary student from the Commonwealth compared with private schools at the highest level of per capita funding (category 12) which received $A873 (primary) and $A1363 (secondary). Yet it is the schools on the lowest level of public funding that are accused of undermining the public schools.

Furthermore, the assertion that federal aid is 'increasingly available to elite "establishment" schools' (presumably those charging high fees) is not substantiated by the facts. Not only do these school receive the lowest per capita grants but these grants are reducing annually in real terms because the formula applied to index the grants does not reflect the full effects of inflation. The grants do not include the betterment element that other private schools receive. In addition, the procedures used to distribute capital funds effectively preclude them from eligibility to receive assistance with renovating and upgrading their facilities. It is a fact that many of these schools do not have the same excellent plant and facilities commonly found in the newer public schools.

It fairly cannot be said that public funding for certain private schools in Australia is 'promoting excessive elitism'. There has been almost no growth in the number of so-called elite schools in the last fifteen years. Growth in the private sector has been almost exclusively in the number of low fee schools which attract the highest levels of Commonwealth subsidy. And, as already pointed out, capital funding is not generally available to schools at the upper end of the scale of tuition fees.

It is hard to believe that the 51,000 children attending some fifty category 1 schools scattered across the nation can be held to be responsible for undermining the quality of education provided for the 2¼ million children in 7625 public schools. After all, if the $A21 million of federal funds involved were to be provided to the public sector it would add less than $A10 per student to the amount spent in public schools. Furthermore, the chances are that for the most part these students would have attended public schools that already have a predominantly middle class composition. Withdrawal of federal funding is more likely to be a threat to the continued operation of low fee schools which receive the largest per capita subsidies than to the high fee schools that receive the lowest per capita subsidies. It is the latter group of schools which have been very active in recent years in establishing foundations as a hedge against the possibility of reduced public funding in the future.

One overwhelming observation which can be made, as Smart clearly demonstrates, is the intensely political nature of the funding issue. The provision of public funding for private schools is an act of political will, the constitutional validity of which, in a number of instances, has ended up by being tested in the courts. As Smart points out, in Australia even a socialist government (albeit one that has deliberately sought to occupy the middle ground in the political spectrum and to cultivate a consensus ethic) finds it expedient to continue public funding to private schools (including those which charge high fees) and, for some of those schools (those which are not well resourced), to expand that support on an extensive scale. Politicians, of course, have a preoccupation with securing and retaining office and hence their willingness to lean towards pragmatism and compromise in the interests of expediency rather than to adhere rigidly to party platform and principle. The ability of pressure groups to influence political decision makers is also critical. The size and political clout of the private school sector is clearly an important factor.

In Australia the private school sector holds strongly to the view that all Australian children are entitled to receive public financial assistance for their education regardless of whether they attend a public or a private school. It is abundantly clear that despite the best efforts of a very vocal minority there is widespread acceptance in Australia for public funding for private schools. The fact that private schools in Australia are thriving is not just the availability of public funding but a result of the very strong community demand and support for private schools. However, private schools need to weigh-up the cost in terms of loss to independence as a consequence of accepting public funding.

Public Accountability

Private schools are accountable for the public funds they receive. Public accountability and prudent public disclosure are seen to be the minimum and understandable price that must be paid by private schools in an effort to resist the seemingly inevitable drift towards some form of centralized control and associated loss of autonomy. Even in America, where there is no direct public funding of private schools, the schools themselves have seen the need to take pre-emptive action to introduce a form of self-regulation in order to stay the possibility of government intervention. A comprehensive accreditation process has been developed as a means of demonstrating the existence of certain standards of education.

Private schools which are in receipt of public funds clearly have an obligation to demonstrate that the funds provided by government are properly accounted for and applied for the purpose for which they were granted. Fiscal accountability of this kind has long been an accepted condition for the receipt of public funding in Australia. However, there are now signs that the nature of these accountability arrangements for federal funds is changing. For example, the legislation authorizing these grants requires each private school, amongst other things, to agree to furnish the Commonwealth Minister for Education with details of the aims of the school, its enrolment policy, its system of governance and the ownership of its capital facilities, a condition which is seen by the schools as intrusive and a threat to their independence. Bearing in mind that education is a state matter and that private schools are registered by the state governments, and that this information is not germane to fiscal accountability or to the determination of a school's funding category, there is understandable concern on the part of private schools as to the underlying motivation of the Commonwealth government for collecting this information.

Furthermore, in the last few years there has been a move in Australia on the part of the federal government to extend accountability arrangements beyond the established forms of fiscal accountability to encompass notions of educational accountability. Private schools are now required to report annually to the federal government (via resource agreements for school systems or accountability statements for non-systemic schools) on the extent to which they are achieving the government's objectives as well as to give an indication as to what else the schools are spending federally provided funds on. Private schools are apprehensive that federal government priorities may take precedence over those determined by school communities themselves, thereby distorting their mission. It is patently obvious that with teachers' salaries claiming such a high proportion of the recurrent budget of most private schools public funds are being devoted primarily to assisting those schools to operate at acceptable levels of resources.

There is also a growing interest on the part of the federal government in obtaining measures of educational outcomes that would reassure it and the community at large that the massive investment of public funds from federal sources in both public and private schools is warranted. A major concern shared by private schools is the extent to which the assessment of educational outcomes will focus attention on the more readily measurable levels of achievement in the acquisition of skills and the recall of factual information to the relative neglect of those which are more difficult to quantify such as the development of desirable attitudes and values and the application of knowledge. Apart from public accountability, private schools are directly accountable to their fee-paying clientele and sponsoring community in a way that public schools in Australia are not accountable.

Public Policy Issues

The provision of public funding to private schools raises a number of questions for public policy. Should constraints be placed upon the demands for diversity and choice in private schooling which are funded from public sources? Is public funding the appropriate mechanism for regulating the size of the private sector? What is the desirable balance between the public and private sectors of schooling? Who should decide what the proportions should be: government (local, state or federal) or market forces? What kind of organizational structure is necessary for the administration of public funding to private schools? Should funding be an entitlement, discretionary or on a differentiated basis according to some formula? Does the form which public funding takes make a difference to the growth and development of the private sector? Clearly there is a need for stability in funding arrangements.

Once in place, public funding is difficult to withdraw without risking considerable upheaval to the education of children.

If there is dissatisfaction and disenchantment with the neighbourhood public school in America, perhaps the American school system is missing out because the private sector, which caters for only 10 per cent of school students, is too small. If this is so, how can the private sector be encouraged to grow to contribute in full measure to choice and quality in education without harming the public sector? Much will depend upon the details of the funding arrangements and the conditions which apply.

One must agree wholeheartedly with Boyd in urging that America should be cautious about emulating the Australian model. Extreme care should always be exercised in translating practices from one society to another without due consideration to the different historical, demographic and social contexts which exist even among countries with somewhat similar traditions. There is always the risk of over-simplification of very complex phenomena.

The suggestion is made in Boyd's chapter that more equitable outcomes would be achieved if the private schools were subject to the same regulation as public schools, perhaps, as has happened in some countries, to integration into the public sector. The point equally might be made, however, that more could be achieved if the public schools were encouraged to develop some of the acknowledged strengths and desirable characteristics of private schools including a greater degree of self-determination. However, it needs to be remembered that in America there is no direct equivalent to the highly centralized public school systems of Australia which remain somewhat remote from the close community involvement that may be more typical of a decentralized public school system.

A fundamental problem for public policy analysis in the area of public and private schools is that the basic and irreconcilable philosophical differences which attend some of the issues do not lend themselves to dispassionate empirical investigation. There are political and methodological difficulties associated with undertaking research in this domain. For some, the public funding of private schools is anathema and for others it is more an article of faith than something for which objective evidence is in the least bit relevant.

Notes

1 Enrolment data from the *National Schools Statistics Collection, Australia, 1985* issued by the Australian Bureau of Statistics, Canberra, April 1986.
2 Figures drawn from the *NCIS Newsletter* volume 4, number 4, July, 1986, published by the National Council of Independent Schools, Canberra.

Part 3
Teachers' Unions

10   Australian Teacher Unionism: New Directions

Jill Blackmore and Andrew Spaull

Introduction

The industrial organizations of teachers employed by Australia's state education departments are popularly known as teachers' unions. With a combined membership of 180,000 teachers, these state unions are among the strongest teacher unions in the world, if measured by organizational unity and level of membership support. Most have over a 95 per cent level of unionization. The pattern of a single organization representing all government school teachers, regardless of sex, function or location, in each state (except Victoria) and the two territories (the Australian Capital Territory and the Northern Territory) is one admired, but not easily attained, elsewhere. This strength and size have ensured that Australia's teachers' unions are now the most visible of state white-collar unions. Furthermore, the single organization of teachers in each state has meant that the teachers' union is generally integrated into state educational policy making. There also exist two national organizations, the Australian Teachers' Federation, whose origins go back to 1921, and the Australian Teachers' Union, formed in 1983.

This chapter will examine the role of teachers' unions in Australian education at the state, local, and federal levels. It will emphasize two new trends that promise to alter future relationships in policy making between unions, educational bureaucracies, and politicians:

(a)   The development of teacher union activity in decision making at the school level and, in particular, in schools in the Victorian state education system. Here, it must be noted at the outset that there have been, and remain, significant differences in the configuration of teacher organizations in Victoria compared with the other states. Further, the roles and influence of the three Victorian teacher unions in the period after 1981 stand as the most successful form of participation in an Australian state education system; however, this achievement has resulted more from their use of interventionist strategies in the political process than from the innate superiority of separate, sectional teacher unions.

(b)   The development of federal teacher unionism, in particular the emergent industrial role of the Australian Teachers' Union. This development rests upon a recent High Court decision enabling, for the first time, inclusion of teachers represented by the Australian Teachers' Union within the federal conciliation and arbitration system, in which teachers and teaching in the state education departments may be subject to the far-reaching implications of federal award decisions.

In order to give direction to this chapter three points of interpretation require identification at the outset:

(i) Unionism/Professionalism

In this chapter we adhere to an essentially 'Australian' position (recently supported from other analyses overseas, Ozga and Lawn, 1981) that in the minds of teacher union leaders and those who study closely teacher unionism, the objectives, policies and activities of teacher unions cannot be crudely delineated between industrial (trade union) and professional (educational) categories. To represent the behavior of teacher unions in this form of traditional categorization is to create a misleading, indeed false, dichotomy in teacher unionism. One cannot separate the 'whites from the yolks' in a teachers' union, even though overseas critics have attempted to do this in their discussion of the strong industrial pre-occupation of Australian teachers' unions. As the historian of the largest union, the New South Wales Teachers Federation (NSWTF), writes (Mitchell, 1985)

> To elevate these distinctions to the level of dogma about professional and trade union behavior is as absurd as it is to deny that teachers' organizations are part of the wider framework of trade unionism. (p. 214) (See also Bessant and Spaull, 1972, pp. 92–6).

(ii) Centralization of Education and Teachers' Unions

Australian teacher unions operating at the state level of education have derived a special power relationship because they deal with a highly centralized state bureaucracy. Their position is analagous to the French teachers' unions position in a centralized national education system. In both countries the modern state apparatus has encouraged, even formalized, the position of state teachers' unions (this has been reinforced in most states by legal recognition in industrial law — see next section). This has meant that in centralized school systems — by definition, devoid of formal recognition of representative and community interests — the state teachers' unions emerged as the only *primary* interest group, and now the *dominant* interest group to challenge the unilateral decision making of the education bureaucracy. Duclaud-Williams' (1985) discussion of the FEN's (Federation Enseignants Nationale) power in French education is appropriate to the Australian teacher union experience. Centralization in education increases union power in the following ways: (i) as the union is relatively weaker than the Minister and Department, it is forced to concentrate its resources at one strategic level, at one point of political access, the Directorate and Minister; (ii) in a centralized system, where policy making is by nature politicized through legislation or ministerial order, decree and administrative regulation, teachers' unions do not have to defend themselves from the accusation that by challenging such decisions they 'are introducing politics into education'; (iii) in a centralized system there are strong political and technical needs to maintain formal consultation and additional sources of information from relevant groups, including teachers (pp. 89–91).

In Australia this has also been accentuated at informal levels: first in the period before 1960 when many education department senior officers had been former activists in teacher unions; second in the current period where ministerial advisers have been recruited from teacher unions' officers and officials, especially in Labor Party government states.

(iii) 'Compulsory' Industrial Arbitration

Several state teacher unions were the first teacher unions anywhere to gain full rights of access to a form of collective industrial negotiations through arbitration machinery which was independent of the state education department. Thus, teacher unions were able to negotiate not only salaries, but other employment conditions, and this was extended to cover conditions of work, for example, class sizes by the 1960s, to a complete coverage of conditions in the current *Victorian Teaching Service Act,* 1983 (Spaull and Hince, 1986, p. 190).

Why did the state, but not necessarily the Education Department, wish to bring teachers under the regulation of compulsory industrial arbitration? It did so, not with an overt desire to control union or professional activity (as occurred in the UK and Canada), but because it upheld the liberal view that government as a model employer should be party to arbitration, and that the 'Australian Experiment' should have its widest application. This view had been encouraged by Labor governments in the Commonwealth in 1911, supported by Queensland in 1915 and 1916, followed by New South Wales (NSW) in 1919, and Western Australia and South Australia in the 1920s. Access to industrial arbitration in Queensland and NSW (and elsewhere) strengthened the organizational power of teachers. This was apparent in the requirement to form a single central union, the immediate expansion of membership, the legal protection of the union and the improvement of teachers' salaries and conditions. These factors provided the unusual picture of strong teacher organization at the time, and in later years, when by 1935 a level of 80 per cent unionization was found among Australian teachers, higher than overseas counterparts.

> Whether in the long view compulsory arbitration helped to engender more conservative and more compliant teacher unionism in Australia is problematic ... What is clear is that the state's intervention, through its industrial relations system, acted as a positive force on the formation and growth of teachers' unions in the twentieth century. This was an important and progressive modification to the centralized control of state education. (Spaull, 1986, p. 26)

The impact of those teacher unions with full industrial bargaining powers on education departments, was acknowledged as early as the Directors-General of Education Conference in 1932 (minutes, p. 86). The NSW Education Department reported that with the advent of collective bargaining for teachers it was necessary for sound relations to be maintained with the NSWTF since 'in these days the term union is not regarded with suspicion or misgivings. In fact it is now quite a respected term'.

In Victoria there is an absence of compulsory arbitration; instead a system of wages (or conciliation) boards exists in which representatives of employers and employees sit as adjudicators. The wages boards were not empowered to register unions, merely to approve groups of employees as well as a number of unions. These principles were carried over into the legislation which established the Teachers' Tribunal in 1946. As a result between 1948 and 1979 the Teachers' Tribunal approved a number of 'breakaway' unions, dissident groups and school principals associations. The new Victorian Teaching Service Conciliation and Arbitration Commission (the VTSCAC) established in 1984, has attempted to recognize only one employee organization for industrial bargaining and dispute resolution processes, but this has been challenged successfully in the Courts by the smallest of the Victorian teachers' organizations the Victorian Affiliated Teachers Federation (VATF). We shall return to the dimension of compulsory arbitration and union formation in the last section of the chapter on the emergence of federal teachers' unions.

Australian Teacher Unionism: The Victorian Case

The State Level

Victorian teacher unionism is different in organization and political style from any other form in Australia. It departs from the typical Australian model of a single, central teachers' union. The Victorian experience has been an organizational malaise based on intense sectional antagonism, fragmentation, and at times inter-union rivalry. This has been partly offset by a level of innovative and progressive policies and practice in the major unions which has recently placed Victoria in the forefront of teacher unionism in Australia.

Victorian teachers take pride that their ancestors created the first modern teachers' union in Australia in 1886. However they are more reticent in admitting that they are still beset with the most fragmented organizational experience. This fragmentation which, as seen earlier, has been the result of Victoria's industrial relation system, has occurred in two ways. First, the formation of breakaways, and for a period, rival unions, from the parent union, in this case the Victorian Teachers' Union (VTU) which was established in 1926. The forerunner of the Victorian Secondary Teachers' Association (VSTA) established 1948, and the Technical Teachers' Union of Victoria (TTUV) established 1967, are classic cases of sectional breakaways of teachers who believed as specialized groups that their policies and interests could not be accommodated in the VTU because of its political domination by the primary school teachers. A similar pattern has emerged more recently amongst school principals, where there has been a tendency to transform their social or fellowship associations into quasi-industrial organizations. For example, the Victorian High School Principals Association (VHSPA), which has existed since 1948, obtained recognition at the Teachers' Tribunal in 1973. The second form of fragmentation is found in the formation of the Victorian Affiliated Teachers' Federation (VATF), or Victorian Association of Teachers as it was called in 1976. It is not strictly a breakaway group in that it seeks to offer an alternative organization to school teachers and other teachers who are disenchanted with militant, 'undemocratic' and 'party political' unions. The group who led the formation were VSTA and VTU members, angered by the VTU's peace moves to the VSTA to forego recruiting and representing secondary teachers, and later the three unions' political and industrial militancy and their acceptance of collective bargaining, which VAT saw as compulsory unionism. Despite its modest success in recruitment mainly from secondary teachers (56 per cent of its membership), VAT was recognized by the Teachers' Tribunal, except for the Technical and Primary Teachers' section. It resembles much of the rivalry between the VSTA and VTU in the 1950s and 1960s, although it is more persistent and vehement. Currently VATF contains less than 2000 members and over 500 of these are in non-government schools.

In July 1984 the three unions (VTU, VSTA and TTUV) established a peak council, the Teachers' Federation of Victoria (TFV). They did so in anticipation of the new VTSCAC recognizing one teachers' organization to represent all state teachers in direct negotiations (collective bargaining) and voluntary arbitration processes (see later). The TFV consists of a governing council of equal number of representatives from the three unions, and a small number of nominated officials and officers (on a rotation basis) who hold

THE 'MAJOR' TEACHERS UNIONS IN VICTORIA

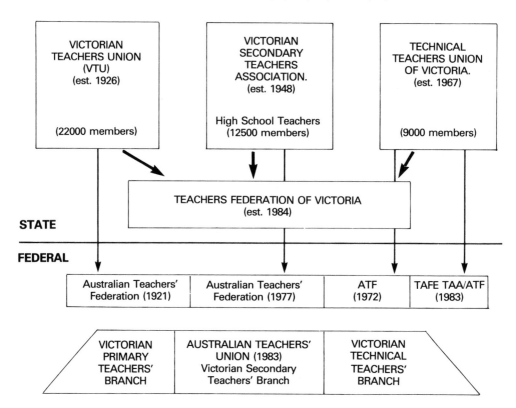

senior positions in the individual unions. Teachers who belong to an individual union are automatically members of the TFV. The TFV acts exclusively on behalf of these teachers and the three unions in all general industrial relations matters, including negotiations on industrial agreements with the Education Ministry. It also coordinates a number of common policies and activities for the three unions, such as the TFV committees and working parties on: the Elimination of Sexism in Education; Health, Welfare and Saftey; Migrant and Multicultural Education; Aboriginal Education; Teachers' Housing; Integration of the Disabled; and State Aid to Non-Government Schools (*TFV Annual Report*, 1985). Increasingly the TFV, rather than individual unions, has conducted negotiations with the state government, the Ministry and Education Department of Victoria. It is now responsible for representing the teachers unions in pre-budget negotiations with the Treasury; it has organized a public relations campaign aimed at restoring confidence in state schooling; and it has prepared detailed responses to Ministry initiatives in restructuring the Ministry and school governance. The apparent successes of the the TFV as a vehicle for formal co-operation between the three unions — in such a short period of time and against the local tradition of union fragmentation and divisiveness — has stimulated discussion for a new form of organization to represent all state teachers. Two propositions under consideration by the individual unions are: the TFV as presently constituted would replace the three unions as such, or that a central union be established in which there will be three separate divisional councils for primary, secondary and technical school teachers.

The government of Victoria's three major teacher unions varies in detail, but all have a common pattern. Rank and file members belong to the organization at the school (or group of schools) level and delegate responsibility for decision making to an annual conference, and administration and policy implementation to a monthly council meeting of about forty teachers and an executive of about ten, the senior executives being full-time. The VSTA and TTUV, as dissenters from the old centralized structures of the VTU, constructed the school as the basic organizational unit.

The VTU underwent significant changes in its basic structures in the mid-1970s. It abolished sectional branches for men and women in the Melbourne metropolitan area, it yielded its right to recruit post-primary teachers (although it added other sections to its membership such as school interpreters), and it devolved some authority for local action to regions, branches and sub-branches, the last being the school. In accord with general moves towards a decentralization of Victorian education, all three unions have established groupings and regions of branches in order to make their organizations more responsive to local issues and as a means of electing members to their governing councils.

The TTUV has special organizational problems due to the diversity of its membership. Branches in secondary technical schools accommodate both trade and academic subject teachers, groups that tend to differ in their training and employment backgrounds and, some have argued, in their educational and industrial outlooks. There are also branches for Technical and Further Education (TAFE) teachers who unlike technical school teachers, are not employed by the Education Department. The TTUV has attempted to cater for this diversity by ensuring since 1980 that TAFE has a separate autonomous organization within the TTUV umbrella. In effect there are two unions within the one organization.

Despite the use of militant tactics by the three major Victorian teacher unions in the late 1970s and early 1980s, it can be argued that in this period they tended to act as dependent institutions in the sense defined by Martin (1975) as:

> ... those reflected in their tendency to react to events rather than shape them ... (such unions) are mostly ... engaged in essentially defensive or protective operations stimulated by changing circumstances outside their control ... (p. 134).

Teacher unions normally behave in this way when fulfilling their basic objective of membership interests, whether it be by resolving individual and group grievances with the Education Department, or responding to variations in existing provisions. However, at a broader policy level the unions exercised a more proactive role in the later 1960s and early 1970s by stimulating significant improvements in teaching conditions and school resources. By contrast, in the more recent period the teacher unions were forced into a more defensive role largely because of government budgetary constraints and a political environment less supportive of state education. In Victoria this reactive stance was particularly evident during the final two years of the state Liberal government.

The changed political and economic environment of the late 1970s and early 1980s created uncertainty within the teacher unions about strategies and tactics. Should teachers accept the changed circumstances and hedge against further attacks, or should they should take the offensive and confront government and public opinion head on with industrial and political campaigns? Underlying these considerations was the issue of whether, and how, the three major unions should combine for a more influential role in educational policy making. There were areas in which combined union action was successful in reversing potentially threatening policy initiatives. An example is provided by the attempt in 1979 to introduce limited-tenure contracts for beginning teachers. The unions sought to embarrass the government about the department's lack of positive policies, not only for those teachers concerned, but for secondary and tertiary students who faced unemployment. The appeal was directed to middle-class and country electorates and their MPs, as well as the general public. The lobbying, public meetings and rallies in Melbourne and the country were reinforced with a number of regional and state-wide stoppages. Significantly, in November 1979 this issue prompted the first joint strike by the VTU, VSTA and TTUV. Union research conducted at the time indicated that there was considerable public support for the unions' view that there are ways of managing a prospective teacher surplus other than by limited-term employment or retrenchments, and positive ministerial negotiations eventuated.

The general trend of teacher unions being forced to adopt defensive positions during the later 1970s has to be modified by examples of individual unions being able to maintain or create policy initiatives. In secondary education the VSTA successfully aided the curriculum reformers' campaign for abolition of external and university entrance examinations at year 12. The union's public activities, and its use of the *Secondary Teacher* to maintain an informed secondary teachers' group, ensured that when the Victorian Institute of Secondary Education (VISE) Council was established in 1977 to administer the Higher School Certificate (HSC), twelve of its Council of twenty-four members would be persons 'with substantial experience in secondary education', a concession which· the government made to reduce the likelihood of trouble with the VSTA. After the establishment of VISE, the VSTA continued to agitate for reforms to VISE itself and to the HSC examinations. Examples of its actions include arguments that secondary teachers (specifically government school teachers) were still underrepresented on the VISE Council (*VSTA News*, 2/80), criticism of the standardization of scores across subjects (*Secondary Teacher*, March, 1980), and encouragement of VISE to accredit the Schools Tertiary Entrance Certificate (STC) as a wholly school-based year 12 assessment.

During the early 1980s the VTU was active in formulating family leave and permanent part-time employment policies to give teachers, especially women, more flexibility in teaching arrangments. Little progress was made on the part-time work policy, but the family leave policy, which provides for seven years extended leave for men and women and the right to return to a permanent position, was finally implemented by the Education Department in November 1984. Since the mid-1970s the VTU has sought a reorganization of the primary teacher promotion system in the light of declining school enrolments (promotion opportunities being tied to size of schools). After lengthy negotiations with the Education Department, the VTU won an agreement for a significant increase in the number of promotion positions in primary schools.

Electoral intervention in 1982 and 1985

The late 1970s and early 1980s were a period of mounting frustration for Victoria's teacher unions. In the defensive atmosphere of those times, conventional union strategies tended to either fail or produce inconclusive results. The unions had developed progressive policies in response to the looming insecurity in the teaching service and structural changes in the education system; what was required was a radical step to give effect to such policies. An active role in the electoral process came to be seen as the only alternative. The move was not without precedent in Victoria. In 1945 the

VTU successfully campaigned for the defeat of a conservative government in order to implement the Teachers' Tribunal. On a smaller scale and with less success, the TTUV, and to a lesser extent the VSTA, had campaigned against state Liberal governments during the 1970s. However, intervention in the 1982 Victorian election was significantly different from these earlier campaigns in terms of the strength of direct support provided to the Australian Labor Party (ALP). In later 1981 and early 1982 the VTU, the least militant of the three major teacher unions, moved to support the ALP in 1982 elections. The VSTA and TTUV followed suit. The move by the VTU was particularly significant. Spaull and Mann (1985) have examined this decision in detail, emphasizing the importance of the VTU's $100,000 donation to the ALP campaign and its grassroots organizational support for ALP candidates. The campaign also won the genuine admiration of the new Minister for Education, Robert Fordham (1982–1985) who developed a special relationship with the unions. Fordham was to become a key figure in the new government, not only in this portfolio but as Deputy Premier in a Cabinet where Premier Cain appeared to give him almost a free hand in education matters.

A key question was whether the teacher unions' campaign of 1982 would be repeated in later elections. Did it signal the start of a long-term and special relationship between the ALP and the teacher unions? Would Victorian teacher unions endorse the ALP in later years, or would it resume the non-interventionist role which is the norm of teacher unions elsewhere, and which had characterized the Victorian unions before 1982? These questions were to be answered in the 1985 state elections.

In 1985 the Victorian teacher unions contributed approximately $70,000 to the ALP's state election campaign. Within the VTU, at least, there was doubt amongst the leadership that its Council would agree to any direct donation at all. Eventually it was decided that the VTU would contribute up to $30,000, but in small amounts directed to selected candidates who could establish a demonstrated commitment to public education. In the weeks leading up to the election the VTU Executive donated about $18,000 in sums of between $500–$3000 to individual candidates. The other two unions donated amounts totalling $50,000. This obviously cautious, piecemeal approach contrasted markedly with the manner in which the VTU had supported the Labor Party in the lead-up to the 1982 election.

Relations with the Labor Government 1982–1986

The relationship between the unions and the Labor Party in government over this period was complex, intense and variable. In its 1982 pre-election platform, the ALP had given undertakings regarding a wide range of issues of importance to the teacher unions — issues both of an educational and an industrial nature. Speaking to the VTU Council prior to the 1985 election, the

VTU's Deputy President presented an analysis of these undertakings and the extent to which they had been met in the three-year period. He concluded in the following terms:

> ... if you in any objective fashion get out the (ALP) policy and examine how the implementation has measured up to the promises, by any measure you will have to say that (it) is a pretty impressive record of delivery on promises ... In our case, we can see that this Minister and this government have held their line very well.

In their subsequent voting the VTU Council endorsed this view (Nash and Spaull, 1986, p. 46).

A major component of the Labor party's election platform had been an undertaking to consult effectively with educational interest groups. Concomitant with this was a promise that decisions would be made 'as close to schools as possible', and that what had previously been seen as a highly centralized decision-making apparatus would be decentralized, with decision making significantly devolved to the local level.

The promise to consult was delivered — at least until 1985. The teacher unions (and the other major 'interest' group, the parents' organizations) were rapidly drawn into an elaborate network of consultations and negotiations. The unions provided teacher representatives on bodies ranging from the state Board of Education to school councils; in between were a myriad of regional committees, selection panels and advisory bodies. Beyond the mechanics of formal representation, the unions became involved in consultation and negotiations in respect of almost all activities of the Education Department — budget proposals, career structures, logs of claims and the detail of their implementation were just a few. For the unions, being consulted by the government and having the opportunity to participate in the Education Department's decision-making processes were important expectations when they had supported the Labor government into power. In the event, however, the experience was not without its difficulties. In the first place, such extensive consultation required considerable time, on the part both of volunteer members and of paid union officials. Over the three-year period the VTU increased the number of its full-time officials by three, and conducted long-running arguments with the Education Department over time-release and subsidy for teachers to undertake consultative activities on the Union's behalf.

A major achievement for the teacher unions has been the long-overdue reform of Victoria's industrial relations machinery. Since the early 1960s there had been almost constant agitation for reform of the Teachers' Tribunal. The unions argued that there were three major deficiencies in the Tribunal's powers and procedures. First, the Tribunal did not normally insist that the employer, namely the Education Department, make a case rebutting or modifying union submissions. Accordingly, in a number of instances the unions were left unclear of the basis on which Tribunal decisions had been reached. Second, the government rarely instructed the government representative on the Tribunal on the stance it wanted adopted, or, on the occasions when it did, these instructions were frequently ignored. As such, it was difficult to discern the government's real position on matters of dispute. Finally, the Tribunal had no powers to resolve industrial disputes.

In 1977 the three unions jointly called for the introduction of direct negotiations and a radical change in the Tribunal's functions so that it could be a tribunal of conciliation and voluntary artibration. At the 1979 elections, the Liberal state government promised reform of the system and this policy was put into effect with the accession of a new Minister for Education. The Minister favoured the introduction of a direct negotiations system, except that compulsory arbitration, not voluntary arbitration, should be available, and that all salary matters should be determined by an arbitral process. In November, 1979 he incorporated these arguments into a new proposal — a Victorian Teaching Service Conciliation and Arbitration Commission. This proposal was rejected by the three teachers' unions who were concerned about the transfer of tribunal powers to the Education Department and the lack of teacher representation on the proposed commission. Instead they called for, and gained, a seminar on industrial relations in the Education Department which led to the establishment of a working party of principal parties in the government education system, which presented its report (known as the Hince Report) in May 1981. The major recommendations of the report (which were to become the elements of the new industrial relations system) were:

- the Education Department (through the Minister) should be the employer;
- the Department and teacher unions should negotiate all claims, including salaries;
- a Teaching Service Conciliation and Arbitration Commission should be established, consisting of a President and other commissioners and consultation with the unions should occur prior to appointments being made;
- where no agreement was reached the parties would proceed to conciliation;
- if no agreement was reached by negotiation and conciliation, the dispute would be referred to arbitration, if both parties agreed; and
- a grievance procedure would be established to assist the resolution of disputes arising from alleged breaches of agreements or determinations. (Spaull and Hince, 1986, pp. 189–97.)

In the event, the working party recommendations were not implemented by the state Liberal government. Under political pressure from the Cabinet, which was concerned about perceptions of 'going soft' on teachers, in November 1981 the Minister rushed through Parliament the *Education Services Act*. It incorporated some sections of the Working Party's report, including the establishment of a Teaching Service Conciliation and Arbitration Commission, but it severely limited the role which direct negotiations could play in determing working conditions. The then Labor Opposition pledged that if elected it would amend the legislation to honour the original intentions of the Working Party Report.

In the three years following Labor's election much of this promise was redeemed. The *Teaching Service Act* (1983) introduced amendments to allow processes of direct negotiations, conciliation and arbitration. The Victorian Teaching Service Conciliation and Arbitration Commission (VTSCAC) was established, with two commissioners being nominated by the teacher unions. Each of the three teacher unions negotiated conditions and staffing agreements for 1983, 1984 and 1985. A log of claims submitted jointly by the three teacher unions proved slow to finalize, but as each union's most important concerns were embodied in their separate logs, this slowness produced little concern amongst members.

As yet VTSCAC has been prevented from supervising and registering industrial agreements and from dispute resolution processes. This has arisen from court challenges to its decision to recognize one teachers' union (the TFV) for purposes of collective bargaining. These delays have been such as to raise serious doubts as to whether the TFV or the three unions will even see in place 'their' new industrial relations machinery. It is rumoured that the Minister now wishes to see state teachers brought under the direct authority of the Industrial Relations Commission of Victoria through the formation of a Teachers' Conciliation and Arbitration Board.

In addition to attending to the mechanics of industrial relations, the Labor government resolved two bitter confrontations which had existed between the teacher unions and the Liberal government: limited-tenure employment of teachers was abolished, and stand-down regulations, which had been introduced in 1980, were repealed. For primary teachers, it was in staffing that the Labor government delivered one of its most valuable pre-election promises. In a period of declining enrolments in primary schools, the government honoured a promise to maintain for the life of the parliament the number of primary teachers which had been employed prior to the ALP taking office. This meant the retention of over 1800 primary teaching positions which might otherwise have been lost, and resulted in some signficant betterments in general staffing ratios and in the provision of teachers for special purposes.

During the government's period in office, however, its relationship with the teacher unions had not been one of uniform harmony. In addition to the problems raised by the widespread introduction of consultative processes, there were other, more specific, thorns. Chief amongst these was the 2 per cent cut to all departments' running costs which was introduced by the 1983 state budget. For the Education Department this cut was translated into, amongst other things, a drastic reduction in the availability of funds to pay for emergency teachers (employed on a casual basis to replace teachers on sick leave, excursions and in-service activities) and a 40 per cent reduction in the number of curriculum consultants available to work with teachers in schools. While some of these cuts were able to be 'negotiated away' in subsequent years, and others offset by ensuring government initiatives, the matter of restrictions on the school's capacity to employ emergency teachers remained a major source of discontent within the teacher unions.

The period between elections, then, was one in which the teacher unions had a far reaching but ambivalent mixed relationship with the government. But does the balance sheet of that relationship add up to a sufficient explanation for the unions' relative hesitancy in backing the Labor Party for the 1985 state election? Nash and Spaull (1986) answer this in three parts:

> First, the unions' relationship with the Labor government had not been uniformly felicitous. There was clearly a debit side, as well as a credit side, to the ledger. While the 'bottom line' of the balance sheet might indicate a marginal profit, the size of this profit was not sufficient. Second, the mood of the membership was uncertain. There were doubts about the future of society, the purposes of schooling and the expectations of teachers. For many members those doubts were undoubtedly being experienced in a very personal way. Finally, the 1985 election did not hold out promise of the dawn of a bright new era. If it resulted in the election of a non-Labor government many small gains for schools and teachers, and some large ones, would probably be lost. If re-election of the Labor government was the result, teachers could look forward at best to a further period of gradual improvement, offset by the kinds of difficulties they had experienced in the previous three years. (p. 54)

Fears held in some quarters before the 1985 state elections that the Labor Government would not be as sympathetic to teachers and their unions as it had during the preceding three years, found greater currency towards the end of 1985. The new Minister for Education, Ian Cathie, quickly demonstrated he was not as willing to involve the unions in the formulation of new policies. At the same time he refused to enter into negotiations with the TFV for new staffing and working conditions agreements. As a result of stalemate, the three unions embarked on limited strike action in October 1985 — the first major stoppages in the schools since 1982. Negotiations were recommended after the stoppages and the unions were able to resist the full brunt of staffing cutbacks, especially in specialist areas. Nevertheless, the familiar battlelines of the past had been redrawn. The Ministry's proposals for ongoing restructuring of control of education/control of schools were rejected by the unions. Thus 'the Development of Corporate Structures of the Victorian Education Portfolio' (1986) which the Minister claimed would improve the efficiency of the Education Department was branded by the TFV — rightly so — as an attempt at recentralization of control of education (*VTU Journal*, August 1986) or another example of 'ministerialization' to quote from Spaull and Hince (1986, p. 100). The Ministry's proposals on reorganization of school based government and administration (*Taking Schools into the 1990s*) was even more provocative. It included the proposal to replace school principals with school managers who would be responsible for the running of the school, not as members of the teaching service, but as state public servants. This proposal was withdrawn following pressure from principals, who remained loyal to their teachers unions. As a measure of the hostility towards the proposal we quote *inter alia* from the TFV response to the overall proposal.

- This report is much more than a proposal for the devolution of powers and functions to schools. It is an attempt to change government education from a public service to a marketable commodity.
- If implemented, it would lead to the abandonment of any attempt to provide equal eduational opportunity for our children and would divide schools into the 'haves' and 'have nots'.
- Staffing will become a nightmare. Current staffing mechanisms attempt to give priority to harder to staff schools, instead, they will be left to compete in a market place. This will severely disadvantage these schools. Local selection of teaching staff would make the participatory process meaningless as the burden on the local community's voluntary involvement would make the system unworkable. An annual relocation of 20 per cent of staff as currently occurs would result in an impossible work load for voluntary committees.
- The potential for conflict is enormous and inevitably schools would be caught up more directly in industrial disputes about matters which are currently handled centrally. This conflict itself would undermine the co-operation necessary to make the educational process participatory and workable.
- The paper gives scant regard to industrial relations or the requirements of central agreements or, for that matter, promotion/qualification structures, and teacher leave rights. It seriously threatens the industrial rights of teachers and conflicts with agreements already in place. (TFV Document 367, 25 June 1986)

The contents of such proposals were cause for alarm; equally the manner in which they had been imposed on the education community further indicated that the consultative partnership between the government and the teachers' unions had been disregarded. This added to the unions' fears that teachers' needs were being abandoned by government policies aimed at cut-backs in public sector funds, working conditions and such initiatives, as teacher health and welfare policies. The 1986 state budget realized the unions' fears.

The unions resorted to a pre-1982 position of combative defence. The Minister has been charged by the unions with desertion of teachers interests; worse, the moderate annual conference of the VTU unanimously passed a

motion of no-confidence in the Minister and requested the government to
replace him (*VTU Journal*, September 1986). At the same time the TFV
launched a public campaign aimed at protecting the state education system
from its public critics. As the TFV President declared in opening the campaign:

> The TFV intends to fight to preserve what it sees as a system under
> attack, not by outside forces, but by the very people who have the
> responsibility for protecting it. (*VSTA News*, 10 September 1986)

Thus, in 1987 and 1988 it appears that the teachers unions will embark
again on limited industrial action. This will cause embarrassment to a Labor
government dedicated to promoting sound industrial relations in education.
Moreover the 'interventionist' days of Victorian teacher unions in the political process seem finished. While it would not seem feasible that the unions
will promote electoral support for the conservative parties at the next elections, it does seem consistent that they will withdraw their support for the
Labor Party. As such they will resume the normal political behaviour of the
teacher unions in the other Australian states.

The Local Level

The organizational structures of the Victorian teacher unions evolved in a
manner which reflected both democratic and oligarchic tendencies, essentially
because of the industrially strategic advantage gained from a strong central
executive, with the freedom to act within broad policy guidelines at the shop
floor level. The particular success of branch (individual school) action in the
earlier VSTA professional campaigns for control of entry and against inspection (1968–74) meant that the strategy soon became a principle of organizational development. Branches always had input into central policy facilitated
by the procedures of the Annual General Meeting (AGM). The VSTA and
TTUV recognized early that the branch was the unit upon which the
strength of the unions could be built as they provided an opportunity for
professional and autonomous decision making.

The balance between centralized control, prescription and local autonomy has been tenuous and sometimes lost, with the tendency for large
unions to bureaucratize in a manner similar to their parent organization, the
employer. For example, the present Industrial Relations Officer with the
Education Ministry and a past President of the VSTA, was concerned about
the traditional, hierarchical organization of branches which divorced decision
making from members, overworked representatives, led to lack of dissemination of information and impeded the ability of branches to resolve issues
quickly. He argued:

> the cornerstone of the VSTA is the branch and many branches are set
> up along lines which actually work against effective membership and

the development of a unified Branch. In many ways, branch organization is the key to increased membership. (*Secondary Teacher*, No
17, 1975, p. 5).

A VSTA 'Think Tank' was proposed in 1974 to disperse the concentration of
branch work away from the few activists who were 'rebuilding the hierar-
chies we were attempting to abandon' (McRae, 1986). The creation of several
specialist branch positions with well defined functions encouraged the formation of sub-committees on the major areas of policy, for example curriculum,
tertiary entrance and assessment. The involvement by VSTA members in
these committees nourished the need of young, well qualified teachers for
professional educational outlets, and established a pattern of local school
organization and teacher involvement engendered by the homogeneity of
experience and training of teachers (see Battersby, 1983). This strength was
further extended into union teacher welfare and professional development
activities. Local VSTA, VTU or TTUV branch representatives were the
agents who could often facilitate swifter action than principals or head office,
the latter renowned for its slowness in decision-making and apparent lack of
concern for individuals.

During the seventies, it was the unions who took the initiative in issue
emergence and policy formation, as well as implementation, on work conditions, qualifications, teacher assessment, curriculum and student assessment.
Whilst the union set the agenda, the central administration and politicians
tended to adopt a reactive, defensive stance. The post-primary unions were
particularly active in cultivating alternative modes of school organization and
curriculum during the seventies, with the establishment of community
schools, vertical groupings of students in mini-schools, and the school-based
Schools Tertiary Entrance Certificate (STC) as an alternative to the external
HSC examination (*Victorian Teacher*, Vol. 3, 1984, p. 7). The union, as such,
was a vehicle for the intellectual energies of teachers. David McRae, one of
the initiators of Sydney Road Community School, ex-Assistant Secretary of
VSTA, former Curriculum Officer with VISE, a member of the Education
Ministry's Policy Advisory Unit, and educational consultant believed the
VSTA acted as a vehicle for radical educational ideas: 'there was no apparent
separation between the idea (of what education should be) and the vehicle for
expression of it ... the union allowed a higher degree of personal commitment on humanistic and effective educational practice' (McRae, 1986).

Unionism was a major influence in the changing organizational structures and decision making patterns in schools during the seventies, and
aroused teacher expectations regarding the level of their involvement in
policy making. The role of the 'branch organization was to transform scattered, individual innovations into considered, tested, general school policy'
(*Secondary Teacher*, Vol. 1, 1975, p. 4). Branch procedures and evolution of
policies on control of entry, inspection, teacher assessment, teachers' rights,
conditions, curriculum and direct negotiation were clearly established and

disseminated through numerous communication channels, publications, workshops and policy committees on sexism, peace education, health and human relations.

Yet union influence in school organization was not uniformly pervasive throughout the state, and there were clear patterns of participation as well as levels of activity within branches which varied by geographical location (rural/urban; western/eastern suburbs). Certain pockets of schools were more prone to activity because of the concentration of first year graduates, still bonded to the Education Department for three years, in the Western and Northern industrial suburban schools which lacked adequate facilities and experienced staff, and had a high incidence of ethnic students, generally from lower socioeconomic backgrounds. Branch action within schools during the seventies in the form of strikes and stop works created divisiveness between unionist and non-unionists; strikers and non-strikers; administration and teachers; those who were signatories to the conditions case and those who weren't. In branches where the staff were more heterogeneous and less politically cohesive, there existed factions of hardliners who followed union policy rigorously on all issues, and those who chose to strike only on certain issues. Many teachers were torn between the immediate daily professional commitment to students and the prospect of long-term benefits to education gained through union action. The job of the branch representatives was to communicate the union position and action to the administration, and to encourage individuals to follow branch policy. In most schools there was a reluctant acceptance of the right of a union member 'not to strike', although some non-strikers would generally offer financial or out-of-hours support. Many non-unionists who agreed with the principle of the issue would refuse to take on 'scab' functions to maintain the everyday functioning of a school and thus mitigate against strike aciton. This was partially the consequence of the widespread dissemination of union literature around schools, available to all in staffrooms, which meant most staff membes were aware, if not actively supportive, of union policies.

One achievement of the professional action program of the early seventies on inspection and teacher assessment by the VSTA was the institution of teacher assessment panels (STEP) and Special Duties Allowance committees (SDA) which allowed elected teacher representatives, together with the Principal, to establish administrative priorities and duties, and determine staffing allocations. The institution of such committees was fraught with difficulties as unionists perceived the informal power networks as acting against the formal structure and procedures being established through union activity. A member of the VSTA Executive queried in 1976 whether 'in fighting for local decision making, the VSTA is promoting its own demise' in that departmental manoeuvres underlying such democratic processes were seen to operate to the detriment of unionists' (*Secondary Teacher*, No. 5, 1976, p. 5). Such observations would be held out by organizational literature questioning the motives behind employers giving in to demands of workplace democracy (Mason, 1982).

Moves towards greater control of the workplace and industrial democracy in Victorian teacher unionism in the mid-seventies was exemplified in VSTA policy on staff exectives. An elected staff executive was to replace the authoritarian, paternalistic control of the principals, the representatives of the Director General and middle managers of the education bureaucracy, in determining the distribution of resources and allocation of duties and staff in schools. Traditionally, the allegiance of the principals lay with the departmental bureaucracy, an attitude bred by promotion procedures dependent on years of service and seniority rather than professional skill or administrative expertise. Interestingly, the school-based administrators (principals) were not included in the departmental policy discussions, but were merely seen to be the implementators of central decisions at the workface. With the increased willingness of the Department to negotiate directly with teacher unions by the mid-seventies, principals saw the need to protect their own positions. Their own associations, such as the Victorian High Schools Principals Association, began to act independently of the teachers' unions. In the technical schools there was not the same division, with a more collegial rather than hierarchical relationship, based on the presence of experienced trade staff (Meier and Welsh, 1981, p. 50). The divisiveness evident in the secondary divisions was less common in primary schools due to the greater acceptance by primary teachers of the paternalistic role of the principal, partially due to training, but also to occupational socialization in a more hierarchical and rigid work situation (Nias, 1985, pp. 105–19). The conflict model of principal/staff relationships which characterized the seventies in the VSTA was exacerbated by the generation gap resulting from the influx of young, highly qualified staff and led to a reassessment of this relationship over executive administrative control (Meier and Welsh, 1981, p. 187).

Those isolated secondary schools which did implement the staff executive policy, generally those with a concentration of radical staff or principals with VSTA membership, (Reid, 1981, pp. 24–5; see also *Secondary Teacher*, No. 18 1976, pp. 6–10) often found the process time-consuming, but fulfilling. A teacher participating in such as experiment in 1978 described the experience:

> One of the most immediate consequences is, of course, a plethora of meetings. We now hold a regular Monday staff meeting after school in order to establish basic school policies. A rotating chairperson system is employed, the chair is never taken by the Principal who is as free as any other to attend or not. Sub-committees have proliferated, rapidly creating a system not unlike the VSTAs own. (*Secondary Teacher*, No. 10, 1978, p. 11)

The elected staff executive, allowing for a limited principal veto on the provision that justification was given, administered all aspects of the schools policy. Staff control of school policy was built into the VSTA policy:

> the staff shall determine how school policy will be decided including the procedures for gauging staff views on school policy, and the means by which, and the extent to which views of the parents, students and the community might contribute to the school policy decision making. (*Secondary Teacher*, No. 1, 1978, p. 16)

Despite its limited application, one of the consequences of the Staff Executive policy and the concept of school-based decision making, was a rethinking of the nature of the principalship, the method of appointments of principals and, by implication, the nature of community involvement in school policy and administration. Technical schools had in theory since 1974 appointed *ad hoc* committees involving parents and teachers for principal selection, with the recommendation finally submitted to the Board of Classifiers, and subject to normal appeal procedures. In practice, the Classifiers, did not always accept the recommendations. The TTUV went as far as advocating local selection of staff, based on the belief that it facilitated a development of a coherent educational policy and was more sensitive to student needs (*TTUV Associate News*, 9 February 1979, p. 10). The VSTA also supported the principle of the local selection of the principal, as it favoured the notion of 'making the principal fit the staff' and not vice versa, but felt some ambivalence regarding the extent and nature of community influence in school policy and how it impinged on professional expertise. The VTU responses were equally cautious, deciding that schools councils should not be the sole determinants of principal appointments, but merely the statutory body to form a 'selection panel' which was equally representative of parents, teachers and administration. One consequence of local selection of school principals was to open up, at least in the short term, the principal class to many younger applicants from the secondary senior teacher class, and primary band 4 with the majority of principal appointments in primary and secondary schools in 1985 made by local selection panels.

The question of 'what is community' has been frequently addressed by each of the organizations due to the constant demands that if local autonomy ws taken to its logical conclusion, individual school policy should be in accordance with community needs. Throughout the successive reconstitutions of school councils in 1976 to include teacher and student representatives, and again in 1981 to give school councils full policy-making powers in all matters, union policy has been for equal representation of parents, teachers and students. This initially antagonized many parent organizations, used to dominating advisory councils. Most councils, when formally constituted, had a minority of teachers, due to community concerns, generally more conservative, that such councils would be run by 'radical teachers'. Teachers manifested similar distrust with the extension of school council powers over all school policy, but in the practical decision making of the new councils were able to locate allies amongst parents and students. In many councils, principals still maintained their privileged positions by virtue of their control of information, liaison role between staff and council, and control of the agenda, and advantage exerbated by the uncertainly of many parents (Gronn, 1983). Initially, with the school councils in an advisory capacity, there was little threatening the professional expertise of teachers, since 'the procedure of making educational policy was to be decided by the whole teaching body' (*Secondary Teacher*, No. 1, 1975). Staff executive policy had also been grounded on the idea of expertise rather than representativeness of the school community. But with the Labor Party devolution policy in action in 1983, the State Board report on principals argued:

> The Ministerial Paper on schools councils established the Governments intention that schools be key units in the education system. School councils, working with state guidelines and industrial agreements, will be responsible for the formulation of overall school policy which will include policies on curriculum and school administration ... the schools policy and resulting education program will be developed through collaboration and negotiation between those groups most directly concerned with schools and will reflect local values, needs and interests. (Victorian State Board, 1983, p. 3)

This was to reduce the mismatch between staff-determined curriculum offerings and the principal as the primary agency of implementation, curriculum advocate and administrator (see Chapman, 1986a). Recent advertisements for a high school principal illustrate how a school council has become the official policy maker.

> The school council has a strong commitment to participatory decision making processes at all levels involving staff, parents and students. The School Council ... contains close and harmonious working relations with the operations of the school via standing committees for curriculum, finance, building and grounds, canteen and communications. (*Education Gazette*, 5 July 1984, p. 445.)

The apparent dissolution of the structural dichotomy between policy and administration in the early phases of Labor government devolution policy laid open the decision making processes to all interest groups, such that a new element of corporatism entered policy making at local level in the eighties (Harrison, 1980). At the same time, the policy/administration dichotomy has been reasserted with the unpopular, and since rejected, Ministerial suggestion that the principals of schools belong to the public and not teaching service, thus opening up such positions to noneducators (*Education Victoria*, Vol. 1, No. 5. 1986, p. 3). The replacement of the Director General (an educator) with a Chief Executive in the Ministry (December 1985) gives similar overtones of corporate management. This constant tension between the process of administrative devolution towards school based decision making and the neo-centalism of educational bureaucrats and the Minister confronted with government and public demands for efficiency and account-ability has yet to be resolved (Blackmore, 1986). It is a tension which exists in the union organizations as well, but with different consequences.

The role of the branch as the unit of decision making in the organiza-tional structure of unions has faced two challenges. First, the earlier reliance on branch action to initiate action was confronted with a concerted attack by the Liberal government (1979–82) and their ability to victimize individual schools. For example, proceedings were instituted against seventeen VSTA members at Preston East Girls High for refusing to use competitive assess-ment. Ministerial initiatives, promoted by the *Education Act* (1981), to return power to the centre were evident in a sequence of decisions made without union consultation on a core curriculum model, the imposition of compulsory Physical Education, establishment of Human and Health Rela-tions Committees, and new increased accountability (see Ryan, 1982). Second, the devolution of responsibility to schools through the Labor gov-ernment's push for collaborative decision making in schools since the 1983 Mininsterial Papers has meant that branch revitalization and membership education have become VTU, TTUV and VSTA priorities in the eighties with in-servicing of branch representatives at the Trade Union Training Authority, workshops to the general membership on negotiations at local level and decision making for school and council representatives (*Victorian Teacher*, No. 3, August 1984, p. 3; *TTUV News*, Vol. 13, No. 8, p. 79). Apart from the general uncertainties created by the extent of the administra-tive and educational changes initiated by the Ministry, union branch lead-ership role has significantly altered. It is far less common for office bearers at the school branch level to be experienced people with official status in school and increasingly branch membership comprises inexperienced and younger teachers.

As the push for democratization of the workplace from the Labor Party Policy Committee converged with the framework of committee systems towards of increased school-based decision making, there was a heightened expectation of teachers, and unionists in particular, to be involved in the decision making in schools. Collectively, these factors set the stage for a unique set of negotiations on school management between the Education Department and the teachers' unions. The democratization of decision mak-ing in educational administration is not exceptional. What was unique was the willingness of the Labor Minister to establish direct negotiations with the unions which led to both separate and joint union industrial agreements between the Minister and the VSTA (1983) and the TTUV and VTU (1984). These agreements determined the nature of staffing, conditions, and school organization (see Agreement Implementation, *VSTA News*, 23 November, 1985). The agreements were welcomed by teacher unionists, as a single Log of Claims sought to replace the need for action on one-off issues with a comprehensive industrial approach. The democratic process underlying the formation of policy at the AGM was retained.

The Agreement was significant in that it institutionalized the committee structures which had partially evolved in the seventies, it consolidated the union branch as the negotiating body for teachers in schools, and established the principle of union representation on major committees. An Agreement Implementation Committee of the Industrial Office of the Education Department was established to resolve any breaches or grievances which could not be resolved in schools. The Agreement was an attempt to standardize conditions across the state. In doing so, it meant some schools in the northern and western suburbs, prepared to be more militant due to poor conditions, had made considerable gains which were lost by the uniformity of the Agreement. Members of such radical unions branches were bitter at the demise of the 1980–1982 policy of needs-based staffing which had given greater flexibility in staffing appropriate to individual schools. Other schools, facing a declining enrolment, found the staffing formula led to difficult decisions regarding the allocation and use of a reduced number of staff, often leading to choices between careers teachers, remedial work or pupil welfare coordinators.

On the whole, there was optimism well into the first year the agreement operated as union branches were seen as 'legitimate organizations' in school administration and policy making and were consulted, often reluctantly, by principals. Many teachers reported that there was less day-to-day conflict between branch and school administration, and that staffs were not divided into opposing factions. These improved relations allowed teachers to look to educational issues of curriculum, transition education and retention. Numerous schools reported increased branch participation and numbers with the withdrawal of union subscriptions restored and industrial peace, with over 80 per cent of all teachers belonging to a union. Others foresaw a new apathy amongst teachers, a willingness to give over trust to the new Labor government, whilst the cynics perceived the unions as being 'hamstrung and de-gutted by the agreements', as 'the cream of our industrial leaders have been enticed into Ministerial appointments' (*Victorian Teacher*, No. 2, 1983, pp. 6–10). This response to the Agreement has hardened in the last three years, as central union officials are seen to be compromised in their close relationship with the Labor Minister (1983–84). One teacher was critical of the mythology and reification of an Agreement that meant disadvantaged schools and committed teachers were forced to accept a lowest common denominator, calling for more flexibility to pursue 'over-agreement' clauses similar to the needs-based principle (*Victorian Teacher*, No. 3, 1985, pp. 17–20). Peter Watkins (1985) reflected that:

> School democracy might also be looked at in a sceptical fashion, as a covert method of controlling formerly militant unions. From this viewpoint it could be argued that increased participation may be a

means to reduce any union discontent and to minimize its effectiveness. By being actively integrated in to the decision making process,
teachers are less likely to act against any decision for which they are
partially responsible. This ensures a high degree of stability in what
has been a highly volatile industrial arena. The resultant stable and
predictable educational situation becomes a major achievement for
politicians extolling a mandate for good industrial relations. (pp.
111–2.)

The industrial agreement in this instance has minimised the ability of
branches to carry out their previously independent action to meet the specific
needs of schools, whilst demanding a commitment to the decisions made by
the administrative committees. The coincidence of the new forms of management in schools with the Agreement and a period of economic contraction,
declining enrolment, and reduced expenditure, have involved and committed union members to decisions which are often detrimental to individual
unionists and the branch itself, most of all to the students and school community. One senior officer of the central administration believed that 'we
have ended up locking schools and the regions into tight details of operation
as a result of industrial agreements. They are understandable but they run
against the general policy of devolution ...' (*Restructuring*, 1985, p. 33). The
centralistic tendencies characteristic of industrial negotiations in order to
establish uniform sets of conditions have therefore tended to reduce flexibility
for individual schools.

The multiplicity of decision-making structures and procedures which
have developed over the past three years have never been closely monitored
or recorded. Some schools run on democratic procedures in a complex
committee systems, and others along more traditional lines, allowing greater
discretionary powers to rest with the principal. School-based decision-
making is still seen to be 'an integral plank of the Government Ministerial
Papers and the Industrial Agreements' (*Teachers' Journal*, No. 10, 1984, p.
112). A VTU survey reported:

The process of change to decentralized decisions according to some
teachers had outstripped teacher abilities to participate in the process.
On the other hand, many teachers have eagerly adopted the philosophy of school-based decision making. They are keenly aware of the
importance of involving the whole community. Teachers report
improved staff morale and job satisfaction. Others say they value
working closely with their collegues on local innovations. (*Teachers
Journal*, 10 July 1984, p. 13).

Lack of support facilities and resources, as well as time allowances for
staff involved in such time consuming processes as program budgeting en-
danger the success of such devolution. Participation has become a useful
argument in the union campaigns opposing the reduction of teaching staff in

a time of declining enrollments (*Victorian Teachers*, No. 5, 1985, p. 5). Despite worsening conditions, union members dominate the administrative, curriculum, SDA and School Council Committees, having the past experience and also a commitment to certain educational policies. This does not necessarily imply agreement on the method of implementation and application but rather that teachers concerned with the theory and practice of teaching and learning perceive their involvement in the union as an essential aspect of their professional commitment and responsibility (see Chapman, 1986a).

The principle of local autonomy in decision making is well exemplified in the issue of curriculum, which was the catalyst for some of the greatest successes and defeats of VSTA policies during the seventies. With the abolition of external examinations except the year 12 Higher School Certificate by 1970, the VSTA stance was to openly confront the selectivity of the HSC exam, and demanded 'staff control of curriculum from K to 12', open tertiary entrance and non-competitive assessment. That is, decisions in schools and classrooms practice should be made by 'highly qualified teaching personnel who are familiar with the schools situation and who have the responsibility of putting the decision into effect' (*Secondary Teacher*, No. 1, 1975, p. 9).

Curriculum was an issue which also created a tension between the centralistic tendencies of a union and the autonomy of school based professionals as resolutions on curriculum at AGM meetings of the VSTA in the early seventies tested adherence to central policy. There was a fear voiced that we have 'replaced the external authority of the VUSEB with another external authority — the VSTA' (*Secondary Teacher*, No. 7, 1976, pp. 9–12). By 1978, the tension was resolved by agreement on central statements of broad principles which allowed school-based curriculum development. 'The educational program and the organizational pattern of a school is the concern of the local community, i.e. the parents, students and teachers associated with the school' (*Secondary Teacher*, No, 1, 1978, p. 16). Most schools had formed permanent or *ad hoc* curriculum committees by the late 1970s. Now, within the expanding social policy of the union, curriculum representatives were to 'develop "community" in your school community' (*Secondary Teacher*, No. 9, 1978, p. 17).

The TTUV had long seen curriculum as an industrial issue, closely bound up with needs based staffing. Staff ceilings and core curriculum, suggested in 1980, were perceived as definite inroads by the Liberal government to remove the right of the school and community to determine curriculum. The TTUV was particularly sensitive because of the massive restructuring, commencing in 1980 with the abolition of the separate administrative divisions between primary, technical and high schools by 1983. Technical school teachers felt particularly threatened and claimed technical schools offered a unique curriculum of 'learning by doing' (*TTUV News*, July 1980, p. 16).

Control of the curriculum has become an industrial issue by the 1980s because it cannot be separated from volatile questions of credentialling, assessment, school organization and structure. It is the focal point of the union's long-term opposition to university influence over what is the 'worthwhile knowledge' to be taught, and how it is to be assessed, in secondary schools. The focus is on the role and composition of the new Victorian Curriculum and Assessment Board (VCAB) recommended by the Blackburn Report, and its first task of creating a single Victorian Certificate of Education (VCE) to carry out the dual functions of certifying the successful completion of twelve year secondary education whilst acting as a selection mechanism for higher education. The VSTA has been singularly active in promoting public debate intended to highlight the oppositional role of the more conservative universities in their refusal to review their own curriculum and teaching practice and selection procedures. Past progressive educational achievements such as the STC alternative to the HSC traditional curriculum are seen to be under threat under the VCE, despite their increasing popularity with over 10 per cent of all year 12 students in over 100 schools participating in an STC course in 1986 (*Victorian Teacher*, No 4, 1985, p. 6). At the same time, the new educational settlement currently under negotiation may diminish the influence of the union and its members on school based curriculum development with the introduction of state-wide curriculum frameworks, and new fields of study and assessment procedures at a time when structural reorganization and drastic financial cuts in professional development and support services by federal and state governments will further undermine teacher autonomy and their ability to influence the direction of educational change.

Finally, the Blackburn Review of post-compulsory education, which recommended the restructuring of years 11 and 12 into senior colleges, caused union concern since such suggestions would fragment the unions' support base, and create a 'lesser' junior system in terms of status, resources and staffing. Teacher unions, included in the Structures Working Party (May 1986) because of their industrial influence and concern to protect teacher security and employment conditions, have claimed success in gaining acceptance by the Working Party of their preferred structural models — a K-12 comprehensive curriculum, clusters of schools sharing resources, or multi-campus complexes under one administration. (*VSTA News*, 6 August 1986, p. 3; *Victorian Teacher*, No 3, 1985, p. 5.) The unions accept the necessity for structural reorganization to better meet children's needs, although they disagree on whether these needs are best served on the organizational premise that 'big is better', but argue that teachers' interests much also be protected during such reform since teacher and student interests are not mutually exclusive.

The devolution of decision making in the eighties has simultaneously facilitated union input into policy making at all levels (through the representation at each level, i.e., on the state board, the regional boards and school councils) and forces unions to respond to administrative restructuring, often with mixed feelings, as in the case of the regionalization of the Education Department in 1984. Although regional offices had been established and regional directors appointed over a decade earlier, their function had been largely to administer centrally-made decisions. The Labor government was now proposing some genuine devolution of control to regions, which would have both a regional director and a representative Regional Board of Education. For the unions, weakening of central control meant the possible weakening of settlements which they looked forward to negotiating directly with their employer and with the government. In regard to regional boards, it also meant participating in consultative processes which would, as noted earlier, be a heavy drain upon their human resources.

In addition to regional boards and new-look school councils, the Labor government also established a state board of education. This body represented not so much a piece of restructuring of the Education Department, but rather an addition to the previous structure. Charged with the responsibility of providing advice to the Minister, separate from the advice he expected to receive from his Department, the Board was representative of teacher and parent organizations and of the administration, both within and outside the government education sector. In most respects the Board and its operation caused the teachers unions little concern, and in fact provided a useful additional avenue for advice to, and influence upon, the Minister. There was, however, a problem with its advice regarding the funding of private schools. Given it composition, the Board would never reach an agreement on this matter which would satisfy the government teacher unions, whose policy was opposed to any public funding of private schools. The Minister's referral of this matter to the Board for its advice merely allowed him to sidestep the difficult political questions for a time, and in the end he referred it to a sub-group of Board members from which the government school organization representatives were excluded. Predictably, this action generated considerable anger from government school organizations. For the most part, however, the state board operated in a non-confronting, advisory fashion.

What then are the implications for the unions' influence in localized decision making and policy in the face of current structural and educational changes? Possible issues are:

1   The concept of 'representativeness' which arises in corporate democratic procedures. This can be illustrated with the example of the makeup of the regional boards and the nature of union influence at this level. Each of the three unions' central councils appoint representatives to the regional boards, together with parent organizations, principals, elected community and departmental representatives. Each of these interest groups have set constituents, an historical relationship between each other and the department, and operate as representatives of the geographical abstract of the region, i.e., a

corporate rather than democratic model. Parents, elected from the 'community' of parents, lack a well defined constituency, agenda, support system or information network or a specific body to whom they are accountable. In such circumstances, teachers' unions (and parent organizations) have both the numbers as well as the support systems at regional level. Even in this climate of consultation and consensus, exclusion of certain interest groups occurs depending on the power balance. One central administrator said that 'there was a feeling in the system that the unions are running the show' (*Restructuring*, 1985, p. 35).

2 Since the union is the only legitimate negotiating body for the teachers, it is the union membership which is bearing the brunt of the participatory process. One effect is that there is 'burn-out' due to overload. Consequently, many teachers are beginning to withdraw from the participatory decision making process to return to classroom duties. A second effect at the organizational level is that the maintenance of a coherent union policy on the diverse issues teacher respresentatives are confronted with is beyond the capabilities of the limited resources of the separate teacher unions. A former member of the VSTA executive indicated that unless the unions amalgamate to pool resources and reduce the numbers of 'representatives' required the effectiveness of union activity will be dissipated (McRae, 1986).

3 Women have not dominated teacher unions at the regional or executive level although they make up 67 per cent of all teachers in Victoria in 1982 (Faneburst, 1982). The failure of the union campaign to achieve equal representation of males and females on regional boards and many union councils and executives reflects more than disinterest of their female members. Studies of the decreasing number of women in senior positions in schools, despite the call for affirmative action promotion policies, indicate that women do not apply in the same proportion as men because they do not feel as competent or capable in administrative and committee executive roles due to lack of experience. Research by Sampson (1985), Faneburst (1982) and Sarros (1984) concurs that women teachers lack the same networking and support in the educational hierarchy as males, and this impedes administrative experience in their early years of teaching. Such evidence appears equally valid for women in unions (Chapman, 1986b). Unless more positive attempts are made to encourage women to move up the ranks, unions will lose a large sector of potential support.

4 The unique relationship between the government and the unions to the exclusion of others is creating some distrust amongst other interest groups and especially amongst education officials at regional and local levels. For example, the current problems of declining enrolments, rationalization procedures and restructuring, critical de-

cisions regarding closure of small schools, the redistribution of resources and staff by amalgamation and clustering of groups of
schools, have largely been left to individual schools or groups of
schools to negotiate, with the assistance of Regional Boards. Some
rationalization has commenced within the climate of uncertainty
awaiting the Blackburn Report's implementation. Lack of consultation and confusion in regions has led first to a Working Party of the
TFV and Education Department officials, and second, to the decision
to form a Task Force to establish procedures, which would (i) maxi-
mize student access to curriculum; and (ii) protect the professional
and industrial rights of teachers (*Victorian Teacher*, No. 4, 1985, p. 3).
Parent organization and regional boards have been critical of the
Ministry regarding the lack of pluralistic consultation in favour of
direct negotiations with the unions on establishing the procedures for
rationalization (Maslen, 1986).

There is also a marked tendency to revert to the centralism in
policy making by the unions which constrains unionists in local
school and regional based decision making situations. The regional
boards' powerlessness regarding staffing and resource allocation is
exacerbated. One Senior Education Officer spoke of meetings at
which:

> The Regional Directors Educational Resource Committee
> gets to a certain point and then we are told 'We can't get any
> further in the discussion on that because the unions are
> talking with the Minister or the Director of Personnel and
> Industrial Relations or the Director of Curriculum — there is
> negotiation going on there and you will not be told about
> it'. (Angus, 1984, p. 31)

Principals, regional directors and parent organizations perceive that
the Minister has made decisions after consultation with teacher unions, and 'quite reluctantly, to save face, with the principals' unions'
(*Restructuring*, p. 49). Regional officers are caught between the
upward policy making of the local school and the downward
neo-centralist and oligarchic tendencies of the parent, teacher organizations and central bureaucrats.

Such accessibility to the Minister at the centre does not guarantee the unions' position in future consultative processes on policy at
any level. Increasingly, the federal and state governments have
chosen to appoint individuals, managerial consultants and public
servants rather than representatives of interest groups on important
policy making and evaluation committees such as the Commonwealth Quality of Education Review Committee (1985) and the
Victorian Structures Project, because of the likelihood of a speedier
and more favourable report in line with government concerns for

efficiency. The neo-centralism displayed by government officials and Labor politicians in the name of efficiency, economy and rationalization indicates that the Labor governments have found that 'representativeness' and 'consultation' are both time-consuming and often openly divergent with government priorities and survival. The appointment of an advisory policy group in the new state Education Ministry is perhaps a signal of reform, even demise, of the currently representative state board. The rhetoric of participation and collaboration so frequently exercised by both unions and the bureaucracy sounds hollow in such circumstances.

5 Collaboration between teachers (generally unionists) and parents on the numerous school based and regional committee structures in a time of relative industrial peace has created an ethos of consensus and mutual understanding. But again, this creates a dilemma for professionals and unionists pursuing professional autonomy and quality education. On the one hand, parent organizations and local parent groups have supported union action on such issues as needs-based staffing, for example, the Five Organizations (*TTUV News*, No, 10, 1979). On the other hand, this search for consensus can favour retention of the status quo rather than promote change. Declining enrolments, dezoning practices, the rhetoric of choice and diversity, economic retrenchment and increased community influence on school staff and policy, have ultimately increased teachers' vulnerability and therefore accountability due to competition for clients.

The incorporation of community and industrial interest groups in policy decisions at both state and local levels evident early in the Labor government's term can seen from two equally valid perspectives. Whilst it originally could be perceived as signallying the influence of unions in government policy-making and increasing autonomy of teachers at the school level, more recent trends in union-employer relationships suggest that the state's relationship with the unions is not necessarily collegial, but rather more manipulative of professional concerns (contrast Beare, 1983). Any appearance of a partnership in policy making is dissipating as teacher unions and parent organizations find themselves defending the state system against its apparent dismantling by ministerial advisors and a critical press upholding a market philosophy favouring privatization. Certainly at the school level, teachers are increasingly cynical as to the impact of democratization on their work situation, and do not regard it as necessarily an empowering process, but rather as giving evidence that the locus of power lies other than at the school level, an unsettling observation when the very nature of teachers' work processes and career structures are under threat (White, 1983 and 1985). Furthermore, any educational settlement negotiated under a Labor government could again be contested under a Liberal government.

Some practical questions need to be asked about school based management. Hewitson (1985, pp. 101–2) argues that it has not proved effective in resolving issues regarding the aims, objectives and content of schooling, for example, witness the continuing battle in Britain between the traditionalists and the progressives. Nor has local community participation in North America for a century resulted in diminishing the 'accountability demand' gap now evident in Victoria. If the current educational political policy makers come to similar conclusions, as it appears they may have, the energy and personnel invested in the school based decision making exercise by the unions is in jeopardy and needs to be reconsidered. Yet the inseparable principles of unionism and professionalism permeate the processes and structures of local decision making in Victorian education, with teachers expecting a say at all stages of the policy process, i.e., problem definition, policy formulation, implementation, evaluation and even demise of educational programs. In a contracting system, different demands will arise and the focal point of the local organization, the union branch, will again need to adapt. Bill Hannan, former editor of the *Secondary Teacher*, ministerial adviser, and now Chairman of the State Board suggests a new conceptualization of the role of the branch:

> Up until 1982–3 the branch's strength was largely measured by their capacity to impose union conditions and respond to provocation ...
> In the future a strong branch will be the one which pervades the school structures and which brings the kind of educational democracy expressed in teacher union policy to bear on the administration and the curriculum of the school. (*Hannan*, 1982, p. 3)

The Federal Level

There have been federal organizations of state teachers' unions in Australia since 1921. For most of this period, and certainly since the early 1980s all state teachers unions have been affiliates of the ATF. It is only during the last decade that the current organization, the Australian Teachers' Federation (ATF), has become an important influence on teacher unionism, and to some extent on national educational matters. Before then, the development of a strong federal body was impeded by its own inertia, state union conservatism and constitutional requirements which, as a result of the *State School Teachers* decision in the High Court in 1929, precluded state-employed teachers from award-making processes at the Commonwealth level (Spaull, 1987a).

Before the mid 1970s the ATF lacked direction and was not a significant factor in the life of Australian teacher unionism. There were forces at work, however, that compelled a larger profile for the ATF. The major impetus to change was the substantial increase in federal funding of schools and accompanying educational initiatives implemented through the establishment of the Australian Schools Commission in 1973. A second impetus to change in the ATF was the significant education reform movement which in the decade from the mid-1960s helped to provide a 'national outlook' in education, as well as generating improvements in teachers' employment, work conditions and teacher education. In general the ATF moved easily into the new political structures and policies which accompanied federal aid to schools after 1972. This was recognizable in its representation of teachers' interests on national educational bodies and policy groups. Also, the ATF enhanced its role through coordination and co-sponsorship of state affiliates' submissions and deputations to federal government departments. There was a noticeable increase in ATF publicity and propaganda, especially during election years (which were frequent during the latter 1970s), and the ATF became actively involved in the annual pre-budget discussions on educational expenditures. Since 1980 the formulation of new areas of ATF national policy has been shaped by some five national committees, whose membership is drawn from the state affiliates, and by ongoing policy research from the ATF and unions' research officers, and the more general activities of the ATF's international committee. There are also smaller working parties on particular topics which emerge from conference or Executive decisions and special conferences, such as the Women Officers' Conference, which also formulate or review ATF policies.

In the early 1980s the five national committees established or continued by the ATF annual conference were: Elimination of Sexism; Curriculum and Evaluation; Youth Policy; Adult Migrant Education; and the International Committee. In 1985 the committees were: International; Schools Commission; National Aboriginal Education; National Economy; and Special Education. The change in orientation of these committees reflects the changing demands on the ATF, and the perceptions by the ATF and its affiliates of new directions in education which have immediate implications for teachers. Thus, the Special Education Committee has now been established because ATF does not have a policy in this area at a time when a number of states are proposing to integrate students with disabilities into conventional schools. The Schools Commission Committee is intended to provide a broad policy base on the area of federal funding and educational activity, and a resource for the ATF representative on the Commission.

The influence of the national committees has been varied. Some like the 'Schools Commission', or the 'National Economy', provide information and direction for the formulation of more general ATF policies in regard to the Commonwealth government and special enquiries such as the Quality in Education Review Committee (1985). Others, such as the committees on Youth Policy and the Elimination of Sexism, although producing comprehensive reports, tended to find much of their work lost in the labyrinth of similar policy concerns in federal and state government departments and the union affiliates. The National Aboriginal Education Committee has been more influential, perhaps because it is not replicating work undertaken elsewhere. It has stimulated policy formulation in state affiliates such as Western Australia and New South Wales and members of the Committee have become closely involved in Commonwealth policy making on aboriginal education.

The ATF's influence on educational policies is difficult to measure. The nature of the 1983 election, with its short lead-up time for campaigning and the party leadership personalities dominating the issues, meant that ATF (or any other group, for that matter) struggled to make a significant impact. Its leaders argued that the ATF campaign had revived public education and state aid as election issues (*Australian Teacher*, May 1983), but if the ATF believed it had influenced the ALP's return to power or the ALP's education policies, then it quickly discovered the realities of dealing with the Labor government. Certainly it found no special place in the governmental process as the Victorian teachers' unions had acquired following their direct support for the ALP in the 1982 state elections. Due to the frustrations of this experience, the ATF shifted the focus of its efforts to the Australian Council of Trade Unions (ACTU) and its efforts against the restraints on public expenditure implied by the 'Economic Trilogy' the government had promised. In an extension of this, an important part of ATF activities during 1985 were directed towards the ACTU Executive and Congress in the hope that the trade union movement would exert some influence on the Commonwealth's education policies where the teacher unions, acting alone, had failed. This shift in strategic emphasis is one of the reasons for the ATF's move to Melbourne in 1986.

The ATF affiliated with the ACTU in 1979. This followed the decision of the Australian Council of Salaried and Professional Organizations (ACSPA), of which the ATF was a long-standing affiliate, to merge with the ACTU. The attraction of affiliation with the ACTU was its key role in national economic and industrial policies. The development of wage indexation policies in the late 1970s had helped to decrease teachers' relative earnings, and the ATF came to recognize that protection of its members' interests required a more direct influence on national economic policy making. Although the decision to affiliate was taken on practical rather than ideological grounds, it prompted an ideological response in some ATF affiliates and led to withdrawal from the ATF by the South Australian Institute of Teachers and the Tasmanian Teachers' Federation. These groups remained outside the formal ATF orbit until the return by the SAIT in 1983 and the TTF In 1984.

The ACTU Executive has supported the ATF and its affiliates in a number of areas of ATF concern, including active endorsement of ATF policies on Aboriginal education and restructuring the national education commissions. Moreover, the ACTU recognized the ATF position that the National Wages and Prices Accord had been breached in relation to the level of Commonwealth funding in government schools and acted on the ATF's behalf in opposing the New South Wales government's proposals to decrease superannuation benefits for teachers. Yet as the President reported back to the ATF in 1985:

> ... if it (ATF) wants more than just 'in principle' resolutions of
> support then it must have the ability to 'deliver' on those issues that
> it has identified as being of critical concern. For example, our effec-
> tiveness on the funding issues in terms of rank and file support and
> mobilization will largely determine the degree to which the ACTU
> will pursue the issue.
>
> Neither can the ATF pretend to be more than it actually is: a
> Federation of State registered unions. The ATF's capacity to deliver
> industrially on a national basis is limited and acknowledged. To this
> extent we are not regarded as central to the pursuit of the ACTU's
> broad industrial strategies. Wishing that things were different does
> not alter the reality of the situation. (Spaull, 1985, p. 17.)

Developments in industrial relations and education in the mid-1980s
period exposed the continuing organizational problems of the confederation
structure on the ATF, especially at its weakest link in the organization, the
national executive. The ATF Executive and Secretariat still have to move
prudently by consultation and co-ordination with the state affiliates. This
was evidenced in the slow process of the ATF forming the Australian
Teachers' Union (ATU) in 1983.

The background to the formation of the ATU can be seen in the long
standing struggle for state teachers to gain access to the federal arbitration
system. In 1928 the Victorian and Tasmanian branches of the Federated State
Teachers' Association of Australia (FSSTAA), a registered employee organization in the federal conciliation and arbitration commission asked the High
Court to rule whether they could receive an arbitrated salaries award, etc. as
a result of a dispute with their employers, the state governments. The High
Court in the *State School Teachers' Case* (1929) interpreted that education was
not an 'industry', or teaching an 'industrial occupation' and therefore state
teachers were not capable of an 'industrial dispute' so necessary for the
federal arbitration process to be applicable, as expressed in the 'industrial
relations' section 51(xxxv) of the Australian Constitution.

> The Parliament shall, subject to this Constitution, have the power to
> make laws ... with respect to: (xxxv) Conciliation and Arbitration
> for the prevention and settlement of industrial disputes extending
> beyond the limits of any one State.

As a result the two branches, and their state union shells, the VTU and TTF,
were despatched to a nothingness in state industrial relations for many more
years, as was the federal union, the FSSTAA, which became the Australian
Teachers' Federation in 1937 (Spaull, 1985).

The decision remained decisive for the next fifty-four years. A 1983
decision of the High Court (in the *Social Welfare Union* case) finally brought
judicial uneasiness about definitions of 'industrial disputes' in the case into the
open, and suggested that muddled thinking in 1929 had resulted in certain

constitutional heresies being committed by later courts (Spaull and Hince, 1986, pp. 240–2).

In June 1986 the High Court went one step further, when in the *State of Queensland v. Australian Teachers' Union and others*, it specifically overturned the *State Teachers* decision of 1929. In doing so, it dismissed the claims of the Queensland government that federal teachers' unions should not be granted federal industrial registration by the Commonwealth Conciliation and Arbitration Commission (see decision, CAC Misc 113/85 MS 7978). As the Chief Justice, Sir Harry Gibbs, stated in rejecting Queensland's appeal:

> Now that the proposition for which *Federated State School Teachers' Association of Australia v. State of Victoria* was regarded as authority, that the occupation which State school teachers pursue is not by its nature industrial, can no longer be accepted, there is no reason why the power given by s.51(xxxv) should not extend to an interstate dispute to which an organization representative of State school teachers is a party. (FC 86/028, p. 7)

His brother judges agreed, with Mason, Brennan and Deane reaffirming the importance of the *Social Welfare Union Case* in extending the coverage of the federal conciliation and arbitration authority.

> Neither the *School Teachers' Case* nor *Pitfield v. Franki* should now be followed. The *Social Welfare Union Case* has undermined the very foundations on which the reasoning in the two decisions was based. There the Court rejected the notion that the meaning of the words 'industrial disputes' in s.51(xxxv) of the Constitution should be ascertained by reference to the word 'industry' viewed in isolation so as to confine the constitutional power to the settlement of a dispute in an industry. Instead the Court emphasized that the words were a composite expression and that as such it should be given its popular meaning so as to embrace a dispute between employer and employee about the terms of employment and the conditions of work ... (pp. 14–15.)

Following the *Social Welfare Union* decision the ATF Executive recommended that a federal registration of state school teachers should be sought through a separate organizational entity to the ATF. In January 1984 this recommendation was accepted by the ATF annual conference and in February ATU applied for registration with the Australian Conciliation and Arbitration Commission. The ATU was to be an organization with a national body and eight branches, one in each state, except for three branches in Victoria to reflect the three existing union organizations. There are no ATU branches in the two Australian Territories because the state teachers' unions there are already registered organizations in the federal arbitration system.

The ATU was not the first teachers' organization to seek federal registration at that time. It had already been preceded by the Teachers'

Association of Australia (TAA) and the Independent Teachers' Federation of Australia (ITFA). The former body was derived from the extremely small conservative Victorian splinter group, the Victorian Affiliated Teachers' Federation, and the latter seeks only to cover teachers in non–government schools.

At present, ATU membership stands at around 85,000 teachers which is just under one half of all eligible teachers. To join the ATU requires an application and the payment of a nominal subscription by an individual teacher. This is in contrast with ATF membership which comes automatically by virtue of membership of one of the ATF affiliates and may help to explain the relatively slow process of ATU recruitment. This is expected to increase rapidly once the ATU seeks and gains a federal award for teachers.

It is anticipated that ATU will obtain federal registration in 1987. It is expected that following this ATF will wind down its operation and become subsumed in the work of the ATU. This will require the support of all the state affiliates of ATF. A second issue that ATU will have to face is whether, having gained registration, the ATU should seek a federal award for teachers. At the ATF annual conference which established the ATU, officials stated that there were no plans to pursue a federal award upon becoming registered; the seeking of registration was essentially a defensive move designed to head off rival organizations. At present, there are few compelling reasons for most teachers to want a federal award, but this can change dramatically and in a short period of time. For example, the Queensland Teachers' Union and Tasmanian Teachers' Federation have already expressed interest in a federal award following state government subvention against public employees in those states. The most obvious and pressing area for a national teachers award, as determined by the Australian Conciliation and Arbitration Commission, will be related to state teachers' conditions of work (such as teachers' contact time, preparation time and class sizes) which now vary considerably from state to state education departments (Spaull, 1987b).

If a federal award for teachers is obtained it will have to be complied with by state government employers. This would tend to increase indirectly the Commonwealth's influence on the school sector, an area where to this stage its activities have been largely confined to financial allocations. An illustration of the impact which federal awards may have on teaching and education is provided by the *Professional Engineers* High Court decision of 1959, which forced state public service boards into a major rearrangement of administrative and classificatory matters for state employed engineers. A federal award for teachers would mean that the state education departments as the delegated employers of teachers would find a Commonwealth agency encroaching on many of their employment policies. The implications of such a new industrial arrangement in state education on the Commonwealth itself, the state governments and the state teacher unions' organization and behaviour will be profound (Spaull and Hince, 1986, p. 244.)

References

ANGUS, L., PRUNTY, J., and BATES, R. (1984) *Restructuring Victorian Education: Some Regional Issues*, Geelong, Deakin University Press.

BATTERSBY, D. (1983) 'The politics of teacher socialization' in BROWNE R.K. and FOSTER L.E. (Eds), *Sociology of Education*, 3rd ed, Melbourne, Macmillan.

BEARE, H. (1983) 'The structural reform movement in Australian education during the 1980s and its effect on schools', *The Journal of Educational Administration*, 21, 2.

BESSANT, B. and SPAULL, A.D. (1972) *Teachers in Conflict*, Carlton, Melbourne University Press.

BLACKMORE, J.A. (1986) 'Tensions to be resolved in participation and school based decision making in Victoria', *Educational Administration Review*, 4, 1.

CHAPMAN, J. (1986a) 'Decentralization, devolution and the teachers', paper presented to the annual meeting of the American Educational Research Association, San Francisco, April.

CHAPMAN, J. (1986b) 'Improving the principal selection process to enhance the opportunities for women', *Unicorn*, 12, 1.

DEAKIN INSTITUTE OF STUDIES IN EDUCATION, *Restructuring in Victorian Education: Current Issues*, Geelong, Deakin University Press.

DUCLAUD-WILLIAMS, R. (1985) 'The FEN', in LAWN M. (Ed.), *The Politics of Teacher Unionism: International Perspectives*, London, Croom Helm.

FANEBURST, L. (1982) 'Positively discriminating', *Victorian Teacher*, 2.

GRONN, P. (1983) 'Talk as work: The accomplishment of school administration', *Administrative Science Quarterly*, 28.

HANNAN, B. (1982) 'The new branch', *Victorian Teacher*, 2.

HARRISON, R.J. (1980) *Pluralism and Corporatism: The Political Evolution of Modern Democracies*, London, George Allen and Unwin.

HEWITSON, M. 'Social accountability in the school system,' in KATZ, F.M. and FOSTER, L.E. *Sociology of Education*, Melbourne Macmillan.

LAWN, M. (Ed.) (1985) *The Politics of Teacher Unionism: International Perspectives*. London, Croom Helm.

McRAE, D. (1986) interview with J. Blackmore, February.

MARTIN, R.M. (1975) *Trade Unions in Australia*, Ringwood, Penguin.

MASLEN, G. (1986) 'The worrying times in our state schools', *Age*, 18 February.

MASON, R.M. (1982) *Participation and Workplace Democracy: A Theoretical Development in the Critique of Liberalism*, Carbondale, Southern Illinois University Press.

MEIER, A.J., and WELSH, D.H. (1981) 'Conflict in Victorian High Schools, 1965–75', MEd thesis, Monash, University.

MITCHELL, B. (1985) *Teachers, Education and Politics. The History of Teachers Organizations in NSW*, St Lucia, University of Queensland Press.

NASH, K. and SPAULL, A.D. (1986) 'Victorian teacher unionism' in SPAULL, A.D. (Ed.), *Teacher Unionism in the 1980s*. ACER, Hawthorn.

NIAS, J. (1985) 'Reference groups in primary teaching' in BALL, S. and GOODSON, I.F. (Eds) *Teachers' lives and Careers*. Lewes, England, Falmer Press.

OZGA, J. and LAWN, M. (1981) *Teachers, Professionalism and Class*. Lewes, England, Falmer Press.

REID, G. (1981) 'Democracy in the staffroom', *Secondary Teacher*, 4.

RYAN, B. (1982) 'Accountability in Australian education', *Disourse*, 2, 2.

SAMPSON, S. (1985) 'Women teachers and promotion: A search for some explanations', paper presented to the Women in Management of Primary and Secondary Education Conference, Canberra, August.

SARROS, A. (1984) 'Not Interested in promotion', *Victorian Teacher*, 1, 1984.

SPAULL, A.D. (1985) 'A history of federal teacher unions in Australia', *ATF Research Papers*, 7.

SPAULL, A.D. (1986) 'The role of the state in the growth of Australian teachers' unions 1916–1925', *History of Education Review*, 15, 1.

SPAULL, A.D. (Ed.) (1986) *Teachers Unionism in the 1980s — Four Perspectives*, ACER, Hawthorn.

SPAULL, A.D. (1987a) 'The *State School Teachers'* case (1929). Revisited', *Australian Journal of Education*' 31, 3.

SPAULL, A.D. (1987b) 'Exploring the Terrain of a Federal Teachers' Award', *ATF Research Papers*, 9, (forthcoming).

SPAULL, A.D. and HINCE, K. (1986) *Industrial Relations and State Education in Australia.* Ringwood, AE Press.

SPAULL, A.D. and MANN, S.P. (1985) 'Teachers unions in Australia: The case of Victoria', in LAWN, M. (Ed.) *The Politics of Teacher Unionism: International Perspectives*, London, Croom Helm.

VICTORIAN STATE BOARD OF EDUCATION, (1983) *Recommendations: the Role of School Councils in the Selection of the Principal.* Melbourne, VGPS, October.

VSTA, Implementation of Agreement Advice 1985, *VSTA News*, February 1985.

WATKINS, P. (1985) 'Collective strategies: Collaborative approaches towards the Administration of education', *Unicorn*, 11, 2.

WHITE, R.D. (1983) 'On teachers and proletarianization', *Discourse*, 13, 2.

WHITE, R.D. (1985) 'Australian teachers and the impact of computerization' in LAWN, M. (Ed.), *The Politics of Teacher Unionism.*

11 The Effects of Teachers' Unions on American Education[1]

Randall W. Eberts and Joe A. Stone

Introduction

After more than two decades of experience with unions in US public schools and despite the vehement opinions of supporters and detractors alike, very little is known about the effects of teacher unions, except that they increase salaries (Baugh and Stone, 1982). McDonnell and Pascal (1979), for example, acknowledge the absence of systematic research on this question, arguing that 'What is available is a collection of untested assertions and anecdotal evidence'. Cresswell and Spargo (1980) draw similar conclusions in a survey of recent research on public school unions.

In this chapter, we want to bring together some of the research we have been conducting as well as research of others to address the basic question: what effect do public school teacher unions have on public education? More specifically, we want to trace the effect of teacher unions to the most important element of education — the student. Research on the influence of teacher collective bargaining in public schools has been primarily anecdotal. Studies of the bargaining process and its effect on the operation of schools typically look at as few as six or seven school districts and rarely more than twelve. The picture that researchers construct of the way teacher unions influence the operation of schools has been sketchy. In reading accounts of how a handful of districts or teachers respond to collective bargaining, one may come across descriptions of behavior that are familiar from personal experience, but one must ask whether such behavior is the rule or the exception.

Our research, conducted over the last seven years with funding from the National Institute of Education, attempts to provide a more comprehensive assessment of collective bargaining by amassing and analyzing data for a respresentative sample of elementary and secondary students and teachers. With these data, we can trace the influence of collective bargaining to its effects on student performance on standardized tests, and to its effects on the cost of providing educational services. While tracing the effects of collective bargaining from the bargaining table into the classroom, we consider the effects of teacher collective bargaining on the mobility of teachers, the allocation of district resources, wage differentials, working conditions, teacher attitudes and job satisfaction, teacher-administrator interactions, administrative discretion, educational policy and practice, the determinants of student achievement, and district operating costs.

There are many aspects of collective bargaining we do not purport to examine. Indeed, we claim only one niche in the literature on teacher unionism: the measurement of the actual effects of collective bargaining on education. We do not ask if public-sector bargaining is consistent with democratic institutions; we simply accept the quite obvious fact that collective bargaining is well established and that it appears to play a significant role in public education. We also do not consider the bargaining process in any detail. We have analyzed the determinants of bargaining outcomes, but only to provide a brief background of the negotiation process and to test if bargaining activity can be considered independently of its effect on the behavior of teachers and administrators. Furthermore, we seek to examine the long-run effects of collective bargaining as an institutional change, not the effects of collective bargaining when negotiations lead to strikes.

This chapter will attempt only to report the findings, not describe in any detail, the methodologies used to produce the results. Such information can be found in our book *Unions and Public Schools* (1984), upon which much of this chapter is based. Before discussing the effects of bargaining, a short description of the teacher union movement is provided in the next section. The third section will present a synopsis of the effects of collective bargaining. The final section contains a brief summary and conclusion.

Teacher Collective Bargaining and Unionism

The establishment of teachers' organizations as recognized bargaining units is a relatively recent phenomenon in the history of American education. While public education experienced general enrollment declines during the 1970s, organizations representing public-school teachers experienced phenomenal growth. Spearheading the growth of public-sector bargaining, the two major teacher unions, the National Education Association (NEA) and the American Federal of Teachers (AFT), increased their ranks from 770,000 members in 1960 to over 2 million by 1985, representing about 86 per cent of the nation's public school teachers.

Four general reasons for the growth of collective bargaining are cited in the literature (Cooper, 1982; Goldschmidt, 1982). The first is the passage of state laws that protect the rights of teachers to seek bargaining recognition. One of the most important changes in the legal structure to accommodate public-sector bargaining was modification of the doctrine of sovereign immunity. The second reason is concern by teachers for their own economic and professional well-being. In addition to their concern about their economic position, teachers also are concerned about their access to, and influence over, educational policy and their ability to maintain a sense of professionalism. Declining enrollments, skyrocketing inflation in the 1970s, and general public discontent with public schools threatened teachers' job security, eroded their purchasing power, and diminished their self-esteem. 'Belt-tightening' is a continued phenomenon of the 1980s. The third reason often cited for teacher bargaining is changes in social conditions and workforce demographics. By the mid-1970s, the teaching force was younger, with a greater proportion of males, and with teachers who had grown up during a decade of protest. The increased militancy and the awareness of change provided a fertile ground for the growth of unionism. The fourth reason is related to the labor movement in general. Unionism in the private sector has been declining, partly because industrial work is becoming increasingly capital-intensive. Education, on the other hand, is highly labor-intensive. As teachers became less resistant to the idea of unionizing, the unions were ready to move. Rivalry between the AFT and the NEA increased their militancy and their fervor to organize.

Legal Structure of Teacher Collective Bargaining

Legal provisions for the conduct of public-sector collective bargaining have come almost exclusively from state governments. Although Congress has considered possible federal legislation to regulate negotiations of public employees, states have assumed the leadership in this matter. Meaningful legislation giving public employees a voice in determining the conditions of their employment was enacted first in the 1960s. Before that time only two states, New Hampshire and Alaska, had statutes that allowed local governments to negotiate with groups representing public employees. Neither state extended to public employees the same rights granted to private employees, however.

The National Labor Relations Act (NLRA) of 1935, later amended in 1947, requires employers to meet and confer in good faith with respect to wages, hours, and other terms and conditions of employment. New Hampshire's law of 1955 and Alaska's law of 1959 did not require or ensure bargaining; local governments were allowed to negotiate only under specified conditions. Permitting private and public employees to bargain, nonetheless, was a major step in treating private and public employees equally in the bargaining arena. Before this time contracts between school boards and teachers' unions were seen as an illegal delegation to school boards of local citizens' sovereign constitutional powers.

Wisconsin was the first state to pass legislation for public employee bargaining that resembled in any way the language found in the NLRA. In

1962 a statute was enacted requiring local governments to bargain in good faith with employee groups. This statute also created administrative machinery to enforce the law. The Wisconsin Public Employee Relations Board was charged with determination of appropriate bargaining units, prevention of prohibited practices, fact-findings, and mediation of disputes.

The enabling legislation passed in Wisconsin marked the beginning of widespread recognition of the rights of public employees to bargain collectively. New York and Michigan passed similar laws within the next five years. By 1974, thirty-seven states had passed some legislation regulating the bargaining of public employees, although statutes varied considerably. Altogether, twenty-seven states provided for exclusive representation of non-supervisory personnel by an employee group, and mediation or factfinding was mandatory in twenty-three states. Strong administrative agencies oversaw negotiations of public employees in twenty-one states, while the same number of states prohibited unfair labor practices and provided some means of enforcement. In addition to such provisions, seven states had impasse procedures that allowed teachers' organizations to go on strike or force compulsory binding arbitration. Four years later an additional seven states had legislation permitting explicit bargaining; seven more states had assigned roles to public-employee-relations boards and permitted strikes by teachers. Thus by 1978, 61 per cent of classroom teachers resided in states that permitted formal collective bargaining in education (Ross, 1978).

Attitudes and Needs of Teachers

Teachers long have carried the banner of professionalism and have resisted the idea of organizing as a bargaining unit. In the early years of the NEA, members felt that the organization's role should be one of promoting the professional side of teaching. Although NEA members were sensitive to their financial needs, the official posture of NEA was one of debate, not collective action (Cooper, 1982, p. 22).

The metamorphosis of teachers from passive professionals to union activists can be understood partially by considering how they see themselves as teachers. A number of studies have been conducted to assess the attitudes of teachers toward their jobs. The picture that emerges shows teachers wanting both respect from the public for their dedication to their profession (Herndon, 1976; Strom, 1979; Lortie, 1977) and the financial rewards they feel should come to skilled professionals (Steele, 1976; Donley, 1976; McDonnell and Pascal, 1979).

Teachers' self-concept on both these counts reached a low point during the 1960s. Educators came to realize that they were underpaid and that their lagging prestige as professionals had suffered even more because of their low wages and limited control over conditions of employment. In addition, as school districts became larger and the number of teacher and administrative personnel increased, teachers felt they were left with little control over their teaching activities.

Thus, teachers saw bargaining as a way to increase their professional discretion through rules to insulate them from external control (Kerchner *et al*, 1980). Some of the rules embodied in contracts, however, have produced a somewhat undesirable by-product. Bargaining leads to greater participation by teachers in decision-making in school affairs (Belasco and Alluto, 1969). Yet participation may not be all that it would appear. In fact, Belasco and Alluto found that too much participation can lead to dissatisfaction, and Eberts (1982) showed that it takes away from instructional time. Nonetheless, the means to greater autonomy, regardless of the increased participation, appears to be a goal of most bargaining units.

The Labor Movement and the NEA and AFT

Since its inception in the early part of this century, the AFT had tried to bring teachers into the mainstream of organized labor. Unlike their considerably more powerful rival, the NEA, the AFT advocated c llective action as the best way to promote the interests of teachers. NEA, on the other hand, preferred what they called a 'professional' approach to employee relations, avoiding the strike and supporting devices such as blacklisting schools that failed to treat teachers properly (Cooper, 1982).

Since NEA membership dwarfed AFT membership during the 1950s by thirteen to one, a general non-union posture of teachers prevailed. In 1961, however, a major victory for the AFT in organizing New York City teachers changed the course of teacher collective bargaining. Donley (1976) describes the AFT victory in New York City as 'probably the biggest single success in the history of teacher organizing in the United States' (p. 46). Indeed the victory in New York City had a profound effect on NEA's attitude toward collective bargaining. Feeling threatened by the sudden popularity of AFT-style labor relations, NEA officially urged bargaining but tempered its support within the bounds of professionalism.

Today, the AFT once again has taken the lead in labor relations. Sensing the nation's concern about teacher competency, the AFT has softened its strong activist and militant stand on bargaining. Instead of pushing for hard line stands on wage demands and bargaining provisions, the AFT has urged its affiliates to establish higher standards — to police its ranks, hold teachers accountable to union standards, and bargain cooperatively rather than contentiously with management. The NEA has also come out recently for increased teacher accountability and a strengthening of professionalism. It is still too early to see how this new stance will be accepted by the rank and file members, especially the old guard members who have fought to make unions a dominant force in education.

Scope of Bargaining

Teacher contracts have matured very quickly in the two decades of recognized bargaining. From the simple beginnings of negotiating only salary and certain working conditions, the scope of bargaining agreements has expanded into areas that traditionally have been administrative perogatives. Teachers now set educational policy; control, to various degrees, personnel matters, including layoffs and promotions; participate in decisions regarding student assignment; and negotiate teacher–student ratios.

Although most of these provisions address teachers' concerns about working conditions, empirical analysis reveals very little significant relationship between district conditions and the presence of contract provisions. In fact, most studies, including our work, show that factors exogenous to district decision-making are the best predictors of bargaining outcomes. Our analysis also reveals that gains in contract provisions are not achieved without costs to the unions. In both Michigan and New York, for example, districts that gained reduction-in-force provisions are more likely to lose class-size limitation provisions than are districts that have not recently gained such provisions. Nonetheless, teachers have acquired a number of noncompensation items that have the potential to limit the flexibility of school management and to increase the costs of public education.

The Educational Process and Collective Bargaining

Collective bargaining takes place basically at the school district level; the student's education takes place in the classroom. For collective bargaining to affect student achievement, its effects must enter the classroom. The obvious primary carrier of these effects is the teacher. The educational process is sufficiently complex that concentrating only upon the teachers, or aspects of the interaction between teacher and student, is not sufficient to assess the overall effect of collective bargaining. Hence we posit a simple model of the educational process that identifies five basic groups of determinants of student outcomes: (i) student characteristics; (ii) teacher characteristics; (iii) time spent by teachers and students performing various tasks; (iv) modes of instruction, and (v) administrator characteristics. Figure 1 depicts the paths of influence between major inputs and student achievement.

By affecting a variety of these inputs in the educational process, collective bargaining can influence student achievement through a number of channels. Table 1 provides a more detailed breakdown of the basic ingredients for the educational process and provides some preliminary hypotheses about how these factors may be affected by collective bargaining.

Figure 1: Path Diagram of Factors Determining Student Achievement

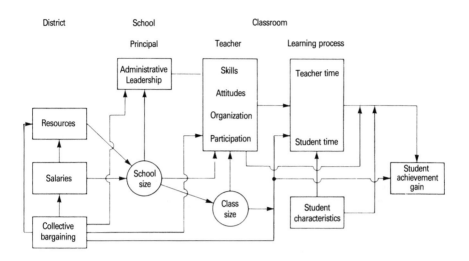

Student Achievement

It is well documented that the abilities and motivation that students bring to the classroom are important determinants of academic success. Many of these are related to home environment, as measured by childhood experience, parental involvement, economic status, and the importance parents place on education. We assume that collective bargaining has no influence on these factors, although the reverse may be true. There may be some instances in which families who have strong preferences about teacher unionism or who have experienced an especially disruptive teacher strike, may send their children to a different district or to private schools, but for our interest we consider the composition of the student body attending a particular school district to be unaffected by the level of bargaining activity.

Teacher Charateristics

Collective bargaining can influence teachers' characteristics in several ways. The first is through mobility. Teachers, either by their own preference or administrative action, may enter or leave a district and, in so doing, change

Table 1: *Determinants of Student Achievement and the Hypothesized Effects of Collective Bargaining*

	Student Characteristics	Time	Mode of Instruction	Teacher Characteristics	Administrative Leadership
Determinants of student achievement	Age Sex Race Childhood experience Parental involvement Exact grade level Economic status Pretest score Attitudes Attendance	Instruction (interaction of time in instruction with characteristics and modes) Preparation Administration Parents	Individualized Size of instructional unit 21+ 14–21 7–13 2–6 Other	Experience (inside and outside school and district) Degree Inservice programs Type of instructor Classroom Aide Specialist Attitudes Degree of participation	Maintenance of order Introducing change Setting clear objectives Supporting teachers Providing rewards and incentives Observing classrooms Allocating resources
Effects of collective bargaining	No hypothesized effect	Has been shown to affect all items Now must show the influence on the effectiveness of time	Size of instructional unit is influenced by staff size, which is influenced by bargained wages	Has been shown to affect all items except degree of participation	Hypothesized constraints on flexibility and on formality of interactions with teachers Possible 'voice' effect

the composition of the teaching staff. A second avenue of influence is through the structure of salary schedules. Since experience and education are given a premium, teachers have some salary incentives to remain with the district and to obtain additional education.

The collective bargaining environment may also influence the attitudes of teachers, especially those attitudes related to working conditions and to their relationship with principals. The formation of certain attitudes may be related to the degree of participation given teachers on policy matters, such as class assignment, student assignment, and curriculum development. Collective bargaining may provide teachers with a greater level of participation but at the same time may cast the administration in an adversarial role.

Teacher and Student Time

The time teachers and students spend on various tasks is an important determinant of student achievement. Collective bargaining may influence the allocation of time by requiring teachers to spend time with union-related business and with coordinating activities.

Methodology

The primary tool of analysis used to examine these relationships is multivariate regression, applied both to cross-sectional and time-series data. The data come from three basic sources. The first is a nationwide sample of 14,000 fourth-graders in 328 elementary schools collected under the Sustaining Effects Study (SES) conducted during the late 1970s under a grant from the Office of Education (now the Department of Education). This dataset is used to look at the effects of collective bargaining on student achievement and district costs. The other two data sets include extensive information about school districts and collective bargaining contracts for every district in Michigan and New York.

Detailed Effects of Collective Bargaining

We maintain that one of the most important, if not the most important, measure of the impact of teacher unions on public education is their effect on student achievement. In pursuing this end, we have considered a host of effects on teachers, administrators, and taxpayers as well as students. Probably the single most important finding of our work is that union schools are more productive than non-union schools for the average elementary student. For extremely above or below average students, however, non-union schools are more productive by about the same margin.

The union productivity advantages arise from two major factors. First, union districts rely to a greater degree than non-union districts on standard classroom instructional techniques, which work best for the majority of students. Significantly below or above average students, however, appear to perform better in nonunion districts, where their exposure to specialized programs and instructional techniques is significantly greater. This standardization of instructional techniques is similar to union behavior in many private sector industries. A second major source of union advantage is the greater effectiveness of instructional leadership activities by school principals in union districts. In organized districts, for example, instructional leadership by school principals may be much more effective both because specific principal actions are conditioned by teacher opinion and because the effectiveness of particular actions is enhanced by improved communication and coordination.

The higher average productivity of teacher unions is not without cost. We find that organized districts spend on average 12 per cent more per pupil than unorganized districts, even with achievement measures and student and community characteristics held constant. What accounts for the higher costs in unionized districts and who bears the costs? There are three general classes of effects: compensation effects, productivity effects, and factor-use effects. We have found, for example, that unionization increased salaries of unionized teachers by 7 to 15 per cent by the late 1970s, as compared to otherwise similar non-unionized teachers. If teacher unions are similar to other unions, the effect on fringe benefits would be at least as large.

As mentioned earlier, union districts are more productive than non-union districts, up to 7 per cent more productive for the average student, partially due to differences in instructional leadership by principals. With respect to factor-use effects of unionization, we find that class-size restrictions, reduction-in-force limitations, and other contract provisions significantly affect the use of resources in unionized districts. For example, the teacher-student ratio in unionized districts is significantly higher than in nonunionized districts. This factor-use effect, however, does not appear to exceed the positive productivity effect.

Of the three unionization effects considered, the productivity effects and factor-use effects appear to be roughly offsetting. That is, the slightly higher productivity of unionized districts is roughly the same magnitude as the cost associated with higher teacher-student ratios in unionized districts. Because the productivity and factor-use effects tend to cancel, the union-induced teacher compensation premium dominates the estimated cost differential. This conclusion is further supported by the fact that multiplying the mid-range estimate of the union salary premium (17 per cent) by the typical ratio of teacher personnel costs to total costs (about 0.7) yields an estimate of the union cost differential (12 per cent) consistent with the midrange of our own estimates (12 per cent). Since the union productivity and factor-use differentials are roughly offsetting, the union cost differential primarily respresents a transfer of benefits from taxpayers to teachers, with little detrimental change in average student achievement.

On a more speculative note, over a much longer period of time the higher compensation in unionized districts could enable such districts to attract and retain more productive teachers, partially offsetting the union cost differential.

Other union effects were also found. Turning to the issue of teacher attitudes and collective bargaining, we found union teachers to be less concerned about personnel policy than non-union teachers, but more concerned about class size. This concern with class size tends to confirm the large implicit price, or compensating wage differential, found for the teacher-student ratio. Union teachers also appear to be less satisfied in general about their workplace than non-union teachers, although this dissatisfaction may be an explanation rather than a consequence, of collective bargaining.

For administrators we investigated the separate and interactive effects of contract provisions in two broad areas of administrative behavior and discretion — resource allocation and educational policy and practice. Significantly, we found that contract provisions follow a clear hierarchy: the presence of particular contract provisions tends to be clearly ordered within major categories, but the provisions remain independent between categories. Our evaluations of the effects of individual provisions indicated that employers and employees tend to disagree more about responses to external events than about events associated with the daily routine of the district. We found significant effects for a number of individual contract provisions on the allocation of district expenditures across various budget categories, with the total magnitude of the effects varying from about 0 to 30 per cent. As indicated above, this range is consistent with our estimates of the effects of collective bargaining on overall costs and teachers' salaries.

For our second broad topic area for administrators, educational policy and practice, we found significant links between contract provisions and modes of instruction (the traditional classroom mode, for example, is more likely to be used in the presence of class-size contract provisions). No significant differences were found, however, between union and nonunion teachers in either the desired level, or the actual level, of teacher participation in a wide range of administrative decisions. What we did find was a persistently positive relationship between the desire for participation and actual participation, whether or not the district is organized. Finally, both union and non-union teachers generally prefer a greater degree of teacher participation in administrative decisions than actually occurs.

Conclusion

Teacher unions have indeed become a crucial force in deciding how public schools are run in the US. In brief, unionized teachers receive higher salaries, teach smaller classes, spend less time in instructing students, and have more time for classroom preparation. The net effect of teacher unions on these important factors in the educational process is to make unionized districts slightly more effective than non-unionized districts in educating the average student. The higher costs associated with union districts, particularly in the form of higher teacher salaries and benefits, far exceed the productivity advantage, however.

Admittedly, we have taken a somewhat simplistic view of the educational process and have glossed over many interesting and important aspects of the bargaining process. Even so, we have examined in a reasonably controlled fashion the effect of unionization on the educational achievements of thousands of individual students and on the operation and efficiency of hundreds of districts across the United States. Our results reflect long-run adjustments by teachers, administrators, and taxpayers to the bargaining environment. Unlike strikes or contract negotiations, these adjustments generally do not make headlines, but they do make lasting changes in American education.

Notes

1 The preparation of this chapter was made possible through an institutional grant from the National Institute of Education to the Center for Educational Policy and Management at the University of Oregon. The opinions expressed in the chapter do not necessarily reflect the positions or policies of NIE or the Department of Education.

References

BAUGH, W.H. and STONE, J.A. (1982). 'Teachers, unions, and wages in the 1970s: Unionism now pays', *Industrial and Labor Relations Review*, 35, 3, April, pp. 368–76.
BELASCO, J.A. and ALLUTO, J. (1969). 'Organizational impacts of teacher negotiations', *Industrial Relations* 9, 1 October, pp. 67–79.
COOPER, B.S. (1982). *Collective Bargaining, Strikes, and Financial Costs in Public Education: A Comparative Review*. Eugene, OR, Clearinghouse on Educational Management, University of Oregon.
CRESSWELL, A. and SPARGO, F. (1980) *Impacts of Collective Bargaining Policy in Elementary and Secondary Education: A Review of Research*, Denver, CO, Education Commission of the States.
DONLEY, M.O., JR. (1976). *Power to the Teacher: How America's Educators became Militant*, Bloomington, In., Indiana University Press.
EBERTS, R.W. (1982). *Unionism and Nonwage Effects: A Simultaneous Equations Model of Public School Teacher Collective Bargaining*, Eugene, OR, Center for Educational Policy and Management, University of Oregon.
EBERTS, R.W., and STONE, J.A. (1984) *Unions and Public Schools: The Effect of Collective Bargaining on American Education*, Lexington, MA, Lexington Books.

GOLDSCHMIDT, S.M. (1982). 'An overview of the Evolution of Collective Bargaining and its Impact on Education', Proceedings of conference on *The Effects of Collective Bargaining on School Administrative Leadership*. Eugene, OR, Center for Educational Policy and Management, University of Oregon.

HERNDON, T. (1976). *NEA Reporter*, April.

KERCHNER, C.T., MITCHELL, D., PRYOR, G. and ERCK, W. (1980). *The Impact of Collective Bargaining on School Management and Policy: A Preliminary Research Report*. Claremont, CA, Labor Relations Research Project, Claremont Graduate School.

LORTIE, D.C. (1969). 'Control and autonomy of elementary school teachers', in ETZONI, A. (Ed.) *The Semi-Professions*. Glencoe, 12, The Free Press.

LORTIE, D.C. (1977). *Schoolteacher: A Sociological Study*. Chicago: University of Chicago Press.

McDONNELL, L. and PASCAL, A. (1979) 'Organized teachers in American schools' *R-2407-NIE*, Santa Monica, CA, Rand Corporation.

ROSS, D. (1978). *Cuebook: State Education Collective Bargaining Laws*. Denver, Colo.: Education Commission of the States.

STEELE, H.H. (1976). 'A teacher's view', *Phi Delta Kappan*, May, pp. 590–2.

STROM, D. (1979). 'Teacher unionism: An assessment', *Education and Urban Society*, 11, 2, February, pp. 152–67.

Part 4
Administration and Reorganization

12 Changing Roles of Australian Education Chief Executives at the State Level

Grant Harman, Frederick M. Wirt and Hedley Beare

Introduction

This chapter is concerned with the changing role of chief executives of education departments and agencies in the Australian states and territories. Its purpose is to explain the aims and methodology of a current research project being undertaken by the authors, and to provide preliminary findings on specific topics.[1]

The term chief executives of education departments and agencies in the Australian states and territories is used to refer to:

(a) Directors-General of the six state education departments and their equivalents in the two territories, i.e., the Australian Capital Territory (ACT) and the Northern Territory (NT);

(b) heads of the separate technical and further education (TAFE) authorities in New South Wales, Victoria and South Australia (in the other three states and in the NT, TAFE is administered by state or territorial departments of education, while in the ACT it is currently under the control of the Commonwealth Department of Education); and

(c) heads of separate statutory tertiary education coordinating authorities in New South Wales, Victoria, Queensland, South Australia and Western Australia.

The aim of the research project being undertaken by the authors is to explore the courses, nature and consequences of the changing role of chief education executives in the Australian states and territories, and also at Commonwealth level. It should be noted, however, that this chapter reports data relating to state and territory executives only. The work is one follow-up of the 1979/80 study of policy-making on the Australian states and territories, directed by Harman and Wirt.[2] That study noted the prevalent belief of Directors-General of education at state level, as well as of others close to them, that their role as departmental heads had dramatically changed. One of us reported:

> In the past, particular directors-general were extremely influential and dominated their respective departments to a large extent; however, over the past decade their traditional dominance has been challenged. Directors-General believe they are being squeezed from all sides with the increasing influence of the Commonwealth government, the growth of professional authority at the school level, and the continuing pressure from the teachers' unions. Teachers and the public still see directors-general as extremely powerful within public education, but they themselves are concerned much more with constraints on their freedom and power.[3]

We were also mindful of somewhat similar role changes with regard to school superintendents in the United States.[4] Because of the rise of many groups who challenge the once unchallenged authority of American school superintendents to determine schooling policy, the administrative environment of these professionals has become very turbulent politically. In additions, the growth of state and federal expectations about new goals for schooling has also intervened on the local scene to create new expectations of what superintendents should do. As a result of this political and mandate turbulence, change in the one-time role of the superintendent as neutral technician to one of negotiator statesman is clearly evidenced. We were led to ask whether a similar shift may operate in Australia.

Methodology and Design

Role is probably one of the most used concepts in the social sciences. It is usually defined as the expectations of significant others of one's behaviour, which shape that behaviour and socializes the holder into its appropriateness. Of course, each person performs multiple roles. Two research questions guided our role focus upon chief executives:

(a) What is expected of public servants in democratic societies, and in particular what is expected of professional public servant executives?

(b) How and why have these executive roles changed over time?

The methodology employed has four basic components. First, the subjects studied are common, i.e., appointed heads of state and territory bodies which supervise primary, secondary and tertiary education, as well as heads of Commonwealth education bodies. Second, we employed a common questionnaire designed to ask these persons how they respond to a set of professional duties. Third, by interviewing all former living executives, as well as

Table 1:   Results of Interviews of Current and Former Chief Executives of Education .

	Interviewed		Not or Not Yet Interviewed
	Current	Former	
New South Wales	2	2	4
Victoria	3	2	3
South Australia	3	3	1
Queensland	2	2	—
Western Australia	2	3	1
Tasmania	1	2	—
Australian Capital Territory	1	1	—
Northern Territory	—	1	4
Commonwealth	3	4	6
TOTAL	17	20	19

current incumbents, we cover more than one generation. One of our respondents (Sir Harold Wyndham) was appointed Director-General in New South Wales as far back as 1952. Fourth, we are asking advice of a small group of informed commentators throughout Australia, including experienced scholars, senior education executives other than chief executives, and former ministers.

This four-fold design was used to avoid asking executives directly whether they believe there has been a change in role, but rather to find the behavioural elements of that change and to tap the perceptions of those who know the scene well as observers or policy actors. If across time answers to the same questions about chief executives behaviour varies, then that may be taken as evidence of role change; if the answers across time do not vary, then we may conclude there is no role change. In short, we do not rely simply on chief executives' own generalized feelings about change, because change is always being discussed in modern societies.

The questionnaire was devised primarily by Beare, with additions from Harman and Wirt. It was field-tested in Victoria, revised to a smaller size, then employed by Wirt, with help from Harman in Queensland, Sydney and Canberra. Table 1 provides information on the interviews completed.

It is important to attempt to link any role change found to factors which lie outside the persons being studied. What explanations are there about how society and role changes are linked? With some minor variations, that literature reports that changes in socio-economic and political environments cause:

(a)   changes in the relative power of social groups;
(b)   changes in group values; and
(c)   changes in the response of the political system to group demands on society.

This is a familiar explanation of social change and its effects, which is found in Marxist, liberal democratic and conservative interpretations of social reality. All three of these, however, give different priorities to what changes are significant or desirable, and what the consequences of such change are. A second explanation follows from the first, namely, that changes in the political system will generate new expectations of the behaviour of all officials about how they should interact in making public policy for the community or society.

Besides the conditions and causes of role change, we are also interested in its consequences. One consequence of importance relates to the implications for the Westminister model of ministerial responsibility and to the relationship between minister and permanent head. Some of our respondents have said straight out that there is no longer such a system in Australia. They point to the other voices to which the minister now listens, and to the trends towards fixed-term contracts and more overtly political appointments of permanent heads and chairmen of statutory authorities. Another consequence of role change relates to training the future pool of Directors-General and heads of tertiary bodies. There is no formal training for these positions, now or in the past, except for on-the-job training in middle and senior executive positions. Our respondents say the position of chief executive has become increasingly 'political'. Most of them began as very 'naive' about politics, and so they had to learn how to do it while on the job. But is there some way of providing 'political' training to educational admininstration? Could or should anything be done in order to improve this quality of the public service and to increase these persons' experience with political learning?

The remainder of the chapter reports data on seven topics: selection and appointment; expectations and achievements; role perception and definition; work activity patterns; working with the minister; relations with senior colleagues; and external relations.

Selection and Appointment

We asked respondents at the beginning of the interviews how they came to occupy the chief executive post and, in particular, how the appointment took place, that is, the procedures involved. Almost all talked freely on this topic.

We must distinguish between the formal process of appointment to the position and its informal aspects. Almost everywhere, and certainly for the current incumbents, the formal process involved advertisement, applications, a selection committee, interviews, perhaps a discussion with the Chairman of the Public Service Board, ministerial decision or recommendation, approval by the Cabinet, and so on. However, for the earlier officers and to some degree this is true of some of the modern ones, that sequence was broken by the informal aspects of the appointment process. Informally, some of the incumbents had political connections, although these were always daintily expressed.

There were probably three main patterns of appointment: the heir-apparent, the two princes fighting for the throne, and the outsider successor. The heir-apparent strategy was clearly characteristic of the earliest appointments, of men who had long service in the Department, always with some early teaching experience. This approach is also evident in the appointment of such Directors-General as Axton in Tasmania and Vickery in Western Australia (since replaced). The dual-princes problem arises with two Deputy-Directors, who have come up through the ranks and have equal qualifications and claims. Sometimes one of these was appointed and the loser would seek early retirement or find an administrative appointment in another branch. Sometimes the dual-princes situation was handled by bringing in an outsider. But this does not occur very often; for example, Western Australia appointed a military officer as Director-General after World War II. While it may be convenient for ministers to use this strategy, desiring to place in office someone sympathetic to their interests, ministers are still left the problem of the intra-departmental contenders.

We were struck by the prevalence of the heir-apparent incumbents, but then we talked to very few who may have lost out in that process. But in the case of Queensland we know that Berkeley was appointed Director-General over Hamilton, the Deputy Director-General, while Hamilton was appointed six months in advance as Chairman of the Advanced Education Board. Similarly in Victoria in 1983, Curry was brought in from one of the colleges of advanced education and appointed over a number of experienced senior officers of the Education Department. We see this is an area ripe for further research on these delicate relationships involved in the three alternatives which we deduced from interviews.

Expectations and Achievements

A number of questions explored these topics. Early in the interviews we asked directly about expectations at the time of appointment. In the expansion of education through the 1950s and 1960s to meet the baby-boom and in response to the Commonwealth ventures, the expectations of Directors-General were largely defined by the term 'institution building'. That refers to expanding the teaching service, altering the curriculum, constructing buildings and all the other attributes of growth. The expectations of the current group, however, refer much more to interactions with newly contending forces in education today. These look more like system-maintenance expectations, that is, struggling to keep the lighthouse going.

The first type found themselves everywhere overwhelmed by demands for education, and their comments explain the course they took in meeting it. These tasks included: expanding secondary education and the high school system, constructing elaborate sets of buildings, removing or decreasing the competitive examination method, and expanding the curriculum. The current set, however, is more preoccupied with the struggle to deal with changes in TAFE, upper secondary schooling and matriculation college institutions, with militancy of teacher unions, and with demands for greater accountability. In short, contemporary administrators must deal with power-sharing. Some of this group also seeks to adopt new management techniques. Central to these is the effort to devolve, not power and authority, but responsibilities. Finally we noted that the early Director-General often spoke about the need to increase the sense of professionalism among teachers; often they might spend their first year in a large number of vists to schools, where they talked with teacher groups particularly about the need to improve their professional standing. Today's Director-General, however, speaks little of this but more of struggling to meet teacher demands on a range of matters.

Later in these interviews we asked about the educational reforms with which respondents were involved during their period in office and that gave them reason for pride. If there is any pattern in the responses, it is that earlier Directors-General, in the time of educational expansion and generous resources, were very proud of the ways they went about meeting the problems of expansion. This group had thrust upon them an enormous set of demands, for which there probably was no precedent in the education history of Australia. It was not simply a problem of providing large amounts of money to build more schools and to recruit and train more teachers; that itself was what might be called a logistic problem. But another part of their problem was how to put those resources together in such a way that their programs improved not only the quantity but the quality of student education. Here, all of the older generation of Directors-General had a sense of their personal influence in riding these currents of change.

As for the incumbents, the distinction should be made between the tertiary heads and the Directors-General. Among the former, there were few specific policies to which they could point, but rather they talked about successfully creating within the colleges of advanced education and universities a sense of trust and understanding of what their agency's role was. An exception to this was the current Chairman of the New South Wales Board of Advanced Education, Ron Parry; he reported success in changing the nature of nursing education in that state, a move he reported was copied elsewhere. As for the current Directors-General, however, they were more likely to talk about coping with constraints. This task meant making difficult decisions about cutting staff and office personnel, closing schools and all the other attributes of system shrinkage. Here too the Directors-General talked about their personal role in seeking to cope amidst constraints.

In asking about barriers to achieving their goals, we were surprised at the variation in answers, which were not simply a difference between the former and the incumbent officers. Some looked upon federal policy action

as a high constraint, but many others did not because they saw it paral-
lelling and hence reinforcing their own concerns and interests. Similarly,
again, state legislation was generally regarded as a constraint by some but
not by others, since that legislation very often reflected their own policies.
Constraints of teachers' unions and equal opportunity or freedom of information provisions were not seen as such by the older Directors-General, but
they are seen this way by incumbents. Limits of funding are seen as a very
high constraint among the contemporary Directors-General, but not, of
course, among the earlier ones, who found public resources pouring in upon
their offices. As for administrative regulations, those emanating from the
Public Service Board are seen as less constraining among the more recent set.
Most in both sets believed that they had the support of public opinion, so
that it was a low constraint for what they had to do; this certainly was the
case for the older Directors-General faced with enormous public demand for
educational services.

Later in the interview we asked whether any significant changes had
taken place in the respondent himself while in office. This is a very introspec-
tive and psychological question, and little was said that can be generalized.
Most found this the most difficult question, quite often occasioning remarks
like: 'Tough one, isn't it?' A few referred to getting tired, others to becoming
more aware of the political nature of their job and to learning how to cope
with that, and some reported no changes at all. If at some later stage of
analysis we can integrate types of executive officers and their behaviours,
relations with others and so on, it would be interesting to correlate these
with the types of answers received here.

Role Perception and Definition

We attempted to explore role perception and definition in a number of ways.
In the interviews, we asked respondents specifically to define the most
important elements of their role as chief executive. Some did not use the
term 'leadership', but rather their answers were programmatic — that is,
they talked about particular things they had to do to carry out specific
programs. Some had to be probed as to their relationship with the minister
— an important part of their role — while in other cases that would be the
first thing mentioned. If there is any gross distinction between the earlier and
present officers, it is between building a new institution and keeping it
working, between innovation on a grand scale and maintenance. Note that
for the first set this required trying to build a sense of professionalism among
the teachers, coalition building for major capital works projects and all the
other system building aspects of the baby-boom period.

We asked respondents about changes in the chief executive position,
especially about new functions added or functions taken away. Among the
older officials, there were few cases of clear additions or deletions in respon-

sibility, although we noted that in an earlier period many Directors-General had responsibilities for more fields, such as recreation, sport and culture. Sir Harold Wyndham in New South Wales may well have been the last of these, as he sat on the committee concerned with the preliminary planning of the Sydney Opera House. But in recent years, responsibility for many functions — such as TAFE, public examinations or secondary school curriculum, as well as the coordination of tertiary education — has moved to new agencies. Consequently, the Director-General is now only one of the chief executives providing advice, and sometimes competing advice, to the minister.

Late in the interviews we asked two other questions on this topic. First, 'Could you describe the picture in your head of your job during your tenure, using several nouns?' and second, 'How were you different from or like your predecessor in this regard?' We noted first a distinction between respondents whose nouns either directly or indirectly referred to leadership, and those who had to be probed in order to have that term come out. Some could say very little about this, while others could rattle off as many as ten items. Some answered in terms of personal qualities, but most gave answers that were task-oriented or which designated actions on their part. As for the difference from their predecessors, one general comment should be made. This was the judgment made in most interviews, that their predecessors were tougher or more 'autocratic' than they were. Only one exception to this judgment appeared. Indeed, those who were in office in the 1960s and early 1970s, often seen now as autocrats, themselves pointed to their predecessors as *real* autocrats.

Work Activity Patterns

We aimed to collect information on time spent on various work tasks; respondents would be asked to review diaries to see how their time was actually distributed on fairly typical weeks. But it became evident early on that this was not useful when we had so many former executives did not have available diaries on such activity. What we did was to ask them to look at a list of specific work activities and to pick those on which they spent most of their time and where they spent least of their time. Eventually, we began to ask them where did they spend at least half of their time.

In those terms, then, most spent most time interacting with senior colleagues. However, the early ones spent less time attending administrative meetings, while the more recent ones spent more, particularly in relation with other departments and the Commonwealth. The earlier ones also spent least time interacting with the minister. Time spent on paper work, writing papers and speeches, was almost without exception, seen as work done *outside* the normal working day, either at home or coming to the office early for an hour or more. The latter strategy did not always work because some eager subordinate would be on his doorstep with some problem — and there went the time for paper work. As for time spent on external relations, a distinction has to be made between the first and later years of the career of a Director-General. Often he would spend the first year putting much emphasis on external relations. This involved visiting schools to talk to teachers, students and parents, or interacting with the media and others. The purpose in both cases was to make oneself familiar with issues and details, to raise the profile of the Department, and to get across the sense of what one was trying to do.

Later in their career, however, the time given to these activities tended to fall off, as one turned more within the structures of government to make and administer policy. Here, the overall picture that comes through is that half one's time or more was spent in interacting with senior colleagues, including administrative meetings.

Working with the Minister

One of the most important and often the most difficult aspects of the role of a chief executive is working with the minister. Many of our respondents had worked with two or more ministers; indeed, some had served up to three ministers over a short space of time. If we characterize the relationship between these two figures from the early period to the present one, it fits the model already referred to. That is, earlier Directors-General were the single and unchallenged adviser to the minister on the professional educational policy aspects; today they are one of several advisers. This change arises because of the new multiple channels to the minister providing advice on education policy. The source of this change is often cited as the Labor Party. A number of respondents pointed to cases of Labor ministers who had been teachers, persons with their own ideas about policy. But the change may have much deeper causes, lying in the increasing demand for education, the differing views of its content and methods, and criticisms of education for not meeting its own goals.

The frequency of interaction with the minister was one avenue for exploring this relationship; it has always varied. We observed the physical proximity of the minister to particular chief executives; we also found that ministers have been much more closely related to education departments than to TAFE agencies or tertiary coordinating bodies. Indeed, in Melbourne the minister is located within the Education Department building, while the TAFE Board is three or four kilometres away and the Post-secondary Education Commission is a 20–25 minute tram ride away in an eastern suburb. Generally the Director-General is located just down the hall from the minister. They talked about 'popping' in and out of the another's offices, or picking up the phone for talks and always, of course, having a regular weekly meeting for 30–60 minutes.

Relationships between the two could change over time. Sometimes they improved, perhaps as a result of good performance by the Director-General and most certainly as trust developed. Sometimes they deteriorated, especially if a minister experienced political trouble from education policy conflicts. Apart from this, however, a pattern was evident. In the early stages of their relationship chief executives sought to educate their ministers on the institution and its policies, thereby putting themselves in a much stronger role with their political master. All of them talked about the necessity to build trust into this relationship, so that the minister could trust the advice of the servant; most of those interviewed thought they had created that trust.

To probe further, we asked respondents for three key incidents to demonstrate their working relationships with a minister in carrying out their duties. Most examples were of relationships with different kinds of ministers, not with the same minister. Characteristically, the incidents formed three patterns. One was cooperative in which the Director-General took the lead, one was cooperative in which the minister took the lead, and one was antagonistic, the two firmly opposed on a specific matter. These are in a descending frequency; the last did not occur often. On antagonistic relations, we asked respondents if they had ever thought of resigning because of such a conflict. One current Director-General said that he had thought about it twice. What often happens in antagonistic situations is that the chief executive writes to the minister, firmly stating objections, but goes no further than that. However, it is on the record should the minister's venture turn out badly. It is important to note that we found none who resigned and went public in such a conflict. This much of the Westminster model is retained.

Finally, initiation of action or policies by the minister has now become a much more common phenomenon. From various states we found examples of major policy or organizational changes that were initiated and pursued actively by ministers, sometimes against the preference and advice of his chief executive.

Relations with Senior Colleagues

In our attempts to understand the role of chief executive within his organization, we asked respondents how they and their deputies divided up the work, and about their interaction with other senior officers.

The deputy question was probed by suggesting that there were two possible models of using the deputy. In the first, the deputy is a jack-of-all-trades, that is, pulled into all kinds of problems as they arise. In the second, the deputy is a specialist, who is assigned particular functions in which he is trained, so that the Director-General could leave that function of the organization up to him. It is clear that there are cases of both of these. It is interesting to note, however, that the Directors-General who reject use of the second model do so because they want somebody to run the organization when they are away and hence to make decisions across the wide range usual for the Director-General. We suspect that in the modern period the jack-of-all-trades type is more common. One matter to be explored further is how the deputy who succeeds to the Director-General position then defines the deputy position.

Interaction was quite frequent with officers below the Director-General whom we will simply call directors, although titles differed. In some cases, directors constituted an executive council, meeting once or twice a month with a formal agenda and reviewing issues so that all senior officers could be aware of what was going on. This council approach, however, might also be only a sounding board for the Director-General's ideas; observers noted that such meetings were most often anecdotal and generated little policy substance. Otherwise, in most cases directors had easy access to the Director-General. Sometimes they were expected to drop in to talk about an emerging issue in order to get the Director-General's preliminary views on the matter. However, it appears that the earlier Directors-General used this style less frequently; they provided a picture of themselves initiating contacts with directors as the occasion arose, but, by and large, using them only to implement policies that they had initiated.

External Relations

The chief officer must relate to a world outside the agency. How did they interact with this external environment of other government agencies, Commonwealth government, school communities, media, teachers' unions, and their counterparts in other states?

What of their relationships with other government instrumentalities had changed significantly during their tenure? Earlier Directors-General talked much about their personal relationships with the heads of these other agencies — the Public Service Board, and the departments of the Treasury and Public Works; occasionally an Under-Treasurer may even have worked early in his career in the Department of Education. But their main accounts were stories of the 'old-boys club' of permanent secretaries known in the English experience. In all cases, however, the expectation was that, whatever the personal relationships, one's case had to be heavily loaded with data in order to justify the priorities of money and other resources they sought. There is also variation among the states in how the public service boards were involved with the administrative personnel who worked in the Department itself. In some places, that involvement has vanished as more responsibilities came directly under the Director-General.

In the recent period, the picture is different, for education is only one of the other government agencies in high competition for constrained resources brought on by a changing economy. In an earlier day, governments could make decisions about resource additions relatively easily when they had many resources. But in a period of constraint, an education agency was in direct competition with everybody else in the game to get those resources. What this may well mean, of course, is that amidst the strong effort to justify priorities decisions had to be made between priorities by someone outside the agency, which is another way of talking about the political function of ministers and Cabinet. But all our respondents were keenly aware that there were two different eras, one of expansion and one of constraint, and that their relationships with other instrumentalities took different forms in these worlds.

Almost every respondent would discuss at length how Commonwealth involvement in education had affected his work. In particular, current incumbents stressed the tremendous influence of Commonwealth activities. One tertiary head explained:

> Our whole life evolves around our relationship with Commonwealth bodies ... We can't move without the stated or perceived wishes of the Commonwealth. The Commonwealth is continually imposing on us things we can't reconcile. On the one hand, they want greater participation by qualified students, and on the other hand greater participation by disadvantaged students. When there is a limit on places, you can't have both!

The tertiary heads in particular provided long lists of constraints they faced from Canberra's involvement — and, of course, they face special problems because of total federal funding of universities and CAEs. But we were struck more by other responses. Some welcomed Commonwealth involvement because it provided substantial funds for education in the state. Some welcomed this involvement because it supplemented and stimulated their own programs; in-service education of teachers was mentioned several times. However, for some particular programs of the Whitlam government, such as Aboriginal education, we did not find such enthusiasm. Indeed, on many of such matters state officers have adopted a strategy of what we might call 'Take the money and run', resisting too detailed interference in how special grants and programs are administered.

Contact with another external source — schools, communities or individual institutions — the pattern was frequent visits by Directors-General in the early years of their term followed by a slackening off later. This is much truer of the more recent Directors-General. As for tertiary heads, their frequency of visits was much smaller than for the Directors-General. Very often the former could wait to be invited to such places; it is not clear that they used such visits very much to project their role and functioning of their office. However, in some cases tertiary heads did make a deliberate practice of scheduling board or committee meetings within tertiary institution locations and so provided the opportunity to view facilities and talk with staff.

What chief education officers got out of such visitations were different. Some were simply stimulated by the contact (Victoria's Lawrie Shears, for example, was very good at the informal exhortation to colleagues at such places). Others saw them as a forum for receiving views rather than trans- mitting them; some would meet separately with the senior students, but almost always with teachers. They also would carry back a sense of which programs were working, as well as specific complaints and details on arising problems. Some undertook regularly to tell complainants that they would deal with their concerns back in their office.

As for contact with the news media, almost every current chief execu- tive detests them and does their best to stay isolated from journalists. Gone are the days when speeches of a Sir Harold Wyndham in New South Wales were printed verbatim on the front pages of the city newspapers; the older men saw the media as outlets for their views and for undergirding their leadership. Today, however, the change is illustrated by Directors-General having press officers who, as one said, can 'talk to those people in their language'. It is also illustrated in the use of the press officer by the minister. Most Directors- General now have a clear distinction in their minds between media questions that are 'political' and hence are for the minister to handle, and others that may deal with 'professional' matters on which they will comment, but with care. Most of them avoid even this contact like the plague; all sense that the media are out to find things wrong; that is the only time when media do talk about education. Officers also believe that when they talk with journalists their views invariably end up in print reading very differently from what they were when spoken.

Much could be said about relations with teachers' unions because comments on this topic were extensive. Earlier Directors-General believed that their relationships with the teachers' unions were cordial, but then again this was before the period of greater union militancy. Many in those times had regular meetings between union and departmental officers that were described often as 'cooperative' and 'cordial', as if they were members of the same club. Indeed, the office of the head of the Tasmanian Teachers' Federa- tion was located down the corridor from that of the Director-General in the education building. However no one today talks much about cordiality, although some occasionally still use that term. Many would use the term 'confrontation', particularly to refer to their predecessor. While all respon- dents know that the relationships have changed, the relationships do vary amongst the states. In Tasmania it is still highly cordial, but elsewhere, at least on occasions, it is very much confrontationist.

On the other hand, among another part of the external world — senior colleagues in other state or territory systems — relations have been and still are warm and close. Everyone knew very well his opposite numbers in other states and territories. Most had known some of them even before appoint- ment to the position, simply because when still deputies many had attended the same national and international meetings. A number made the point that several were personal friends and they would go to social functions or even go abroad together; often they retained the friendships after leaving office. It is also clear that the tertiary heads have developed their own interstate organization to facilitate advancing their interests.

Discussion

In conclusion a few overall impressions should be stated. In the first place, everyone we talked with believed that the role of chief executive had changed importantly and that the change was one from being the chief adviser to the minister on education policy — the closed model — to one in which there were many channels for policy advice — a pluralistic or open model. Second, most pointed to several factors that contributed to these changes:

(a) The Labor Party's suspicion of the neutrality of permanent civil servants whom they had seen working against them when they served the Liberal Party. This is not totally true, of course, because in some cases substantial changes were brought on by a Liberal government, as in Victoria. It is clear, however, that in many cases the Labor Party has had a suspicion of this group and would like to see a change to something like a rotatable set of permanent heads, who did not have a speciality in a particular field. Also, the constituency of the Labor Party in the teachers' unions has provided a natural source of advice on education policy.

(b) Many refer to the unrealized expectations of many citizens that followed the great investment in education twenty years or more ago. Their point was that too many citizens expected too much was going to occur for their children with more expenditure on education. The high rate of youth unemployment in recent years has been disenchanting, and consequently resentment against professional advisors was natural.

(c) The constricted economy was everywhere pointed out as a factor which not only reduced the flow of public resources to Canberra and the states, but which forced upon top education administrators the new role of making decisions with less money. That decision-making meant that one had to devise priorities about the sources of expenditure and then to sell those priorities to a minister, who obviously had his own list of priorities derived from his own political environment.

These three changes were highly publicized because they occurred in every state and in Canberra, and were also visible in the UK and US. The general public and governments could all agree that it was necessary to cut back and that this would not be a short-run problem. This combination of causes for changing the roles of chief executives suggests that Australia is not simply a disaggregated collection of six states and two territories, but rather it resonates to broad national and international developments. What, then, are the implications for the future role of these officers? Is it the case, as some of our respondents have said, that the Westminster model no longer truly exists? If so, what then should be the role of the Director-General and teritary head, when such offices no longer are the sole authority on education policy? Finally, as this role evolves from one of a neutral technical leader to one of negotiator among competing interests, what are the implications for preparation for this role?

Notes

1 The authors acknowledge financial support and other help provided by the University of Melbourne, the University of Illinois at Champaign–Urbana and the University of New England.
2 This research was conducted under the auspices of the US–Australia Education Project, with financial support provided in Australia by the Commonwealth Government through the Education Department and Development Committee, and in the United States by the Ford Foundation through a grant to Stanford University. See the eight monographs from the project published in 1980 by the Centre for Study of Higher Education at the University of Melbourne.
3 HARMAN, G., (1985) 'Handling education policy at the state level in Australia and America', *Comparative Education Review*, 29, 1, February, p. 31.
4 See, for example, WIRT, F.M. and KIRST, M.W., (1982) *Schools in Conflict: The Politics of Education*, Berkeley, McCutchan.

13 State-Wide Educational Reform and Administrative Reorganization: Australian Experience in American Perspective*

William Lowe Boyd and Judith D. Chapman

In Australia, as in the United States, major educational reform efforts are underway on a state-wide basis. In both countries the broad-scale reforms being undertaken present a major test of the ability of authorities to achieve significant system-wide change. Of course, this is not the first time either country has attempted substantial programs of school reform. It is fair to ask, therefore, whether current efforts have profited from the lessons of the past. Put another way, are the new reforms likely to be more successful than those of the past? This chapter addresses these questions with evidence drawn from the most ambitious of the ventures now underway in Australia, that ongoing in the state of Victoria. In examining the Victorian exercise in decentralization, devolution, and school improvement, the discussion here focuses on the reasons for the reorganization effort, the effect of the effort to date, and the implications for educational policy and political and administrative theory.[1]

In brief, this research found that, although the devolution effort has accomplished part of its objective to share decision-making more broadly, the implementation of the plan has suffered from a neglect of the retraining and in-service activities needed to facilitate learning the new attitudes and roles fundamental to the new style of collaborative management which was mandated. Nevertheless, the reform effort has been successful in bringing about a tremendous change in the thrust of administration and in the content and semantics of discourse about school administration and school-

*This chapter is adapted from CHAPMAN, J. and BOYD, W.L. (1986) 'Decentralization, devolution, and the school principal: Australian lessons on state-wide educational reform', *Educational Administration Quarterly*, 22, 4, Fall.

community relations in Victoria. How much of this shift in attitude will become permanently translated into practice will only be revealed with the passage of time.

Introduction

Like most other countries, neither Australia nor the United States has a spectacular record of successful school reform. Current efforts at decentralization in Australia are only the most recent of numerous attempts, since World War II, to reduce what many observers agree is the excessive centralization of the nation's state-wide school systems.[2] By contrast, recent American reform efforts have increased centralization as a by-product of measures designed to correct deficiencies associated with the decentralized character of US schooling.[3] Thus, the widespread effort today to pursue excellence in American education follows on the heels of the ambitious, but only partly successful, 'Great Society' effort to achieve full equality of opportunity through schooling.

The high expectations raised in the US by the Great Society programs of the 1960s and the rather disappointing results which followed — not only in education but in other social policy arenas as well — prompted intensive efforts to analyze and evaluate what went wrong. As a result, there now is a vast literature on policy and implementation analysis and much more knowledge and sophistication about the complexities and problems of designing and executing successful social programs.[4] However, research on implementation problems, as well as that on the organizational characteristics of schools, sometimes seems to imply that nothing will work.[5] By contrast, the literature on the 'effective schools' movement provides prescriptions that promise success.[6]

Born as a reaction to the influential Coleman and Jencks studies that suggested schools make little difference, the effective schools movement has sought to identify the key attributes of schools that are unusually successful in fostering student achievement.[7] Among these attributes, the research stresses the importance of a strong sense of community and commitment among school staff members, and the role of principals as key actors in promoting this sense and overall school improvement.[8] Given the widespread concern for school effectiveness, the Victorian venture in Australia is of particular interest because it seeks school improvement through democratic, school-based management, with extensive community and staff involvement which necessitates a revised management role for principals.[9]

Although some American school districts have experimented with school site management plans intended to increase the decision-making power of school staff and school advisory councils, no American state has undertaken as broad and ambitious an initiative in devolution to the school level as has Victoria.[10] Indeed, the centralizing thrust of many states' plans for excellence actually is reducing local school level discretion today. This trend flies in the face of what we have learned about the importance of school staff involvement in the design and implementation of successful reforms, making the opposing trend in Victoria all the more important to observe.[11]

Given the bold reach of the Victorian initiative — to mandate community and staff participation in curriculum and school improvement, budgetary decisions, and even selection of new principles in a large state school system — composed in 1982 of 2140 schools; 40,775 teachers; and 584,781 students — one may ask how the authorities have planned to attain these goals.[12] This is no simple question because the key findings of American implementation studies have emphasized the loosely coordinated nature of schools, the wide discretion of service-level staff in implementing policies, and the frequent reality of resistance or superficial compliance in response to mandates from above.[13] As a result, successful school reform seems to require more a 'bottom-up' than a 'top-down' management approach.[14]

Ironically, Victorian authorities have used an essentially 'top-down' approach in pursuit of their 'bottom-up' objective of devolution. Still, their neglect of the lessons of American implementation analysis is far more understandable than is the corresponding ignorance or amnesia shown by US policy makers in many of the state-wide reforms now underway.[15] On the positive side, the Victorian venture has been pursued more systematically and resolutely than any previous attempts at devolution in Australian state education departments. However, the effort has been sadly lacking in training and in-service support activities designed to clarify and facilitate the transition to the dramatically new roles and relationships that have been mandated. As a result, there has been a great deal of confusion and school principals, in particular, have felt 'left out on a limb' in a most tenuous position. Nevertheless, the venture already has begun to significantly alter the character of educational administration and school-community relationships in Victoria. Consequently, it is well worth examining for the insights it provides into administrative reorganization, school reform, and the difficulties of transforming existing practices and attitudes.

Background

Developments in Victoria to 1983

The past two decades have been a time of transition in the administration of education in the state of Victoria, Australia. The basic administrative structure established under the Education Act of 1872 created a highly centralized state system in which all major functions were under the supervision of officers of the Education Department, located in Melbourne, the state capital. The chief executive officer was the Director-General; he was responsible to the Minister of Education in the Victorian parliament for the administration of the Education Act. All major decisions, both professional and managerial, were made by the senior officers of the Education Department. Schools were evaluated annually by inspectors of the Department. The principal acted as an agent of the Department, implementing policies and decisions made by officials in the central office.

Gradually, in the period between 1968 and 1981, some elements of power were relinquished by the central authorities. Recognizing that the traditional system could no longer provide effective administration for a rapidly expanding and increasingly complex system of 2000 schools, it became the Liberal (Conservative) government's policy to decentralize administrative arrangements. Mr T J Moore, Assistant Director-General of Education, explained the Liberal policy of decentralization in 1975:

> Decentralization is a matter of government policy and so far as education is concerned, the process has two distinct dimensions. One of these has been associated with the creating of [eleven] regional directorates and the other with the granting of increased autonomy to school principals.[16]

In 1980, a government review of education policies culminated in the publication of a *White Paper on Strategies and Structures for Education in Victorian Government Schools*.[17] Among the major initiatives embraced in the White Paper were:

— the reorganization of central office, regional and school levels to achieve increased devolution of power and responsibility to local and regional units;

— the expansion of the role of regional office in providing services to schools, in contributing to policy formulation at the central level, in coordinating activities and undertaking planning, in becoming a focus for accountability within the region and in serving as a direct link from school to central office and the Ministers;

— the encouragement to schools to take greater responsibility in developing educational policies and curriculum; the allocation to the principal of the responsibility to prepare school policy in consultation and agreement with the School Council;

— the provision for principals to participate in the selection of teaching staff;

— the expansion of the role of School Councils in respect to the appointment of principals and deputy principals and the planning of buildings and facilities.

A management consultant group was retained to develop a detailed plan for the implementation of the objectives of the White Paper. The *PA Report*, which they produced in September 1981, provided a blueprint for the work of an Implementation Task Force. Although both the *White Paper* and the *PA Report* endorsed measures to increase administrative accountability and efficiency as well as to broaden participation in decision making, some observers felt the thrust, especially in the *PA Report*, was more inclined toward efficiency than participation.[18]

In the remainder of 1981 and the first part of 1982 there were massive structural changes at the central and regional levels of the Education Department. In the midst of these changes came a further dramatic change. In the election of April 1982, the Liberal government was toppled from power after ruling in Victoria for over twenty-seven years. The new Labor government halted further implementation of the *PA Report* and undertook a Ministerial Review of Education that lasted from May to August. The results of that review were published in a series of ministerial papers in which the new government announced its intention to go well beyond the plan of the Liberal government in terms of devolution of authority. It established as a major objective a shift in the focus of education to the school level. Embodied in the ministerial papers was the principle that all sections of the school community should work together as partners in the interests of school and students. Particular emphasis was placed upon:

— genuine devolution of authority and responsibility to the school community;
— collaborative decision making processes;
— a responsive bureaucracy, with the main function of serving and assisting schools;
— effectiveness of educational outcomes; and
— the active redress of disadvantages and discrimination.[19]

1983–1986: The New Style of Management

In April 1983 the restructuring of the Victorian Education Department entered a new, school-based phase, when the centrally located Primary, Secondary and Technical Divisions were disbanded. For the first time in the history of the Victorian Education Department, principals would relate not to a primary, secondary or technical school administration but to their regional office: The only exceptions to these arrangements were in the area of school staffing and in those areas which traditionally had not been handled by the teaching divisions, notably teachers' salaries, superannuation and leave.[20]

To facilitate the transition to this dramatically altered organization, the Director-General provided principals with a stuctural diagram identifying central task areas. Regional Directors were expected to provide principals with a chart showing regional patterns of organization. Principals were requested, in future, to refer all inquiries and communications on matters previously handled by the teaching divisions to their regional office. Beyond this no major in-service for principals was provided.

On 12 December 1983, the State Minister of Education released a statement on the role of principals. While reiterating the central role played by principals in the life and work of the school, the statement emphasized that 'this important leadership function is to be exercised in cooperation with the School Council and the staff of the school'.

> The principal carries out the dual role of being both the representative of the Education Department and thereby responsible to the Director-General and also being executive officer of the School Council, responsible to the School Council for the implementation of Council policies and decisions on all matters within its jurisdiction. The principal carries ultimate responsibility for the administration and organization of the school, though this responsibility is to be exercised in consultation with staff.[21]

In the same month, the Education Act of 1958 was amended to provide that 'the school council shall determine the general education policy of the school within guidelines issued by the Minister'.[22] At the same time, changes were made to the composition of School Councils to provide for a higher proportion of teacher representation. These amendments placed a new emphasis upon local responsibility *and shared decision making on educational matters*.[23]

In the internal administration of the schools, administrative committees were established to offer advice to the principal on the implementation of the Industrial Agreement (union contract) and on general school operation. While principals retained the right of veto on the administrative committees, reasons were to be given for any advice that was disregarded.

In sum, a striking feature of the Victorian experience is the broad scope of the effort and the fact that each year has seen further sweeping changes. Early in 1986, Geoff Maslen summarized the major developments up to that date:

> For six years, since 1980 when the former Liberal government set about restructuring the Education Department, the government school system has been hit by one momentous change after another ... These past six years have seen school councils given extensive new powers, including a say in the appointment of the school principal and substantial authority over the curriculum. New regional boards have been set up; school inspectors — and corporal punishment — abolished; high and technical school divisions scrapped, and even the 114 year-old Education Department [structure] itself done away with.
>
> The Blackburn inquiry into the senior years of schooling called for a transformation of the curriculum, certification and organization of the last two years of school, and these changes, too, will begin to take place this year.
>
> Statewide, Victoria is experiencing a profound downturn in school enrollments. This, coupled with politically imposed modifica-

tions to the education system, is forcing local communities to contemplate the closure of long-established schools, their merger with neighboring schools or the creation of clusters and multi-campus schools . . .

[Following a welcome period of tranquil labor relations] industrial conflict surfaced again [in 1985] after a new Education Minister, Ian Cathie, took over the portfolio . . . The [teachers] unions responded to the new Minister's attitude and the government's [retrenchment] actions by staging a series of strikes in protest. Victoria was thrown once more into the turmoil that had marred the school system throughout the 1970s.[24]

The Causes of Reorganization: A Theoretical Perspective

The forces that precipitated the reorganization of the Victorian education system are consistent with theory on the evolution of state educational policy-making structures, particularly as it has been developed by Joseph McGivney.[25] However, Victorian developments illustrate a stage of development not yet experienced in the American context. In the United States, Iannaccone produced the seminal conceptual work on the evolution of state policy-making arrangements in education in 1967.[26] By means of a secondary analysis of studies of educational policy-making in eleven states, Iannaccone developed a typology of four stages through which states seemed to move in terms of relations between interest groups and governmental policy-making bodies.

Reflecting American's tradition of decentralization and local control of education, Type I involved 'locally-based disparate' linkages between localized groups and school districts, on the one hand, and state policy-making bodies, on the other. Type II, the 'statewide monolithic', reflected movement from Type I to an arrangement in which the state education association of teachers and administrators mediated competing demands and presented unified proposals to the policy-making bodies. Type III, 'statewide fragmented', developed when a variety of forces, most notably the emergence of conflict between labor and management, broke down the consensus that permitted a monolithic coalition and unified proposals. Iannaccone's Type IV, the 'statewide syndical', was based on developments in a single state, Illinois, where a 'School Problems Commission' had been created, providing a formal structure bringing together interest group leaders and state legislative and executive leaders.

As McGivney and others have noted, Type IV proved to be the most problematic feature of the conceptualization since no other state has moved in this direction and the School Problems Commission has not continued to function as Iannaccone described it. In his revision of the typology, McGivney emphasizes Iannaccone's focus on societal movement in the direction of increasing bureaucratization. McGivney develops this theme as the 'centralization imperative' and cites evidence supporting a trend toward increasing centralization of state policy-making structures in the United States. Thus, he proposes a new Type IV, the 'statewide bureaucratized', the only pure example of which in the US is our one statewide school system, in Hawaii. McGivney concludes that,

> The reconceptualized fourth stage in the state politics of education typology appears to be a viable and useful substitute for Iannanccone's earlier conceptualized Type IV. It fits well in considering Switzerland, West Germany, and Australia, all of which function as highly bureaucratized political systems in terms of education.[27]

While Australian states began with centralized, statewide school systems, there is no reason to think that the exotic environment of the Antipodes would cause such arrangements to remain static and not evolve over time. Indeed, their experience abundantly demonstrates that they are not immune from the centralization imperative. This dynamic has led to excessive bureaucratization and, concomitantly, to powerful statewide teachers unions forged to bargain forcefully with the central bureaucracy. In fact, the extraordinary degree of centralization of authority and policy-making in Australian state school systems is legendary and the subject of numerous discussions about possible reforms among scholars, overseas visitors, and policy makers.[28] Part of the problem, as Hedley Beare notes, probably arises from population growth unaccompanied (until recently) by structural reform of the increasingly vast statewide school systems. As he remarks, 'at federation each of the states contained about as many people as would be contained now in one of the regional growth centers like Albury-Wodonga, or Canberra, or Newcastle'.[29]

In the case of Victoria, there is substantial evidence that the centralized bureaucracy became so top-heavy and unwieldy that it began to lose effective control over the statewide system.[30] One theoretical implication of this development is that it would be more accurate to refer to the driving force as a 'bureaucratization imperative' than a 'centralization imperative', since the latter suggests centralized control while the reality may be that control is *fragmented* at the top. Thus, in Victoria the need for administrative reorganization and decentralization became increasingly apparent to those familiar with the system. Philip Creed reports that Alan Hunt, who became Minister of Education in 1979, stated that:

> within the first ten days of his Ministry he found no clear lines of communication, a high degree of duplication and triplication and that the fundamental maxim that an organizational structure must be simple to be effective had not been applied.[31]

More significantly, Creed notes that:

the clear perception around the corridors of the Department was that Hunt had been appointed to 'tidy up' the largest government department. He was understood to be a Liberal Party strong man who was encouraged to restore order in industrial relations with the three major teacher unions and to put departmental affairs in order.[32]

In view of the evolution of the Victorian state-wide school system, it seems appropriate to propose a new stage V in the theory of structural evolution, which can be called the 'statewide decentralized bureaucracy' stage (see table 1). But there is no reason to believe that structural evolution will stop at this stage either. If the reforms achieved at this stage prove inadequate for the efficient delivery of high-quality education responsive to local and regional needs, we could see movement toward a stage VI, which might be characterized as a 'decentralized: federation' stage. Indeed, Hedley Beare anticipates this stage when he observes that the Redcliffe-Maud Royal Commission study in Britain:

> suggests that several Australian school systems have grown far too large and that the 'state system model' is no longer appropriate or efficient. One could argue that Australia, with a population of 14.5 million, might be better served by having about twenty-nine systems, but that there should be at least fifteen. The fact that all the state systems have felt the need to regionalize seems to argue for the Maud conclusions. Could not the education regions in each State become semi-autonomous school systems? ... If a school system is viable in Canberra, why not one based on Newcastle and its environs, or on Wollongong and its region? Since 70 per cent of Australia's population lives in ten major cities, surely geographical dispersion cannot be used as an argument against setting up at least some urban systems?[33]

If developments in stage V in Victoria are to become fully effective, it seems there will need to be a period of stability soon when the numerous changes can be consolidated without further changes being heaped on top of them. A problem evident both in the Chapman and Boyd research and in Creed's illuminating account of the change process is that a high degree of dislocation and confusion has been generated by the continuing onslaught of structural, procedural, and personnel changes. Stage V should get, and no doubt will receive, a fair trial in Victoria before policy makers begin to think seriously about stage VI possibilities.[34]

For American policy makers, developments in Victoria should be of more than mere academic interest. As a by-product of the state-wide 'excellence' reform movement in American education currently, there is a substantial trend toward centralization of educational government at the state level and a concomitant erosion of the already depleted residue of local control of schools. Consequently, observers have begun to worry about this trend and

Table 1: The Stages of Evolution of State Policy-Making Structures: From Decentralization to Centralized Bureaucracy to Decentralized Bureaucracy

	Stage I	Stage II	Stage III	Stage IV	Stage V
Type of influence structure	Localistic decentralized	State-wide monolithic	State-wide fragmented	State-wide bureaucratized	State-wide decentralized bureaucracy
Decision-making process; loci of accommodation	Each local unit and legislature	Informal state-wide coalition	Governor legislature courts	Bureaucracy	Partnership: center regions schools

Source: Based upon McGIVNEY, J. (1984) 'State educational government patterns', *Educational Administration Quarterly*, 20, 2 spring, p. 56, who in turn builds upon IANNACCONE, L. (1967) *Politics in Education*, New York, Center for Applied Research in Education.

to propose structural alternatives capable of meeting the demand for increased effectiveness and efficiency in schooling while avoiding excessive centralization and preserving flexibility and local or parental choice. One interesting discussion of this type is by Denis Doyle and Chester Finn, whose interest in fostering school-level decision-making has parallels in the Victorian emphasis on devolution to the school-site level.[35] Thus, there are good reasons for policy makers in both hemispheres to watch with interest the progress and performance of the Victorian venture, the subject to which we turn now.

Implementation and Consequences of Reorganization

The Historical and Socio-Political Context of Reform

The problems encountered in Victoria in implementing decentralization and devolution have, in large measure, as historical basis. From 1872–1968, the Victorian Education Department operated strictly on the principles of centralized bureaucracy. All the educational administrators had been schooled in this tradition; they had undertaken their initial teacher training and received their early professional experience within this context.

The period 1968–1981 heralded the first major shift to a more decentralized system. With virtually no additional preparation or training,[36] principals were told 'to run their own schools'. Heavily reliant upon departmental support, principals came to expect to be the prime decision makers and ultimate source of authority in the schools. With varying degrees of success, they adjusted to this new role.

The years 1981 through to 1984 saw two successive governments conduct major reassessments of the education system. Poised to implement its policy of decentralization and devolution at the school level and having already effected changes at the centre and region, the Liberal Party was ousted after over twenty-seven years of state government. Administrators, many of whom had been actively involved in the discussions that had contributed to the publication of the Liberal government's *White Paper on Restructuring Education*, were confronted with a new Labor government with vastly different values from those of its predecessor. As a Regional Director of Education observed:

> From January–April 1982 the position was clear. Then with the new government, the school was given greater discretion. The devolution to schools was much greater than expected and this was done with a new set of values.

In trying to overcome what one high-level administrator said was 'over 100 years of the colonial management mentality of the British Empire and East India Company', the Labor government faced the problem that there was no strongly articulated majority sentiment for sweeping devolution. Instead, support came mainly from Labor party intellectuals and state-level teachers unions and parent organization leaders. At the grass-roots, both teachers and parents seemed to be either ambivalent or only mildly supportive of devolution. And when the time came to devolve further powers to the regional level, even the state-level union and parent leaders became less enthusiastic when they recognized, as noted earlier, that regionalization ran counter to the interest they had developed in centralized bargaining power. Indeed, a survey of opinion in 1984 about progress in restructuring Victorian education — commissioned by the State Board of Education and conducted by a study team from Deakin University — found agreement that 'devolution to regions has stalled'.[37]

Lessons Honored, Neglected and Learned

Those who have studied administrative reorganization in government agree that such efforts rarely achieve success in terms of the usual goals of increased efficiency, effectiveness, or responsiveness.[38] As March and Olsen observe, in a recent review of the literature:

> In terms of their effects on administrative costs, size of staff, productivity, or spending, most major reorganization efforts [at the federal level] have been described by outsiders, and frequently by participants, as substantial failures. Few efficiencies are achieved; little gain in responsiveness is recorded; control seems as elusive after the

efforts as before ... The same conclusions have been reached about reorganizations at the state and local level in the United States ... and about reorganizations at the national level in other countries.[39]

Yet, the usually limited success of reorganization efforts in terms of their professed goals does not mean they are useless. They nevertheless may have both significant short-run and long-term effects. Speaking of the former, one of the most astute students of bureaucracy, Herbert Kaufman, provides a more realistic standard against which to judge the success of reorganization ventures:

> The consequences of reorganization are frequently profound. But the profound, determinable consequences do not lie in the engineering realm of efficiency, simplicity, size, and cost of government. Rather, the real payoffs are measured in terms of influence, policy, and communication ... Thus, a leader who transfers, combines, and splits organizations in government for engineering purposes will usually find that nobody can be sure whether any progress has been made toward those goals ... In contrast, a leader who shifts organizations around to confer power on selected people or remove it from others in order to mold government policies, and to impress on everyone what his or her values and priorities are, will more often be rewarded with a sense of having expended political resources for significant accomplishments. The calculus of reorganization is essentially the calculus of politics itself.[40]

Effects on influence
As Kaufman and others have noted, one of the main effects of reorganization usually is to redistribute influence. In Victoria, it is clear that some substantial change has occurred in this regard. Many relationships have been altered and many people have been forced to play new roles. Principals must consult and involve many more people in decision making than heretofore, and our data clearly show that they feel they have lost power. The establishment of administrative committees within the school and the changing composition and function of school councils ensured that the balance of power between principals and members of the school community, in particular between principals and members of the teaching staff, was dramatically altered.

> Principals found themselves beset by a struggle for power and this after 112 years in which the principal, at the school, was considered omnipotent. (Regional Director)

Moreover, despite the rhetoric of collaboration, some principals found that:

> Among the new participants in the collaborative process were those who were unwilling to participate honestly in collaborative decision making ... Such participants revealed a greater preparedness to play

power politics and use negotiation rather than really enter the spirit of collaboration.

Implementation problems

The findings presented in the Chapman and Boyd study show a variety of reasons why principals have found it difficult to move to a fully collaborative decision making model. Although the devolution effort has accomplished part of its objective to share decision-making more broadly, it is clear that the implementation of the plan has suffered from a rather gross neglect of the need for retraining and inservice activities designed to foster the learning of the new attitudes and roles that are fundamental to the new style of management which was mandated. While such activities could hardly remove all the obstacles associated with participants' political interests, it is obvious that not just principals, but all the players in the redefined game, have needed help to think through and to begin to play the new roles.

Indeed, an enormous amount of momentum is needed to change a system with more than 2000 schools and 40,000 teachers. Changed administrative arrangements require that an entirely new communication network be established. The new 'appropriate' people must be identified, working relationships must be built up: New values require that the heritage, the folklore, the 'understanding' of people in the system be reassessed; this within a context where many people are experiencing personal and professional threat and insecurity.

Notwithstanding the problems associated with the implementation of any system-wide change however, much of the confusion and anxiety associated with decentralization and devolution must in this instance be directly attributed to the nature of the implementation process. First, directly related to the lack of in-service support was the insufficient provision of financial support:

> Regionalization sounds very good in principle. The mistake the government has made is that you can do it without additional cost. If you want something to be cost-effective you centralize; don't decentralize. If you want a high level of expertise duplicated twelve times around the state in the regions, it is going to cost money. Unless the government is going to accept that, in my view regionalization will never come anywhere near the expectations of it. (Principal of a technical school)

In addition, the entire process took place with considerable haste.

> The suddenness of it all could have been better perhaps. You live day to day in a school so the changes seem sudden. It's been an exciting time, although you see many frustrated people and you wonder whether the extra effort is worth it. There has been increased stress, and this gets passed on — the administration pass their frenzy down the line. There is generally too short a time in all areas.

Also, sources of power and resources which had been evident under the traditional bureaucratic arrangements were not precisely transformed and delegated. Principals could no longer act with the certainty of the past.

> Had the central authority clearly indicated to principals their degrees of freedom, principals may have acted more confidently. (Regional Director)

Further, the advantages of devolution were at no time communicated to principals in sufficient detail to enable them to fully understand and accept the policy. Principals' fears of the new and unexplored was never significantly allayed.

Finally, the government's perceived disrespect for principals created considerable animosity:

> The problem for the Principals Associations is that they are being ignored by the higher policy makers. Principals do not appear to have much impact. Principals are being treated together with teachers. It is difficult for some who see this as being forced to 'eat humble pie'. (Principal of a country high school)

> There is so much doom among principals because their feelings are hurt about not being consulted. They have lost their power. (Principal of a country high school)

> All these new arrangements seem to be designed to cut down the powers of the principal. While there were only a few autocratic principals, they have been portrayed as the norm. Principals have been forced to defend their positions. (Principal of a suburban high school)

One Regional Director confirmed the importance of this factor:

> On the one hand principals should accept government policy and do it. This however has been difficult when they have felt 'put down' by the Minister and the unions.

This resentment was compounded when, as one secondary school principal reported:

> Unfortunately the VSTA (Victorian Secondary Teachers Association) representative often knows what is to happen in schools *before* the principal.

Effects on policy
Beyond enhancing feelings of political efficacy, the redistribution of power through devolution should result in discernable shifts in policy in the directions favored by the reorganization designers. Here, again, there are some signs of progress. Consistent with the thrust of the ministerial papers, people

are being forced to think about the nature of the educational program at the school level. Indeed, curricular leadership has emerged as an important attitubute for applicants for principalships in the early rounds of appointments in which the school community, for the first time, has participated in the selection process.

As principals and their collaborators are encouraged to pay more attention to curriculum and instruction, the government's goal of school improvement stands a better chance of being achieved. But the lack of necessary support from consultants at the regional level remains a major constraint. As one person remarked in this respect, 'Without direction, school-based curriculum development is hopeless'.

Communicating the government's intentions
Reorganization provides an important means for governments to convey and advance their priorities and values. Indeed, it has been argued that reorganizations often are long-run successes, despite being short-run failures, precisely because of the power of their rhetoric and symbols to change the climate of opinion over time.[41] It is in this respect that the chief legacy of the Victorian devolution venture is likely to be found. By changing language and thinking about administration and participation in government schools, devolution may in time produce significant change in practice.

Already, there has been a tremendous change in the content and semantics of discourse about school administration and school-community relations in Victoria. In pursuit of a collaborative, non-hierarchical approach to management, new relationships are being explored and negotiated. Although this sometimes is a tense exercise, there is evidence that parents, teachers and principals are moving toward greater collaboration. In many ways, one of the greatest difficulties is that between educators and the public, where a tradition of only very limited parental involvement in decision-making is hard to overcome. Here, Victorian government leaders seem to sense March and Olsen's insight that 'reorganization can be viewed as a form of civic education'.[42] But to succeed they also must have the political good fortune to be able to persist patiently in their efforts.[43]

If Victorians seem most concerned with an issue out of fashion in the United States — who runs or controls schools, as opposed to US concern about the content and quality of schooling — Americans nevertheless can recognize and learn from the alternative route they have taken to achieve school improvement. Since both the effective schools literature and the implementation literature show that a collaborative process is central to successful school reform, it appears that American educators need to give greater attention to the democratic quality of the management process, and particularly so in light of the centralizing trends in many states. While the Victorian experience shows again that one cannot mandate new approaches, provide little by way of support services, and expect to get quick results, it nevertheless illustrates the extent to which thinking and, ultimately, practice can be redirected by the rhetoric and symbols of forceful leadership. Just as the Reagan administration has prompted a remarkable degree of change in American schooling through aggressive use of exhortations from the 'bully pulpit', so too may the Victorian Labor government be remoulding education in the 'Garden State' 'down under'.[44]

Notes

1 Data for this chapter are drawn primarily from CHAPMAN, J. and BOYD, W.L. (1986) 'Decentralization, devolution, and the school principal: Australian lessons on state-wide educational reform', *Educational Administration Quarterly*, 22, 4, fall. The authors conducted in-depth interviews in 1984 with a broad range of participants in the Victorian reform effort, from senior officers in the Education Department down to school level personnel, including principals, teachers, and parents active in school affairs. Data on developments in 1985 and 1986 are drawn from follow-up interviews with key participants and observers and from other studies of the Victorian reorganization effort which are cited below.

2 See BEARE, H. (1983) 'The structural reform movement in Australian education during the 1980s and its effect on schools', *Journal of Educational Administration*, 21, 2, summer, pp. 149–68; and BESWICK, D.G. and HARMAN, G.S. (1983) 'Education policy in Australia', Research Working Paper No. 83.7, Melbourne, Centre for the Study of Higher Education, University of Melbourne.

3 There are some 15,000 American school districts compared to six state and two territorial school systems in Australia. For comparisons of trends in the two countries, see MURPHY, J. (1980) 'School administrators beseiged: A look at Australian and American education', *American Journal of Education*, 89, 1 pp. 1–26; and BOYD, W.L. (1984) 'Competing values in educational policy and governance: Australian and American developments', *Educational Administration Review*, 2, 2, spring, pp. 4–24.

4 See, for example, NAGEL, S.S. (Ed.), (1983) *Encyclopedia of Policy Studies*, New York, Marcel Dekker, Inc., and MANN, D. (Ed.), (1978) *Making Change Happen?* New York, Teachers College Press.

5 See, for example, MANN, D. (Ed.) *op. cit.*, and the collection of studies in BALDRIDGE, J.V. and DEAL, T. (Eds) (1983) *The Dynamics of Organizational Change in Education*, Berkeley, CA, McCutchan.

6 For a discussion and assessment of the implications of this literature, see ODDEN A. and WEBB L.D. (Eds), (1983) *School Finance and School Improvement Linkages for the 1980s*, Cambridge, MA, Ballinger.

7 COLEMAN, J.S. et al., (1966) *Equality of Educational Opportunity*, Washington, D.C., US Government Printing Office; JENCKS, C. et al., (1972) *Inequality: A Reassessment of the Effect of Family and Schooling in America*, New York, Basic Books.

8 See COHEN, M. (1983) 'Instructional, management, and social conditions in effective schools', in ODDEN, A. and WEBB, L.D. (Eds), *School Finance and School Improvement Linkages, for the 1980s*, Cambridge, MA, Ballinger.

9 Ministerial Papers 1–4. ('Decision making in Victorian education'; 'The School Improvement Plan'; 'The State Board of Education'; 'School Councils') Issued by the Minister of Education, Melbourne, Victoria, March 1983.

10 See the discussion of school site mangement plans in GARMS, W. GUTHRIE, J. and PIERCE, L. (1978) *School Finance: The Economics and Politics of Public Education*, Englewood Cliffs, NJ, Prentice-Hall, pp. 277–94.

11 See the collection of studies in MANN, D. (1978) *op cit.*

12 The second smallest of the six Australian states, Victoria is the most densely settled, with about 26 per cent of the nation's population. It is about the same size as Great Britain and a bit larger than the state of Utah. The school system figures given here are drawn from COMMONWEALTH SCHOOLS COMMISSION (1984) *Australian School Statistics*, 1st edn. Canberra, Commonwealth Schools Commission, January, pp. 5, 24 and 32.

13 Again see the useful collection of studies in MANN, D. (1978) *op. cit.*

14 See especially MANN, D. (1978) 'The user-driven system and a modest proposal' in MANN, D. *op cit.*

15 On the cultural similarities and differences between Australia and the United States that may determine the relevance of the lessons of one for the other, see HANCOCK, G., KIRST, M. and GROSSMAN, D. (Eds), (1983) *Contemporary Issues in Educational Policy: Perspectives from Australia and USA*, Canberra, ACT Schools Authority and Curriculum Development Centre. Also see WEST, P. (1983) 'Australia and the United States: Some differences', *Comparative Education Review*, 27, 3, October, pp. 414–6.

16 MOORE, T.J. (1975) 'Administration in the late 1970s 'Proceedings of a seminar for principals and senior teachers, Continuing Education Centre, Wangaratta, Victoria, Australia, Series 3, No. 1, *Educational Administration*, p. 26.

17 *White Paper on Strategies and Structure for Education in Victorian Government Schools*, Melbourne, F.D. Atkinson, Government Printer (1980).

18 See BATES, R. (1983) 'The socio-political context of administrative change and the metaphorical negotiation of education reform in Victoria', paper presented at the annual meeting of the Australian Association for Research in Education, Canberra, November; and SELLECK, R.J.W. (1983) 'Is he to be a little Lord God Almighty?' — A reflection on the study of the history of education', *History of Education Review*, 12, 1 pp. 1–14.

19 Ministerial Paper No. 1, 'Decision Making in Victorian Education', *op. cit.*, p. 4.

20 Norman Curry, Director General of Education, Victorian Education Department. Memorandum for Principals, Staffs and School Councils of all Schools, Officers in Charge of Units, Regional Directors of Education, Branch directors, Unit Coordinators, 28 March 1983.

21 Robert Fordham, Minister of Education, State Government of Victoria. Memorandum for Principals of Schools, Presidents of School Council, 12 December 1983, p. 2.

22 Norman Curry, Director General of Education, Victorian Education Department. Memorandum to School Council, Principal and Staff, all members of the school community, 31 January 1984.

23 For an examination of the changing relationships between principals and members of the school councils, see CHAPMAN, J.D. (1984) 'An attitudinal profile of principals, staff and community representatives on Victorian high school councils', *Educational Administration Review*, 2, 2, autumn, pp. 118–29.

24 MASLEN, G. (1986) 'Year of upheaval as educators ring the changes', *The Age*, 4 February.

25 McGIVNEY, J.H. (1984) 'State educational governance patterns', *Eductional Administration Quarterly*, 20, 2, spring, pp. 43–63.

26 IANNACCONE, L. (1967) *Politics in Education*, New York, Center for Applied Research in Education.

27 McGIVNEY, J. *op. cit.*, p. 58.

28 It is said, for instance, that there was a time when school principals in New South Wales could not replace a broken window in their building without securing approval from the central office in Sydney. For examples of the scholarly discussion, see WALKER, W.G. (1970) 'The governance of education in Australia: Centra-

lization and politics', *Journal of Educational Administration*, 8, 2, May, pp. 17–40; and BEARE, H. (1983) *op. cit.*

29 BEARE, H. (1983) *op. cit.*, p. 158.

30 This is the view expressed by numerous 'insiders' and well-informed observers the authors interviewed, such as Professors Grant Harman and David Beswick, of the University of Melbourne. Professor Harman, now at the University of New England, was selected by Minister of Education, Alan Hunt, to draft the influencial *White Paper on Strategies and Structures for Education in Victorian Government Schools* (Government Printer, Melbourne, 1980). See HARMAN, G. (1985) 'The White Paper and planned organizational change' in FRAZER, M., DUNSTAN, J.F. and CREED, P.J. (Eds), *Perspectives on Organizational Change: Lessons from Education*, Melbourne, Longman Cheshire.

31 CREED, P.J. (1986) 'Implementing Structural change in a state department of education', paper presented at the annual meeting of the American Educational Research Association, San Francisco, April, p. 5. See also DUNSTAN, J.F. (1986) 'The impact of changing values on organizational structures in education', paper presented at the annual meeting of the American Educational Research Association, San Francisco, April; and FRAZER M. (Eds) (1985) *op. cit.*

32 CREED, P.J. (1986) *op. cit.*, p. 3.

33 BEARE, H. (1983) *op. cit.*, p. 159.

34 Insofar as further decentralization is concerned, the reality is that the powerful statewide teachers' unions have an interest in maintaining their centralized bargaining powers. This fact already has impeded progress toward full regionalization. As Creed reports, 'The view of many senior officers is that significant progress towards decentralization cannot be achieved until personnel operations are decentralized and devolved to match the significantly decentralized curriculum and facilities functions. However, as the Director-General at the time pointed out, attempts by departmental administrators to devolve personnel functions have met considerable teacher union opposition' (CREED, P.J. (1986) *op. cit.*, p. 23).

35 DOYLE, D.P. and FINN, E., JR., (1984) 'American schools and the future of local control', *The Public Interest*, no 77, fall, pp. 77–95. See also the discussion in BASTIAN A. *et al.*, (1985) *Choosing Equality: The Case for Democratic Schooling*, New York, The New World Foundation.

36 See CHAPMAN, J.D. (1984) 'A descriptive profile of Australian school principals' Canberra, Commonwealth Schools Commission for a discussion of the formal preparation in educational administration of Australian principals.

37 The Deakin team interviewed fifty-five people, ranging from parents, teachers, and principals up through regional directors, senior officers in the central administration, and all the members of the State Board of Education. See BATES, R. *et al.*, (1984) *Restructuring Victorian Education: Current Issues. A Report to the State Board of Education*. Geelong, Deakin Institute for Studies in Education, November, p. 143.

38 See KAUFMAN, H. (1977) 'Reflections on administrative reorganization', in PECHMAN J. (Ed.), *Setting National Priorities: The 1978 Budget* Washington, D.C.: The Brookings Institution; MARCH, J.G. and OLSEN, J.P. (1983) 'Organizing political life: What administrative reorganization tells us about government', *American Political Science Review*, 22, June, pp. 281–96; ROURKE, F.E. (1984) *Bureaucracy, Politics, and Public Policy*, 3rd edn,. Boston, MA, Little, Brown, and Company.

39 MARCH, J.G. and OLSEN, J.P. (1983) *op. cit.*, p. 288.

40 KAUFMAN, H. (1977) *op. cit.*, pp. 403 and 405–6.

41 MARCH, J.G. and OLSEN, J.P. (1983) *op. cit.*, p. 288.

42 *Ibid.*

43 *Ibid.*, p. 287.

44 For perceptive discussions of the Reagan administration's effective use of the 'bully

pulpit', see JUNG, R.K. and KIRST, M.W. (1986) 'Beyond mutual adaptation, into the bully pulpit: Recent research on the federal role in education', *Educational Administration Quarterly*, 22, 3, summer, pp. 80–109; and JUNG, R.K. (forthcoming) 'The federal role in elementary/secondary education: Mapping a shifting terrain' in BOYAN, N. (Ed.), *Handbook of Research on Educational Administration*, New York, Longman.

14 State-Wide Arrangements for Organizing Australian Education

Grant Harman

Introduction

On 12 November 1985, with little, if any, advance notice, the Victorian Minister for Education, Mr Ian Cathie, announced a new set of major organizational changes in public education for the state.[1] He also announced that the office of Director-General of Education had ceased to exist since the Education Department had been replaced by a Ministry of Education and that the Director-General of Education, Dr Norman Curry, had resigned as Director-General and had accepted the new position of Chariman of the Library Council of Victoria.

This announcement was both surprising and important for a number of reasons. It was surprising because the major restructuring of the Victorian Education Department begun in 1979 by the Liberal Minister for Education, Mr Alan Hunt, and largely continued along the same lines by his Labor successor, Mr Robert Fordham, appeared to be still incomplete. It was also surprising that Mr Cathie intended to appoint a new permanent head and presumably cause a spill of at least a number of senior executive positions when Dr Curry and other senior executives of the Education Department had been appointed only some four years or less — and some of them had been appointed under the Labor government's administration.[2] It was important in that it marked the end in Victoria of the long-established position of Director-General (or Director as the post was earlier styled), a position and nomenclature which has been employed also in each of the other states for a long period. The change raised the question of whether the move to the new title of Chief Executive for the head of the Ministry of Education implied that a non-educator might be appointed, or that the post was to be seen more in terms of management than educational leadership. The announcement was also important in that it marked recognition by another state of problems relating to co-ordination within the education portfolio and coordination between education activities and other activities of government. The Minister began his announcement with a clear statement of purpose:

> Today I announced far-reaching changes to the administration of education in Victoria aimed at achieving two important and related purposes — to expedite the process of devolving functions and authority to schools and regions and to improve the coordination of policy, resources and planning across the portfolio.[3]

The Minister's announcement was of particular fascination to the author for two reasons. First, for a number of years I have been interested in questions relating to the coordination of education activities both within different sectors of education and across whole education portfolios. In 1980, for example, I prepared a detailed consultant's report which dealt with some of these issues for the Keeves Enquiry into Education in South Australia.[4] Second, in 1980 I had argued in two separate settings that the then proposed reorganization in Victoria ideally should address questions of organizational arrangements and coordination across the portfolio. I have documented elsewhere[5] that, in a paper given at a panel discussion in July 1980 at the University of Melbourne on Alan Hunt's *Green Paper*, I criticized the limited focus on government schools in a paper claiming to be addressing 'Education in Victoria', and the failure of the document to address important questions about coordination and the relationships between different sectors of education and the agencies responsible administratively for these. Apart from this, once I was involved in the preparation of the *White Paper*[6], which was eventually tabled in the Victorian Parliament by Mr Alan Hunt (then Minister of Education) and Mr Norman Lacy (then Assistant Minister of Education) on 10 December 1980, I raised the issue in private discussions with the two ministers. From memory, Mr Hunt said that he agreed with many of my arguments, but that his major concern was reorganization of the Education Department and that he had proceeded already too far down a particular track to broaden the interests of the restructuring exercise, at least in the short-term. However, Mr Hunt did agree to a change in the title of the White Paper from *White Paper on Strategies and Structures for Education in Victoria* to *White Paper on Strategies and Structures for Education in Victorian Government Schools*.

The purpose of this chapter is to address a small number of issues relating to state-wide arrangements for organizing education in Australia, and particularly in the larger states. The chapter briefly reviews what information is currently available about the new Victorian reorganization, explains why ministers and governments are becoming increasingly concerned about problems of coordination, comments on approaches used in other states, suggests a few broad principles that might guide plans to develop state-wide organizational arrangements and finally sets out one possible scheme that appears not to have been considered to date as an option.

Information on Victorian Plans

At the time of writing, only limited information was available on the details of the new administrative pattern in Victoria. Although a restructure project team was working to develop detailed advice that soon would go to the Minister, all it had available was a copy of the Minister's statement of 12 November 1985 and a short article by the Minister published in *Education Victoria* in February 1986.

As already noted, in his statement of 12 November 1985, the Minister explained that the two purposes of the changes were to expedite further devolution of functions and authority to schools and regions, and to improve coordination. On coordination he explained:

> A greater degree of coordination between schools, TAFE (technical further education) and higher education is required so that flexible pathways can develop between education sectors. The achievement of comprehensive growth policies also requires sectors to operate within a common policy framework. Moreover, education will be increasingly required to act in concert with other agencies in order to support Government policy objectives.[7]

The statement of 12 November 1985 included the accompanying diagram (figure 1), and commented in particular on four special features in the new Ministry — the Education Executive Committee, a Portfolio Policy Coordination element, a School System Coordination element, and a Portfolio Resources Management element. Three of these clearly will have education system-wide functions. The Education Executive Committee will be chaired by the Minister and will comprise the Chief Executive of the Ministry of Education, and the chairpersons of the Victorian Institute of Secondary Education (VISE), the TAFE Board, the State Board of Education and the Victorian-Post-Secondary Education Commission (VPSEC). Significantly, in discussing this Committee, the Minister said that each of the agencies 'will continue to operate autonomously but the Chief Executive will offer advice on all aspects of the portfolio, as well as being responsible for the school system'.[8] On the Portfolio Policy Coordination element, the Minister said that the aim would be to draw together information and advice from across all agencies in the portfolio 'so as to support a corporate management approach and allow for program coordination and a review on a cross-sectoral basis'.[9] Finally, he also stated that the Portfolio Resources Management element:

> will be responsible for ensuring that resources across education sectors are utilized to meet educational priorities. The coordination of facilities, personnel and industrial relations policy is involved.[10]

The Minister's article of February 1986 provided little additional detail. However, it did reinforce the point that concern about coordination was in

Figure 1: Revised Organisation of the Victorian Ministry
of Education

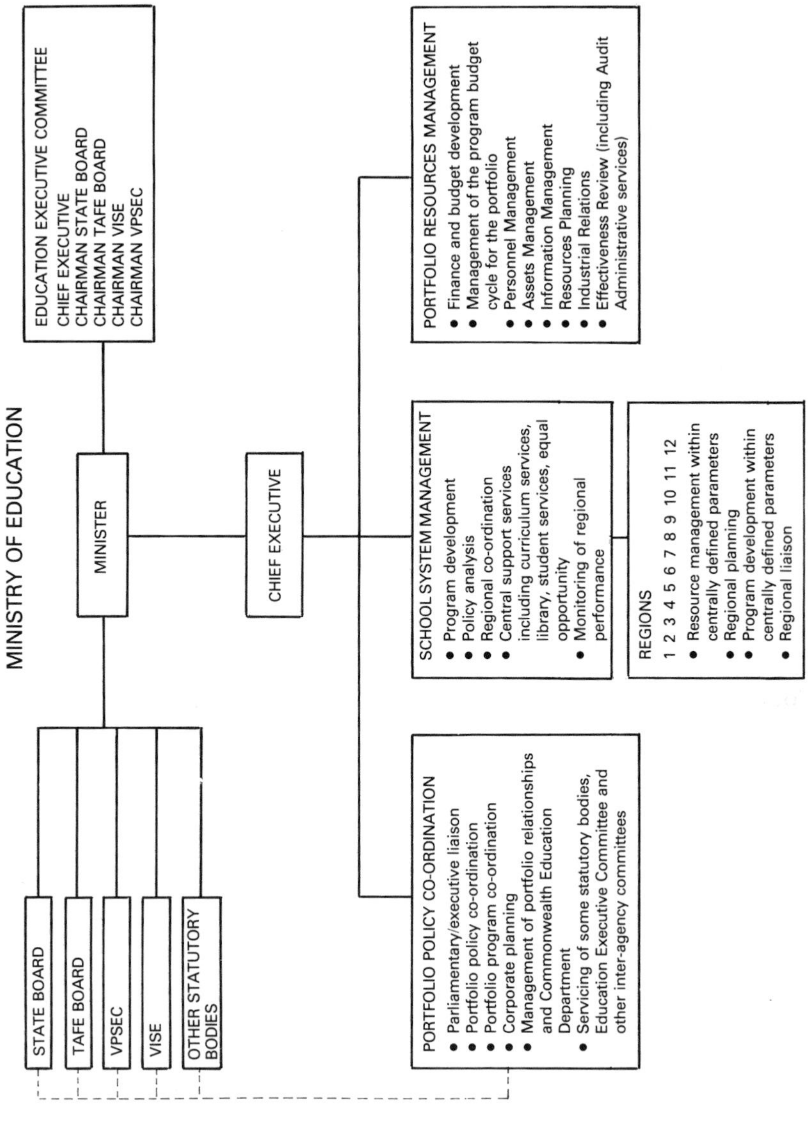

MINISTRY OF EDUCATION

EDUCATION EXECUTIVE COMMITTEE
CHIEF EXECUTIVE
CHAIRMAN STATE BOARD
CHAIRMAN TAFE BOARD
CHAIRMAN VISE
CHAIRMAN VPSEC

PORTFOLIO RESOURCES MANAGEMENT
- Finance and budget development
- Management of the program budget cycle for the portfolio
- Personnel Management
- Assets Management
- Information Management
- Resources Planning
- Industrial Relations
- Effectiveness Review (including Audit Administrative services)

MINISTER

CHIEF EXECUTIVE

STATE BOARD
TAFE BOARD
VPSEC
VISE
OTHER STATUTORY BODIES

SCHOOL SYSTEM MANAGEMENT
- Program development
- Policy analysis
- Regional co-ordination
- Central support services including curriculum services, library, student services, equal opportunity
- Monitoring of regional performance

REGIONS
1 2 3 4 5 6 7 8 9 10 11 12
- Resource management within centrally defined parameters
- Regional planning
- Program development within centrally defined parameters
- Regional liaison

PORTFOLIO POLICY CO-ORDINATION
- Parliamentary/executive liaison
- Portfolio policy co-ordination
- Portfolio program co-ordination
- Corporate planning
- Management of portfolio relationships and Commonwealth Education Department
- Servicing of some statutory bodies, Education Executive Committee and other inter-agency committees

fact related to the likely restructuring of post-primary schools arising from recommendations of the Blackburn Report and concern about cross-sectoral transfer of students. Apart from this, the Minister stated that the new arrangements would provide for 'strategic and integrated management', 'a capacity to effectively review programs and plan for the delivery of education services in a restrained resource environment', and the development and implementation of 'corporate information systems to support the management of an integrated education portfolio'.

One striking feature about Mr Cathie's proposals for reorganization is that the rationale for change was expressed largely in the language of management. Note the use of words and terms such as 'corporate management approach', 'capacity to review programs' and 'restrained resource environment'. In many respects there is a close similarity between Mr Cathie's statements and what Mr Alan Hunt said some five years earlier.

The Growing Concern About Coordination

Concern about the need for more effective coordination for education at state level is a fairly recent phenomenon in Australia. It has sprung essentially from dramatic changes in the scale, diversity and overall size of public education enterprises, and from recognition that administrative arrangements developed late last century, and modified only marginally since then, are often unable to cope adequately with the demands placed on them today. Associated with this are new demands and pressures resulting from the complications of federalism for education, the increased politicization of education, changed management practices in public administration at state level, and demands for budgetary constraints.

The administrative pattern for education in each of the six states was remarkably stable for a long period. It developed in the decades immediately prior to federation, when colonial governments in turn decided to provide education themselves on a major scale as opposed to subsidizing education provided by churches and other bodies, and so set up systems of free, compulsory, public schooling. In each case, a government department of education or public institution was established, responsible to a Minister of the Crown. Uniformally across the six colonies these education departments developed highly centralized administrative systems, for their concern was to provide a common service to all citizens and their families, whether they were located in metropolitan or country areas.

Over the years, with population growth and the development and expansion of secondary education, technical education, teachers' colleges and universities, the responsibilities of state education departments grew. But in most states until well after the second world war, all substantial public education enterprises other than universities (and in some cases institutions like agricultural colleges controlled by state agricultural departments) remained under the direct control of education departments. Thus co-ordination of activities and of advice to Ministers provided few difficulties. Director-Generals were clearly and unambiguously the senior advisers to their Ministers. While there remained a single state university (or perhaps two universities in the case of New South Wales from 1949), there was no competition for scarce resources between relatively autonomous tertiary educational institutions and it remained relatively easy for the Director-General and/or Minister to relate informally to one or two University Vice-Chancellors. Further, until the early 1960s, the only major interest of the Federal government in the education sector was in universities.

Since 1960s, however, the situation has changed dramatically. The size and scale of education as a public enterprise has changed substantially. The Federal Government now has a major interest in schools, TAFE and CAEs (Colleges of Advanced Education) as well as in universities and often is a key force of initiative and change in education policy; in each state there are a number of separate tertiary education institutions often competing for scarce resources; and in all states new education agencies or departments have been established to administer or co-ordinate specialized functions. The result is that, instead of one department and one senior adviser, Ministers now have a number of departments and agencies under their control, each headed by a senior executive. Frequently these various bodies iron out boundary disputes, matters of conflict and other problems through consultation, but from time to time Ministers find they must adjudicate between conflicting advice and demands. Apart from this, they are often concerned about possible overlap between the functions of different agencies, about difficulties for transfer of students and educational cooperation resulting from institutions and programs being controlled by different departments or boards, about possible inefficiencies resulting from duplication and competition, and about difficulties in presenting a single overall state viewpoint to Commonwealth education authorities and ensuring that education policies harmonize with government efforts in related fields.

In essence, what we are witnessing is a recognition that the traditional late nineteenth century administrative arrangements with various *ad hoc* adjustments (such as the creation of separate departments or boards for TAFE, coordinating agencies for tertiary education, and the creation of special agencies to handle the registration of teachers, fixing of teachers' salaries, and the administration of the High Schooling Certificate (HSC) examinations and related matters) over the years are not adequate to meet today's demands, and that new arrangements are necessary. But significantly to date, no state has tackled questions of coordination and the overall design of administrative arrangements directly as a single major issue of concern, but rather a number of states have tackled these questions, as the Victorian Minister appears to be doing, as parts of efforts of change where questions of coordination and overall administrative arrangements are not of primary concern.

Approaches of Different States

Apart from Victoria, to my knowledge New South Wales, South Australia and Queensland have tackled the problem of coordination across the education portfolio. There have also been discussions about the overall administrative design for education in the ACT as the territory moves to some form of territorial government, and discussions of aspects of coordination from time to time in Tasmania and Western Australia.

Being the largest state, it is not surprising that New South Wales has an elaborate set of administrative machinery for educational governance. By 1980 it had separate departments of education and technical and further education, a higher education board (which in 1975 had replaced three separate coordinating bodies for universities and colleges of advanced education, and Adult Education Board, a Nurses Education Board, a Teacher Housing Authority, as well as five universities, over twenty colleges of advanced education, and a number of other statutory boards, such as the Board of Senior Secondary Education. In that year the New South Wales Government set up a new over-arching authority, the Education Commission of New South Wales. Establishment of the Commission was the result of years of pressure exerted by the New South Wales Teachers' Federation and from commitments made by the Australian Labor Party in the early 1970s and again in the 1976 General Election campaign, which resulted in a Labor government led by Mr Neville Wran assuming office.

The Education Commission consists of thirteen members, comprising six appointed by the governor (one the full-time Chairman), five elected members (one elected by primary teachers, one elected by secondary teachers, one elected by TAFE teachers, one elected by the Executive Council of the Federation of Parents and Citizens' Associations in New South Wales, and one elected by the Council of the Federation of School/Community Organizations of New South Wales) and two ex-officio members (the Director-General of Education, and the Director-General of Technical and Further Education).[11] The Commission has two main statutory functions — employment of teachers, and provision of advice on policy across all sectors of education. No detailed assessment is yet available on the operation and effectiveness of this interesting body, but it is widely believed that matters relating to its functions as the employer of school teachers and TAFE teachers absorb most of its time and attention. Certainly there is little evidence to suggest that it is a major force in overall planning and policy development.

In South Australia the innovation for state-wide coordination has been establishment of an Office of the Minister, under the control of a senior public servant but one of lesser seniority than either the Director-General of Education or the Director-General of TAFE. This development resulted from recommendations made by the Committee of Enquiry into Education in South Australia, chaired by Dr J.P. Keeves. The Keeves Enquiry was given a number of terms of reference. One directed the Enquiry specifically to examine and make recommendations on:

> the organization of the Education Department, the Department of Further Education, the Childhood Services, including responsibilities for the management of financial, human and other resources, the relationship between the three organizations, and any rationalization which might be desirable.[12]

The Enquiry recommended the establishment of an Education Policy and priorities Executive comprising the Minister as Chairman, and the heads of the various departments and agencies of the portfolio including the Director-General of Education and the Director-General of TAFE. It saw as desirable:

> that the Education Policy and Priorities Executive should evolve as a corporate management group for the management of certain aspects of the education portfolio, particularly those concerned with inter-sectoral matters.[13]

The Enquiry also recommended establishment of an Office of the Minister of Education to ensure consultation between sectors and the provision of coordinated advice to the Minister, to facilitate forward planning, to monitor education policies and programs of the Commonwealth, and to ensure that all relevant authorities are kept informed of ministerial discussions.[14] More recently the South Australian government has appointed two separate ministers in the education area, one with special responsibilities for TAFE, higher education and employment and the other with responsibility for all other education activities.

In Queensland the problems of coordination have been less severe than in the larger states, particularly since TAFE has remained administratively under the Education Department and the government of Queensland has been less inclined than some other administrations to create new statutory bodies within the education portfolio. However, in 1979 a Select Parliamentary Committee recommended abolition of the Board of Advanced Education and replacement by a Ministry of Post-Secondary Education, separate from the Department of Education. No action was taken on this recommendation, but in 1984 the senior posts in the Department of Education were reorganized to provide for a new post of Assistant-Director General in charge of the post-school area and colleges. This means then that through the Education Department the Minister can be provided with advice across the whole education portfolio, although the Board of Advanced Education, the colleges of advanced education and universities would probably dispute the competence and capacity of the Department to provide detailed, expert advice on many aspects of higher education.

Some Principles and One Possible Model

In the Australian context, a number of features appear to be desirable in any state administrative system concerned with the delivery of particular education services. In the first place, an administrative system for education should be highly sensitive to the purposes of education and to the special characteristics of education activities. Education needs somewhat different arrangements to those appropriate for such purposes as the collection of taxes, the enforcement of laws, and the provision of garbage services. Among other things, the arrangements need to be client oriented as far as possible, they should provide teachers and other professionals with a great deal of autonomy in their work, and they should provide a variety of mechanisms to gain advice and input for policy from both the broader community, and from those affected directly by the activity and from professional personnel. Second, in the Australian context I would want to stress the desirability of a large measure of decentralization and devolution. For one thing, day-to-day decisions in any organization should be taken as close as possible to the workface or to points of organization-client interaction; for another, especially in Australia, there is always a strong tendency towards central control. Third, within the bounds of resources, structures should facilitate the maximum degree of choice by students, parents and communities. Fourth, arrangements should be economical and efficient and should encourage flexibility, adaptability, diversity and regular review of functions and evaluation of achievements.

Apart from these general characteristics, it might well be considered that overall state-wide arrangements should have some special characteristics including:

(a) simplicity, with as far as possible the functions and responsibilities of various agencies and bodies being clearly specified and accepted;

(b) avoidance of proliferation of separate bodies on the one hand, but on the other recognition that diverse and conflicting demands often cause great strain on an organization;

(c) avoidance wherever possible of duplication of function and the likelihood of friction and conflict; and

(d) mechanisms to provide effective coordination of activities and advice, and forward planning and policy capacity.

One of the central questions to face in the overall design is what kind of body or mechanism should be at the centre to provide for the necessary coordination and overall policy and planning capacity. A number of options or combinations of them have been suggested or tried. These include:

(a) advisory committees (such as that suggested by Mr Cathie, and consisting of the Minister as Chairman and including heads of all departments and major agencies);

(b) statutory authorities (such as the Education Commission in New South Wales); and

(c) ministerial departments (which could have a range of other functions as well).

Most, if not all, of the three options or combinations of them have strengths as well as weaknesses. For example, a super advisory committee chaired by the Minister would depend very much for its effectiveness on the energy and skill of the Minister, and on the quality and size of the secretariat which services it. If such a body was serviced by the major department of the portfolio, the heads of other agencies might well have concern about its independence from that department. The statutory authority is more independent than a traditional department and is less likely to be drawn into day-to-day squabbles. It can also take a more independent and critical stance in terms of policy advice. But on the other hand, it is often much slower than a department in formulating policy advice, since generally statutory bodies are made up largely of part-time members who have other time commitments. The ministerial department provides for more rapid decision-making and, unlike statutory authorities, all senior people give their full-time to the enterprise and are readily available to provide advice and carry out administrative tasks. Apart from this, the ministerial department provides for easier overall coordination across the various policy domains of government; as Wettenhall says, 'the more we use statutory authorities the harder it is to ensure the harmony of governmental operations as a whole.'[15]

One option that has not been tried is an arrangement whereby a relatively small ministerial department is employed as the main policy, planning and coordinating body for the portfolio, while a number of different statutory bodies are used to perform specialized administrative functions, or to organize or control particular sectors. This arrangement is set out in figure 2. Alternatively, at the second level, a mixture of department and statutory bodies could be used; however, coordination of the activities of one or more departments by another department could be difficult unless the coordinating department's powers and responsibilities were clearly spelt out. Another possibility would be to have a number of largely autonomous regional school authorities or boards, instead of one central schools authority. Such an arrangement would be broadly similar to that which operates in Britain, where the Department of Education and Science is concerned with broad policy questions, and effective control of schools lies with local education authorities (LEAs), organized on a regional basis, while the main responsibility for the coordination of advanced level post-school education lies with the University Grants Committee (UGC) and a parallel agency for polytechnics, National Advisory Body (NAB).

Figure 2: Suggested Administrative Structure for Education at State Level

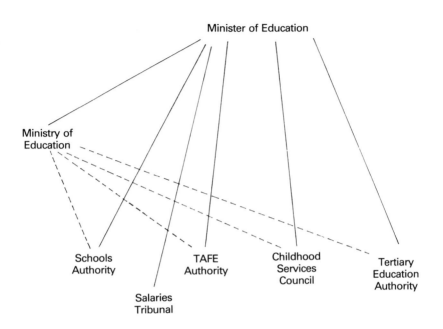

Notes

1 Memorandum from Ian Cathie, Minister for Education, addressed to 'All Officers and Employees of the Ministry of Education and of School Councils', 12 November 1985.

2 These included the Executive Director (Schools), three Branch Directors in Educational Programs, and thirty-two other middle management positions.

3 Memorandum of 12 November 1985, p. 1.

4 HARMAN, G. (1980) *Administrative Structures for Providing Education Services at State Level*, Melbourne.

5 HARMAN, G. (1985) 'The White Paper and planned organizational change' in FRAZER, M. DUNSTON, J. and CREED, P. (Eds) *Perspectives on Organizational Change: Lessons from Education*, Melbourne, Longman Cheshire, pp. 155–88.

6 *White Paper on Strategies and Structures for Education in Victorian Government Schools*, Government Printer, Melbourne, 1980.

7 Memorandum of 12 November 1985, p. 1.

8 *Ibid.*, p. 2.

9 *Ibid.*

10 *Ibid.*

11 CATHIE, I. (1986) 'Devolution: Key to the restructuring, *Education Victoria*, 20 February.

12 HARMAN, G. (1980) *op. cit.*, pp. 38–9.

13 COMMITTEE OF ENQUIRY INTO EDUCATION IN SOUTH AUSTRALIA (1981) *Education and Change in South Australia: First Report*, Adelaide.
14 *Ibid.*, p. 5–5.
15 WETTENHALL, R.L. (1973) 'Fitting into the framework of government' in HARMAN, G.S. and SELBY SMITH, C. (Eds) *Designing a New Education Authority*, Cariberra, Education Research Unit, Research School of Social Sciences, Australian National University, p. 63.

15 Reorganization in Education in a Climate of Changing Social Expectations: A Commentary

Phillip Hughes

Introduction

The five chapters of parts 3 and 4 highlight some interesting characteristics of educational policy in Australia and the United States and also some interesting distinctions between the two countries. Chapter 13, for example, points out that the current US emphasis on quality in education has led to a greater centralisation of power and particularly at the state level. In contrast, the chapter notes the emphasis in Australia, using the state of Victoria as an example, on decentralization of decision-making, on devolution of responsibility and on wider participation of parents and teachers in the policy process.

This assessment, like others in the different chapters, is perceptive and revealing. It could, however, be misleading if it were taken at face value. For example, some people might read into the chapters the implication that the distinctions between Australian and US policy processes and organizational structures are growing greater since they seem to be moving in opposite directions. This is only so, however, if the starting points of the movements are the same. In fact, as I will emphasize below, the starting points are quite different. The traditional distribution between local, state and federal power in education in Australia on the one hand and the United States on the other is quite different and the current moves tend to be making them more similar rather than more different. In addition to this, moves in the two countries are much more complex than might appear. For example, devolution is not by any means an unequivocal emphasis in Australian education as will be seen below. While there have certainly been substantial attempts at devolution there are also moves in certain areas towards greater central control. Thus, if we were to interpret devolution as a positive process we would have to record some gains and some losses.

There are further complexities in the interpretation. As pointed out, the major reason for devolution has been the attempt to develop a higher quality education. Some of the findings of the effective schools research have been taken to imply the need for more responsibility at the individual school level. While this is true it is not the whole truth. It is interesting that the Commonwealth government initiative, the Quality of Education Review Committee (QERC, 1985) in looking at what must be done to improve quality in education, gave considerable emphasis to common needs which were felt by the schools and which should be expressed at the system level. The Committee called for greater accountability of schools to the system with this accountability reinforced by agreements by Commonwealth and state governments. Similarly, in the United States, while one response to the call for quality in education has been to insist on legislative requirements at the state level there are other powerful arguments which would tend to move in the opposite direction. The influential book by Theodore Sizer (1985), *Horace's Compromise*, emphasizes the vital importance of giving schools and their teachers the power to make many curriculum decisions at the school level. In both countries then we do not have unidirectional changes but rather more complex currents of change.

These chapters represent a significant contribution to our understanding of the contemporary scene. Becuase of their emphasis on what is currently happening it may also be useful to see their significance in the context of the history of education in both countries and the broader social setting.

Changes in Victorian Education Are Part of a Wider Context of Change

Many of the chapters related to Australian education have related particularly to one of the six Australian states, Victoria. It may be difficult to relate the significance of these changes, firstly to Australian education, and then to American education, without putting them in a broader social context. That context will also allow readers to see the more broadly-based chapters on Australia in a more revealing light.

Australian education systems in the past have been more remarkable for stability than for rapid change. In the period immediately following 1870, the various Australian states passed education acts to move from the dual systems involving church and state control, to a clearly defined state control. The pattern adopted claimed to be 'free, compulsory and secular' the 'free' aspect related to the provision of elementary education without cost; 'compulsory' implied obligatory attendance between the ages of 6–12; and 'secular' implied that any provision for religious teaching was to be outside the normal teaching program. The main emphasis was on the control of schools, placing them under the direction of state departments of education, headed by a specially appointed educator in a public service position, responsible to a Minsiter for Education, a political figure. No role was given to federal government, since no such government existed. The commitment of the various Education Acts, was to provide 'equal education for all', with 'equal' being seen in the sense of uniform provision for all (Phillips, 1985).

The efforts of the early years went to strengthen this pattern with the production of prescriptive school syllabuses by the central administration, and for specifying content and standards of achievement. Procedures for supervision, and for assessment of teaching and the results of teaching, were controlled centrally: teachers had much less say than formerly on the nature of their tasks; parents had none at all.

The first fifty years of this century brought substantial development, but within this framework of state control. The universities were set up under state acts. The education system extended its reach to include primary, secondary, technical and teacher-training sectors, under the same departmental control. The federal government, initiated in 1901, had no role in any of these sectors. The impact in Australia of overseas influences was indirect, springing from the immigration of people from Britain and Ireland, in particular. In addition, Australian-born education directors such as Frank Tate and Peter Board began to play an important role and their own acquaintance with the reading of overseas educators began to liberalize the thinking about education.

It was in this period that overseas educators were invited specifically to comment on Australian education. This pattern was inaugurated through an ambitious project, the New Education Fellowship (NEF) Conference in 1937. NEF became a significant Australian influence through people such as Tate and Board, and in this venture brought to Australia many overseas visitors who held meetings in all the Australian states, involving a wide cross-section of teachers and those in the general community who were interested. The conference was significant in that it opened up a series of visits by 'critical friends' whose comments developed a surprising consistency. Following this conference, I.L. Kandel (1938) of Columbia University said:

> ... there is undeniably efficiency of a sort, but it is purchased at the price of unrest among teachers, of public interest not always properly directed, and of confusion of aims and purposes. In the interests of efficiency, again, the prevailing note among teachers is conformity ...'

This view was to be re-stressed and expanded by others, pointing to the over-emphasis on uniformity, the restricting effect of centralized administration and of external examinations and of the lack of general public involvement.

One of the most detailed and influential critiques was by R. Freeman Butts, also of Columbia, in 1954. He emphasized the problems set by centralized policies and administration, the inspectorial system, fixed syllabuses for each state, a hierarchy of subjects biased towards the academic, the effects of external examinations and the demands of university entrance. He said of public involvement:

> ... the centralized Departments of Education in Australia, for all their power are hemmed in by parliament, by cabinet, by appeals and arbitration boards, by public works departments and by treasury and budget officials. These are all outside the fold of professional educators. It is assumed that these groups are qualified to make decisions about education but it is also assumed that other non-professional persons in the community are not expected to be able to make qualified or valid judgments about education'. (Butts, 1955)

This viewpoint was taken up again by Robert Jackson, University of Toronto, on a visit sponsored by the Directors-General of Education. He indicated his opinion that the situation resulted from

> ... an unusual combination of the philosophy of the welfare state and a type of thinking developed in a country where it is not too difficult to survive without much planning and undue effort. (Jackson, 1962)

He went on to make a number of recommendations, including the need for a greater increase in involvement of the public, to obtain interest in and support for education.

The moves identified as necessary by these writers, namely support for education decentralization of decision-making, gained strength in the 1960s. Queensland, New South Wales and Tasmania established regions under Area Directors, with defined powers, still responsible to a central Director-General. Further steps, leading to a greater relaxation of centralization, were made firstly by delegating greater authority to school inspectors and, more recently, to school principals. As this was occurring, there was a parallel move towards broadening the base of decision-making by involving teachers, parents and students. This, of course, represented a much more radical form of decentralization and of participation. This was taken up first in Tasmania, where a government committee in a report, *The Role of the School in Society* (Hughes, 1968), recommended mechanisms at the school and regional level for community participation. A more substantial move was to be recommended for the Australia Capital Territory. Since 1913, this Territory had had its schools administered by the New South Wales Department of Education. The rapid growth of Canberra in the 1960s, together with dissatisfaction over education in the territory and the difficulty of influencing a distant administration in Sydney, led to a strong move for an independent education authority. Initiatives from parent groups in the community led to the establishment of a working party, chaired by Sir George Currie. The report of the working party (Currie, 1967) recommended an independent authority which would devolve very considerable powers to each school, where responsibility would be taken by a board representative of teachers, parents and students. While this move was not immediately successful it was representative of a considerable movement towards greater participation in the decisions in education by those who were affected by them.

The period since 1970 in Australian education has been one of unprecedented contrasts, even of paradox. It began as a period of considerable activity in education, accompanied by massive increases in expenditure. There was a mood of optimism: the long struggle against shortages of personnel, buildings and other resources seemed to be in the past. That optimism was to be remarkably short-lived and to change to an atmosphere of doubt and questioning. It is paradoxical that the fundamental approach to education in a period of shortage was one of optimism: as those shortages began to disappear through an unprecedentedly large increase in resources, the mood appreared to be one of pessimism or, at best, uncertainty.

Major features of the period may be identified as follows:

- an increased involvement of the national government in education;
- a clear identification of needs in education and an explicit statement of values;
- a significant commitment of finance to specific programs in education;
- the involvement of the national government in curriculum development;
- a growing emphasis on school-based curriculum development as an aspect of school-based decision-making;
- the beginnings of real participation in decisions for teachers, parents and students;
- a reduction in external controls, partly through a reduced use of external examinations;

and, later:

- an intense debate on the nature of education, including the means for public accountability, the satisfactory development of minimum 'basic skills' and the perceived dichotomy between 'open education' and 'traditional education';
- a deeper concern about the education of girls, and particularly youth unemployment, and the consequent concern for the school-work interface;
- the recognition that Australia was now a multicultural society with an obligation to recognize the validity and worth of a variety of cultures;
- the more obvious impact on education and on society as a whole of pressure groups espousing particular causes.

The most obvious factor in the education scene has been the increased role of the federal government in education. A listing of the committees and their timing establishes the point. They include the Murray Committee on University Education (1957); the Martin Committee on Tertiary Education (1964); the Science Facilities Program (1964); the Secondary Schools Libraries

Program (1968); The Neal–Radford Report (1972); the Karmel Committee on Australian Schools (1974); the Hughes Committee on Education in the ACT (1973); the Fry Committee, on the Education of Young Children (1973); the Kangan Committee on Technical and Further Education (1974); the Report on Open Tertiary Education (1974); the Williams Committee on Education and Training (1979); the Auchmuty Committee on Teacher Education (1978) and the Karmel Committee on Quality of Education (1985).

The national government commitment to education was limited first to university education, extending next to technical education. It was only with the Science Facilities Program that its support was extended to schools and then only to the provision of buildings and equipment to non–government schools. The Libraries Program took a further step, providing buildings, equipment and materials for libraries in government and non–government schools. The Neal–Radford Report was to signal a further extension, the development of a Commonwealth teaching service. The major involvement, however, was still to come in a move whose final dimensions and magnitude are still uncertain. This was the development of the Schools Commission, following the Report of the Karmel Committee (Karmel, 1973), a Report which was given rapid and massive support through legislation by the Labour government in 1973.

Federal involvement was to deepen in another fashion with the decision to accept the recommendations of the Hughes Committee (Hughes, 1973) and thus to take direct responsibility for a school system, the ACT Schools Authority. This Authority was set up as a participatory body, involving parents, teachers and community representatives, responsible to the Federal Minister for Education. The Authority was notable for the responsibility given to individual schools, and exercised through school boards, in the key areas of curriculum, staffing and finance.

The federal government was active on a larger scale through the Schools Commission with respect to increased participation. In spelling out the values which lay behind its program recommendation, the Karmel Committee had listed:

- equality
- diversity
- devolution of authority
- community participation
- responsiveness to change.

The Report had stated clearly its position with respect to participation.

> The Committee favours less rather than more centralized control over the operation of schools. Responsibility should be devolved as far as possible upon the people involved in the actual task of school- ing, in consultation with the parents of the pupils whom they teach and, at senior levels, with the students themselves. Its belief in this

grass-roots approach to the control of the schools reflects a convic-
tion that responsiblity will be most effectively discharged where the
people entrusted with making decisions are also the people responsible for carrying them out, with an obligation to justify them, and in
a postition to profit from their experience (Karmel, 1973, p. 9)

The Schools Commission programs have actively encouraged the support of
this idea. Their program funding has introduced an aspect of flexibility and
individual choice where previously there was little opportunity to do other
than continue previous programs. Their Disadvantaged Schools Program and
Innovations Program were both based on the principle of decision-making
by individual schools and communities and have therefore had an important
effect, not only through the program itself but through the additional recognition and capability given to local initiatives. The scale of this movement is
indicated by the fact that the Innovations Program alone has supported over
2000 projects. In addition, the Commission has funded a School and Community Project to act as a linking network and resource centre for the
enormous range and variety of community-based initiatives in schools. Many
of these initiatives transferred to later Schools Commission programs, the
Transition Education Program, and later the Participation and Equity Program.

Simultaneously with this encouragement of devolution and participation
from the national level, the states and territories have taken initiatives.
Victoria, South Australia and the Australian Capital Territory require their
schools to establish boards or councils of a representative nature and these
bodies have powers defined by legislation. In Tasmania and Queensland,
schools have been given the power to establish their own boards but are not
required to do so. In New South Wales the Department of Education has
established a special and senior post in community involvement to encourage
participation.

In a further move, the Education Commission in New South Wales, the
major policy-making body includes parents as well as teachers and other
community representatives.

In spite of these moves towards the inclusion of parents and other
groups in policy-making, there appears to be a slowing down in the momentum of this movement. The early changes which led towards involvement in
curriculum, in staff selection and in finance have tended to be halted by the
opposition of teachers' unions in the case of staff selections and the complexities of government audit and control procedures in the case of finance. It
may not be merely coincidental that this loss of impetus occurs at the same
time as a lack of general public support for increased resources in education.

The federal government later proceeded to institute a Curriculum Development Centre (CDC) to look at national initiatives with respect to the
curriculum and an Education Research and Development Committee
(ERDC) to look at national priorities in educational research. After an initial

flush of enthusiasm each of these bodies has had its mandate wiped out or diminished. ERDC has disappeared by political fiat, ostensibly as a cost-cutting measure. Such of its functions as continue do so within the Commonwealth Department of Education. CDC, once a statutory body with its own Act and the power to develop and retain its own funds, has now been made an arm of the Schools Commission, responsible to the Minister through the Chairman of the Schools Commission. The Schools Commission, in its turn, has had most of its financial role removed from it and transferred to the Department of Education. The reason given for this in the Minister's press statement was to enhance the policy-making role of the Schools Commission. However that may be, the Chairman of the Schools Commission will now be merely one adviser to the Minister amongst many others when it comes to disbursement of funds for capital and recurrent purposes to schools throughout Australia. The situation seems to have some parallels with changed role of the Director-General. Again we see the pattern of ministerial advisers in education being appointed directly to the Minister's own office. This of course, radically changes the nature of the advice given to the government and to the Minister in that there will be less publicly available advice offered and more confidential advice.

The third area of Commonwealth initiatives in education is through funding mechanisms, such as PEP, the Participation and Equity Program, and BLIPS, the Basic Learning in Primary Schools Program. Under these programs money is available to departments and to schools for quite specific purposes, with a requirement to report on the achievement of these purposes. That this has become a much more deliberate policy is evident from the Report of the Quality of Education Review Committee, (QERC). In that Report, which was accepted by the government almost in toto at the time of its reception, the general principles for the funding of programs for primary and secondary education were spelt out very precisely (Karmel, 1985).

QERC represents a major change of emphasis. It claims specifically that the emphasis with respect to Commonwealth support should move from inputs to outcomes. The Commonwealth would set, maintain and monitor its own priorities in education. The states and the schools would have indirect input to the process only.

In all these aspects, the Commonwealth which made the first major steps towards devolution, has clearly moved in the other direction, largely to provide itself with more control over policy, and over expenditure. As we will see the states were making similar moves.

Harsher Climate Has Affected the Nature of Educational Change

During the 1980s, and in the latter 1970s, the high political priority of education was substantially diminished. This may have been caused partly by the exaggerated rhetoric of the earlier period which portrayed education as the solution to a variety of social ills. In both America and Australia this rhetoric led to high, and highly unreal, expectations. Much of the rhetoric was from politicians, but educators enjoying the warm sunlight of political approval, did little to dampen those expectations. As the economic climate became harsher, bringing very high levels of youth unemployment, schools were portrayed less as part of the solution, more as part of the problem. This is exemplified by the comments of the Australian Minister for Industry, Technology and Commerce, Senator Button, speaking to a national seminar on business and government.

Senator Button told the audience that education in Australia was failing business:

Our education and training system has largely abstracted itself from the needs of industry and commerce, leaving much of its output without the necessarily basic skills, he said.

But more significantly the vast majority leave school with only a mental void concerning industry and business.

There were enormous deficiencies, especially in secondary schools, including a failure to address the hard disciplines where 'environmental studies find much more favour than physics and [students take] film appreciation rather than chemistry. (*CANBERRA Times*, 5 June 1986, p. 1)

It is in this climate that much of the recent reorganization of Australian education is occurring, both at the national and state levels. As has been mentioned, the Commonwealth government removed from its Schools Commission most of its executive powers, making it into a largely advisory body. The Curriculum Development Centre, a national body had its independent status removed.

Movements of equal significance took place at the state level. One such has been the change of power within state systems of education, and specifically, the reduction in power for state directors-general and the corresponding increase in power of state ministers of education. This is exemplified in chapter 12, which clearly outlines the relative changes in the positions of director-general and ministers. Why has it occurred? A number of reasons apply.

1 The reduced acceptance of 'expert authority' in general, whether the expert is a Director-General or the principal of a school.
2 The increased influence of pressure groups in our society.
3 The great visibility of educational activities and decisions with particular emphasis on the role of television. The Minister for Education can and does make decisions on the spot in television interviews

rather than wait to seek further advice. There is an understandable reluctance to seem indecisive or in need of expert opinion.

4   The realization by individuals and groups that for difficult decisions in education the Director-General can only say no. Only the Minister can say yes. This is because the decisions which reach the Director-General are only those which cannot be approved within existing policy. If they can be approved it will have already been done. The Director-General, however, cannot of himself change existing policy but must refer to the Minister. Most people perceiving the effect of this chain will shortcut this procedure and go direct to the Minister.

5   A further major cause is the broader social role accepted quite universally for education. Education has convinced its audience that it is linked with 'life changes'. Such a valuable commodity is likely to continue to receive enhanced attention and greater political input.

6   In an effort to meet the complexities of the current situation governments in Australia have restructured their own functions and operations and have asked for, and implemented, restructuring of departments of education. This restructuring has normally increased the power of the political arm in contrast to the public service arm of government. Premiers' departments now play a more active controlling role rather than public service boards. Premiers and ministers appoint their own advisers from political ranks in order to implement their own agenda, thus further distancing the Director-General from the area of decisions. In all this, of course, we are coming closer to the US situation where the senior advisers for politicians go in with the one election and out with another. The role of continuing public servants in such a situation is much more exclusively an instrumental one.

The last reason listed above mentions the restructuring which is taking place throughout the states. That restructuring has been a feaure of the 80s. As mentioned in the earlier chapters, the Victorian restructuring commenced in 1980 under a Liberal government and has continued in various stages under a Labor government. The most recent phase of this restructuring is the appointment of a Chief Executive Officer, as the advisor to the Minister over the full range of the portfolio, in the same sense as the traditional role of the Director-General of Education. As the name implies, however, the conception is quite different. In Queensland, the Report *Education 2000* proposes substantial changes to the education system. In Western Australia, a former Federal Minister of Education, Kim Beazley, chaired an enquiry, the *Beazley Report* (1984) whose substantial recommendations for change are now being implemented through Government policy. In South Australia, the two Keeves Reports (1983 and 1984) led to significant restructuring of the Education Department. In Tasmania, the *Review of Efficiency and Effectiveness of the Education Department,* (Hughes, 1983) was commissioned by a Labor government, and accepted and implemented by the succeeding Liberal government. That review again involved a substantial restructuring.

What is the common thread, if any, linking these separate actions? Hedley Beare, one of our contributors, draws one conclusion in another of his articles.

> Firstly, then, the most obvious commonality is that every restructuring has aimed at clarifying the lines of control, which appear to have been obfuscated by the movements of the 1970s. In particular, ministerial control and responsibility appear to have been reaffirmed by means of simplified lines of reporting. Yet there is no possibility that the simple bureaucratic pyramids of power which characterized the 1960s could be rebuilt, and the new structures have had to accommodate the new patterns of power-sharing and participation which the past decade threw up.
>
> The 1970s, it appears have gone far enough in establishing heterogeneity, diversity, local initiatives, progressive reforms. Now is the time to redraw the lines of control so that the people responsible for the system's health will have agreed communication channels, well-defined authority structures, so that the system itself has purpose and coherence. It is an act of unity in diversity.
>
> The restructuring also means a re-grouping of resources now grown scarce. They are a response to declining resources for education and so are aimed at cutting back on dead-wood and administrative slack and at producing financial accountability. Systems cannot now afford overlap, duplication, and time wasted on activities where there ought to be collaboration. Quite bluntly, no system can now afford to pay for that kind of luxury. (Beare, 1985)

The changes described in the earlier chapters thus have about them a quality of ambivalence.

This ambivalence is evident in the account of the teachers' unions in Australia, with particular emphasis on Victoria. On the one hand the unions have been traditionally opposed to the centralized bureaucratic pattern of Australian education. In situations as different as the Australian Capital Territory and Victoria they have actively supported a process of devolution to the schools. This has left them, however, in a difficult situation in exerting influence — since they now have to deal with, not one head, but many. It also highlights a certain inconsistency in their own structure, which remains largely centralized in contrast to the more devolved pattern of system decision-making in general.

The ambivalence exists, also in the account of the changed and changing role of the director-general. Viewed from one aspect, it is a reaction against an over-centralized decision-making pattern. When seen, however, not just in contrast to some devolution to schools but also the enhanced activity and direct influence of ministers, the direction of the change is not so clear. The Boyd and Chapman chapter includes the quotation from Kaufman, that one of the main effects of reorganization is to redistribute influence. While this is an obvious comment, it appears that the reorganizations which have occurred have frequently not been explicit about their intentions in the redistribution of power or else the results have differed from the stated intentions. Perhaps part of the difficulty lies in trying to interpret events while we are too close to them. Again Boyd and Chapman make the comment that reorganizations are often long-term successes despite being short-term failures, because of 'the power of their rhetoric and symbols to change the climate of opinion overtime'. This may well be the case, but it makes it more important to us to attempt to discern what changes are likely (and desirable) in the longer term.

It will be seen from the above that the 1970s and 1980s represent two distinct periods of major restructuring of education in Australia. The first period needs to be seen as part of a major effort at upgrading education. Education was seen as an important political priority and broader social aims were to be an important part of the educational changes. It is in the context of these changes that the movements of the 1980s need to be seen. Chapter 13 pointed out that in the US there had been some reaction against schools following the generally supportive atmosphere of the great society debate and that these reactions were now leading to a pressure for greater centralization. Something of the same reaction occurred in Australia follow-ing the strong social emphases of the Whitlam Labor government and its educational initiatives through the Schools Commission. It is necessary to see the Victorian initiatives outlined in the chapters above as one part of this pattern. That part has emphasized devolution to the school community of substantial powers, including collaborative decisions on such vital issues such as the curriculum and the appointment of staff, but this is only part of the story. Many factors, but notably a harsher economic climate, have made a substantial impact on the directions of organizational change. Those direc-tions, while still retaining elements of devolution, also involve a clearer central control, but a more explicitly political control.

Directions for the Future?

The picture with respect to educational policy and participation in policy-making is very complex. As has been pointed out, the distinction between patterns in the US and those in Australia is evident, but not as clear-cut as might first appear. This is largely because the individual patterns in each country are also complex, giving some indications of directions for change, but also exhibiting contrary tendencies. This section will examine the major results. emerging from the chapters presented earlier, and also will speculate on some of the directions of future change.

The experiences, as analyzed earlier, indicate a number of benefits emerging from the process of devolution of decision-making to schools. The advantages include the following:

- teachers in schools show enhanced morale due to their more direct involvement in educational decisions;
- the involvement has given greater impetus to the professional development of teachers, who now see direct benefits from such development;
- teachers indicate feelings of greater trust and confidence in the organization;
- teachers indicate a greater commitment to the implementation of the curriculum, arising from their involvement.

These advantages have been accompanied by associated costs, not necessarily causally related to the process itself. The costs include:

- a reduction in morale for principals and senior officers because they see substantial limitations on their own power and effectiveness;
- uncertainties concerning the nature and level of responsibilities because of the continuous nature of policy and organizational change;
- less effective teaching, because of the multiplicity of duties and tasks for teachers outside the classroom;
- more pressure and anxiety reported by teachers;
- feelings of disappointment arising from unreal expectations.

This is a complex balance-sheet to assess — part of that assessment will relate to the judgment as to whether the costs are a necessary result of the devolution process, or merely a short-term effect, or a result of the particular ways in which the process was introduced.

The studies of the role of teacher unions also reveal a mixed balance-sheet. One issue is that of political alignment by the union, i.e. association with a particular political party; in Australia that has led to some substantial short-term gains, but at the cost of long-term advantage. The union which becomes too strongly linked with one political party is secure only if it can guarantee the success of that party in elections. A further dilemma emerges from the US study. Strong teacher unions are likely to improve working conditions, but at the expense of variety of situation and approach. This will probably mean an advantage for some students, associated with disadvantage for those at the upper and lower ends of the scale. Once again, this does not seem to be a necessary result of the process.

Education in Australia and the USA is clearly in a state of major reassessment, reconceptualization and redevelopment. What of the future? It seems that the reforms so far put in place may not yet have reached the real focus for improvement — teacher, student and classroom, together with the factors that directly affect performance and response in that setting. Studies to emerge over recent years are beginning to redirect attention to those areas.

It is of vital importance that these studies be taken into account. I would mention specifically studies such as *Horace's Compromise* (Sizer, 1985), *A Place Called School: Prospects for the Future*, (Goodlad, 1984), *The Shopping Mall High School: Winners and Losers in the Educational Marketplace* (Powell, Farrar and Cohen, 1985).

These studies focus on what happens in schools as the central concern, and look at broader educational and social issues, including reorganization, in terms of the effects at the school level. Obvious as the benefits of this approach seem to be, it is one to which not enough attention has been paid. The work reported in this book is as encouraging in our hopes for benefits in education as is the process by which it derived. The open and frank exchanges on our concerns, issues and efforts is of enormous benefit. Each country gains benefits from a study of the way that familiar issues emerge in a different cultural setting. It is certain that the honesty and clarity of these exchanges can only be of positive help.

This exchange raises wider questions on our capacity to learn. Immediately before reading through these chapters I was given the task by UNESCO of conducting an evaluation of the implementation of their program in China, South Korea and the Philippines. In preparing for this task I was struck by its complexity, in terms of the very substantial cultural and ideological difference between the countries. In the actual investigation and discussions which ensued, my perception of those differences was sharpened. But my realization of the commonality of many issues in education was also heightened. The benefit comes not so much through direct lessons to be learned, but through a deeper understanding of our own situation after viewing it from a different context.

References

BEARE, H. (1985) 'Changing structures in education', paper presented to the 1985 Seminar on Catholic Education, 26 June.

BEAZLEY, K. (Chairman) (1984) *Education in Western Australia*, Report of a Committee of Inquiry, Perth, Government Printer.

BUTTS, R.F. (1955). *Assumptions Underlying Australian Education*, Melbourne, A.C.E.R.

Canberra Times (1986). 'Timid bureaucrats bashed by Button', 5 June, p. 1.

CURRIE, G. (1967). *An Independent Education Authority for the Australian Capital Teritory*, Report of Working Party. Canberra, Australian National University.

GOODLAD, J. (1984). *A Place Called School: Prospects for the Future*. New York, McGraw-Hill Book Co.

HUGHES, P.W. (Chairman) (1968). *The Role of the School in Society*, Hobart, Education Department of Tasmania.

HUGHES, P.W. (Chairman) (1973). *A Design for the Governance and Organisation of Education in the A.C.T.* Canberra, Australian Government Publishing Service.

HUGHES, P.W. (1983). *The Review of Efficiency and Effectiveness of the Education Department*. Education Dept., Hobart, Tasmania.

JACKSON, R.W.B. (1962). *Emergent Needs in Australian Education*, Melbourne, A.C.E.R.

KANDEL, I.L. (1938). *Types of Administration*, Melbourne, A.C.E.R.

KARMEL, P. (Chairman) (1973). *Schools in Australia*, Canberra, Australian Government Publishing Service.

KARMEL, P. (Chairman) (1985). *Quality of Education in Australia*, Report of Ministerial Review Committee, Canberra, AGPS.

PHILLIPS, D. (1985). *Making More Adequate Provision: State Education in Tasmania, 1939–1985*. Hobart, Education Dept. of Tasmania.

POWELL, A., FARRAR, E., and COHEN. D. (1985). *The Shopping Mall High School: Winners and Losers in the Educational Market Place*. Boston, MA, Houghton Mifflin Co.

SIZER, T. (1985). *Horace's Compromise*. Boston, MA, Houghton Mifflin.

Notes on Contributors

TERRY ASTUTO is Assistant Professor in the Department of Educational Administration at Teachers College, Columbia University, New York.

HEDLEY BEARE is Professor of Education at the Univesity of Melbourne.

IAN BIRCH is Associate Professor and Head of the Department of Education at the University of Western Australia.

JILL BLACKMORE is Lecturer in the School of Education at Deakin University.

WILLIAM LOWE BOYD is Professor of Education, Division of Education Policy Studies, College of Education, Pennsylvania State University.

JUDITH CHAPMAN is Senior Lecturer in the Faculty of Education at Monash University.

DAVID CLARK is William Clay Parrish Jr. Professor of Education in the Curry School of Education at the University of Virginia.

BERRY DURSTON is Executive Director of the National Council of Independent Schools, Canberra.

RANDALL EBERTS is Associate Professor of Economics at the University of Oregon.

GRANT HARMAN is Professor of Education and Head of the Centre for Administrative and Higher Education Studies at the University of New England.

PHILLIP HUGHES is Professor of Education and Head of the Department of Teacher Education at the University of Tasmania.

BETSY LEVIN is Dean of the School of Law at the University of Colorado.

DON SMART is Senior Lecturer in the Department of Education at Murdoch University.

ANDREW SPAULL is Reader in the Faculty of Education at Monash University.

JOE STONE is the W. E. Miner Professor of Economics at the University of Oregon.

FREDERICK WIRT is Professor of Political Science at the University of Illinois.

Index

aboriginal education, 226–7, 260, *see also* National Aboriginal Education Committee
Aboriginal Education (1985), 30, 45
Aboriginal Land Rights, Royal Commission into, *xii*
aborigines, *ix*, *x*
academic ability, *see* public and private schools
academic standards, improvement of, 48–9
Aitkin, D., 168–9, 180
Alluto, J., *see* Bellasco
Altbach, P.G., *see* Kelly
America and Australia
    links between, *xi*, 6
    similarities between, 4–5
American academic interest in Australia, 6
American Association for Australian Literary Studies, *vii*
American Association of Colleges for Teacher Education, 66
American Constitution, *see* Constitution
American Department of Education, *see* Education, Department of
American Education Consolidation and Improvement Act (ECIA), 21, 54
American education
    excellence in, 48, 50, 56
    and 'new basics,' 51
    perceptions of problems in, 57–8
American education policy
    see also education policy
    bilingual students and, 68
    central elements of, 73–4
    changes in, 48, 72–3

and character building, 59, 70
and competition, 59, 65–6
and the Courts, 100–19
decentralization of, 54–5
devolution to States of, 48–9, 59, 71–2
federal involvement in, 49–52
future, 73–4
local initiatives in, 50
and perforance standards, 59, 66–7, 73–4
under Reagan administration, *see* Reagan
American Educational Research Association, *vii–viii*, 20
American Federation of Teachers, 173, 234, 237
    and merit pay legislation, 65
Amiot, A.A., *see* Clark
Andrews, N., 176, 180
Angus, L., Prunty, J., and Bates, R., 222, 231
Arnove, R.F., *see* Kelly
Astuto, T.A., 7, *see also* Clark
Auchmuchty Committee on Teacher Education (1978), 300
Australian Capital Territory (ACT)
    see also Hughes Committee
    creation of independent education authority in, 298
    Schools for the ACT, 177, 183
Australian colonies, *x*
Australian Commonwealth, *see* Commonwealth
Australian Conciliation and Arbitration Commission, 229
Australian Constitution, *see* Constitution

313

Educational Researcher, 75
Educational Statistics, National Center
    for (Amer.), 62
educational voucher plan, 177–8, 179, *see
    also* tuition fees; *and* tuition tax
    credits
Elementary and Secondary Education
    Act (1965, Amer.), 72
enrolment data, *see* schools
equal employment opportunity
    programs, 30
equal opportunity in education, 22, 29–
    31, 50, 102, 113–18, 297, 300
Equity and Choice Act, The (1985,
    Amer.), 64
Erck, W., *see* Kerchner
Erickson, D.A., 180, 181

Fane, G. (The Fane Report) (1984), 38,
    45
Faneburst, L., 222, 231
Farrar, E., *see* Powell
Federated State Teachers' Association of
    Australia (FSTAA), 228
Finn, C.E., 163–4, 181, *see also* Doyle
Ford Foundation, *viii*
Fordham, Robert, (Australian Minister
    for Educ., 1982–5), 204, 283
foreign student assistance, *see* overseas
    students, aid to
Fraser, Malcolm (Australian Liberal
    Government, 1976–83), *xiii*, 7, 13,
    19, 24, 35, 38–9, 44, 132, 141, 143–
    6, 152, 160
    and financial responsibility for
        universities, 90
    and State aid to education, 165
Frazer, M., Dunstan, J.F. and Creed,
    P.J., 281
freedom of expression in school
    environment, 107–11
freedom of speech and the law, 108
French education system, 5, *see also*
    teacher unions
Friedman, M. and Friedman, R., 176,
    181
Fry Committee on the Education of
    Young Children, 300
Fulbright Fellowships, *vii*
Future Shock, 12

Gardner, D.P., *see* National Commission
    on Excellence in Education (NCEE)

Gardner, E., 48, 75
Gardner, W.I., 177, 181
Garms, W.I., Guthrie, J.W. and Pierce,
    L.C., 180, 181
Garms, W.I., Guthrie, J. and Pierce, L.,
    279
Garms, W.I. and Kirst, M.W., 174, 181
Ginsburg, M.B., Meyenn, R.J. and
    Miller, H.D.R., 231
'global village', the, 129–32, 136–7
Goldring, J., 45, *see also* Goldring
    Committee
Goldring Committee on Private
    Overseas Student Policy (Aus.), 31,
    see also overseas students
Goldschmidt, S.M., 234, 245
Goodlad, J., 308
Gorton, Senator, *see* Martin Committee
Grattan, M., 169, 181
Gronn, P., 215, 231
Grossman, D.L., 14, *see also* Hancock
Guthrie, J., 2, *see also* Garms

Hancock, G., Kirst, M.W. and
    Grossman, D.L., 3, 4, 14, 280
Hannan, B., 225, 231
Hanson, W. and Weisbrod, B.A., 180,
    182
Hardin, R., *see* Barry
Harman, G., *viii*, 11, 167–8, 182, 249,
    251, 263, 281, 293
Harrison, R.J., 215, 231
Hartle, T., *see* Doyle
Harvard, Chair of Australian History, 6
Hawke, Robert (Australian Labor
    Government 1983–86), *xiii–xiv*, 7,
    8, 13, 19, 21–45, 132, 135, 141–43,
    184, 215–6, 220–21
Hawke and Reagan education policies,
    comparison of, 44
Heritage Foundation, *Mandate for
    Leadership*, (Amer.), 62
Herndon, T., 236, 245
Hertling, J., 68, 70, 75
Hewitson, M., 224, 231
higher education (Aus.)
    see also Fane Report *and* tertiary
        education
    demand and supply of places in, 35–
        6
    funding, 35–7
    policy, 23–4
    privatisation of, 38